JUSTICE AND NATURAL RESOURCES

Justice and Natural Resources

An Egalitarian Theory

CHRIS ARMSTRONG

UNIVERSITY PRESS

OXFORD
UNIVERSITY PRESS

Great Clarendon Street, Oxford, OX2 6DP,
United Kingdom

Oxford University Press is a department of the University of Oxford.
It furthers the University's objective of excellence in research, scholarship,
and education by publishing worldwide. Oxford is a registered trade mark of
Oxford University Press in the UK and in certain other countries

© Chris Armstrong 2017

The moral rights of the author have been asserted

First Edition published in 2017

Impression: 2

All rights reserved. No part of this publication may be reproduced, stored in
a retrieval system, or transmitted, in any form or by any means, without the
prior permission in writing of Oxford University Press, or as expressly permitted
by law, by licence or under terms agreed with the appropriate reprographics
rights organization. Enquiries concerning reproduction outside the scope of the
above should be sent to the Rights Department, Oxford University Press, at the
address above

You must not circulate this work in any other form
and you must impose this same condition on any acquirer

Published in the United States of America by Oxford University Press
198 Madison Avenue, New York, NY 10016, United States of America

British Library Cataloguing in Publication Data

Data available

Library of Congress Control Number: 2016960742

ISBN 978-0-19-870272-6

Printed in Great Britain by
CPI Group (UK) Lts, Croydon, CR0 4YY

Links to third party websites are provided by Oxford in good faith and
for information only. Oxford disclaims any responsibility for the materials
contained in any third party website referenced in this work.

Acknowledgements

I have been working on this book for roughly half a decade, and have racked up a number of debts along the way. A Mid-Career Fellowship from the British Academy during the academic year 2012–13 provided much-needed time to make progress on the manuscript. Visiting fellowships at the Centre for Democracy, Peace and Justice at the University of Uppsala, at the Centre for the Study of Social Justice at the University of Oxford, and in the School of Philosophy in the Australian National University provided space away from the distractions of my home university. I have also benefited greatly from the broad community of people now working on egalitarian theory, global justice, territorial rights, and natural resources. For comments on various chapters—and in some cases the whole manuscript—I would like to extend my sincere thanks to Ayelet Banai, Megan Blomfield, Gillian Brock, Alex Brown, Daniel Callies, Simon Caney, Ian Carter, Dimitris Efthymiou, Anca Gheaus, Bob Goodin, Clare Heyward, Holly Lawford-Smith, Duncan McLaren, Alejandra Mancilla, Andrew Mason, Darrel Moellendorf, Shmulik Nili, Kieran Oberman, David Owen, Ed Page, Fabian Schuppert, Henry Shue, Annie Stilz, Kit Wellman, Leif Wenar, Scott Wisor, and Lea Ypi. I would also like to thank audiences at the University of Amsterdam, the Australian National University, the University of Bristol, the University of the West of England in Bristol, University College Dublin, the University of Durham, Humboldt University of Berlin, the London School of Economics, McGill University, the University of New South Wales, the University of Oslo, Nuffield College Oxford, the University of Salamanca, the University of Southampton, the University of Uppsala, the University of Utrecht, the University of Vienna, the University of Warwick, and the University of Zurich. I would like to extend special thanks to those who participated in a symposium on my book-in-progress at the Goethe University Frankfurt during January 2016, including Darrel Moellendorf, Merten Reglitz, Daniel Callies, Eszter Kollar, Anca Gheaus, and Ayelet Banai. All of these interlocutors have helped me to sharpen the arguments presented here, though I am aware that many of them continue to disagree with some, and sometimes much, of what I have to say.

Chapter 3 draws on my paper 'Natural Resources: The Demands of Equality', *Journal of Social Philosophy* 44/4 (2013): 331–47. Chapter 5 draws on 'Justice and Attachment to Natural Resources', *Journal of Political Philosophy* 14/2 (2014): 48–65. Chapter 6 draws on 'Against "Permanent Sovereignty" over Natural Resources', *Politics, Philosophy and Economics* 14/2 (2015): 129–51. In each case the text has been revised substantially.

Finally, I would like to dedicate this book to those who have given me so much support while I wrote it: for Sophia, Felix, Leonard, and Yasmin, with love.

Contents

Introduction	1
1. Resources and Rights	9
2. Equality and Its Critics	29
3. The Demands of Equality	62
4. Rewarding Improvement	93
5. Accommodating Attachment	113
6. Against Permanent Sovereignty	132
7. Perfecting Sovereignty?	150
8. Resource Taxes	177
9. The Ocean's Riches	201
10. The Burdens of Conservation	220
References	248
Index	262

Introduction

Conflicts over natural resources are impossible to ignore in our world. We know that the tribespeople of the Amazon have been brutally dispossessed as great swathes of rainforest are destroyed. We understand that a key factor in many of the civil wars which have devastated African communities is the struggle to gain control over supplies of oil, diamonds, and gold. We may even remember that a relentless thirst for natural resources spurred Europe's colonization of the world, shaping the very boundaries of nation-states in its aftermath. Countries such as Argentina, the Ivory Coast, and the Gold Coast (now Ghana) were even named after the resources to be found (or pillaged) there. Others (including Nigeria, Cameroon, Senegal, and Gambia) were named for the rivers which sustained local communities.

As resources are consumed ever more frenetically, struggles over them show no sign of disappearing. The desire to exert control over as yet untapped natural resources has motivated new territorial claims over the Arctic region, and seen millions poured into deep-sea mining technology. Political scientists have often predicted that 'water wars' will be a feature of our future, although thankfully those predictions have not yet been borne out.[1] We know that many economies in the Middle East have been transformed by the discovery of oil, and by the conflicts which have sometimes followed. But these conflicts are not confined to geographical 'hot spots'. Rather disagreements about who owns resources, and how they should be used, are endemic. In the Scottish independence campaign of 2014, debates about the viability of a Scottish state frequently turned on rival claims about who would end up owning North Sea oil, and even what price it might be expected to command in the coming years. As I write, many Canadian citizens are campaigning to raise awareness of the environmental impact of oil pipelines, and tar sands exploitation, on virgin forests and on the indigenous people who live in them.

It is abundantly clear that natural resources matter to people. All of us need some resources if we are to survive—including water, air, light from the sun, and some land to stand upon. Others are so valuable that states which possess large reserves of them have a guaranteed source of income (though whether that income will be turned into sustained economic growth, or shared with ordinary citizens, is another matter entirely). States jealously guard their sovereignty over the resources in their territories, individuals defend property claims over resources discovered on their land, and communities argue about just who has the right to fish in which waters. While the 'resource curse' literature has suggested that in weak states bountiful resources can provoke coup attempts and civil war, this only illustrates, and brutally so, that resources are so valuable to people that they are willing to risk their lives—and kill—over them.

The fact that natural resources matter to people has prompted much discussion of the fairness or justice of patterns of access to or control over them. And this discussion is important. After all, few of us would accept a situation whereby whoever happened to physically control a resource at any given time was therefore able to retain all of the benefits flowing from it—or indeed a situation whereby conflicts over resources were settled by superior force.[2] If not, we need a normative account of how rights over natural resources—and any duties attaching to them—should be shared between us. We might, for instance, be prepared to argue that if we all need water, and if there is more than enough freshwater in our world for everyone to drink, then we each have a *right* to enough to live by. Or we might endorse a still more demanding principle of justice. A theory of justice selects and defends principles which are especially stringent—especially morally grave or serious—such that we can properly call for their enforcement. Entitlements of justice are weighty enough that individuals whose claims are not met can properly enjoin coercive institutions to defend them, or even, potentially, take action to defend them themselves. Duties of justice are weighty enough that those who refuse to abide by them can, in principle, be obliged to do so.[3]

One aim of this book is to provide a conceptual architecture for thinking about issues of natural resource justice, including a definition of natural resources, and accounts of the key resource rights that agents might enjoy, and of the nature and significance of what I will call special claims over resources. Recent years have witnessed a welcome resurgence of interest in issues of natural resource justice (partly explained, no doubt, by increasing awareness of environmental degradation and resource scarcity, partly by a continued concern for enduring global inequalities, and partly contingent on the wider surge of interest in the nature and justification of territorial rights more broadly). To a large extent the conceptual architecture I provide could be of benefit to people whether they agree with my own approach or not, and in that sense I hope that it might advance debates on natural resource justice in its own right. But more importantly, the book defends one particular theory of natural resource justice, which I call a global egalitarian theory. Such a theory holds that the proper scope of (at least some, significant) principles of justice is global, and that as far as justice goes our goal should be to promote equality between people, wherever they live in the world.[4]

STRUCTURE OF THE BOOK

Roughly speaking, the first five chapters of this book develop an egalitarian theory of natural resource justice. These chapters argue for the superiority of an egalitarian theory versus various non-egalitarian alternatives, and defend the egalitarian perspective from some serious challenges which have been levelled at it. But they also defend a specific interpretation of the demands of equality when it comes to natural resources, and in that sense they engage critically with some existing egalitarian accounts of natural resource justice. Many prominent egalitarian views have argued that natural resources are normatively special in some sense; some of them have even argued that natural resources are the *only* thing egalitarians ought to care about the distribution of. They have also often argued that the goal of egalitarians must be a strictly equal division of natural resources—or, more commonly, of their economic value. My own position differs from those views, as will become clear. It rejects the view that natural resources are the only sources of advantage with which egalitarians should concern themselves. Instead it seeks to reclaim them as one (albeit important) source of advantage amongst many. It argues for a welfarist account of equality, and claims that we ought to seek not the equalization of natural resources (or resource value) but rather equal access to wellbeing. Equal access to wellbeing is in turn served by access to a set of advantages and disadvantages which goes far beyond natural resources (although they are an important element). Although debates about the precise role that natural resources should play in an egalitarian theory may sound somewhat arcane, I will show that divergent views about the demands of equality when it comes to natural resources have considerable implications for debates about appropriation, climate justice, and justice between generations.

The structure of the first half of the book is as follows. Chapter 1 defines natural resources, clarifies what we should expect a theory of natural resource justice to do, and introduces a conceptual account of the most important rights which agents might have over natural resources. It also discusses the diversity of natural resources, and draws out some of the ways in which this might matter for a normative theory.

Chapter 2 argues for an egalitarian approach to issues of natural resource justice, as opposed to a more modest account focusing on people's basic rights, for instance. Although protecting basic rights is urgent and important, doing so is not sufficient for justice. The chapter presents an account of why equality matters, and unpacks some of the implications of an egalitarian view. It also addresses some important challenges to that position. For example, it has been argued that the drive to equalize advantages only arises between people who are already united in a certain kind of relationship. Furthermore, it is sometimes argued that divergent endowments of natural resources are inconsequential for economic development, and that (so long as everyone has access to a certain minimum) we need not concern ourselves with the justice of their distribution. It has also been suggested that egalitarians pay insufficient attention to attachment, and the ways in which particular people have come to value particular resources; and that they neglect the fact that communities often act on their resources so as to make them more economically valuable, possibly deriving special claims over them as a result. I respond to each of these challenges, though in the case of special claims the response will continue throughout subsequent chapters.

Chapter 3 clarifies the place that natural resources should have within an egalitarian theory, as one important set of advantages and disadvantages amongst many which drive access to wellbeing. It critically engages with—but rejects—arguments which suggest that natural resources are the only things that matter from the point of view of distributive justice, and views which hold that even if we should care about some broader category of advantage, natural resources or their value are the only thing we should *distribute* so as to bring us closer to equality. It claims instead that natural resources are, in a slogan, 'tremendously important but nothing special' as drivers of human wellbeing. It draws out the implications of this view for important questions about natural resource appropriation, climate justice, and intergenerational justice.

Chapter 4 introduces the topic of special claims over natural resources, with which any egalitarian theory must grapple. Whilst all of us might have general claims on the world's resources, it is possible that *some* agents have especially strong claims over *particular* resources. If these special claims can be defended, their existence may trouble the view that the distribution of natural resources, or the benefits and burdens flowing from them, is 'morally arbitrary'.[5] The chapter investigates whether plausible special claims can be grounded on what I call the 'improvement' of natural resources. In particular it draws out a responsibility-catering principle which would secure a claim, for improving agents, over the economic value which is added to a natural resource when it is improved. If that principle can be defended it might provide defenders of national claims over natural resources, for instance, with an argument for reducing the scope of egalitarian redistribution across borders. Even if the 'unimproved' value of resources is vulnerable to calls for redistribution, the improved portion of a resource's value might properly be reserved for the community which has brought it into existence. This chapter, however, raises several doubts about responsibility-catering claims over 'added value'. The upshot is that rather less flows from improvement—and indeed the distinction between improved and unimproved resources—than is sometimes thought to be the case.

Chapter 5 considers a second kind of special claim, this time from what I will call 'attachment'. It is often (plausibly) suggested that natural resources do not only matter to people as interchangeable fuels for various economic activities. Perhaps some natural resources matter *in particular* to some people, as non-substitutable supports for their most central life-plans. If so, egalitarians might wrong those people if they recommend that we redistribute resources without regard for the way people are attached to them. This chapter shows that egalitarianism does not require us to do so. A variety of theories of justice, my own included, have reason to take seriously the central projects which give meaning and purpose to individual lives; and egalitarians accordingly have reason to investigate how and to what extent attachments can be accommodated within an egalitarian theory. I argue that egalitarians can and should care about these attachments, and moreover that we can be much more permissive towards them than has sometimes been alleged. But pointing towards attachment does not give us reason to believe that some people's life-plans matter more than others, and it does not give us reason to abandon egalitarianism as a theory about natural resources.

If the first half of the book sets out an egalitarian theory of natural resource justice—in which natural resources are set in their proper place—later chapters switch focus to the question of how justice might be brought closer. Even if we possess a good conceptual account of the demands of justice, when it comes to natural resources, it is a different question how we might bring it closer to fruition—or how, to be specific, we might promote greater global equality. Now we might, at this point, throw up our hands and say that the job of the theorist has been done: that it is the goal of political theorists or philosophers to clarify ideals, but the work of politicians, economists, administrators, or—just possibly—ordinary citizens to argue about how they might best be implemented. But that is not the move I want to make. Instead these chapters investigate some ways in which we might advance egalitarian justice. It is not my intention, to be clear, to provide a full 'theory of transition', or indeed a deeper theory of social and political change. Rather (and more modestly) my intention is to identify some promising avenues for reform which might bring about, even if an inch at a time, a more just world.[6] Even if the theorist is by no means uniquely qualified to assess the possibilities for reform which our world offers us—in fact he or she may be no better qualified than the next person—if we are committed not only to analysing the world but also to changing it, the task of identifying the glimmers of light that the contemporary world offers us cannot be ignored.

The second half of the book proceeds as follows. Chapter 6 addresses the status quo within international politics, which is dominated by the institution of 'permanent sovereignty' over natural resources—by way of which individual nation-states enjoy extensive and for the most part exclusive rights over the resources falling within their borders. Egalitarians have often assumed that such a regime of national control cannot be defended, but that remains to be demonstrated in light of some sophisticated defences of state or national rights over natural resources which have been made in recent years. These allege, variously, that nations or states have improvement- or attachment-based special claims over the resources in their territories, or that tolerating a regime of national or state control is conducive to justice goals such as the protection of self-determination, the meeting of citizens' basic rights, or the effective custodianship of natural resources. I critically assess these various arguments, and show that they are not sufficient to justify the institution of permanent sovereignty—and, indeed, that in many respects they count against it. Moreover, I show that even insofar as those arguments possess some normative weight, they are compatible with a significant dispersal of resource rights away from individual nation-states, both downwards towards local communities, and upwards towards transnational and global agencies.

The conclusion might then be that we should try as a matter of urgency to transcend the institution of permanent sovereignty, or at the very least to seriously qualify it. But perhaps such a judgement would be too hasty. Chapter 7 considers the view that we should not attempt to transcend or radically reform permanent sovereignty, but that we should rather seek to further entrench it. Perhaps permanent sovereignty is a potentially radical principle, inasmuch as it promises to make natural resources work for the citizens of each country (even if doing so will do nothing to rectify inequalities between countries). Moreover, putting resources to work for the poor of a country might be thought to be an achievable goal, whereas the radical reforms sometimes embraced by global egalitarians may have much less certain prospects of success. In this chapter I scrutinize the idea that our priority ought to be to reform the international trade in resources so as to protect the rights of citizens, and specifically to deliver upon an ideal of 'public accountability' in resource sales.[7] I suggest that egalitarians can offer conditional support to such accountability reforms, insofar as they promise to promote equality (though I also show that their promise in this regard is limited). But I suggest that they cannot be considered a replacement for more ambitious egalitarian reforms. I also directly confront the pragmatic challenge, which alleges that whereas some mooted global egalitarian reforms are highly ambitious, an advantage of proposals for reforming the resource trade is that they depend only upon a principle (of popular sovereignty over resources) which already has a basis in international law. Negatively, I show that the place of such a principle in international law is quite uncertain; this reduces the supposed pragmatic advantage of accountability reforms, and their purported superiority over more ambitious egalitarian reforms. More positively, I agree that it is important for egalitarians to identify at least some achievable reforms by way of which we can make significant advances on the status quo. Even if this goal should not operate as a constraint upon theory, it nevertheless represents a worthwhile endeavour if our theorizing is to make a difference. This lays down a challenge which the subsequent chapters of the book attempt to meet.

Introduction 7

Chapter 8 examines some of the best-known suggestions for advancing justice when it comes to natural resources: resource taxes. Although taxes have occupied much of the attention of theorists of natural resource justice, they are but one among a considerable set of options we have for advancing justice. I therefore begin by addressing some general questions about when, why, and on what we should levy taxes. I also address some concerns about taxing natural resources in particular, and clarify the role resource taxes can play in the egalitarian project. The chapter goes on to investigate what the precise tax base should be if we ought indeed to adopt at least some natural resource taxes. One of its principal conclusions is that a single undifferentiated global tax on natural resources is unlikely to serve justice well. Moreover, it is likely that progress in achieving global resource taxes will be built incrementally, rather than being achieved at one stroke. For both reasons it is worth investigating some proposals for more specific resource taxes. The chapter concludes with brief discussions of user charges on common-pool resources, carbon taxes, and a tax on Sovereign Wealth Funds.

Chapter 9 discusses the resources contained in or under the world's oceans, resources which have been somewhat neglected by political theorists but which are hugely significant for important ecosystem processes and which have potentially vast economic value. It outlines the political struggle which has been waged over the resources contained in the world's oceans in recent decades, in which the protagonists have locked horns over whether these resources should be brought under the control of individual states, left largely unregulated, or else globally managed as part of humankind's 'common heritage', and exploited in such a way as to ameliorate, rather than intensify, existing global inequalities. The chapter discusses two contrasting sets of resources in some detail. First it discusses the case of fishing rights, in which we have seen a mixture of extended state control and unconstrained exploitation in the area beyond state jurisdiction; it shows that this approach has comprehensively failed to deliver on either intra-generational justice or sustainability, and sketches some alternative proposals which would serve justice better. It then discusses the mineral resources contained in the portions of the seabed which still fall beyond state control. Agreement has been reached, under the auspices of the International Seabed Authority, to harness the exploitation of these potentially valuable minerals to promote global equality. Though challenges remain, this chapter welcomes this development and identifies some wider lessons we might draw from it for the struggle to put resources to work to promote global equality. One of them is that institutions which are capable of promoting equality already exist, and that sizeable constituencies, particularly in the developing world, have already challenged them to do so. That is a challenge which the developed world has not met well to date. But in the interests of intra- and intergenerational justice, we must hope that their intransigence can be overcome.

Chapter 10 discusses the allocation of the burdens on conservation. It is plausible to think that justice requires the conservation of at least some resources at least some of the time, whether this means simply letting them be—so that, for instance, they can go on delivering vital ecosystem services— or actively sinking time and money into their protection from various threats (or indeed their restoration if such threats come to fruition). But when resources are conserved, this can generate costs, and this chapter discusses where those costs should fall. Our answer to this question will have major distributive consequences. It is often said that, if we want to continue to enjoy a safe climate, we ought to 'leave the oil in the soil'—as well as the gas, and the coal. But doing so would have distributive consequences, not least for those who currently rely on fossil fuel extraction for their livelihoods. I draw out an account of when it is appropriate to pool these costs globally. One consequence of the arguments of this chapter is that a common picture of natural resource justice—under which agents or communities with valuable resources are taxed so as to shift funds in the direction of those without—must be rendered more complex. In at least some significant cases, justice likely requires transfers in the direction of agents or communities who currently control valuable resources. I conclude by examining some of the institutions which already exist, and which might help us to ameliorate global injustice by spreading the benefits and burdens flowing from natural resources more equitably. Along with other chapters in the second half of the book, the aim is to sustain a sense of possibility—a sense of the many ways in which injustice might be ameliorated, and equality promoted, if we only possessed the political will to do so.

ENDNOTES

1. Barnaby 2009.
2. Though for an excellent account of the role which the principle of 'might makes right' nevertheless plays in resource politics globally, see Wenar 2016a.
3. For a brief overview of various definitions of distributive justice, see Armstrong 2012, chapter 1.
4. Leading global egalitarian accounts include Beitz 1979; Tan 2004; Caney 2005a; and Moellendorf 2009.
5. Beitz 1979.
6. For a good account of the nature and demands of 'transitional theory', see Sreenivasan 2012.
7. Wenar 2016a; see also Pogge 2002, chapter 8.

1

Resources and Rights

Poets, philosophers, and prophets have long told us that the world is a treasury, a storehouse, and a cornucopia. It overflows with resources which humans can put to use, and those uses are as many and various as the resources themselves. Some of them are familiar: consider the air that we breathe, the warmth from the sun that makes our world habitable, or indeed its light, which stimulates the plant growth upon which terrestrial ecosystems depend. Other benefits these resources bestow upon us are only now coming to be understood: consider, for instance, the complex role of the oceans or the ice-caps in processes of climate regulation. These examples hammer home, in fact, how narrow the margins are within which life can flourish. Meanwhile resources can impose burdens too—as when a malaria-infected mosquito bites a sleeping child, or a tropical typhoon tears down a village. Indeed, the very same resources can produce both benefits and burdens: rainwater sustains crops and can be captured for drinking, but excessive rainfall lowers plants' nutrient levels and causes landslides and soil erosion. Literature both secular and religious teems with examples of too little rain, or too much.

Potentially, any of these benefits and burdens can be of relevance to a theory of justice. A theory of natural resource justice will define and allocate a set of resource rights, determining who can justly derive which benefits in which circumstances, or who has the right to make decisions, say, about how resources shall be used. It will also stipulate a set of duties specifying ways in which resources should not be used, or must be protected, who must bear which burdens, and when we should refrain from interfering with other peoples' access to resources. Since we now know that the world is not quite a cornucopia—since we are coming to accept, grudgingly, the ways in which its bounty is limited—it will specify and constrain the way in which resources can be used.

The purpose of this chapter is primarily to clarify the content of a theory of natural resource justice, by defining both natural resources and the rights we might have in relation to them. It also makes clear which questions will fall inside and outside the scope of this study. Section 1.1 explains how we will understand 'natural resources', and emphasizes their diversity. It is important to be clear at the outset, though, about what work we are asking a definition of natural resources to *do*. Some accounts of justice stipulate that natural resources are the only thing which we should seek to regulate shares of. On some views, for instance, whereas we are all entitled to equal shares of the benefits flowing from natural resources, the products or social goods we make out of them are immune to redistributive claims.[1] Quite how we define natural resources then becomes tremendously important—insofar as that definition must stake out the very boundaries of a theory of distributive justice. Alternatively it might be thought that although principles of distributive justice apply to many sources of advantage, of which natural resources are but one, there is something *special* about natural resources from the point of view of justice which suggests that distinct principles should apply to them.[2]

I reject both of those claims. Natural resources are hugely important from the point of view of justice, but they are emphatically not all that matters. They are (merely) an (important) subcategory of the goods to which an account of justice ought to apply. As I make clear in Chapter 3, I also reject the idea that there is anything 'special' about natural resources from the point of view of justice such that even if they are not the only correct distribuenda for a theory of justice, specific or custom-made principles or constraints must apply to their distribution. As such little hangs, from a normative point of view, on quite how we distinguish natural resources from other goods, in order to investigate the implications of a broader egalitarian account for natural resources we need a *descriptive* definition of what natural resources are before we can draw any conclusions, to be sure, just as we would need a descriptive account of what education or healthcare were before we could capture egalitarianism's implications for those issues. But that definition does not then define the territory of an account of distributive justice; it merely allows us to capture a subset of its implications. The descriptive definition offered in section 1.1 allows us to distinguish natural resources from other goods for the purposes of working through those implications, but it does not mean that the self-same principles should not apply to other goods. Natural resources, I will indeed suggest, are an interesting place to start in working through the implications of an egalitarian account of justice; but they would be a very bad place to finish.

Section 1.2 addresses some of the finer questions about precisely what the scope of an account of natural resource justice should be, and defends further the approach taken in this book. Section 1.3, finally, offers a conceptual account of the rights which a theory of natural resource justice will seek to allocate. I sketch a list of eight key resource rights (each of which will imply accompanying duties) and suggest that as well as being conceptually distinct, these rights could in practice be separated and allocated between different agents. By the end of the first chapter we will have clarified what we can expect an account of natural resource justice to *do*. Chapters 2 through to 5 will defend one such account, and Chapters 6 through to 10 will illustrate some of its implications.

1.1. DEFINING NATURAL RESOURCES

We will define natural resources rather conventionally: they are raw materials available from the natural world, which are (therefore) not produced by humans but which are nevertheless useful to them. Such a definition distinguishes them from the *products* or artefacts which people make, often using natural resources as building-blocks (and if not, then certainly using products which are themselves made, at some point of regress, out of natural resources). Whereas products do not exist unless a person intervenes to create them, natural resources are naturally occurring: they would be 'there' whether there were human beings or not. The German equivalent, *Rohstoff*, or *raw stuff*, captures this point well: natural resources are the raw materials we are confronted with in coming into existence in the world, with which we can potentially support our various (and competing) human projects. The trees of the forests, the water of the rivers and oceans, and the mineral and petrochemical wealth lying under the soil and the seas are familiar enough examples. But we can also include the air that we breathe, wild (uncultivated) plants and animals, and the energy contained in wind, waves, and sunlight.[3] So too can we include the land itself. Land after all possesses the same key normative features as other resources: whilst all of us require some land to live upon, none of us is responsible for creating it.[4]

Of course, the distinction between raw materials and artefacts will often mark out differences of degree, rather than type; there will be cases which appear less than clear-cut. Perhaps a wild peach tree is an instance of a natural resource; but what if it turns out to have grown there because I threw a peach-stone over my shoulder? Will it now count as an artefact, a natural resource, or an object which is somewhere in between? The answer is presumably the latter. Perhaps just where on the continuum it falls depends on whether I meant it to grow or not. Political theorists disagree about just how profoundly we need to intervene in natural processes for the products emanating from them to start counting as artefacts rather than natural resources. Is picking up an acorn enough to indicate to others that I now have a claim over it, or that it should not be considered a natural resource any longer? Or must I do something further to that acorn, such as plant it in the ground and water it? In Chapter 4 we consider arguments about just what constitutes the 'improvement' of natural resources, and what normative implications may flow from acts of improvement. But in principle, improving acts can reduce the 'naturalness' of particular objects, and shift them further along the continuum towards artefacthood. For now, note that the definition of natural resources as objects not created by anybody is familiar enough and informs the treatment of natural resources under international law. That is, although international legal instruments often show a lack of precision about *exactly* what natural resources are, they tend to converge in specifying them as raw non-human-made materials taken from the bounty of nature.[5] That definition often leans on a distinction between 'natural wealth' and 'natural resources' in which the first corresponds to the sources of such materials (rivers, forests, the atmosphere, the ecosystem generally) and the second refers to the materials contained in them (such as fresh water, trees, and gases) which can potentially be isolated, removed, or consumed.[6] Some such definition has also informed well-known discussions of natural resources within the literature on distributive justice.[7]

We shall focus on natural resources which are 'available' to humans because, as far as a theory of justice is concerned, natural resources become interesting insofar as they are potential sources of benefits and burdens to people. If a vein of metal ore was contained within the centre of the earth and we knew that it could never be accessed under any circumstances, and that it could impose neither benefits nor burdens to people now or in the future, it would be of no salience to a theory of justice. But the most unpromising resources can turn out to be of use in one way or another. Even apparently inert resources can often be used as building-blocks, defences against flood, or objects of devotion. Some of them might just be beautiful, or offer us encouragement by the simple fact of their endurance. If it is conceivable that a resource might be of any benefit to people—even people living some distance into the future, possessed of technology we do not yet possess—that suffices for it to become of interest *as* a resource from the point of view of justice. The same would apply if we knew that it produced burdens (or might produce them in future)—if living near it made life more difficult, or expensive, or upsetting. It is with the benefits and burdens associated with resources that a theory of resource justice concerns itself.

These benefits and burdens are manifold because, as I have noted, we interact with natural resources in a bewildering variety of ways: we eat them, or drink them, or use them to produce food, breathe them, worship them, burn them for warmth, use them to scatter the ashes of our dead upon, enjoy the views they provide, benefit from their shade or the defence they offer us against flood or desertification, benefit from their ability to absorb greenhouse gases—and the list goes on. Not all of these benefits and burdens can be reduced to the narrowly 'economic', although many natural resources are of course bought and sold on open (and increasingly global) commodity markets. Natural resources also have cultural or symbolic uses: in some places in the world the ways of life of entire communities are bound up in following wild animals or fish in their regular migratory paths (as with the Saami herders we will discuss in Chapter 5); or with the never-ending pursuit of scarce fresh water (think of the nomadic peoples of the Rift Valley in Eastern Africa, moving from place to place in search of drinking water for themselves and their livestock). Many of us simply find natural resources such as trees, waterfalls, and rolling hills attractive, and prefer lives in which we are exposed to (some forms of) 'nature' rather than lives in which we are deprived of access to it. Perhaps the existence of a 'nature' independent of human activity provides an important context for our lives, beyond and irreducible to our quotidian concerns.[8]

Given our focus on the benefits and burdens flowing from natural resources, a theory of natural resource justice need not call, in the first instance, for the redistribution of natural resources themselves. In some cases, to be sure, it will. For instance, if we all have an entirely predictable need for fresh water, justice may demand that we move fresh water itself (or products containing water) to those who need it. But even here, it will usually be possible to help those currently deprived of water to develop infrastructure to better capture it themselves, because water cycles through a vast global hydrological system, and nowhere is it entirely lacking. Often we will have reasons of justice to prefer *not* moving resources: that might be disruptive or inefficient. Given that we are interested in resources as sources of benefits and burdens, it is a welcome fact that in practice we can usually share streams of benefits without moving resources themselves. The trees of the tropical rainforests are (literally) rooted to particular places, but they provide benefits to all of us, including carbon sequestration. Since their capacity to absorb carbon dioxide is limited, justice demands that we share that capacity appropriately, and may also demand that we share any costs of protecting the forests. But it does not demand that we move them. The extraction or consumption of many resources—familiarly oil, or minerals, but not only them—can be taxed, so that the economic benefits arising from them can be shared between all of us, whether we ever come into contact with them directly or not. If protecting important resources imposes burdens—such as financial burdens—then these too can be shared. Justice requires, first and foremost, that benefits and burdens are properly shared, and it may turn out that in relatively few cases will this actually require moving resources themselves.

1.1.1. The Diversity of Natural Resources

Natural resources are by no means an undifferentiated category of goods. There are important differences between natural resources, and at least some of these plausibly have implications for the ways in which we should think about them from the point of view of justice. Although these differences have received little attention from theorists of natural resource justice to date, they are worth considering.

First, we should recognize that natural resources deliver benefits in different ways. Two features are particularly important here. On the one hand, some streams of benefits are excludable whereas others are non-excludable. A benefit is excludable when the agents who control a given resource can practically prevent others from deriving that benefit flowing from it, and non-excludable when they cannot (or when it is very costly to do so). On the other hand, some benefits are subtractive but others are non-subtractive. A benefit is subtractive when an agent, in the act of deriving a benefit from a good, necessarily reduces the scope for others to do the same, and non-subtractive when the consumption of one agent does not diminish the supply available to others. These features identify ideal types, and in practice both excludability and subtractiveness are best thought of as matters of degree. Moreover, the degree of excludability and subtractiveness is going to be partly contextual, depending on factors such as population levels. Looking at a beautiful mountain is typically viewed as enjoying a non-excludable benefit. But conceivably, if the valley before the mountain is crowded enough, my enjoyment could deprive another of benefits. Cooling my feet in the icy water of a mountain stream is plausibly thought of as enjoying a non-subtractive benefit, because it is not going to make that water significantly less cool. But if enough people did the same the water would warm up.

Armed with these distinctions, we can distinguish between different classes of benefits, of which three are especially important. Resources deliver *pure public goods* when benefits are non-excludable and non-subtractive. They deliver *collective goods* when benefits are non-excludable but subtractive. Finally, they deliver *private goods* when benefits are excludable and subtractive.[9] I take it that an adequate theory of justice should not be exclusively concerned with goods which are privately owned and where others can be excluded from the benefits flowing from them. If we care about private goods because of the wellbeing they allow individuals to enjoy, for instance, then we must recognize that individuals can also enjoy—or be denied—important sources of wellbeing as a result of differential access to collective or pure public goods.[10]

Some benefits deriving from natural resources clearly exhibit the features of pure public goods: if I obtain pleasure from gazing at the trees in a forest, I do not prevent you from doing the same, and I do not typically diminish the beauty left for others to admire. Some exhibit the features of collective goods: if I own a forest which absorbs carbon dioxide, I cannot prevent you from benefiting from its ability to absorb that gas—but the more of your gas it absorbs, the less it can of mine. Others exhibit the properties of private goods: if I burn a piece of coal in my hearth, you cannot; every bit I burn diminishes the benefits available, but I can prevent others from enjoying the warmth it produces. Some resources, of course, have competing uses as either private goods *or* public goods (imagine a tree which can either be felled for timber, or left standing so that it can sequester greenhouse gases, or simply go on being beautiful). I assume that a theory of natural resource justice should tell us how to allocate benefits of all of these kinds, but they may pose somewhat different normative challenges. Theories of natural resource justice to date appear to have overwhelmingly focused on the challenge of sharing natural resource benefits *qua* private goods. But tailor-made guidance on other categories of goods—such as key collective goods—is also required. Chapter 10 discusses one important case, that of rainforest protection.

Second, some natural resources are non-substitutable supports for basic human rights, because they are in and of themselves necessary to human survival. Two key resources in this category are fresh water and air. I argue in Chapters 2 and 3 that an account of natural resource justice ought to defend sufficient shares of those natural resources specifically and non-substitutably necessary to the meeting of basic human rights: that concern for the supports for basic human rights should place a firm constraint on any inequalities which might otherwise be morally acceptable. Other resources, however valuable, are not non-substitutable supports for basic rights. This is not to say that they are entirely substitutable sources of benefits. It might well be that particular people are committed to important projects which are dependent on secure access to particular resources (see Chapter 5). But certain resources are distinctive first inasmuch as they are indispensable supports for the most *basic* functionings, and second insofar as they represent vital supports for *anyone's* life, no matter which projects they happen to be committed to. This is enough to single them out as supports for basic human rights.[11]

Third, return to the distinction present in international law between natural resources, and the source of those resources: natural wealth. This captures something important, which is that all natural resources are the products of natural processes. Another way of capturing the same point is to distinguish, as environmental scientists do, between ecosystems and the ecosystem services they provide us with. Some of these systems function incredibly slowly, producing services (including natural resources) over vast periods of time. Such resources—including oil, coal, natural gas, and many minerals—will not be replaced by those systems during the lifetime of present generations, and indeed perhaps not within the lifespan of the human species as a whole. We therefore call such resources non-renewable, or non-replenishable. Other systems function much more rapidly, so that we can use the resources emanating from them secure in the knowledge that they will be replaced very soon. Rainwater would be a prime example, or the light from the sun. We call those resources renewable or replenishable.

The difference between renewable and non-renewable natural resources may also have implications for justice. In relation to renewable resources, we face the task of ensuring the continued functioning of the ecosystem processes which give rise to them. If ecosystem health is ensured, a ready supply of the requisite resources 'naturally' follows. We face questions, to be sure, of how to share access to those resources; but we also face questions about how to *protect* the ecosystem processes from which they emanate. They pose an additional normative challenge about how to fairly share the costs of conservation, potentially including both direct costs and opportunity costs for those charged with protecting them (see Chapter 10).

All of this diversity need not, to be sure, affect the kind of account of distributive justice we are committed to: it does not tell us whether we should generally favour egalitarian or sufficientarian principles, for instance. But it can affect the implications of any account: it should mean that within the remit of an egalitarian account we have reason to protect basic entitlements to some natural resources even where this is not otherwise demanded by our egalitarianism, for instance. We will explore some of those implications further in later chapters.

1.2. COMMODITIES, RESOURCES, AND JUSTICE

In this section I discuss two issues arising from the conceptual framework set out in section 1.1. Addressing each helps to clarify the objectives of the present account.

1.2.1. Natural Resources and Commodities

A theory of natural resource justice assumes that we can intelligibly formulate principles of justice to govern the ways in which the benefits and burdens flowing from natural resources ought to be allocated between people (including, potentially, both present and future people). Those benefits and burdens are a 'distribuendum' which ought to be of interest to people with a whole range of views about justice. A global egalitarian, for instance, might call for the radical redistribution of at least some of those benefits and burdens, assuming that our world is presently characterized by considerable injustice. As we will see in Chapter 2, a 'minimalist' about global justice might defend, more modestly, a universal entitlement to the resources necessary to meeting one's basic rights, or to living a life of a decent standard. But this theory too could have revisionist implications.

Perhaps sweeping global principles of resource allocation ought to be rejected, though, on the basis that they are insufficiently sensitive to the ways in which people come to be attached to natural resources. Treating natural resources as an undifferentiated class of goods which we can blithely move around the planet in order to maximize utility, or satisfy equality, for instance, would be to wrench them free of their social context, a context in which for many people they are much more than mere interchangeable sources of benefit. Perhaps the 'initial' distribution of resources was basically haphazard. But over time the haphazard becomes the status quo, and people factor control over local resources into their most central life-plans. If so, then one view would be that when people have strong attachments to particular natural resources we ought to *exempt* them from principles which would seek to advance some pattern or other of resource allocation. On that view we ought to circumscribe the remit of a theory of natural resource justice: we ought to protect important commitments to natural resources, that is, by removing some of them from the domain of principles of resource justice. A theory of natural resource justice would then focus not on natural resources generally, but rather exclusively on natural resources which were already bought and sold as 'mere' commodities, on the assumption that only then can we be sure that they are not the subject of significant attachments.[12]

Now, one response to such a view would reiterate that a theory of natural resource justice will not always—and perhaps not even often—call for us to wrench resources out of their social context and spirit them elsewhere. We can share the sequestering capacity of the forests fairly without moving trees around, and in that sense attachments can remain undisturbed. If we take attachments seriously we might respect them, in this case, by granting secure access to forests. It is not obvious that taking them seriously requires us to give forest-dwellers exclusive ownership of sequestering capacity.[13] And if we care about the potential of some resources to drive economic development, a plausible option if we wanted to share those opportunities most widely would be to tax those resources. In principle taxes could allow agents not to develop or destroy the resources they are particularly attached to.[14] A second response is to reiterate that a theory of natural resource justice will not treat natural resources as mere commodities, valuable only in light of their ability to fuel economic processes. As I have argued from the start, resources can fuel wellbeing in much more various ways than that; and taking due heed of the role of resources in sustaining human wellbeing will also count against treating them as commodities alone (on which see section 1.2.2).

But let us attempt a more fundamental response here. What if it *were* true that there was a clear tension between global justice theorists' redistributive ambitions and important attachments? How should we respond? We should grant it is true that resources are often important to people in ways which are not well captured when we depict them as economic commodities. But we should firmly reject the claim that the right way to respond to this fact is to remove the resources in question from the remit of principles of justice. It is possible—and desirable—to recognize the significance of the attachment people feel to natural resources without going that far. To the contrary, we need a theory of justice to tell us why attachment matters, and how we ought to weigh it alongside other sources of claims over resources. I suggest in this book that egalitarians both can and should pay far more attention to important attachments than they have sometimes done to date. But if we are to take attachment seriously as a distributive constraint then we must do so for reasons of justice. We must confront the difficult task of constructing an account of how different claims of justice ought to be integrated within a single theory. To say that a particular natural resource ought to be left with the person who needs it in order to pursue some vital life-project does not mean that we should say it is not a natural resource, or not a valid token for discussion under a theory of natural resource justice. It is to say that those projects matter from the point of view of justice, and to spell out the implications of those projects for a just distribution of resource rights.

This allows us to understand better what it might mean to describe a conception of natural resources as 'intentional'. Avery Kolers has suggested that theorists of global justice tend to treat natural resources as though they come into the world with value, and uses, already attached to them. But of course their value, and their uses, depend upon the projects and technologies which human communities have. To advance a purely physical conception of natural resources is to tear them out of this social context, and to misunderstand their nature as partly 'social' entities, whose value is highly dependent on social context.[15] A conception of natural resources should be 'intentional', by contrast, in the sense that a particular piece of matter should not count as a natural resource unless it is used in certain ways by the community which currently controls it. In describing natural resources we are describing, in that sense, materials which have already become embedded in particular (typically, for Kolers, economic) processes.[16]

I agree that it would be highly misleading to assume that the value or uses of natural resources are somehow 'natural' themselves, rather than context-specific. For example, in Chapter 4 I discuss the familiar distinction between improved and unimproved resources, and suggest that such a distinction cannot turn on the idea that there is some portion of the value of any given resource which is somehow 'natural' or asocial. The exchange values of both improved and unimproved resources are contextually determined. The question is how we accommodate such facts within an account of natural resource justice. My account accommodates them first by construing natural resources as goods which are potentially of use to humans. If a substance cannot deliver benefits to (current or future) human beings, it is of no interest to a theory of natural resource justice—and as such, the set of goods falling into the category 'natural resources' will ebb and flow with the development of technology, for instance. Second, in Chapter 4 I will argue that when it comes to distributing the value even of unimproved natural resources, this value cannot be seen as a purely natural asset (whatever that might mean), but rather as a social one. This has two implications, as we will see: that the unimproved/improved distinction is normatively less interesting than has often been supposed; and that the argument for redistributing natural resource values is much more similar to conventional egalitarian arguments for redistributing social assets than has sometimes been assumed.

The way in which natural resources are conceived as intentional goods on Kolers's account, by contrast, leads us astray. On this account goods only count as natural resources when they *are being* used in certain ways, rather than when they have the potential to be used to serve human ends; and whether something counts as a natural resource depends only upon the actions of the group or agents currently controlling it. I suggest in Chapter 5 that this is deeply counter-intuitive. When an agent controls a good which could deliver huge benefits to another agent—saving them from a life of misery, or imminent death, say—the first agent cannot end the conversation about justice by declaring that they are not using this good in a particular (economically intensive) way, and hence that there can be no question at all, from the point of view of justice, of them sharing it with the needy *because it is not a natural resource*. We have every reason, then, to restrict our discussion of natural resources to those goods which potentially deliver benefits to human beings. But we have every reason to resist the much more restrictive definition Kolers recommends.

1.2.2. The Limits of Justice

A theory of natural resource justice will give us reasons to prefer one distribution of benefits and burdens over another, by showing that this distribution is more faithful to the demands of justice. Its subjects are people, living or as yet unborn. Such a theory seeks to advance the interests of human beings, and to constrain the ways in which people sometimes use (or overuse) resources at the expense of others' interests. But a large moral question looms in the background, which is the question of the constraints humans ought to place on their use of natural resources not in light of each other's claims, but in light of the claims of other species or of 'nature' in general. Perhaps any plausible moral view will recognize reasons why particular natural resources should be preserved independently of the benefits they deliver to people: for instance, a given resource might have intrinsic value, or deliver important benefits to other species. If so, there may be constraints on how humans should consume natural resources which do not derive from the consideration of human interests.

For instance, in what follows I will occasionally discuss examples where people have argued about how to distribute between themselves rights over animals such as reindeer, or fish. But one view might be that people cannot have any rights over animals, or at least that there are some ways in which they ought not to benefit from them (eating them, say, or experimenting on them). This brings us to some contentious questions in meta-ethics. It is certainly plausible that morality requires constraints on our use of resources above and beyond the demands imposed by a theory of distributive justice. We might then envisage a division of labour whereby a moral theory determined which benefits people might permissibly derive from animals, say (and we could imagine a range of answers to that question), and a theory of distributive justice determined how those permissible benefits should be allocated between people now or in the future. Resolving the first moral question would easily occupy a book of its own, but it seems to me to be independent from the second question, which is the one I will pursue. Even if it were true, for instance, that we ought never to derive benefits from animals, neither the individual arguments in this book nor the shape of the argument as a whole would be affected. When I talk of the distribution of benefits, for instance, readers can imagine that I am talking about permissible benefits. When individual examples involving reindeer or fish crop up, these animals could be substituted with abiotic resources without any loss of meaning.

Still, the question of whether and how we ought to defer to putative non-human interests is an important one, even if I will not pursue it. We can observe, though, that the account of natural resource justice defended in this book will, even if this is not its target, protect putative non-human interests or putative intrinsic value much better than either current practices, or indeed a more minimalist account of natural resource justice. This is because I believe that a defensible theory of natural resource justice will by itself engender much greater restraint in resource consumption than occurs at present, and therefore go some way to alleviating the concerns of defenders of 'nature'. This is so for at least three reasons. First, taking the demands of intergenerational justice sufficiently seriously will likely give us reason to preserve resources much more effectively than we have done for centuries, and indeed to radically alter—and radically constrain—the ways in which we currently consume precious resources. Undoubtedly a belief in the intrinsic value of those resources, or in the right of other sentient beings to make use of them themselves, would add further strength to the injunction to do so. But we need not lean on any particular account of the intrinsic value of nature, or of animal rights, to arrive at the conclusion that our current habits in consuming the resources of the world are in need of urgent reform.

Second, one feature of our world is that communities such as states currently monopolize both the benefits and the burdens flowing from the natural resources in their territories. One important set of burdens is the *opportunity costs* of consuming resources. If an agent or a community refrains from consuming some precious resource, he, she, or it loses out on the economic development opportunities which would have accrued had the resource in question been consumed. As environmental consciousness develops, these agents are frequently enjoined not to destroy precious biodiversity, unspoiled wilderness, or resources, such as rainforests, which deliver important global public goods. But by and large, it is not those who do the enjoining who will bear the opportunity cost. It is the agent who controls the resource in question who is being asked to forego opportunities—opportunities which others may be able to avail themselves of. In a context where some of the world's most precious resources are contained in developing rather than developed countries, this produces considerable distributive unfairness, and understandable resistance on the part of locals to injunctions from outside to conserve these resources. But I will argue in Chapter 10 that there are often good arguments why the opportunity costs of the conservation of precious resources ought to be pooled globally—why outsiders, that is, should mitigate the costs borne by locals who currently control resources, when justice requires their preservation. If such transfers occurred, a major impetus towards their destruction would be removed.

Third, considering the variety of ways in which even *present* people benefit from natural resources should itself seriously constrain our consumption of them. In practice we often take a rapacious and short-term attitude towards natural resources such that present economic benefits override any other considerations. Liberal economic theory has a habit of treating the non-exploitation of resources as a form of wastefulness. We are all too wedded to the habit of identifying benefits with economic benefits, and natural resources with raw materials for industry, agriculture, and energy generation. But we benefit from natural resources in many more ways than this, and taking those benefits seriously will often itself give us good reason not to consume them so frenetically. If I happen to derive comfort, in this world, from the knowledge that at least some of the natural world lies undisturbed and unravaged by humanity, then taking this benefit seriously already counsels in favour of conservation. Chapter 5 makes the case that resources can have cultural or symbolic value to particular people, that their attachment to such resources is normatively important, and that their desire for continued access to those resources will at least sometimes defeat the claims of others who would consume those resources in the interests of economic development. An egalitarian theory ought to take seriously the diversity of ways in which people benefit from exposure to natural resources, only some of which actually involve consuming them. If it does so, the possibility of their degradation is qualified. An important part of the solution to the worry about our rapacious and destructive attitude towards natural resources, then, is precisely to recognize the diversity of ways in which they can be of benefit to people, and also to properly recognize the benefits which they ought to be allowed to deliver to future people. That might not capture all of the reasons why we ought ever to protect natural resources from threats, but it is sufficient to establish that a properly broad theory of natural resource justice itself has strong reasons to reject the relentless pursuit of short-term economic benefits.

1.3. RESOURCE RIGHTS

A theory of natural resource justice will specify a set of rights and duties dictating what we can, and indeed must, do with regard to resources. In this section I describe a set of eight core resource rights. There are many things we might be permitted to do with natural resources. Rights over resources might therefore be unpacked in various ways, to distinguish their various 'incidents'.[17] We require a list which is reasonably concise, but which still incorporates all of the main contenders. Such a list should capture both the main things which individuals can do with natural resources, and the main things which groups or institutions such as states can do with them. My list is intended therefore to be capable of capturing the content of both what are conventionally understood to be rights of property, and rights of jurisdiction. We are able to question, once we have such a list, which resource rights individuals ought to have, and also to assess arguments for states' rights over natural resources. As such, individual rights of property, and states' rights of property or of jurisdiction, are both possible outcomes of an investigation into natural resource justice. But it remains to be seen whether they can be justified.

The list of resource rights is as follows:[18]

1. *Access* is the right to interact with a resource in a non-subtractive fashion. Visiting a resource, or handling it in a non-damaging way, would count as accessing it, assuming this did not diminish the amount of benefits available to others. Taking pleasure in the beauty of a river would too.

2. *Withdrawal* is the right to obtain subtractive benefits—to obtain or remove resource units for one's use, or to consume and thereby remove their capacity to provide the same benefits for others. Consuming a resource entirely would count as an instance of withdrawal, as when we burn a non-renewable fossil fuel. So too would locking it in a vault and hence preventing others from accessing it.

3. *Alienation* is the right to sell a resource, and thereby transfer to another one's existing rights over it. If I have the right to withdraw a quantity of coal from a coal-seam but pass that right on to my friend, I have exercised a right of alienation.

4. The right to *derive income* is the right to obtain proceeds from transferring rights over a resource, or from allowing others to benefit from it. If one is able to sell a resource, to retain the money gained thereby is to exercise the right to derive income. Charging others to benefit either subtractively or non-subtractively from a resource one has rights over—such as charging people to sit in the shade of your tree, or to eat its apples—is also to exercise the right.

These four rights describe the ability to directly enjoy or transfer benefits from a resource. We could usefully call them *first-order rights*. But there is a second set of rights which are, in essence, rights to distribute, condition, or constrain the ways in which others can derive or transfer benefits. We could call the following four rights *second-order rights*:

5. *Exclusion* is the right to determine who can access and withdraw a resource, and therefore includes the right to forbid others from doing so. To be the gatekeeper of a public park, or to hold the key to a store of coal, is to exercise the right of exclusion.

6. *Management* is the right to set rules for *how* resources can be accessed or withdrawn, and conversely to make decisions about whether and how particular resources ought to be protected. Forbidding people from using wood to fuel open fires, but permitting its use in house- and boat-building is to exercise the right of management, as is passing a regulation forbidding the enrichment of uranium. So is requiring everyone to prune their apple trees in the autumn.

7. The right to *regulate alienation* is the right to set rules about how rights over resources can be sold or otherwise transferred. To forbid the bequest of a resource is to exercise the right to regulate alienation, as is to stipulate the conditions (such as democratic consent) under which agents (such as individuals, or collectives) can transfer any rights they hold over resources.

8. The right to *regulate income* is the right to set rules about who can derive income from resources they have rights over, and how. Setting minimum or maximum prices for particular benefits would count as an exercise of this right, as would setting rules about how the income from selling resources or hiring out their benefits should be shared between agents (e.g. by imposing taxes, or requiring rights-holders to pay dividends).

These eight rights capture the most important things we can do with regard to resources, and our entitlements of justice, I suggest, can in turn be captured by pointing to one or some combination of them. Notably, the four first-order rights are the typical prerogatives of individual owners, whereas the four second-order rights are typically the preserve of governing authorities such as states (in which case we tend to call them rights of jurisdiction). But there is nothing natural about such a division of labour, and allocating rights in one way rather than another requires a principled justification.

Whenever any combination of these rights is held by any combination of agents, duties will be imposed on others. I will not attempt to delineate these duties here: that would be an exhausting project. Suffice to say two things: first, that the duties involved will include both positive and negative duties (and the very same right will frequently, and perhaps always, invoke both kinds of duty). Someone's right to access a resource can generate, for instance, a (negative) duty on all other parties not to interfere with her access, and may generate a (positive) duty to provide that resource in the right circumstances. To give an example, insofar as someone's basic human rights depend upon consumption of air, this can generate (negative) duties not to hinder that consumption, and also (positive) duties to improve air quality or, in emergencies, to supply air itself. Second, as the last example already indicates, the duties that arise will be complex and sit with different agents. They will, moreover, generate remedial duties when imperfectly observed. Rights, at least on an interest theory, will generate complex 'waves of duties' which resist simple characterization.[19] It will sometimes be worthwhile, in what follows, to delineate specific duties attendant on the rights I have described. But attempting an exhaustive account would be a forlorn (and tedious) project.

1.3.1. Allocating Rights

The rights described in section 1.3 are both conceptually and practically separable. Hence we should not be misled into assuming that they naturally cohere into a single and simple notion of 'ownership'. Honoré's account of the incidents of property makes this point very clearly. As he puts it, 'Historically there have been many reasons for separating the standard incidents into two or more parcels. Indeed, historically speaking, the metaphor of splitting may mislead, for in some cases full ownership has been built up from the fragments, not vice versa.'[20] Such fragmentation is by no means exceptional or aberrant.[21] Thus to ask 'who owns natural resources?' is certainly an unhelpful question, *if* that question obscures possibilities under which all of the various rights over resources are not concentrated in the hands of single agents. Ownership might be the outcome of an argument about resources but it ought not, at the risk of begging the question, to be its starting point. We can say the same for the traditional understanding of jurisdiction or 'permanent sovereignty' over natural resources (see Chapter 6). The four second-order rights need not be allocated of a piece to single agents or communities, and the possibility that they should not must remain open.

Within debates about natural resource justice to date, the battle lines have, however, frequently been drawn around competing visions of ownership. One view much evident in historical political thought holds that the world's resources were originally unowned, but that individuals could derive rights of private ownership over such resources (subject to some keenly contested constraints or provisos: see Chapter 2). Against that view, some have defended forms of collective ownership, under which we should all exercise joint control over the world's resources. Alternatively, perhaps we are each entitled to an equal individual share of natural resources. International law, by contrast, has endorsed a principle of 'permanent sovereignty' over those resources contained within individual nation-states which is often interpreted to include ownership of those resources.

It would be a mistake to suppose that the task of a theory of natural resource justice is in the first instance to adjudicate between these competing visions. Our task is to take seriously the various claims of justice which we might have over natural resources. Taking them seriously might then push us some way *towards* one vision of ownership or other. In fact, I believe that we would be ill-served by an assumption that all resources should be either individually, collectively, or even nationally owned. Justice, more likely, demands a patchwork allocation of resource rights so that *some* resources might be owned by individuals or collectives, but for others no single agent will exercise a full set of rights.

This view might appear unduly controversial. Consider individual ownership again. Even if individual ownership should not be theoretically privileged, we might think that it is so widespread an economic and political practice that there must be *something* to be said for viewing it as a default position. In response it is worth reiterating that in practice separating the incidents of ownership is utterly commonplace. To illustrate that point, imagine a small, sunny Mediterranean nation-state. As a citizen of the European Union (EU) (at the time of writing), I have the right to enter that territory, which will also allow me to avail of the right to *access* at least some of its resources: that is, to enjoy non-subtractive benefits from those resources (swimming at its beaches, enjoying its sunshine, walking its olive groves). But I will not, in all likelihood, have rights of alienation or exclusion.

On the other hand I might happen to own a part-share of one of those olive groves. This might include the right to *derive income* (perhaps I have a right to 20 litres of olive oil per year, or the proceeds from selling those litres). But that right to derive income need not actually be accompanied by rights of *access* (someone who was not a EU citizen, and who was not entitled to enter the country, could still have the same right to specific proceeds[22]). It might but need not be accompanied by the right of *alienation* (I may be unable to trigger the sale of the olive grove, though if it were sold I might be entitled to a portion of the proceeds). And it may not be accompanied by rights of management or withdrawal either. On the other hand, if I *were* a citizen of the EU, then I (along with all other EU citizens) might have some rather diluted management rights over the olive grove, assuming its owners derive benefits from the EU's Common Agricultural Policy (which brings in train certain rules about land use), and assuming that the EU will separately prohibit use of certain pesticides and fertilizers, for example. Though we need not labour the point further, it is also both conceptually and practically possible to enjoy other bundles of resource rights—to have rights to management and exclusion without rights of alienation, or without rights to derive income, for example.[23]

Separation of these individual rights is not just hypothetical, but is practised every day. We routinely find, in economic life and legal reality, agents who act as 'trustees' (enjoying rights of exclusion and management, say, but not rights of alienation or income-derival); 'shareholders' (enjoying the right to derive income alone); 'authorized users' (enjoying the right to access the resources of, for instance, public parks—but none of the other rights); 'proprietors' of various collectively managed natural assets (including rights of access, some rights of withdrawal, and rights of management and exclusion); and so on.[24]

The task of a theory of natural resource justice, then, is not in the first instance to adjudicate between competing conceptions of ownership. It is to answer the question where and to whom, at the bar of justice, rights (and any correlative duties) with regard to resources are to be allocated. It might well be that our answer to that question will fall short of endorsing national ownership, or even a strong version of individual private ownership. In Chapter 6 I examine arguments in favour of the doctrine of permanent state sovereignty over natural resources, and find it unsupported by considerations of justice. In Chapters 4 and 5 I examine arguments grounding special claims over natural resources, and show that, in general, they also fail to demonstrate that a strong version of private ownership of resources is demanded by justice, with the implication that we could justly place significant constraints on the ability of agents to achieve a full and exclusive set of rights over particular natural resources. In the process we will vindicate not just the conceptual possibility but the desirability of dispersing resource rights amongst a variety of agents. The answer to the question about ownership, then—which of the conventional visions of ownership should we choose?—might therefore be none of them.

This opens up considerable possibilities from the point of view of an account of justice. Perhaps justice dictates that we should decouple some of the most significant rights from each other. Even if we allow some agent to control or directly derive substantial benefits from a resource, we might qualify their right to earn income from it by hiring those benefits out to others.[25] That alone would actually be a rather limited inroad on the 'myth of property' insofar as it would leave the rest of the bundle with the agent in question. Other inroads are possible, which would allocate rights of access or withdrawal to other agents, at least *in extremis*. Splitting rights in such ways might help us to accommodate the general claims which all of us putatively have over natural resources alongside the special claims which some of us have over some resources. Achieving justice in the face of competing claims over those precious resources requires an open mind.

ENDNOTES

1. That view broadly overlaps with the school of thought known as left-libertarianism. See the discussion in Chapter 3.
2. See for instance Risse 2012. I discuss this argument further in Chapter 3.
3. The fact that *energy* can count as a resource means that it may be a little clumsy to talk of resources as raw *materials*. In any case, we have to conceive of the raw materials or building-blocks available to us as comprising both matter and energy.
4. See e.g. Risse 2012; Casal 2011; and Steiner 2011b. Land reclaimed from the sea might be an exception.
5. For a clear account of the overlapping definitions of natural resources within international law, see Schrijver 1997 (especially 12–16).
6. Schrijver 1997: 19. For the purposes of compiling statistics on natural resources and economic growth, by contrast, the OECD suggests that 'Natural resources are natural assets (raw materials) occurring in nature that can be used for economic production or consumption.' Organisation for Economic Co-operation and Development Glossary of Statistics: http://stats.oecd.org/glossary. Natural resources are being defined too restrictively here, because they can be beneficial in a wide variety of ways, not all of which will best be captured by the idea of *economic* production or consumption (see section 1.2).
7. The pioneering accounts of Charles Beitz, Brian Barry, and Thomas Pogge do not offer a precise definition of natural resources, but each appears to assume that by contrast with social products they are not created by humans, and hence represent non-human-made raw materials. Beitz 1979: 137; Barry 1982; Pogge 2002: 196–7, 201–7. Leif Wenar defines natural resources as 'non-manufactured and unprocessed, non-human objects with a value in use'. Wenar 2016a: 202. Mathias Risse's theory identifies the same features (Risse 2012).
8. Goodin 1992: 38–40.
9. There is of course a fourth category: goods whose benefits are excludable but non-subtractive are commonly called 'club goods'. But they are much less significant for our purposes. For a discussion, see for instance Cornes and Sandler 1996.
10. Compare, for instance, Dworkin's account of equality of resources, which is exclusively concerned with privately owned goods. Dworkin (2000: 65) suggested that an adequate theory of equality must find some way of integrating a concern with public goods, but his theory leaves the challenge to one side.
11. For a groundbreaking account of such rights, see Shue 1980.

12. Kolers 2012. I examine this view more closely in Chapter 5, where I show that it has objectionable implications.
13. Armstrong 2015.
14. This would depend upon both the precise tax base and the tax rate. See the discussion in Chapter 8.
15. On this point see also Hayward 2006.
16. Kolers 2014.
17. The notion of 'incidents' of ownership comes from Honoré 1987. The famous eleven incidents of ownership delineated by Honoré include six rights. These differ somewhat from the eight resource rights I suggest. For one thing, I subdivide some of Honoré's rights (Honoré describes a 'right to use' which on a wide interpretation adumbrates what I am calling both rights of access and rights of management; he also describes a 'right to the capital' which adumbrates both the right to withdraw and the right to alienate). We need to keep open the possibility that parties might have the right to access a resource without the right to manage it (or vice versa), or the right to withdraw it without the right to alienate it (or vice versa). For another thing, I include what I call *second-order rights* which regulate the ways in which rights of access, withdrawal, alienation, and income-derival can be exercised and by whom.
18. The list of rights is substantially based upon the pioneering work of Elinor Ostrom. See e.g. Ostrom 2000: 339. The right to derive income, to regulate income, and to regulate alienation are my own additions, however. I have also amended the ways in which some of the other rights are described. Christman (1994) suggests a partially overlapping list including rights to possess, use, manage, alienate, transfer, and gain income from property, but excluding second-order rights.
19. Waldron 1989.
20. Honoré 1987: 187.
21. As one leading legal account of property has it, 'property institutions diverge enormously in the range of elements they comprise'. For instance, what we might call 'use-privileges' are often separated from the right to accumulate wealth from a resource: 'The shareholders in a public company or the beneficiaries under a large trust have private wealth—cashable claims on scarce resources—without necessarily having any substantial use-privileges over the items vested in the company or trustees.' Harris 1996: 28; 27. Defenders of global distributive justice might observe the reverse too: that a party (or community) might enjoy the right to access or use a resource without having claims to derive (all of the) income from it.
22. The shareholder's dividend is a very common example of a right to derive income divorced from other resource rights. See Harris 1996: 27.
23. To enjoy rights of management and exclusion without rights of access, alienation, or derival of income is the conventional legal situation of a trustee, another very common role.
24. For a slightly different but overlapping typology of status-types, see Ostrom 2000: 340. See also Ostrom 2003.
25. As suggested by Christman 1994, chapter 9.

2

Equality and Its Critics

Natural resources are potentially useful to people, and yet none of us is responsible for their existence. Those twin ideas have resonated within political philosophy for centuries. The conclusion that philosophers have frequently drawn is that natural resources represent a 'common bounty', a 'common treasury', or a 'common storehouse' for the satisfaction of human desires and projects over which nobody *initially* has a greater claim than anybody else. Some such view represented a shared starting point for seventeenth-century thinkers including Hobbes, Locke, Grotius, and Pufendorf. These theorists all believed that people could derive what I will call special claims over resources. For instance, by working on a tract of land, or its resources, I might be said to 'appropriate' it—to become its rightful owner. All of these theorists agreed that individual appropriation of natural resources from the 'common storehouse' could be justified. But they also believed that there must be some kind of distributive constraint upon each person's freedom to annex resources in this way.

The two ideas continue to reverberate within contemporary debates on global justice. Charles Beitz famously argued that the uneven distribution of natural resources across the earth was 'morally arbitrary', and that it would be wrong for this distribution to confine some communities to relative poverty and to grant others easy access to wealth. As Beitz put it, 'The fact that someone happens to be located advantageously with respect to natural resources does not provide a reason why he or she should be entitled to exclude others from the benefits that might be derived from them.'[1] Geography, we might say, need not be not destiny. The argument is grounded on much the same ideas: that natural resources are a source of advantage; and yet that nobody appears, on the face of it, to have a greater claim to the benefits and burdens flowing from these resources than anyone else. Beitz also held, therefore, that one agent's (or one community's) ability to derive benefits from natural resources must somehow be constrained in light of others' claims. Many have followed in his footsteps since.[2]

But as the long history of debates on resource justice amply illustrates—and as contemporary debates continue to reveal—there is room for considerable disagreement about just how strict any constraint on agents' holdings ought to be. The argument that one agent's appropriation ought not to leave others on the brink of death is, to be sure, relatively uncontroversial.[3] It can safely be observed that none of us could survive without air and fresh water, and it is also evident that supplies of both are more than sufficient for everyone in the world to meet their basic human rights. Everyone needs air to breathe, and fortunately air is abundant and non-excludable. Humans are also estimated to require 2.5 to 3 litres of water per day for drinking, or a total of 30–50 litres if cooking and sanitation needs are also taken into account.[4] If so, global supplies of fresh water are more than sufficient to meet the basic rights of all. Only twelve of the world's countries have access to less than 1,000 litres per person, and only one (Kuwait) has access to less than 100 litres per capita.[5] It might then be thought that any distributive theory which fails to call for secure access to those resources for all is unappealing. The upshot would be a constraint on everyone's freedom to annex resources or their benefits: nobody must deprive others of the resources necessary to meet their own basic rights.

Such a constraint would be very important, but it would only take us so far. This is because whereas some natural resources are needed by all humans, a great surplus would remain which are merely likely to be useful for a variety of human activities, as opposed to being strictly needed by anyone. Should we care, from the point of view of justice, if some agents end up holding more of this surplus, and others less? When one agent seizes for himself a disproportionately large share of their benefits, is this necessarily to do a disservice to the claims of others? Might justice require not only the protection of our basic rights, but also that our ability to access the benefits and burdens flowing from natural resources remains *equal*?

This chapter examines conflicting views on this question. One point is worth bearing in mind before we begin. When we discuss the constraints of justice that ought to apply to natural resources, the various views we will consider disagree about not only the distributive *principle* such a constraint should enact, but also about the *scope* of any constraint. In the work of philosophers like Locke, for instance, the primary question appears to be how the private ownership of natural resources ought to be constrained. But even insofar as they have shared a focus upon ownership, philosophers have often disagreed about whether we should only be concerned to regulate ownership arising from the initial appropriation of resources, or whether we should also seek to regulate holdings which arise through subsequent transactions. Some accounts of natural resource justice apply a constraint only to initial appropriation, but not to what people subsequently do with their resources, so that skewed holdings which would be intolerable if they were the result of initial appropriation become tolerable if they arise through voluntary gifts or bequests on death, say. Some accounts would constrain appropriation and bequests, but not in-life gifts.[6] Still others—including most of the views under discussion in section 2.1—regulate holdings however they arise.[7] My own focus in this book will be broad: as I understand it, any and all of the benefits and burdens arising from natural resources are an appropriate topic for a theory of justice, even if some of these benefits and burdens accrue to non-owners (or even if there are no private owners at all). The discussion that follows serves to illustrate the diversity of views on natural resource justice, however, and the criticisms I make of the various views stand irrespective of our question about scope (an issue we return to in Chapter 3).

We will focus in sections 2.1 and 2.2, then, on the question of the *distributive standard* any constraint should enforce. If we are concerned about justice and injustice in resource holdings—or, more broadly, in receipt of the benefits and burdens arising from natural resources—according to what principle should we seek to constrain them? A first view, which we can associate with the school of thought known as right-libertarianism, suggests that holdings should be relatively unconstrained, perhaps because individual appropriation can be expected to be beneficial to all. A second view is a 'minimalist' one which suggests that holdings are just whenever all individuals retain access to the natural resources necessary to meet their basic human rights. I set out and criticize both views in section 2.1. The criticisms I make point forward to an egalitarian constraint. Section 2.2 defends such a constraint more explicitly. On the egalitarian view I will defend, holdings are just only when they pay proper regard to the value of equality. This need not mean that inequalities in natural resource shares are always and everywhere intolerable. But it does mean that inequalities stand in need of justification—and that, since equality has considerable value, the justification needs to be a compelling one.

The rest of the chapter deals with some challenges to an egalitarian view. Engaging with them is worthwhile in its own right, but also helps us to better understand the nature of an egalitarian theory of resource justice. The first challenge is as follows. The approach I defend in this book is one which holds that inequalities matter wherever, or between whomever, they occur. It matters that a person's life goes well, and each person's life matters equally. To the extent that natural resources represent important sources of wellbeing, we have reason to object to inequalities in the distribution of those benefits and burdens. But it has been claimed that inequalities are not automatically unjust, and rather are only to be considered unjust when they apply between people united in some specified kind of social relationship. On some views, as a result, inequalities outside an individual country's borders simply do not matter from the point of view of justice. In section 2.3 I show how egalitarians should respond to this 'relational' challenge. I then deal with another important objection. We should be interested in the distribution of the benefits and burdens flowing from natural resources, I suggest, insofar as those benefits and burdens make a difference to how people's lives go. But it has been argued that plentiful resource endowments are either irrelevant to countries' economic growth, or a veritable 'curse' for countries seeking to grow their way out of poverty. The normative conclusion which is sometimes drawn from this is that we need not care, from the point of view of justice, if some countries have more abundant shares of natural resources than others. If so, the many pages filled by learned disquisitions on resource inequality represent a wasted effort. In section 2.4 I show how egalitarians should respond to this objection. Finally, section 2.5 briefly introduces some other challenges to a global egalitarian theory which I will engage with in the remainder of this book.

2.1. RIGHT-LIBERTARIAN AND MINIMALIST CONSTRAINTS

2.1.1. Right-Libertarianism's Weak Constraint

As a philosophical view right-libertarianism argues for very weak constraints on natural resource holdings.[8] Right-libertarians claim that the world's resources are initially un-owned and hence that appropriating them denies no one of their rightful property. They also claim that humans individually own their own bodies and hence their labour-power. From these premises (world non-ownership and individual self-ownership) they typically derive two claims: one is that an agent's self-ownership carries over into very strong claims over any natural resources she is able to appropriate; the other is that the quantity of resources she is able to appropriate should be relatively unconstrained. Why might we accept those conclusions? A starting point for many accounts is John Locke's case for the institution of private property, which leant on both direct and instrumental arguments. The direct argument suggested that self-ownership fairly straightforwardly generates claims in the things one has mixed one's labour with: since one owns one's labour just as securely as one owns one's body, if anyone else removed the resources one has 'mixed' one's labour with, that would be tantamount to the theft of one's body (or at least a part of it).[9] The instrumental argument pointed to the various social and economic advantages of a regime in which private appropriation is permitted, contrasted with the (supposedly wasteful and unproductive) effects of a regime of non-ownership (or, alternatively, joint ownership). Both considerations, right-libertarians argue, counsel in favour of relatively unconstrained appropriation, and a robust set of property rights in the objects which are appropriated.

In light of its social advantages, Locke argued that private property could justly be made out of the 'fruits of the earth'—without the appropriator owing compensation to others—just so long as 'enough and as good' was left for others.[10] The precise meaning, and implications, of his famous 'proviso' has engendered much debate ever since, with libertarians on both the right and the left claiming it as their point of inspiration.[11] On the right, the task of unpacking and defending some version of that proviso was most notably taken up by Robert Nozick, who argued that appropriation is not unjust if it leaves no one worse off than they were before appropriation occurred. Of course it might appear that every time someone else appropriates a resource which had initially been un-owned, my position is worsened—in the sense that I now have a smaller range of resources to appropriate myself, in which case my liberty has been reduced. But notoriously elusive though his argument was here, Nozick's point appeared to be that although my range of liberties may have been reduced, my overall level of wellbeing may not have been. Considered along some suitable standard of wellbeing, overall I may actually benefit when others appropriate resources, not least if they are then able to create economic opportunities which I can avail of.[12]

On Nozick's view the efficiency of free markets means that his proviso is unlikely to be violated in practice.[13] Like Locke he appeared to believe that the productive capacities of free enterprise would unleash great economic advances, which would serve to lift the position of the poor on a rising tide of opportunity. Indeed, Nozick offered us scant examples of how the proviso *could* be violated. A violation would, to be sure, arise in a situation where everyone habitually used an un-owned waterhole for drinking, but one agent then appropriated the waterhole and forbade others from using it, thus rendering them unable to survive as they had before. Appropriating the waterhole and charging for water would also, other things being equal, leave people worse off. But imagine that one day it becomes apparent to the members of a community that the local water*hole* could be turned into a water*mill*. Its members race to appropriate it, and the person initially standing closest wins the race. Our lucky appropriator might then build his mill, creating jobs for the excluded and allowing them to purchase water from him with part of their wages. This new industry might make the lucky appropriator as rich as Croesus, but as long as the excluded are still able to drink—indeed, are now able to earn (albeit relatively meagre) wages from him—their wellbeing might in fact have increased. If so how can there be any complaint in justice?[14]

One response would target the way in which Nozick defines a worsening of someone's condition. On Nozick's view, worsening (apparently) means setting back someone's material wellbeing. But contrast this notion of material worsening with what we might call 'opportunity worsening'. Appropriations which increase (or do not diminish) our present level of material wellbeing might nevertheless leave us newly dependent on others, vulnerable to their whims, and with radically restricted opportunities to maintain the kind of freedom and autonomy that theories of justice—including right-libertarian ones—profess an interest in.[15] A first objection therefore holds that, even in the absence of the immediate worsening of someone's material wellbeing, setbacks to their opportunities might still be objectionable at the bar of justice. And these setbacks can have very significant consequences: although the waterhole example I discussed is rather other-worldly, it is not difficult to see how concerns about restricted opportunities could resonate with debates about climate justice, for instance. Imagine instead, then, that initially countries make 'subsistence emissions', employing only a small part of the carbon-sequestering capacity of the atmosphere.[16] But what if one rushes to industrialize, appropriating such a large share of its capacity that, although others are not denied the ability to make subsistence emissions, neither are they able to industrialize themselves? The industrializing country might have raised the absolute material wellbeing of people in other countries, for instance by developing new consumer products or the medicines that great wealth makes possible. But still, the opportunities of other countries have now been radically and permanently curtailed. And this appears objectionable.

A second objection would question the baseline against which Nozick's proviso operates. The proviso appears to ask us whether poor individuals in capitalist economies are nevertheless better off than they would be in a world where no private property existed. Even if the answer will often be yes, why is this the appropriate comparison? Why is it *enough* to say that a regime of strong and unconstrained private property rights makes us better off than a world of non-appropriation? Can it not be relevant that there are alternative (or, perhaps, accessible alternative) scenarios in which the poor are even better off?[17] Those might include worlds in which appropriation was subjected to a more rigorous egalitarian constraint (indeed, even revising Nozick's proviso to incorporate some notion of opportunity worsening might push it in an egalitarian direction, at the same time as making it more likely that the proviso will be violated in market societies[18]). By comparison to such principles a situation in which the fast or the strong—early appropriators, in short—are able to make far greater gains than others may lose appeal. Right-libertarians may well point to the overall benefits of a system whereby individuals are able to freely appropriate from nature, then, as opposed to a system whereby resources cannot be owned, or whereby their use remains subject to the kind of vetoes associated with joint ownership.[19] But it is doubtful that these suffice to justify the unconstrained inequalities which can be produced by such unilateral appropriations. Thus it appears we can say that the constraint argued for by Nozick is necessary, but not that it is sufficient, to secure justice. We lack clear arguments why some more demanding constraint is not also required.

2.1.2. Minimalism's Basic Rights Constraint

On a 'minimalist' view justice permits any pattern of holdings which is compatible with all individuals maintaining access to the objects of their basic human rights. When applied to natural resources this has negative and positive implications. Negatively, the view rules out any individual holdings—or acts of appropriation—which prevent others' basic rights being met. Positively—subject to certain conditions—justice may demand that we provide others with the natural resources necessary to securing their basic rights. But once everyone's basic human rights are secured, a minimalist account recommends no further constraints. These views claim that it is important that basic rights are met, and that the goal of making sure everyone lives a life above a threshold marked out by basic rights has independent moral value. They deny, however, that justice places further constraints on holdings and that inequalities, in particular, are objectionable in and of themselves.[20]

Minimalism about natural resource justice has a distinguished philosophical pedigree. If it was a commonplace of seventeenth-century thought that the earth was originally given to humankind in common, our collective ownership of the world and its fruits was held necessarily to place a constraint on permissible holdings. Whilst some of these views used the fact of collective ownership to support egalitarian conclusions, others held, more modestly, that private acquisition, though otherwise tolerable or even desirable, should not leave others indigent. Such ideas have been given renewed currency in Mathias Risse's theory of global justice. According to his view, whilst there may be demands of 'reasonable conduct' which constrain holdings in a broadly egalitarian fashion, the demands of justice proper are much more modest. Although egalitarianism might be appropriate *within* communities, we ought (only) to embrace a basic rights constraint on permissible distributions *between* communities.[21] As far as cross-national comparisons are concerned, justice is satisfied when everyone has what he or she needs in order to meet their basic human rights, and this not only places a constraint on permissible holdings, but may require us to take positive action to protect others' ability to access essential natural resources such as fresh water.[22] Consider a striking example suggested by Risse in which the population of the United States shrinks to two people who are nevertheless still able, through some security technology or other, to exclude all outsiders from the land and other resources of that territory. Would such exclusion not be objectionable from the point of view of justice? Imagine that it left at least some outsiders unable to meet their basic rights. Wouldn't accepting that outcome require us to place far too much weight on the claims of initial appropriators, vis-à-vis the claims of people in general to make use of the world's resources? On Risse's account, to be sure, outsiders do not necessarily have a claim to the *particular* resources contained in the United States; but we do have symmetrical claims to support ourselves with the resources the world makes available to us, and respect for our basic rights to that extent constrains the amount of resources that any agent(s) can control.[23]

We can find further support for broadly minimalist views within recent debates on global justice. For David Miller there can be positive duties of justice, in the right circumstances, to help other societies meet the basic human rights of their members. If outsiders non-culpably lack access to the natural resources necessary to meeting those rights, for instance, it could be incumbent upon others to grant them material assistance. But unequal shares of natural resources do not in and of themselves raise problems from the point of view of justice.[24] Whilst Miller did once suggest that unequal access to natural resources might stand in need of correction,[25] his more recent work does not make any such claim, and instead develops arguments why nations might have claims over the particular resources in their territories which would defeat programmes for egalitarian redistribution (see section 2.5). John Rawls, similarly, suggested that in a just 'Society of Peoples' each community was to be treated as the custodian of the natural resources within its territory, and denied that unequal shares of those resources constituted an injustice standing in need of correction. So long as well-ordered societies observe a duty of assistance—a duty, that is, to help 'burdened' societies construct and maintain the kind of decent social and political institutions which would allow them to support the basic human rights of their own members—then justice is satisfied without recourse to equalization.[26] Observing that duty might conceivably require transfers of natural resources in urgent cases, but other means of encouraging the development of stable institutions are probably more likely to succeed. Either way, equalization of resource shares would not be part of the moral picture at the international level.

Is the minimalist view defensible? Natural resources exhibit what Rawls called 'moderate scarcity': though they are not so abundant that conflicts over their distribution cannot arise, neither are they so scarce that our most basic claims cannot be met.[27] Given that there are more than enough resources in the world for everyone to obtain what they need for their survival, it is hard to see why any view which did not allow them that minimum should be accepted. To put it another way, it is hard to see what claims insiders (or owners) might have over natural resources which are *more* weighty than outsiders' (or non-owners') dependence on them for their very existence. It therefore appears that any plausible view should indeed defend a basic rights constraint on permissible distributions. Why, though, grant the negative claim endorsed by the minimalist view, to the effect that once basic rights are met any remaining inequalities in their distribution should not concern us from the point of view of justice?

Strikingly, at the global level the minimalist view is vulnerable to some of the same challenges that face the Nozickean view. In one important respect the minimalist view is certainly more demanding, inasmuch as at least on one version it can demand—as a matter of justice, rather than charity—that we positively protect others' access to essential resources, rather than merely refraining from depriving them of resources. But in other respects it is not obvious that it is any more demanding. Although the minimalist view will rule out appropriations which tip other people into circumstances where their basic rights are not met, so of course will the Nozickean view (because doing so will count as making them materially worse off). In cases where appropriation makes people worse off but does not jeopardize their basic rights, the minimalist view is *less* demanding than the Nozickean one (the Nozickean view will rule out any appropriation which makes someone materially worse off; but the minimalist view will only rule out such appropriation where this threatens basic rights). As with the Nozickean view, furthermore, minimalists have no principled objection to holdings which significantly restrict the opportunities of others, just so long as basic rights are secure.

But we should reject any view of natural resource justice which shows no concern with inequalities in their own right. Consider once more the case of climate justice. As part of the critique of right-libertarianism's weak constraints I called to mind an example (and not too far-fetched an example) in which one nation rushed to industrialization, thus depriving other countries of the possibility of ever doing the same. The Nozickean view would not rule this out, because the industrializing nation does not make other nations worse off (in Nozick's sense), even though it radically and permanently reduces their opportunities. The minimalist view would appear to support the same conclusion: given that other nations are still able to produce subsistence-level emissions, any inequality here is unobjectionable. But this seems deeply unfair. Recall, further, Risse's striking example of a two-person United States controlling vast swathes of natural resources. I suggest that the example is indeed a forceful one, but that it is too forceful for the good of his own theory. On his account the actions of these two people are objectionable whenever they leave outsiders unable to meet their basic rights. But if basic rights outside this counterfactual US *were* secure, justice would not rule out a situation in which these two individuals excluded everyone else from the entire sum of natural resources contained within that vast territory. Risse's theory tells us that these two individuals might be acting *unreasonably* and that outsiders might, without committing an injustice, attempt to enter the depopulated United States.[28] But assume our two individuals are successful in excluding them. Do they act unjustly, in excluding outsiders who may be vastly worse off than themselves? On the minimalist view, they do not.

The most telling objection to this conclusion therefore closely resembles the objection to the right-libertarian view. The conclusion allows some individuals to live lives of great luxury, whereas others may live lives which are considerably less comfortable, simply because the former are able to annex resources before others do. Their ability to annex those resources is not dependent upon effort or hard work—in Risse's example, we are asked to imagine that our two individuals simply benefit from an electronic surveillance system which makes border control easy—and may track features (such as geographical proximity) for which individuals are not responsible. Both Risse and Miller claim, to be clear, that communities *are* responsible for at least a significant portion of the value of the resources within their territories (see section 2.5.1). But whereas they make that factual conjecture (on which I cast doubt in Chapter 4), their view does not make control dependent on whether it is in fact the case. Equality would not be a demand of justice whether it was true or not.

My challenge thus far has concentrated on how to share some of the benefits flowing from natural resources. But minimalism also experiences difficulties in providing persuasive guidance on burden-sharing problems. Humankind faces many collective problems, of which one of the most discussed in recent decades has been climate change. Assuming that mitigating climate change requires sacrifices, we require an account of how those sacrifices should be distributed globally. On this question Rawls's minimalist view is silent; although his theory famously included a brief discussion of intergenerational justice at the domestic level, it offered no explicit guidance on the global question of who should make the sacrifices required to avoid dangerous climate change. Risse and Miller have given the problem explicit attention, but their contributions further reveal the difficulties a minimalist account faces. Although he calls it a 'tentative' proposal, Risse provides a fairly plausible answer to our question of how to share mitigation burdens, which allocates costs to states in line with both their current emissions levels and their ability to pay.[29] But the proposal is an answer to a question about the demands of 'reasonable conduct', and *not* a question about the demands of justice. Those demands are not established explicitly, but the general contours of his account would suggest the following: if one set of states were to load the burdens of tackling climate change onto others, in a way that exacerbated existing inequalities but did not jeopardize anyone's basic rights, it would not act unjustly.

Miller's response, by contrast, is considerably more demanding at the bar of justice. His answer to our question about mitigation burdens is twofold. First, we should exempt countries with endemic poverty from making any material mitigation sacrifices; their need to develop their way out of poverty is more pressing. Second, countries *not* burdened by endemic poverty should shoulder equal burdens. The principle of 'equal sacrifice' does not mean that countries should cut emissions by equal amounts, since the same quantity of cuts would be more costly to achieve for some countries than for others. Rather it means that the degree of material sacrifice borne by different countries should be equalized.[30] As a solution this is imperfect, I would suggest, because it does not track relevant background inequalities well enough. Miller's proposal could well mean that wealthy countries end up cutting emissions by considerably less than poorer (but not indigent) countries. Whether this is so will depend on how economically valuable emissions are for each country: if a given quantity of emissions deliver £1,000,000 of economic benefits to a wealthy country but only £750,000 to a poorer country, then Miller's scheme will enjoin the latter to cut more, since its cuts come more 'cheaply'. This, however, may aggravate existing inequalities in access to wellbeing. A more satisfying egalitarian proposal would distribute the costs of mitigation in such a way as to reduce background inequalities, rather than intensify them.

But the most important point to note about Miller's suggestion is not that it is imperfectly egalitarian, but precisely that it *is* an egalitarian answer, however imperfect. In dealing with a collective problem which requires sacrifices from all of us, Miller suggests, an egalitarian answer is the most plausible response. Miller's way of registering this point without abandoning minimalism as a general view about global justice is to claim that the argument is only egalitarian in a 'shallow' sense: the idea is that a benefit (or, here, a burden) should be distributed equally unless anyone has a special claim justifying departures from equality. A 'deep' reason for favouring equality, by contrast, would be (additionally) grounded on some idea of the equal status or social standing of its subjects.[31] I examine some arguments for supposing that the scope of egalitarian concern need not be global in section 2.3. The crucial point to note for now is Miller's acceptance that only an egalitarian answer to this type of problem will be a plausible one (whatever the right egalitarian answer turns out to be). Egalitarians will endorse that judgement, and argue that it should be applied (at least) to the whole range of benefits and burdens emanating from natural resources.

In this section, I have claimed that views which are silent about inequalities in the benefits and burdens flowing from natural resources are insufficiently demanding. To the extent that those benefits and burdens can make our lives go better or worse, I suggest that we have reason to object to unequal access to them. Section 2.2 presents the case for a global egalitarian theory of natural resource justice more positively.

2.2. TOWARDS EQUALITY

It is a philosophical commonplace that each person has equal moral value, and that how one person's life goes is just as important as any other's. Notably, as human beings we all possess, to some degree, the capacity to form and revise plans for our lives.[32] Equal concern and respect is the price to be paid in light of our status as agents. Now many views—indeed all reputable views—hold that people are deserving of equal concern in some sense. What is distinctive about egalitarianism is the belief that taking our moral status as agents seriously justifies significant limits on distributive inequalities. Given that people have in common the capacity to form and revise plans for how their lives go, to experience pleasure and suffering, and to form valuable relationships, and given that their ability to do so can be expected to depend, among other things, on access to various external goods such as natural resources, good grounds must be provided for denying them equal access to those sources of advantage.

Whereas minimalist views may only be concerned with how well people's lives go in some absolute sense—for instance, they may hold that the demands of justice are exhausted if everyone leads a life in which their basic human rights are protected—egalitarians are interested in how well people's lives go in a comparative sense. Even if everyone's basic rights are secure, it still matters if some people's lives go *better* than others.[33] Moreover, egalitarians value (greater) equality non-instrumentally. Minimalists might agree that we can have instrumental reasons to care about particular inequalities: even if inequality does not matter in itself, they may say, we sometimes have grounds to object to it on the basis of its effects. Egalitarians may also object to those effects (and, to that extent, value equality instrumentally too). But they will claim that inequalities do not only matter because of those effects, or when they are associated with such effects. Inequality is objectionable simply because it involves some people's lives going better than others.

Believing that equality is an important value is of course not tantamount to believing that it is the only value which matters. Egalitarians are frequently pluralists inasmuch as they believe that more than one value can come into play when we normatively assess a given state of affairs. Values such as efficiency or liberty may also have moral weight. In at least some cases those values will lead us to modify the demands of equality when it comes to producing 'all-things-considered' judgements about what we should actually *do*. The defining feature of egalitarianism is simply the claim that equality does have significant value, and that accordingly it should be given significant weight in assessing the justice of particular distributions. Egalitarians believe that equality is important and that although it may not always be triumphant in cases of value conflict, its value should not be traded away easily.

By way of example, consider the relationship between equality and efficiency (or the idea that higher levels of aggregate wellbeing are morally preferable to lower levels). Derek Parfit has rightly suggested that even if egalitarians accept what he calls the Principle of Equality—the view that inequality is bad in itself, and that moves towards equality should count as improvements, other things being equal—they may also endorse what he calls the Principle of Utility, which holds that it is also better if people are better off rather than worse off.[34] If raising aggregate wellbeing (or Utility) has non-negligible value, this implies that we should at least sometimes choose outcomes in which everyone is better off, at the expense of some inequality. The pluralist egalitarian might agree that equality provides us with a reason for *not* doing so, but this reason can be overruled if the increases in wellbeing are significant enough. Still, even when equality loses out in this way its appeal is not quashed, and if circumstances change its demands may come to the forefront once more.

From the point of view of equality, natural resources gain interest insofar as they are capable of delivering benefits and burdens to people, thereby making their lives go more or less well. As we saw in section 2.1, egalitarians have accordingly objected to unilateral appropriations of resources which thereby leave inferior opportunities available to others. An egalitarian approach to natural resources has often been defended within contemporary debates on global justice, from Beitz onwards.[35] It has also been defended by adherents of the view known as left-libertarianism. Left-libertarians (like right-libertarians) endorse a reasonably strong version of self-ownership; but they also believe that we come into the world facing an array of natural resources which no one is responsible for creating, yet which can allow us to advance our various plans and projects, or our wellbeing broadly construed. Since no one has a better claim than anyone else to make use of these resources, left-libertarians believe that our licence to appropriate the world's spaces and resources should be subject to a strict 'egalitarian proviso'. This might be thought to have the implication that no one can justly appropriate more resources than everyone else could. Alternatively (and this is the view generally favoured by left-libertarians) we might tolerate disproportionate appropriation but demand that over-appropriators compensate others to make good any disadvantage otherwise arising from their over-appropriation.[36] In Chapter 3 I will make clear some disagreements between the left-libertarian view and my own. But all of these views draw on the same intuition—that insofar as no one has any better initial claim on natural resources than anyone else, the benefits and burdens flowing from them should be distributed in such a way as to promote equality in human wellbeing. If we all matter equally, if we all have the capacity to experience wellbeing, and if our success in doing so will likely depend upon our access to goods such as natural resources, then we have reason to believe that our claims on those goods are equal. I have employed several examples in section 2.1 in order to show that the thought that we should defer to the value of equality unless powerful reasons can be provided for departing from it has considerable intuitive appeal. But in section 2.3 I examine some arguments for not extending the scope of egalitarian concern in this way.

2.3. RELATIONISM VERSUS NON-RELATIONISM

The view I outlined in section 2.2 reflects what has been called a 'humanist' or 'non-relational' approach to the scope of egalitarian concern. Once we have identified advantages which all humans have reason to value, and once we have accepted that all humans are the ultimate units of equal moral respect and concern, it would be arbitrary to distribute such advantages unequally unless powerful reasons can be provided for doing so. Accepting without good reason an unequal distribution of the benefits and burdens flowing from natural resources, say, fails to treat moral persons with sufficient respect. In advancing that argument I have not claimed that we need to know anything more about the humans concerned than the fact that they *are* humans (wherever they may happen to be).[37]

This relatively straightforward view, however, is rejected by 'relationists' about the scope of egalitarian justice. Relationists hold that at least one *further* fact must obtain before the commitment to distributive egalitarianism becomes appropriate.[38] Specifically, 'relationist' views hold that the strictures of egalitarianism only apply to people once certain social relations hold between them. The best-known relational views emphasize the normative salience of the existence of social cooperation, or (some) people's shared subjection to coercive institutions, or the pervasive mutual impact of people's actions. The mere existence of inequalities, on these relational views, does not require principled justification. What requires justification is the way in which institutions or practices endorse or sustain inequalities—allowing, for instance, arbitrary features of persons to influence distributive patterns.[39] On such views, it is because we belong to shared enterprises, or share in our subjection to certain coercive institutions, or shape the circumstances in which others must make decisions about their lives—and because these relationships make a difference to our life-chances—that equality as a distributive ideal becomes relevant. Rather than some transcendental moral principle, it is a standard to which we hold the concrete practices in which we are embedded. If there are humans who fall outside the scope of those practices or relations, then whatever we might owe them, from a moral point of view, it must be something less demanding than distributive equality.

Now relationism is a diverse family of views, insofar as there is disagreement about the precise further fact (or combination of facts) which triggers egalitarian concern; but some such view is embraced by each advocate of a minimalist constraint on resource holdings discussed in section 2.2 (including Rawls, Miller, and Risse). Notably, each believes that inequalities are objectionable *within* individual societies, because such societies *are* characterized by, variously, the presence of social cooperation or of coercive institutions or of a 'basic structure' of institutions which has a pervasive effect upon citizens' life-chances. It is these relations to which the strictures of egalitarianism are to be applied. But beyond the boundaries of the state each of these theorists defends a more modest account of justice. They do not claim, that is, that there are no requirements of justice at the global level. But the minimal standards which do apply relate primarily to the protection of basic human rights, and not to the mitigation of inequality. These theorists therefore believe that inequalities in access to natural resources *between* communities do not require the same justification that would apply to inequalities *within* communities. Indeed, on the global scale these theorists are not only minimalists about natural resources, but about all of the goods relevant to distributive justice: justice requires the protection of basic rights, but it does not constrain inequality.[40]

The debate between relationism and non-relationism is by now rather well worked, and rather than rehearsing that debate in full here I will confine myself to outlining three responses that non-relationists have made to the challenge from relationism. A first response has engaged with the relationist challenge empirically, and claimed that each 'further fact' suggested to date— be it the existence of coercion, of relations of reciprocity, or of mutual pervasive impact—fails to mark out nation-states as distinctive. At least some practices or institutions beyond the nation-state can be shown to exhibit the relevant features, at least to some significant degree. Consider coercion, for example: we might point out that more or less coercive institutions exist at the global level, or even that the borders of nation-states are themselves coercive.[41] Similar points might be made with reference to the cooperative practices which sustain a global economy. They can certainly be made with reference to the impact that our decisions (such as decisions to exploit natural resources) can have upon people in distant parts of the globe, and climate change presents but one example. In the evolving debate so far, relationists who wish to restrict the scope of egalitarian justice to the nation-state have failed to identify features of social life which cleanly demarcate the domestic from the global.[42] The implication appears to be that the scope of egalitarian concern cannot be cleanly restricted either.

A second and more fundamental response has denied that the relevant relations (even if they did more or less cleanly map onto an empirical difference between domestic and global levels, which we have reason to doubt) possess the profound normative significance that relationists have claimed for them. The non-relationist might admit that coercively imposing an inequality, say, is objectionable, but deny that the coercive imposition of an inequality is *necessary* in order for us to consider it unjust. Relationists have provided better reasons for believing that the relational genesis of an inequality is a sufficient reason for objecting to it than they have for believing that it is *only* in light of some relational genesis that we can legitimately object to an inequality.[43] Indeed, it might be argued that many of the reasons relationists have provided for objecting to inequalities—that they allow our lives to go better or worse on the basis of arbitrary features about us, for instance— possess a normative force which relationism can ill contain. For instance, if it is unfair for co-citizens to face different prospects in life simply because they were born into different classes or ethnic groups, why is it any less unfair for people to face radically divergent prospects simply because they were born into different countries?[44]

We have already seen, in fact, that the view that we should endorse equal shares of some advantage unless good reasons exist for not doing so *is* defended, at times, by critics of global egalitarianism. Miller, for instance, leans on such a principle in establishing a fair distribution of the burdens of mitigating climate change; Risse also sketches a broadly egalitarian answer to the same quandary, although he considers it an answer to the question of what is 'reasonable', and not what is just. Both of them would also accept the same idea when it comes to intra-state inequalities. But then why, globally, do inequalities not even require justification? Indeed, on this point these relational critics of global egalitarianism often turn out to inhabit a rather odd position: whereas their official view appears to be that global inequalities *do not stand in need of justification at all*, because the demands of equality only arise given specific social relations—which, in their view, only exist domestically—they also frequently produce arguments to the effect that global inequalities *are justified* on the basis of, for instance, the fact that some nation-states have conserved or depleted their resources, or made good or bad decisions more broadly. If global inequalities do not stand in need of justification in the first place, this kind of argument is simply superfluous: there would be no good reason to redistribute resources even if they did not apply. So does the unequal distribution of natural resources require justification or not?

We might put further pressure on the relationist view as follows (and this is our third objection). Many relationist views see their goal as fairly allocating the product of some cooperative scheme (in this case, one which putatively coincides with a particular nation-state). But *before* we can think about the distribution of this product, we need to know that the scheme in question had a good claim over the raw materials it employed in order to create it—that is, the land and other resources it claims control over.[45] But what might such a claim be based upon? And what if different communities want to use the same land and resources, or to use common-pool resources such as the global atmosphere's absorptive capacity? We seem to require some normative standard for adjudicating between these rival claims. But it is hard to see how this can be anything other than a non-relational standard. It is also hard to see why anything other than an egalitarian standard will be persuasive. Consider again Risse's example of a depopulated United States. The implication of Risse's theory is that so long as outsiders can meet their basic rights with what they have, two people could, without committing an injustice, control a territory the size of the United States, and all of its resources. Indeed, the implication of his theory is that, from the point of view of justice, no justification for such control is even needed. The non-relationist egalitarian, by contrast, believes that such an annexation of resources would depend upon a very strong justification—and given that the lives of the two individuals in question matter no more than those who are thereby excluded, it is difficult to see what a satisfactory justification could be. Non-relationist egalitarians will argue, as Merten Reglitz has recently done, that a requirement not to use 'more than an equal share of whatever is available to humanity that can make human lives go well' is an independent moral constraint upon any practice or community.[46]

In light of all these responses, non-relationists consider the claim that the egalitarian impulse is somehow arrested at the borders of any individual state to be uncompelling. Indeed, a common rejoinder to theories which seek to restrict the scope of egalitarian concern to the level of individual nation-states is that such theories improperly conflate the questions of which features are likely to *motivate* people to make the sacrifices necessary to promote the ideal of equality, and the separate question of when those sacrifices are *justified*. That citizens in one country often appear reluctant to make sacrifices for distant others is undeniable; but we should not treat this as an unalterable fact,[47] or conclude from it that they are not, in fact, required to make such sacrifices. In the case of natural resources, the actions of one community can impose burdens on other communities, or deprive them of potential benefits. The minimalists I discussed in section 2.2 do acknowledge principled constraints upon such activities, but those constraints relate exclusively to the protection of basic human rights. Such a constraint, I have argued, is inordinately weak; justice is not only a matter of whether people can lead lives free from misery and hunger, but also about whether they can flourish—and it matters whether some are able to flourish to a greater extent than others.

2.4. THE 'RESOURCE CURSE'

Perhaps, though, egalitarians' concern with unequal resource endowments is unnecessary. It has sometimes been argued that shares of natural resources— even if they are very unequal—are simply not very consequential for economic development. Of course all communities will rely on minimal shares of natural resources in order to secure the basic rights of their citizens. And sometimes, for minimalists, shortfalls in meeting those basic rights can mean that positive duties of justice fall on outsiders. But as Rawls pointed out, many countries possessed of abundant shares of natural resources simply squander them, falling into spirals of bad governance, civil strife, and economic stagnation— that is, they suffer from some version of the so-called 'resource curse'. On the other hand many countries with meagre shares do very well regardless. In light of these facts, why insist on equal shares?[48] Mathias Risse has also suggested that (domestic) institutional health is much more significant for economic development than relative resource shares, and that this counts against a focus on distributing resources.[49] Shmuel Nili has claimed that there is simply no evidence that greater resource endowments are a spur to development, and hence that the quest to equalize the distribution of resources is unmotivated.[50]

Such claims threaten to terminate the discussion of natural resource inequalities before it has begun, and I will therefore examine, in this section, how strong the evidence is for the argument that resources do not matter for economic development. Before we begin, that claim must be distinguished from two others that need not detain us. First, I will not consider the claim that large resource endowments are actually *bad* for communities, for instance in the sense that they necessarily have negative implications for growth or institutional quality. Such a claim, I note, would not count against a focus, by theorists of global justice, on the unequal distribution of resources. Quite the reverse: if this claim *were* true, it would give us a reason *for* caring about their distribution: natural resources would then be an important burden and it might, plausibly, be unfair for some countries to suffer from such a burden whereas others do not. To sustain the desired conclusion—that egalitarians should stop worrying about unequal resource endowments—the argument must be grounded on the claim that the impact of unequal resource wealth is neutral (or very close to it). It is this claim that I examine in what follows.

A second claim would be that resource endowments are not a direct spur to development, but rather assist development only insofar as they boost some other factor such as institutional quality. The claim that the influence of resource is 'mediated' by institutional quality has also been made by both Risse and Nili.[51] To conclude that this counts against egalitarian concern with relative resource shares is, however, a puzzling move. For the egalitarian concern with relative resource shares to be intelligible, it is enough that resource shares have *some* influence on development. We need not claim that their influence is direct, or indeed that plentiful resources are sufficient to guarantee development. After all nobody, surely, believes that providing books to schools is sufficient to guarantee good educational outcomes. Presumably their impact is 'mediated' too, in the sense that they can help teachers teach better, or students learn better—whereas if no one picks them up, their effect will be nil. Still, if we discovered tomorrow that, say, schools in the north and south of a country were receiving radically different quantities of books, the egalitarian would rightly be concerned—rightly concerned, that is, unless she knew for sure that supplies of books could never make a significant difference, even in combination with a range of other factors, on the outcomes that matter. Egalitarians can say the same thing about natural resources. The only claim that could justify a termination of egalitarian concern would be the claim that resources do not matter for development whether directly *or* indirectly.[52] That claim, then, is where the action is. In what follows I provide several reasons for doubting it.

2.4.1. What the Resource Curse Literature Reveals

Let us begin, then, by considering the empirical evidence on the resource curse. It is important to note at the outset that the nature of and mechanisms involved in the curse are complex and contested. Consider the famous case of oil rents. It is often said that oil rents (when compared to other sources of national income) tend to secure relatively meagre progress in securing development and better governance. There are a variety of explanations for why this might be the case. Attention has gradually shifted from economic factors and onto 'political' factors instead.[53] Probably the most powerful explanation for the putative underperformance of oil-rich states suggests that access to large oil rents means that governments have no need to resort to the taxation of the general populace. Relying on taxation usually has a positive effect on the development of stable and effective systems of governance, for the simple reason that citizens are resistant to paying taxes in the absence of transparent, accountable, and more or less competent administrative structures, and in the absence of a pay-off in the effective provision of public goods. But if oil-rich governments are able to bankroll their activities with oil rents instead of tax revenues, this renders them much less dependent upon the consent of the governed, and gives them little incentive to deliver effective administrative structures.[54] This fact has been held to explain why resource wealth appears to correlate negatively with democracy;[55] combating the curse, by contrast, is thought to require the strong checks and balances characteristic of a healthy democracy.[56] It has also been thought to explain the poor correlation with economic growth, as public goods such as education and infrastructure which might prepare a more sustainable seedbed for long-term growth are neglected, and rents are instead dissipated among elites.

In recent years it has become clear that the evidence for a natural resource curse is more complex than this suggests, however. Three points are in order. First, it is controversial how widespread a phenomenon the curse is. For one thing, it is increasingly recognized that the curse is evident principally in countries whose income is highly dependent on exports of oil, rather than resources in general.[57] For another thing, some countries appear unaffected by the curse. The study of Latin American countries, for instance, has revealed no correlation between oil and conflict, and the region's oil states are actually twice as likely to be democratic as its non-oil states.[58] There also appear to be strong threshold effects in the relationship between resource revenues, good governance, and economic growth, which undermine any across-the-board claim that resource shares do not matter for development. Adherents of the curse typically acknowledge, for instance, that in initially well-governed countries natural resources are a boon to economic growth. (Consider, by way of example, the divergent growth paths of Norway, Sweden, and Denmark after Norway, once considered the 'poor man' of Scandinavia, discovered Western

Europe's largest reserves of oil and gas. Those reserves now produce fully a third of Norwegian government revenues.[59]) Finally, recent analyses suggest that far from being an inevitable drag upon development, any negative correlation between resource wealth and growth is historically very specific. According to Michael Ross—perhaps the most famous theorist of the resource curse—there simply was no curse before about 1980. Moreover, between 1990 and 2006 oil-exporting states grew about 40 per cent *faster* than the rest of the world.[60] It begins to look very much, then, as though grand claims about the weak (or even negative) impact of resources on development and governance are hard to sustain. According to Ross, analysts of the resource curse—himself included—may simply have inferred too much from the failure of weak states, especially in Africa, to cope with the increased volatility of international energy markets during the 1980s.[61] The role of donors and international consultancies in encouraging and arranging the accumulation of debt for infrastructure in boom years should also not be disregarded.[62]

Second, claims about the relationship between resource wealth and either institutional quality *or* economic growth have turned out to be based upon some dubious benchmarks for comparison. Typically analysts have compared the future growth prospects of countries which have reached a particular level of economic development at T^1 on the back of selling resources, with the prospects of countries which had already reached roughly the same level of development *without* selling resources in large quantities. On this specific comparison, countries in the latter category are often found to have better long-term growth prospects. But it should not be surprising that countries which have reached, say, middle-income status by developing manufacturing rather than relying on resource exports enjoy better long-term growth prospects; one will have built up productive infrastructure, whereas the other may not.[63] But what this does not tell us is whether among countries which *start* from the same position (that is, with similar initial levels of development or infrastructure), those which discover oil turn out to perform better or worse than those which do not. According to this more instructive comparison, some studies have found that the discovery of oil correlates *positively* with growth and institutional quality, and that this becomes more obvious when we actually engage in historical time-series analysis of countries' development paths.[64] The positive effect on growth might be smaller than we might expect in light of the massive scale of oil rents, but still, on this comparison, having oil looks to be better than not having it.[65] Moreover, it has recently been shown that oil states have outpaced non-oil states in generating improvements in important indicators of wider wellbeing such as child health and mortality rates.[66] It has also been demonstrated that resource abundance is positively correlated with years in education (for boys and girls) and with life expectancy.[67]

Parallel points can be made about the purported link between oil wealth and institutional quality: once more, the resource curse literature has erred in 'comparing newly enriched oil countries to a new peer group of middle- and high-income states, whose institutions have developed over many years. This makes the nouveau riche oil states look institutionally stunted.'[68] When comparing states with similar levels of *initial* development, those which discover oil have been found to perform no worse in terms of institutional quality,[69] or indeed better,[70] whilst other studies have found that 'increases in natural resource income are associated with increases in democracy'.[71]

Even for countries afflicted by it, then, the resource 'curse' has now come to look less like a curse and more like a (somewhat mixed) blessing.[72] It might well be true, to be sure, that advancing economically via oil rents is not the optimal development strategy. For instance, oil-based growth may not be as sustainable, or as broadly beneficial, as advancing via the production of high-tech consumer products.[73] But if breaking into those lucrative markets is difficult, the recourse to resource exports might be the best chance some countries have to escape poverty. Thus even if the impact of oil rents is often disappointing, it could *also* be true that as far as both economic development and good governance are concerned, having oil is considerably better than not having oil, *and* that having abundant shares of natural resources is the most likely way for some poor countries to achieve economic progress.

Third, the erstwhile claim that resource-rich countries enjoy relatively poor rates of economic growth has often turned out to be founded upon a highly counter-intuitive definition of what qualifies a country as 'resource-rich'. We might think that it is relatively obvious which countries are resource-rich and resource-poor. For instance, we might intuitively define 'resource-rich countries' simply as those countries which have more valuable reserves of resources compared to others. But this is not the sense of 'resource-rich' with which analyses of the economic resource curse have typically operated. Rather a country has been considered resource-rich *when a high proportion of its national income comes from resource sales*.[74] This might be the case, however, simply because its other industries produce relatively little. On the basis of such a definition, we could describe a country like the United States as resource-poor, given that only around 2 per cent of its GDP comes on the back of its extractive industries. But by any sane standard, the US has tremendous resource wealth. Indeed, that resource wealth was crucial in its rise to global pre-eminence.[75] By contrast, a country which has much more meagre resources than the US would be labelled resource-rich purely because its national income was heavily *dependent* upon exporting those resources. This suggests a disconnect between the theory of the economic resource curse and empirical research into its genesis. Whereas the theory of the resource curse holds that it is increases in the presence of resources per se which brings in tow weak growth, the major empirical studies on which the theory is based have typically studied the effects of resource dependence rather than resource abundance.[76] But given that resource wealth has been *defined* in terms of dependence upon resource exports, the finding that other sectors of an economy are often relatively weak, for example, would hardly be surprising.[77]

This assumption within the 'resource curse' literature is seldom discussed, but has to be borne in mind when we evaluate any empirical claim (insofar as such claims have survived closer scrutiny in any case) that levels of resource wealth correlate poorly with economic growth. On a more intuitive index of resource wealth that conclusion could be radically undermined. For instance, if we rank countries according to the market value of known resources in their territories we arrive at the startling conclusions that African countries are far poorer in subsoil resources than, for instance, members of the (mainly wealthy) Organisation for Economic Co-operation and Development. Working from World Bank calculations, Paul Collier has estimated that the average square kilometre in Africa contains $25,000-worth of known subsoil resources, whereas the equivalent area in the average OECD country contains $125,000-worth. We might conjecture, of course, that the *unknown* resource wealth of Africa is likely to be closer to the OECD average. But we do not know; and in the meantime the image of Africa as 'resource-rich' has a strong whiff of myth about it.[78] This, too, must place serious pressure on any claim that resource-rich countries exhibit poor economic growth. The great resource endowments of OECD countries do not appear to have inhibited their development.

2.4.2. What the Resource Curse Literature Does Not Reveal

Recent empirical work, then—as well as greater clarity about what scholars of the resource curse have in fact claimed to establish—suffices to cast serious doubt upon the thesis that resources do not matter for development. Recall that the claim that egalitarians should not care about the unequal distribution of natural resources cannot be based upon the idea that resources are not the only thing that matters for development. Neither could it be based upon the idea that their impact is indirect—or even, for that matter, that they are not the most important contributor to economic development. For the egalitarian's concern for their distribution to be unmotivated, it would have to be the case that they do not contribute to development at all, even in an indirect way. In fact, I have suggested that any empirical claim that resource wealth correlates poorly with economic growth is seriously troubled when we inspect the finer details of the resource curse literature. Resource wealth might not always be as great a boon to national economic development as we would expect it to be; but the momentum of the recent debate suggests that at least in terms of growth, it is better seen as a somewhat mixed blessing than as a curse. Findings to the contrary, it turns out, have drawn their inferences from a rather limited range of cases (and a rather limited time-period), and have moreover been based upon some very questionable benchmarking assumptions.

One thing we have learned, to be sure, is that resources are not always as tremendous a source of progress as we might expect. Indeed, all too often enormous resource endowments have converted into relatively modest progress in advancing human wellbeing—and especially the wellbeing of the worst-off in resource-exporting countries. But it would be a momentous mistake to conclude from this that the distribution of the benefits flowing from natural resources is normatively uninteresting. There is a significant difference between the claim that resource wealth *does not here and now* convert into sustained increases in national income, say, or into the secure advancement of the interests of the poorest, and the claim that it *cannot* (or, perhaps, cannot feasibly) make such a difference. Only if the latter were true would inequalities in resource distribution become normatively uninteresting. To the contrary, if there are means by which resource wealth could convert more reliably, or more significantly, to wellbeing, they would be deserving of our attention. Moreover, the *reasons* why resource endowments do not convert into greater gains in wellbeing, including for the poorest in our world, may themselves be a proper object of normative enquiry.

Imagine, then, that resource wealth in one country did fail to convert into improvements in citizens' lives, perhaps because oil rents were squandered by a despot and his clique. We cannot draw from this failure the conclusion that resource wealth does not matter to individuals; instead, we have every reason to investigate ways of making resource wealth work better for citizens. For instance, it is often argued that policies which would see rents shared more fairly between citizens would be a considerable boon for economic development and the relief of poverty.[79] Such policies might ameliorate the effects of the so-called resource curse: if the problem in resource-cursed countries is that states have a ready supply of funds and need not rely upon citizens' cooperation, it has often been noted that delivering funds directly into the hands of citizens would reverse this situation.[80] In the second half of this book I will investigate a series of policies—such as resource taxes, or transparency or accountability reforms—which might enable resource wealth to advance individual wellbeing better. Only if we knew that such proposals could not succeed would the termination of interest in relative resource endowments be justified.

Moreover, we should pay close attention to the structural context in which the so-called resource curse operates. One factor in the relative underperformance of resource rents (in advancing the wellbeing of poor citizens) is undoubtedly the corruption and venality of local leaders who are prepared to sell resources in secrecy and dissipate much of the proceeds. But as recent analyses have emphasized, this process also depends upon the readiness of outsiders to buy resources from unrepresentative ruling elites. Indeed, the willingness of outsiders to buy oil and minerals without demanding anything in the way of accountability or transparency from their vendors may sustain, and even incentivize the emergence of, unrepresentative regimes.[81] The normative conclusion to draw from this is as follows. It is undeniably the case that some countries share the benefits arising from their natural resources very badly, that dictators use resource profits to fund their own lavish lifestyles, and that often a large proportion of resource rents are squandered. But it would be a perverse theory which held these facts as evidence that 'we' ought not to care about their distribution, not least if 'we' play a part in making these facts true. The often disappointing impact of resource exports might be in part an artefact of the relationship between the developed and the developing worlds, and the former may have an important role to play in making resources work better for everyone in our world, and not only the advantaged.

It is also significant that the structural background against which developing countries operate is not determined by those countries alone, but is influenced by global trade rules and falls out across a background of massive and entrenched inequality. For instance, many resource-rich countries secure massive rents from exporting resources such as oil. But their ability to do so is influenced by their bargaining power within a competitive global marketplace. Whereas a country like Saudi Arabia typically retains 80 or 90 per cent of the market value of the oil it extracts, for some countries in Africa—typically recent entrants to the oil trade, with weak economies and little in the way of infrastructure—the bargains which have been struck have often been far less favourable. As we will see in Chapter 7, some of these countries have retained a mere 5 to 10 per cent of the market value of oil extracted in their territories. Moreover, the fact that extraction has been the preserve of multinational corporations (and that international financial institutions have actively discouraged the development of local extractive infrastructure) partly explains the poor record of such extraction in leading to increases in local employment, skills, and infrastructure. But again, these facts are not unalterable, and part of what makes them true at present has been the decisions of the developed world and of international financial institutions. It might be that shifts in global trade rules, or in the policies of international institutions, hold some promise too for making resources work better for the poor.

In this section I have rejected the claim that the relationship between resource wealth and growth is sufficiently weak that we need not care about unequal access to resources. For one thing, there are grounds for doubting the empirical claim that resources make no difference to development. For another, I have argued that claiming that resources are simply ineffective in stimulating economic growth threatens to deflect our attention from some of the global factors which *make* it the case that their contribution to growth is often disappointing. On both grounds, we should reject the argument that egalitarians should not be interested in their distribution.

2.5. SPECIAL CLAIMS OVER RESOURCES

I want, finally, to point forward to one other challenge which I will address more fully in subsequent chapters of this book. To introduce some terms I will be using throughout the book, natural resources' usefulness to us all—along with the fact that none of us created them—suggests that we all have a *general claim* upon them. I define general claims as any claims that can be registered by all agents of a theory of justice. Individuals might be said to have a general claim over those types of resources—such as air and water—necessary to their survival. But over and above that, they might be said to have a general claim on the large surplus of the world's resources which no one needs for his or her survival. The egalitarian claim is simply that the salience of resources to individual wellbeing means that unless we have a compelling reason for doing otherwise, the benefits and burdens they deliver ought to be distributed in line with the value of equality.

But this may not be the end of the story. Perhaps we *do* have compelling reasons for departing from equality, and perhaps these reasons, if taken seriously, will reduce the scope for the egalitarian distribution of these benefits and burdens. These reasons might lie with the *special claims* that some of us have over natural resources. By contrast to general claims, special claims will always be particular in two ways: they will be claims which *some* of us can register over *specific* natural resource tokens. A special claim will be met by assigning an agent rights over *this* natural resource, because of some feature of that agent's relationship with it. In what follows I will briefly introduce two kinds of special claim, show how they might be thought to pose a challenge to an egalitarian account of natural resource justice, and begin to suggest how egalitarians should respond to that challenge. But properly speaking, this response takes place across much of this book (and, in particular, within Chapters 4, 5, and 6).

2.5.1. National Responsibility and Special Claims from Improvement

One reason for reticence about equalizing the benefits and burdens arising from natural resources would suggest that the current distribution of those resources across the world—or at least the economic value they have at any given time—is not an 'arbitrary' fact but rather something which individual communities are at least partly responsible for. For instance, agents may have altered the properties of particular resources—hardening them or purifying them, say—with the result that they are now more useful and more valuable. If that is the case then in redistributing those resources—or their economic value—we deprive communities of something they can plausibly be said to be entitled to. This argument suggests, in short, that communities possess what I call a *special claim from improvement* over local resources. The claim need not, of course, be that communities are entitled to the *entirety* of the value of the resources within their territories. A more moderate claim might be that they are responsible for a substantial part of that value. But if special claims over even a substantial part of the value of those resources exist, this might motivate resistance to egalitarian principles of natural resource justice.[82]

Four responses to this argument are appropriate. First, even if it were true that individual communities are responsible for some or even a substantial portion of the value of the resources within their territories, this would not rule out all egalitarian redistribution. Egalitarians could find space to heed special claims from improvement. They might, for instance, claim not that the value of (or benefits and burdens flowing from) natural resources should be equalized, but that the *unimproved* value of such resources should be equalized.[83] This is not to say that the 'cut' between unimproved and improved portions will be easy to make. But it is not obvious that the difficulty of making a cut counsels in favour of leaving resource value where it is, as opposed to equalizing at least some portion of it. Thus even if minimalists are right that there are some special claims from improvement at the national level, this would circumscribe rather than rule out the scope for egalitarian redistribution.[84]

Second, even if national special claims do exist, we still require an account of just how they ought to be catered for within a theory of justice. This is a question regarding not the justification but the content of special claims over natural resources. Troublingly for the minimalist, there is no easy short-cut to the conclusion that we should grant ownership of natural resources to communities which have improved them in some way; some accommodation of special and general claims which falls short of granting ownership to national claims might be defensible. I will argue that this is indeed the case.

Third, we can cast doubt on both the strength and normative implications of any special claims from improvement that national communities might make. As I argue in Chapters 4 and 6, many of the resources contained in particular communities have not been directly improved at all (in the sense that their properties have not been altered through human intervention, so as to increase their economic value). Supporters of communal claims sometimes turn, at this point, to more general processes by way of which communities determine, for instance, the property rules for the use of resources (an activity which, as a result, serves to influence their economic value) or provide infrastructure which makes their extraction and improvement cheaper or easier (ditto).[85] In such ways the present value of the resources within a community *may* be a fact for which that community is substantially responsible even if any given natural resource has not been improved by directly changing its properties. In Chapter 4, however, I also cast doubt on this revised view.

Fourth, even if it is the case that, other things being equal, an agent who improves a resource so as to directly increase its value generates some kind of claim over the proceeds, it is not clear that the scope of those claims can themselves go un-circumscribed by egalitarian principles. For even if we care about the claims agents generate when they improve, we may also care about agents' opportunities to engage in improving acts in the first place. Imagine a situation in which the world offers more than enough resources for everyone to meet their basic needs. But as in Risse's powerful example, a small number of people succeed in fencing off a massive swathe of territory containing abundant and eminently improvable resources. Everyone else is left with enough resources to meet their basic needs, but no more, and with (we stipulate) no option of improving those resources. Over time, our fence-makers improve the resources within their new territory, and claim the (enormous) proceeds of that improvement. The new value which those resources have is attributable to their own purposive action. On the other hand, no one else has had the same opportunity to improve those resources. In these circumstances, their claims appear attenuated. Plausibly, our view on the extent to which agents can permissibly reap rewards from making improvements to resources must depend *itself* on some prior account of what degree of resources people rightly have access to. By contrast, if minimalists want to suggest that our fence-making improvers have good claims from improvement, then this must be because they have already assumed that our opportunities to improve the resources of the world need not be equal. If so, we need to know what that assumption is grounded upon, because it cannot be the fact of improvement itself. For all of these four reasons, pointing to special claims from improvement does not count against an egalitarian theory of natural resource justice, even though such improvement *might* generate entitlements that egalitarians have reason to respect. We will see in later chapters how far those claims take us.

2.5.2. Special Claims from Attachment

The European colonization of what is now the United States of America involved many evils. Huge numbers of indigenous people were killed, starved of their livelihoods, stigmatized, and marginalized. One of the complaints of the survivors—a complaint repeated by their contemporary descendants—is that they were forcibly removed from land and other resources, interaction with which had defined their lives and their individual or collective identities.

Of course, many indigenous people were subsequently 'rehomed': given new places to live in often far distant parts of the country, and alternative means of employment. The fortunes of people relocated in this way have typically been bleak, though, even though we *might* think that they now have the opportunity to lead lives which are more materially comfortable than their old ones. Perhaps, in some cases, they have access to just as much land and resources as they (or their ancestors) did. But the claims Native Americans themselves make are typically to the *actual* land and resources on which their lives were based. As we noted in Chapter 1, natural resources do not only matter to people as interchangeable ingredients for economic development. Often natural resources matter *in particular* to some people, as non-substitutable supports for their most central life-plans. If so, it might be thought that global egalitarianism threatens to wrong these people if it aims to redistribute resources without regard for the way some people are *attached* to certain resources.

I have already anticipated the appropriate response to this argument: global egalitarianism does not require us to redistribute natural resources without regard to the way in which people are attached to them. Negatively, it may be false that global egalitarianism necessarily requires the redistribution of natural resources, or at least many such resources. Positively, a variety of theories of justice may have reason to take seriously the central projects which give meaning and purpose to individual lives. And if so, egalitarians will accordingly have reason to investigate how and to what extent attachments can be accommodated within an egalitarian theory. That question is the subject of Chapter 5. I argue there that special claims from attachment are structurally different from special claims from improvement: the former target *how much* an agent is entitled to, registering a claim over value whose existence is attributable to an improving agent; the latter target *which* resources any extant entitlement ought to be met with, with the argument seeking to convert a general claim into a special one. I will suggest that egalitarians can and should care about patterns of attachment, and moreover that they can be much more permissive towards them than has sometimes been alleged. But attachment does not provide us with reasons why some people's life-plans (or wellbeing) matter more than others, and does not give us reason to abandon global egalitarianism as a theory about natural resources.

ENDNOTES

1. Beitz 1979: 138.
2. E.g. Barry 1982; Risse 2012.
3. Such an idea was a commonplace amongst the philosophers mentioned in the first paragraph of this chapter, and many of their contemporaries. For a useful overview see Van Duffel and Yap 2011.

4. Gleick 1998a.
5. Food and Agriculture Organization's 'Aquastat' (Information System on Water and Agriculture): http://www.fao.org/ag/agl/aglw/aquastat/dbase/index.stm (2004). The major issues we currently face arise not from global or even national scarcity, but from local scarcity, from the weaknesses of water-harvesting and transporting infrastructure, and from the fact that patterns of local access to basic supplies of water are conditioned by existing inequalities. Moreover, climate change is widely expected to exacerbate local—and perhaps eventually generate national, or even global—scarcity.
6. See e.g. Steiner 1994.
7. To give some examples, Robert Nozick's right-libertarian theory applies its famous proviso to holdings arising from later voluntary transactions and not only to initial appropriations (Nozick 1974: 180). Risse's theory places a basic-needs constraint on tolerable distributions that is not defeasible by any later transfers or actions (Risse 2012: part 2). Peter Vallentyne's and Michael Otsuka's egalitarian theories both require taxation of gifts that disturb equality as well as initial appropriation. Vallentyne 2012: 163; Otsuka 2003, chapter 1.
8. Some right-libertarians, such as Narveson (1999), suggest that appropriation should not be constrained by justice at all. If my arguments against very weak constraints are successful they will apply *a fortiori* to any such view.
9. There has in fact been considerable disagreement about precisely what labour-mixing involves, and how it grounds property rights on Locke's account. Libertarian theorists—both right and left—are in dispute about whether just appropriation is conditional on actually labouring, on the creation of value in improved objects, or merely on the staking of a claim over a natural resource. In Chapter 4 I discuss improvement-based special claims, and in Chapter 5 I discuss Simmons's version of the labour-mixing argument which grounds claims on the integration of control over objects into one's purposive projects, and hence produces what I would call an attachment-based argument (Simmons 1994).
10. A second proviso nullified claims where those fruits were then left to spoil. The invention of money reduces the significance of this proviso (Locke 1960).
11. On the precise demandingness of Locke's famous 'proviso', see for instance Waldron 1979. Barbara Fried considers the fact that the proviso has also been adapted by right- and left-libertarians as evidence that it 'lacks any determinate operational implications' (Fried 2004: 84).
12. Nozick 1974: 178–82.
13. Nozick 1974: 182.
14. I develop this example from one which Nozick himself briefly outlines. He does, intriguingly, suggest that there is a limit to the price which our appropriator could charge the excluded for water, but does not offer any account of how a fair price could be determined (Nozick 1974: 180).
15. As powerfully argued by Cohen 1995, chapters 3 and 4. Otsuka rejects Nozick's proviso for similar reasons, in favour of an egalitarian constraint. Otsuka 2003: 23.
16. For the contrast between 'subsistence' and 'luxury' emissions, see Shue 2014, chapter 2.

17. See Wenar 1998: 815, and Cohen 1995, chapter 3. Waldron (1993) suggests that advocates of property regimes have a special justificatory burden towards those who will be poorest under the regimes they argue for.
18. Cohen 1995: 87.
19. As did Nozick (1974: 177), pointing towards a variety of 'familiar social considerations' favouring free markets.
20. In that sense minimalism overlaps with the view known as sufficientarianism, on which see Casal 2006.
21. Risse (2012: 113) describes his view as a 'minimal' conception of collective ownership.
22. Risse 2014.
23. Risse 2012: 90.
24. Miller 2007. A minimalist view on natural resource justice—according to which outsiders' claims on the natural resources within a territory are overridden by insiders' interest in collective self-determination, unless outsiders' basic human rights are at stake—is also defended in Moore 2012. See also Nine 2012.
25. Miller 1999, chapter 10.
26. Rawls 1999. There is, note, some disagreement about whether the duty of assistance is a duty of justice or a less stringent humanitarian duty. See Armstrong 2009b.
27. Rawls 1971: 110.
28. Risse 2012: 90. I interrogate Risse's reasons for rejecting an egalitarian account further in Armstrong 2014a.
29. Risse 2012: 202–6.
30. Miller 2009.
31. Miller 2009: 140.
32. Egalitarians need not assume that people possess such a property to equal degrees. Indeed, they might even be committed to ignoring or disregarding the extent to which people differ in those properties beyond a certain degree. Carter 2011.
33. See e.g. Temkin 2015.
34. Parfit 1997.
35. Beitz 1979; Barry 1982; Casal 2011.
36. See e.g. Steiner 1994; Otsuka 2003; Vallentyne 2012.
37. For defences of the humanist or non-relational view, see Caney 2011; Gilabert 2012.
38. For the contrast between relationist and non-relationist views about the scope of equality, see Sangiovanni 2007.
39. See e.g. Tan 2012.
40. For more on the contrast between minimalist and egalitarian views on global justice, see Armstrong 2012, chapters 2 and 3. As I make clear there, some minimalist views also claim that the terms of global cooperation ought to be fair or non-exploitative in some sense. But that demand does not, on their view, push us to endorse global egalitarianism.
41. Abizadeh 2007; see also Armstrong 2009a.
42. Indeed, some relationists have taken precisely the existence of global forms of coercion, or cooperation, to imply that we should be fully-fledged global egalitarians. See e.g. Beitz 1979; Moellendorf 2009; and Tan 2012. Although there is a

dispute between non-relationists and these global relationist egalitarians, in a globalized world its implications are comparatively modest, and I confine myself here to arguing against statist varieties of relationism.
43. Caney 2008; Abizadeh 2007.
44. See e.g. Caney 2005a.
45. Barry 1982.
46. Reglitz 2015: 2.
47. For instance, it might be argued that states do much to sustain allegiance to fellow citizens vis-à-vis distant others (and could presumably act otherwise). For a recent argument to that effect, see Axelsen 2013. For an innovative argument about the roles states could play in fostering sympathies more amenable to global egalitarianism, see Ypi 2012.
48. Rawls 1999: 108.
49. Risse 2005; also 2012: 63–9.
50. Nili 2016a.
51. Risse appears to believe that the egalitarian concern for divergent resource levels is embarrassed if high levels of resources are not sufficient to guarantee wealth, but are in fact 'mediated' by other factors such as institutional quality. Moreover, he claims that, since the significance of resources is in supporting institutions, if rich countries uphold their duty to assist poor countries in building (minimally decent) institutions, 'no further worries regarding under-appreciation of resources should arise' (Risse 2005: 358, 366. See also Nili 2016a).
52. A claim which Nili (2016a: 142) also makes: 'there currently exists no social-scientific argument that natural resource abundance makes a significant contribution (however indirectly) to individuals' economic prospects'.
53. Such as the upward pressure large resource exports place on exchange rates, thus making other exports uncompetitive in overseas markets—the so-called 'Dutch disease'.
54. See e.g. Chaudhry 1989; Sachs and Warner 1995; and Fearon 2005. Non-reliance on taxes is a matter of degree: Ross (2012: 31) estimates that oil states are about 30 per cent less dependent than other states on taxes.
55. Ross 2001.
56. Robinson, Torvik, and Verdier 2006.
57. Karl 2007; Ross 2012: 1 ('the resource curse is overwhelmingly an oil curse').
58. Ross 2012: 146 (conflict); Ross 2012: 85 (democracy).
59. Nili (2016a: 144) claims that we cannot know that a country like Norway would not have grown just as quickly without oil, given the quality of its institutions. Perhaps we simply cannot isolate the impact of resource rents. The best response to that, I suspect, is to ask whether we would say the same of Qatar, Kuwait, Brunei, United Arab Emirates, and Saudi Arabia, each of which are in the world's top-ten countries according to GDP per capita, but none of which is famed for the quality of its institutions.
60. Ross 2012: 196.
61. Ross 2012: xiv.
62. Stevens, Lahn, and Kooroshy 2015: 15.

63. Given for instance the 'enclave' nature of extractive industries, which often fail to sustain local employment or to develop local infrastructure. For more on this, see Chapter 7.
64. Haber and Menaldo 2011.
65. Alexeev and Conrad 2009: 587, 595. See also Brunnschweiler and Bulte 2008: 259 ('mineral resource abundance seems to have a positive overall effect on economic performance') and Stevens, Lahn, and Kooroshy 2015: 14 ('If a country is starting from "nothing", economic growth based on extractive resources looks like rather a good option'). Recall also Ross's finding that, post-1990, oil states have grown faster than non-oil states.
66. Ross 2012: 3.
67. Stijns 2006: 1075.
68. Ross 2012: 213.
69. Alexeev and Conrad 2009.
70. Brunnschweiler and Bulte 2008: 254.
71. Haber and Menaldo 2011: 3.
72. Kennedy and Tiede 2013.
73. This is the conclusion reached by Alexeev and Conrad (2009: 587): 'countries that are rich only because of their natural resource wealth are likely to grow relatively slowly after that wealth has been mostly depleted. But they will, on average, remain wealthier than they would have been without natural resource wealth... It may be the case, however, that natural resource-induced growth is less beneficial over the long term than growth generated by industry, exports, or education.'
74. E.g. Ross 2001; Collier and Hoeffler 1998; Sachs and Warner 1995.
75. According to one study, on a suitable measure of resource abundance the richest countries are in fact Australia, Canada, New Zealand, and Norway. Brunnschweiler and Bulte 2008: 253.
76. Brunnschweiler and Bulte 2008: 253. As the authors note, this mismatch raises the possibility that theorists of the resource curse are wrong about the direction of causality involved in the 'curse'. Whereas institutions cannot plausibly influence initial resource abundance, it is much more plausible that they can influence resource dependence (for instance by failing to develop other sectors of an economy once income streams from resources are present). If so, the claim that resource wealth undermines institutional quality is doubly embarrassed: it may be that it is poor institutions which engender resource dependence, and not the other way around. See also Stijns 2006.
77. Note that I am not objecting here to the use of measures of resource dependence in analyses of the resource curse *tout court*. It might be perfectly sensible to employ a measure of resource dependence when investigating political effects whereby leaders in resource-exporting countries become less reliant on citizens' cooperation (see e.g. Wiens, Poast, and Clark 2014). The remarks in this paragraph concern the theoretical salience of measures of resource dependence (as opposed to abundance) when assessing the connection between resource wealth and economic growth. If claims about the weak relationship between resource wealth and economic performance turn out to be based upon indices of dependence rather than abundance, this seems to me to undercut the normative conclusion

drawn by scholars such as Risse and Nili, to the effect that varying resource endowments do not matter for growth.
78. Collier 2010b: 119.
79. Segal 2011.
80. Moss 2011; Sandbu 2006; Sala-i-Martin and Subramanian 2003; and Palley 2003.
81. Pogge 2002; Wenar 2016a.
82. Miller suggests that communities are responsible for a substantial part of the value of the resources within their territories. Miller 2007, chapter 8. The argument that agents have influenced the value of the resources they control also plays a role in Risse's rejection of egalitarian principles of natural resource justice (Risse 2005: 362–3).
83. See e.g. Steiner 1994.
84. In fact, I will argue in Chapter 4 that the distinction between 'improved' and 'unimproved' portions of value cannot bear the normative weight often placed upon it. The implication I draw is that even the 'improved' portion of value might be vulnerable to calls for redistribution.
85. See e.g. Moore 2012.

3

The Demands of Equality

Chapter 2 argued in favour of an egalitarian account of natural resource justice. But what distribution of natural resources, or the benefits and burdens flowing from them, should egalitarians favour? One common—and, we might think, perfectly obvious—answer would be equal shares. To be sure, the idea of sharing out all natural resources themselves would be an odd one. And on what basis would we share them out, in any case? By weight? Or volume? Alternatively, perhaps their economic value might be shared through some system of taxes and transfers. Proposals along just those lines have a long and distinguished history. Thomas Paine claimed that each of us is 'a joint life proprietor, with the rest, in the property of the soil, and in all its natural productions, vegetable and animal'. He argued passionately for a right to a basic capital stake for all, and a basic income for people over fifty years of age 'in lieu of the natural inheritance, which, as a right, belongs to every man'.[1] Eighty years later Henry George argued on a similar basis for a tax on the unimproved value of land and its resources, with the proceeds being shared equally.[2]

In more recent debates about global justice, Beitz argued that even if we lived in a world of self-contained societies, the 'arbitrary' and highly unequal distribution of natural resources between societies would still be troubling from the point of view of justice. Rather than allowing societies to suffer (or prosper) as a result of this uneven distribution we should instead embrace a principle which would distribute the value of natural resources so as to at least mitigate the inequalities emanating from it.[3] Since then many others have argued for principles which would equally distribute the value of the world's natural resources, again chiefly because of the moral arbitrariness of their distribution.[4]

This chapter will argue that the equal shares principle has exerted a regrettable hold on egalitarians, and ought to be rejected. It is vulnerable to two major objections. First, strictly equal shares are unattractive in light of people's different capacities to convert resources into what matters morally: actual wellbeing.[5] Second, inequalities in natural resource holdings are not the only inequalities which ought to concern us, and, as such, insisting on equal shares of natural resources (or their value) *in particular* is unwarranted. On both counts, equal shares ought to be rejected.

I press those objections in section 3.1, against left-libertarian arguments, which are notable for their insistence that only natural resource inequalities are correctable at the bar of justice. Against that view I suggest that whilst natural resource inequalities are important, they are only one among a broad set of inequalities that egalitarians ought to be concerned with. Moreover, I suggest that left-libertarians face a dilemma inasmuch as they sign up to responsibility-catering principles. It is precisely because nobody created natural resources, they argue, that none of us has any responsibility-based claim to greater shares than anyone else; the artefacts we produce with our labour, on the other hand, are ours in a deep sense because they are the products of our own efforts. But there are many other inequalities we face when we come into the world, and for which we appear no more responsible. The left-libertarian must then either claim that these other inequalities do not matter (thereby undermining his claim to track responsibility, and presenting him with the challenge of specifying why *some* inequalities for which we are not responsible are nevertheless acceptable); or he must claim that these other inequalities can also be presented as inequalities in access to natural resources— stretching that category so that the results converge, or nearly converge, with the liberal or socialist egalitarian views that they claim their view presents an alternative to. At present prominent left-libertarians have not seized either horn of the dilemma decisively. Although some of them stretch the category of natural resources, thereby expanding the set of goods which can be redistributed, the resulting distributions will still not eradicate involuntary disadvantage.

The rest of the chapter proceeds as follows. Section 3.2 briefly addresses, but rejects, some pragmatic arguments in favour of equal shares. Section 3.3 argues that we should seek to equalize across a wide category of advantages and disadvantages, and that we can, within specified limits, conceive of advantages and disadvantages as *substitutable* across these categories. The limits to substitutability, though, do not give us reason to insist on equal resource shares. Given this, we should favour 'equalizing' or 'equality-promoting' shares of the benefits and burdens flowing from natural resources. That fact has important implications for a variety of debates relevant to natural resource justice. Section 3.4 sets out some of the implications for natural resource appropriation and for climate justice. Section 3.5 sets out some of the implications for discussions of intergenerational justice. Section 3.6 briefly sums up, and discusses some of the issues which arise once we select wellbeing as the 'metric' for our egalitarianism at the global level.

3.1. AGAINST NATURAL RESOURCE EXCEPTIONALISM

I will suggest in this chapter that natural resources are not the only sources of advantage and disadvantage which ought to matter from the point of view of justice. Egalitarians also ought to care, for instance, about the impact of people's internal endowments, which give them unequal abilities to convert the same resources into wellbeing, and which also—in the world we all inhabit—give people hugely unequal earning power. This undermines approaches which define natural resources as the one thing a theory of justice should seek to equalize holdings of. It also undermines approaches which seek to equalize opportunities for wellbeing rather than resource shares, but which nevertheless claim that when seeking to equalize those opportunities, natural resources (or resource values) are the only thing we should distribute between people. Contrary to the first view, natural resources are not the correct *equalisandum* for justice. And contrary to the second view, they are not the right *distribuendum* either.

The kinds of disadvantage we all face, in coming into the world, are multifaceted. Some people are lucky enough to receive bequests from dead relatives. Some of us are raised to speak languages, or display social mores, that give us better access to desirable opportunities. Some of us face prejudice, closed doors, and violence on the basis of sex, sexuality, ethnicity, religion, or disability. Some of us live in countries which have, over centuries, built up considerable civic and economic infrastructure (sometimes bankrolled by the exploitation of others). Some of us are born in countries which have already obtained access to lucrative service industries, or which produce high-end consumer products, whereas others are born in countries shut out from those markets by skewed rules of international trade or by the huge start-up costs involved in accessing those markets. It is sometimes argued that relative supplies of natural resources are not very decisive in determining the wealth of a community, and that variables such as institutional quality matter much more. But even if this were correct (and we saw in Chapter 2 that the associated claims are complex and contentious), an egalitarian could ask why the fact that individuals are born into communities with wildly varying levels of institutional quality or capacity would be any *more* defensible a generator of inequality than the fact that some are born into resource-rich countries and some into resource-poor ones. If we are concerned to neutralize or at least mitigate unchosen disadvantage, then it is worth pointing out that all of these things constitute inequalities for which the individuals born into our world cannot plausibly be held responsible.

Consider, by contrast, the left-libertarian view. The right-libertarians discussed in Chapter 2 cleave to a strong conception of self-ownership, and place few or no constraints upon individuals' ability to appropriate natural resources. As such, right-libertarianism is a recipe for disastrous levels of inequality. The defining feature of left-libertarianism, on the other hand, is that it marries a commitment to individual self-ownership with the idea that we are all co-equal owners of the natural resources which are already 'out there' when we come into the world. On the latter point, some left-libertarians consider themselves to be presenting the most plausible version of Locke's famous proviso—a strictly egalitarian one. If justice requires that when we appropriate we leave 'enough and as good' for others, this could be taken to mean that we must leave everyone else with the opportunity to appropriate an equal share. If we over-appropriate, by contrast, we should compensate others for, or 'pay rent' on, the disproportionate share of the world's resources we come to control. Some of these scholars consider themselves to be walking in the radical footsteps of Thomas Paine and Henry George when they defend, for instance, a global basic income reflecting each individual's share of the world's resource rents.

One defender of the claim that natural resource values are the solely appropriate distribuendum for an egalitarian theory is Hillel Steiner. For Steiner things are axiomatically either natural resources—in which case we have symmetrical claims over them—or they are the products of labour—and hence there can be no redistributive claim over them. In that sense natural resources—or, to be specific, resource values—are the only contender in the search for an appropriate target for redistribution.[5] Importantly, the theory is also intended to enact a choice/circumstance distinction: it is because no one is responsible for creating natural resources that we all have a symmetrical claim over them, whereas the fruits of our own labour—which we are presumably responsible for choosing to exert, or not—are properly considered immune from redistributive projects.

However, this view struggles to insulate distribution from the influence of unchosen circumstance. Consider, first, that for Steiner natural resource value is both the equalisandum and the distribuendum of justice: natural resource value, that is, is what we should have equal shares of, and is also the (only) thing we should distribute in order to promote equality. The first claim will necessarily be rejected by anyone favouring a welfarist (or capability-oriented) view of equality. For assuming that people have unequal abilities to convert resources into wellbeing (or capabilities), equal shares of resource value will leave some worse off—and perhaps much worse off—than others through no fault of their own. There might, to be sure, be cases where it is contentious where we should draw the line—witness the extensive debate about when expensive tastes should be subsidized, and whether we are responsible for them (see section 3.6)—but there will also be easy cases—such as involuntary disability—where sharing resource value equally serves egalitarians badly.

Even if we leave that issue to one side, the view faces further problems on account of its insistence that natural resources should be the sole distribuendum. Consider the challenge of inheritance. Imagine that at T^1 we all individually enjoy equal shares of the value of the world's natural resources. Over time some of us will make more of our shares than others, and we might then at T^2 seek to pass those (purportedly earned and legitimate) advantages onto others. If the practice of bequest is tolerated, it becomes possible for some of us to transfer the fruits of our own labour—to which we may have perfectly good title—to our descendants, and in so doing disrupt the pursuit of equality. That, though, could see some faring better or worse in life as a result of decisions for which they are not responsible. Like many egalitarians, Steiner rejects any right of inheritance.[7] But in order to be able to reject it—and to maintain his theory's exclusive focus on natural resources as the proper distribuendum—he must treat the assets of the dead *as natural resources*, regardless of their actual properties. In blocking inheritance it is not only the raw natural materials formerly owned by the dead which are declared fit for egalitarian redistribution, but also the products of their labour (their Beatles records, perhaps, or their poetry, or their shares in telecommunications companies). These latter are seen by Steiner to in some sense 'revert' to natural resource status upon the deaths of their owners; indeed they must be understood in this way, for otherwise there could be no redistributive claim on them. These are not virgin raw materials in our (or indeed the conventional) sense of the term because they have been improved—perhaps beyond all recognition—by human beings, and may even have been created by them.

The unequal earning power attached to the labour of the living also represents a challenge. Living people are, for Steiner, entitled to what they produce with their own labour: if an agent produces something by her own efforts, then—so long as she did not use a disproportionate share of resources in so doing—that thing is hers in the very deep sense that there can be no redistributive claim on it whatsoever. On this point many egalitarians might express concern, since people have very unequal capacities to labour, or abilities which command very different market values, and hence unequal opportunities to transform their symmetrical stock of natural resources into valuable commodities. What would become, on such a scheme, of the weak and the infirm and the sick, or people whose talents were not in demand? Will the theory endorse inequalities flowing from varying internal endowments? Steiner accepts that an account which focused exclusively on natural resources *conventionally* understood would be 'insufficiently egalitarian' in concentrating on 'external' at the expense of 'personal' resources.[8] But his response is to define internal endowments themselves—or, at least, the 'germ-line genetic information' coded in our DNA—as natural resources upon which there is an egalitarian redistributive claim.

This move is problematic. First, and less importantly, note that it requires further stretching of the definition of natural resources. The point about human germ-line genetic information, a critic might say, is that it *is* produced by humans: without humans making the decision to reproduce, there would be no future humans, and no germ-line genetic information. We cannot say the same for (wild) trees, or coal, or sand. As such, its description as a natural resource has struck many as odd. It might be responded that although individual humans appropriate genetic information in deciding to reproduce, they do not create that genetic information from scratch.[9] That is true, but the difference with other natural resources persists: unlike any other purportedly 'natural' resource, human genetic information simply would not exist without human intervention.[10]

Second, and more importantly, the egalitarian redistributive strategy, as applied to germ-line genetic information, is unsatisfying in that it is incapable of delivering on the choice/circumstance distinction which supposedly animates the theory. By way of remedy for the inegalitarian effects of parents' appropriation of germ-line information of varying earning power, the suggestion is that we tax the appropriation of genes linked to superior earning power, and compensate those who appropriate genes linked to inferior earning power.[11] This move raises obvious epistemic challenges, because it requires us to use genetic codes to estimate, as a basis for taxation, the future earning power of children. In fact the challenge looks to be more than epistemic, since the future earning power of children is likely not to be *determined* at the time of conception.[12] In any case taxing *parents* now for the (estimated future) earning power of their children can hardly prevent children from later benefiting unequally from their unequal talents. At best the taxation of parents may narrow likely inequalities, by making the parents of 'gifted' children poorer on average, and hence less able to pass *some* of their erstwhile advantages on to their children.[13] But—as Steiner acknowledges—this will serve to narrow inequalities between children and not to eradicate them. As such the theory's ability to prevent children from benefiting from unequal talents is distinctly limited. In its drive to eradicate the influence of brute luck it is already required to expand its conception of natural resources in two unfamiliar ways, with the implication that natural resources can be the products of human labour, living or dead. But it remains incapable of eradicating undeserved disadvantage because in order to do so it would have to tax the earning power of living generations (something which left-libertarians refuse to countenance). In the absence of such a move, left-libertarians offer an incomplete egalitarianism.

I have suggested that Steiner's theory errs both in depicting natural resources as the equalisandum for an egalitarian theory, and in depicting them as the distribuendum. But not all left-libertarian views share these two features. Some view opportunity for welfare or wellbeing as the equalisandum of a theory of justice, at the same time as holding fast to the idea that it is only shares of natural resource value that we should redistribute in order to move closer to equality. Prominent defenders of such a view are Michael Otsuka and Peter Vallentyne.[14] Like Steiner, both hold that the egalitarian should aim to distribute shares of natural resource value so as to advance equality, but unlike Steiner both argue that our aim in so doing should be to ameliorate inequalities in opportunities for welfare (Vallentyne calls his argument, as a result, not an equal shares view, but an 'equality-promoting view', insofar as it seeks to use natural resource value to advance us towards equality of opportunity for welfare, and as a result will likely demand that we disburse that value very unequally between different individuals[15]). Their theories would therefore go some way to redressing inequalities contingent on disabilities, or other unequal capacities to convert natural resources into wellbeing. In that respect the two theories represent an advance. I also endorse a welfarist conception of egalitarianism, and unpack some of its implications across the remainder of this chapter. But note that, as far as Otsuka and Vallentyne's positions go, *neither theory would equalize opportunity for wellbeing.* They would not do so because each is committed to viewing natural resources as the sole distribuendum for equality.[16] Inequalities would therefore remain for which the individuals bearing the brunt of them cannot be held responsible. Put simply, the problem is that the pot of natural resource value is insufficient to fully ameliorate undeserved inequalities in wellbeing. By way of illustration it is estimated that, globally, resource rents make up, on average, around 4 to 5 per cent of each country's GDP. The sale of natural resources, though an important source of income for many countries, is dwarfed in significance for most by income from services, intellectual property, and so on[17]—but insofar as these are 'earned' by the exercise of our labour-power (however unequal, and however arbitrary the demand for any particular kind of labour), they are not up for grabs. Although the depiction of opportunities for wellbeing as the equalisandum is therefore to be welcomed, the simultaneous endorsement of natural resources as the distribuendum leaves the project of equalizing those opportunities severely hampered.[18]

* * *

The arguments of this section have sought to undermine one variety of what we might call 'natural resource exceptionalism'—that is, the idea that there is something normatively distinctive about natural resources which determines the way we ought to think about their distribution. That variety suggests— though the struggle to hold onto the idea can involve various contortions— that natural resources are the only set of goods we should be interested in when it comes to redistributive justice. I have suggested that it is uncompelling. But there is another, albeit more mild, version of natural resource exceptionalism which we might briefly consider. This version suggests that the argument for sharing natural resources is especially *straightforward*, because it can, for instance, be made without reference to any relational facts about human interaction. Natural resources are distinctive in the sense that we can easily imagine worlds in which they, and they alone, should be subject to redistribution; arguments for sharing other goods, by contrast, must depend upon additional considerations (such as relational facts).

In a world which does in fact display considerable interdependence—like ours—that argument might be of purely hypothetical interest (likewise, the argument will have little interest for those who already believe that humanism or non-relationism settles the question of the scope of egalitarian concern). But the ghost of the idea might remain in the belief that the argument for redistributing natural resources is especially 'pure' or uncontroversial. In my view, however, this supposed advantage is not obvious, and it is worth briefly demonstrating why. Beitz famously suggested that a resource redistribution principle could apply even in a counterfactual world of autarkic nation-states, whereas broader distributive principles might depend upon empirical claims about the effects of globalization, or the emergence of global social cooperation. Unequal resource benefits would require correction *even if* globalization had not occurred, because this represents a pernicious form of inequality for which its victims (and beneficiaries) cannot be held responsible.[19]

But the claim that unequal resource benefits are objectionable whether or not they are produced within the ambit of a global form of social cooperation fails to identify anything special about natural resources. If the intuition underlying that claim is that arbitrary factors ought not to influence our prospects, then we would surely be led in the direction of a global egalitarian principle which *also* sought to correct inequalities arising from climate, geography, natural events, and unequal personal endowments. We cannot rule out such possibilities by suggesting that these advantages or disadvantages are not social products and are hence inappropriate objects for distribution, because such a response would undercut any resource redistribution principle too. We seem to be required to say either that principles of justice apply only to social products (in which case they apparently never apply to natural resources), or to say that they apply to inequalities whether produced by social cooperation or not (in which case singling out natural resources alone for equalization is unjustified).

Even *if* we accept that they are 'manna from heaven', then, natural resources do not appear to be the *only* thing which their holders are not responsible for creating, and over which claims might therefore appear to be weak. We should instead ask whether, *from the point of view of people coming into the world*, there is anything normatively distinctive about natural resources at all. We are each of us born into situations of quite multifarious but nevertheless unearned advantages and disadvantages, many of which do not have much obvious connection with natural resources, but which are likewise unchosen by their recipients.

Finally, though we have seen that he rejects equal shares, we might note that a similar thought about the special non-created nature of natural resources animates Risse's claim that a specific 'ground of justice' applies to them, entailing specific and separate distributive constraints. But although his theory of global justice treats natural resources as a special category of goods over which special claims are uniquely weak—not least since, by contrast to other goods, no one created them—elsewhere he appears to concede the case against exceptionalism. Recall from Chapter 2 his claim that outsiders might justly try to enter states which are underusing the resources in their territories. It has rightly been suggested in response that immigrants would then gain access not only to natural resources—over which claims are weak—but also to public goods and cultural resources which *were* created by particular communities.[20] By way of reply Risse asks, in relation to 'cultural and institutional accomplishments', 'But does this mean that, say, the current generation of Americans is more entitled to the legacy of their ancestors than anybody else? If so, it cannot be because they themselves have done any work to create what by stipulation now is a legacy.' To the contrary, he concludes (correctly in my view) that 'contemporary Americans have the same sort of relationship to the legacy left to them by their forebears as they have to the natural resources and space of the earth: for any given individual, these things are like manna from heaven'.[21] That argument is, I would suggest, absolutely right—but also fatal to his variety of natural resource exceptionalism.

3.2. PRAGMATIC ARGUMENTS FOR EXCEPTIONALISM

At the level of principle, egalitarians should eschew the view that it is only the distribution of natural resources that ought to concern us, in favour of a more broad-based focus on whatever advantages and disadvantages actually make a difference to our wellbeing. But perhaps there are good pragmatic reasons to favour equal shares of the benefits and burdens arising from natural resources *amongst* the advantages that a theory of justice seeks to equalize. It has been suggested for instance that a policy advocating equal resource values enjoys strategic or practical advantages that other egalitarian strategies do not. It might be that the drive to equalize holdings in a whole series of social goods presents theories of justice with a set of epistemic difficulties, since doing so would require us to possess facts about innate capacities, individual choices, and so on. By contrast, establishing and then taxing (unequal) holdings of resources might be relatively straightforward from the practical point of view. We might also think, along with many economists, that taxing natural resources is relatively efficient (in the sense that it is less prone to producing disincentive effects) than taxing other goods such as income.[22] Indeed, we might even think that taxing natural resources is less likely to interfere with liberty than taxing other social goods. Finally, we might believe that even if natural resource inequalities are not the only undeserved inequalities, it might be relatively easy to *persuade* people to rectify them, and that taxes on natural resources are likely to command especially broad philosophical or political support.[23] In sum, even if inequalities in natural resource values are not all that should matter to egalitarians—even if natural resources are but a subset of the concrete drivers of human wellbeing—they may represent an area in which progress towards equality can relatively easily be made. If so, it could be that pursuing equal shares of natural resource value represents the most feasible way of making progress towards equality more broadly construed.

It seems to me that these various considerations have some force. However, they offer no support to the argument for equal shares. An egalitarian could agree that there are good practical reasons for prioritizing the pursuit of natural resource taxes, and affirm that this is indeed an area in which the chances of success are relatively good (on which see Chapter 8). She could even agree that natural resource taxes look especially attractive because of their efficiency and their (relatively small) effects on liberty. But that does not commit us to any particular view on how to disburse the *proceeds* from such taxes. We could accept all of these arguments for natural resource taxes and simply say: grant all of the proceeds to whoever is worst off in the world according to our preferred metric. We could even say, in fact, that if it is true that we are unlikely to be able to directly attack other inequalities any time soon, this makes it all the more important that we should use the proceeds to ameliorate whichever inequalities concern us most, rather than restricting our attention to one subset of inequalities that coincide haphazardly at best with overall access to wellbeing. The equal disbursement of proceeds from natural resource taxes would, notably, shift funds from resource-rich but generally poor countries, to resource-poor but generally rich countries.[24] But from an egalitarian point of view this would be myopic.

3.3. AN EQUALITY-PROMOTING CONSTRAINT

Given the poverty of both principled and pragmatic arguments for equal shares, we have no good reason to insist on them. Resource benefits should rather be harnessed to redress inequalities in access to wellbeing more broadly. This conclusion assumes that as a source of benefit or burden, the benefits and burdens arising from natural resources can offset, or compensate for, inequalities arising from at least some other sources. It assumes at least the moderate *substitutability* of different categories of advantage.²⁵ Different advantages can be considered morally substitutable when an agent lacking one advantage can properly be restored to parity with others by giving her a different kind of advantage, and where that substitution is not the occasion of a significant moral loss.

There may, though, be limits to the moral substitutability of different types of advantage. Insofar as there are such limits, we will have reason, within a broader egalitarian account, to still favour equal shares of one kind of good or other. Even egalitarian accounts concerned with a considerable range of goods might still find reason to 'hypothecate' some of them. Hypothecation occurs when an egalitarian selects out a good or perhaps several goods and demands (perhaps roughly) equal shares *of these goods*, regardless of the distribution of other valued goods. In so doing, they will treat some goods as morally incommensurable with others, so that advantages or disadvantages 'elsewhere' are not held to compensate for or offset unequal holdings in these specific goods. To give an example, we might be strongly committed to the political principle of 'one person, one vote'. We would then believe that unequal shares of income, say, ought not to be offset by giving extra votes to the poor. Alternatively we might believe that inequalities in access to valued social positions ought not to be compensated for by giving those thereby deprived more money, or greater shares of healthcare. Perhaps some kinds of discrimination are so demeaning that in an egalitarian society we should not be content even if they are compensated for. Hypothecating a good suggests that there is a distinctive wrongness about its unequal distribution which cannot or should not be offset by providing additional shares of other goods.

In many cases we will accept a degree of substitutability between goods: for example, many egalitarians will be content with a society in which some have chosen more leisure and others more income. But most, I suspect, would not accept complete substitutability. One reason for insisting on equal shares of particular goods—which is again rather pragmatic—would apply if we knew that inequalities in the distribution of those goods would persistently and invasively lead to inequalities in our holdings of other goods. Perhaps in societies characterized by widespread injustice we know that inequalities in education lead—because it has a partly 'positional' character—to pervasive inequalities across the whole of economic life. For that reason we might have especially strong strategic reasons to favour equality in educational provision.²⁶ Alternatively the thought may be that in a society (or world) committed to social equality or equality of status, we will have good reason to insist on equality with regard to certain goods.²⁷ To formulate the principle more carefully, it seems plausible that we have a reason to hypothecate goods wherever there is a history of inequality of status (such as entrenched gender or ethnic inequality), where that inequality of status is bound up in unequal shares of the good in question, and where, more positively, hypothecating that good is likely to be successful in breaking the chain of disadvantage. If women or certain ethnic groups have been deprived of equal access to certain jobs or colleges (and if, as often happens, their failure to permeate those sectors has served as perverse proof of their inferiority), we might have strong reasons to seek equal access to those jobs or colleges even if those women or ethnic groups have excellent opportunities elsewhere. A commitment to equal status provides us with a reason to disdain certain inequalities which we would otherwise accept, especially when the inequalities of status are profound and enduring.

But our question is not the general defensibility of considering all goods as substitutable.[28] Rather our question is: even if the egalitarian case for hypothecating some goods is sound, why hypothecate natural resources in particular? It seems possible that the idea of equality of status can lead us some way in that direction. We know that women have been excluded from property ownership in many countries (including ownership of land and other natural resources), and that these inequalities are bound up, in a complex way, with the view of them as less than full citizens (by which we mean that their inferior access to resources is both a cause, and an effect, of their inequality of status). In such societies, addressing gender inequalities might plausibly entail ensuring that women have roughly equal access to, say, land ownership.[29] There are also many indigenous communities, members of which have been deprived of access to valued natural resources, *and* been the subject of enduring inequalities of status, with regard to whom the same argument is plausible. In such cases hypothecating equal natural resource benefits makes egalitarian sense—if it promises to be effective in weakening the cycle of disadvantage in question. But it is important to note that this is not an argument for equal shares of natural resources *simpliciter*. Instead it is an argument that we sometimes have reasons to favour greater equality of resources in some communities, across certain social groups. The thought fails to support equal shares of natural resource benefits across the board.

* * *

I have suggested we abandon the twin assumptions that only natural resources matter from the point of view of inequality, and that egalitarians must demand equal shares of the benefits flowing from them. If as egalitarians we ought to care about a whole range of inequalities, a policy aimed at sharing natural resource benefits equally will be defectively egalitarian. Given the poor correlation between natural resource wealth and overall shares of important goods, such a policy would often move funds *from* people who are, in fact, doing very badly overall in terms of wellbeing, and give them *to* people who are doing considerably better. Even in cases where natural resource benefits do correlate well with shares in other goods—where those with fewer natural resources are also worse off in other ways—such a policy would still be insufficiently egalitarian, because it would give precisely the same share of natural resource benefits to the rich as it would to the poor of the world. Even if there are good strategic reasons for pursuing the taxation of natural resources, egalitarians ought to reject equal distribution of the proceeds.

What, though, are the implications of dropping those assumptions? The more we embrace the substitutability of different forms of advantage the more it becomes possible (and important) to say that egalitarianism is a theory about *how much* people get overall, and not a theory of *which things* people get. It is a theory which concerns itself first and foremost with overall levels of advantage and only sometimes, in special cases, with the way in which particular advantages are distributed across persons. On the first question egalitarianism then begins to look like a rather permissive theory, insofar as there will be a great number of different distributions of advantage across persons which are compatible with justice.

What can we say positively about the demands of equality with regard to the benefits and burdens flowing from natural resources? First, we will sometimes want to avoid gender- and ethnicity-based inequalities in resource benefits, especially in societies with a history of exclusion from resource ownership where this exclusion has fed into a vicious cycle of prejudice and stigma. This will provide support for active measures to enhance resource rights for such marginalized groups. But whilst there can be reasons to prefer equal resource benefits in particular cases, this does not generate an argument for globally equal benefits.

Second, egalitarians should also seek to (modestly) constrain otherwise acceptable inequalities by defending a basic entitlement to some essential natural resources. Here we will want to say roughly that humans are entitled to sufficient shares of those natural resources necessary for them to meet their basic human rights. In making this claim we reconnect with the tradition of Paine, George, and their forebears—many of whom insisted that each person had the right to use the common stock to ensure their subsistence—as well as with some more recent commentators. Such a principle is capable of commanding broad support. Even those with a more modest account of global justice will find reason to object to a world in which many people are deprived of access to resources which are key to human wellbeing. All human beings, simply as human beings, will unavoidably require certain quantities of specific natural resources such as fresh water and clean air. Although it would be perverse to stipulate any entitlement to *equal* shares of fresh water, it makes sense to guarantee the minimal shares sufficient to support basic human rights. We do so because these specific resources serve basic interests in non-substitutable ways. The basic rights constraint is important because when we come to discuss natural resource appropriation or climate justice (see section 3.4) we might reach the conclusion that *all* the unused benefits arising from natural resources (properly available to our generation) should go to the world's worst-off. That conclusion needs to be moderated by a respect for the basic rights of everyone, including those who are already faring disproportionately well.

Securing basic rights will not exhaust the total benefits arising from natural resources. There will remain a large 'surplus' of benefits which may be vulnerable to redistribution in the interests of global justice. Still, even if we accept an egalitarian account of global justice this does not lead inexorably to the conclusion that this surplus ought to be distributed evenly. More likely, it ought to be distributed—for egalitarian reasons—with a strong priority towards the worst-off individuals across the world, measured in terms of overall access to wellbeing. We ought to favour then, third, 'equalizing' or equality-promoting rather than equal shares of benefits.

The proceeds of any such redistribution are likely to be best used in a variety of ways which have relatively little directly to do with natural resources (including funding progress in dealing with endemic diseases, for instance, or supporting primary education in the developing world; see Chapter 8). But in many cases they will also be well spent on major infrastructure projects where the connection to resources is closer, such as projects designed to secure stable and sustainable access to key resources such as clean fresh water, to fund 'technology transfer' schemes to spread green technologies in the developing world, and to fund the protection of natural resources of common concern to all of humankind, such as the polar regions or the rainforests. This allocation will be informed by a desire to reduce global inequalities and to advance intergenerational justice.

3.4. CONSTRAINING APPROPRIATION

Egalitarians should seek to distribute all of the benefits and burdens relevant to justice in such a way as to equalize access to wellbeing. In the (likely) event that doing so is not possible at any given point in time—in the event, that is, that egalitarians have the opportunity to influence some but not all benefits and burdens—then they should pursue an equalizing strategy: they should distribute whatever goods are at hand so as to reduce as much as possible the broader inequalities we care about. In many cases this plausibly means giving disproportionately large shares of these goods—natural resource value, for instance—to the worst-off overall. In the rest of the chapter I illustrate some of the implications of that view. One of the major areas of contestation within discussions of land and natural resources has long been the extent to which given agents are at liberty to appropriate natural resources from common stocks and convert them into private property. It is sometimes suggested in debates about rights over land that this has become an essentially historical question. Barring the high seas and the polar regions, we live in a more or less wholly appropriated world; Locke's suggestion that those who do not consent to a particular sovereign could begin their own commonwealths elsewhere has been rendered irrelevant by the virtual demise of *terra nullius*. What an investigation of limits to appropriation can tell us now, if anything, is how appropriation could have justly occurred, and this might have lessons—though likely not straightforward ones, given the complex facts of history—for present distributions.

But even if the original appropriation of land is of mainly historical interest, appropriation is a live, contemporary, and important issue when we switch our attention to other natural resources. Apparently unowned natural resources are still being appropriated on a continual basis: individuals collect rainwater for use in drinking, cooking, and cleaning, or harness energy from solar radiation to use in domestic heating; corporations are exploring for oil in the deep sea hundreds of miles from the nearest inhabited land (see Chapter 9); all of us have 'carbon footprints', in the sense that we are all, albeit to wildly differing degrees, continually consuming the capacity of the atmosphere or other carbon sinks to absorb greenhouse gases. Meanwhile valuable minerals and fossil fuels are being extracted from under the territories of nation-states, and whereas international law grants nation-states sweeping privileges over 'their' natural resources, at the level of theory their right to do so and to retain the proceeds is a live rather than a settled question (see Chapter 6).

The question of limits to appropriation is therefore a stubbornly significant one, with an important role to play in, for instance, discussions of climate justice. Just how much of the atmosphere's carbon-absorptive capacity can each of us justly consume? Just how much solar energy, or oil, or wind-power can someone utilize without committing an injustice? We saw in Chapter 2 that Locke's famous (but ambiguous) answer to that question suggested that there was a moral limit to appropriation where it ceased to leave 'enough and as good' for others to appropriate. That apparently simple claim has, we saw, been taken up in very different ways, but on one version it generates an *egalitarian* proviso according to which we commit an injustice—and owe compensation, at the very least—when we appropriate more than a symmetrical share of natural resources.

However, it is hard to see how such a restrictive egalitarian limit on appropriation can be defended. A necessary move here is to distinguish between a 'narrow' egalitarian proviso and a 'broad' one. A narrow egalitarian proviso places limits on appropriating natural resource benefits in particular, and hence rejects appropriation beyond symmetrical shares even when this might usefully offset other inequalities. A broad egalitarian proviso will allow appropriation beyond symmetrical shares where this usefully promotes equality across the whole range of goods relevant to distributive justice. A welfarist egalitarian could allow appropriation of benefits for each agent until such a point that their access to wellbeing became equal; that would place much stricter limits on some agents' appropriation than on others. And the broader the range of goods we are willing to treat as potential distribuenda, the better the prospects for equalizing access to wellbeing *tout court*. The permissible appropriations under such a principle might be very unequal indeed, if they usefully alleviate significant inequalities in the holdings of other goods.

This has important implications for the practice of regulating acquisition, as can be illustrated through the example of climate justice. The principle of equal per capita greenhouse gas emissions enjoys considerable support in discussions of climate justice, and is often taken to be justified on much the same grounds as the purported entitlement to equal natural resource benefits: in the light of the fact that no one has created the atmosphere's capacity to absorb greenhouse gases, we might ask whether there can *ever* be good reasons to allow some agents to generate more emissions than others.[30] But it is not difficult to provide such reasons. A principle which specifies equal per capita emissions but ignores the scale of the other impacts we make on the carbon cycle (such as, perhaps, protecting or enhancing carbon sinks such as rainforests) is myopic. It is unduly restrictive to focus on one kind of carbon 'debit' alone, to the exclusion of other debits and of possible 'credits' generated by our other activities.[31] At the bar of justice a principle of equal per capita emissions is unduly generous to agents who already enjoy greater shares of other important goods, vis-à-vis those whose lives are blighted by poverty, underdevelopment, and a general lack of opportunities. This is not to deny that an equal per capita emissions principle would represent a great advance on the status quo; but it is far from optimal from the point of view of equality.

Consider finally the question of burdens. Egalitarians have for centuries been vexed by the idea that some of us come into the world with inferior opportunities to harvest the opportunities that natural resources offer to our species. But burdens can be just as significant, and the inequality of the burdens we face can be just as undeserved. Imagine two communities possessed of equal natural resource wealth, but one of which is, through no fault of its own, a victim of a terrible disease spread by mosquitoes (or contaminated water, or radioactive gas seeping from nearby rocks). Although benefits (and especially the economic value of the world's resources) have attracted disproportionate attention, a consistent egalitarian will call for the equalization of (at least) these benefits *and burdens* (or *net* benefits, we might say). And if the arguments of this chapter are sound, burdens as well as benefits should be distributed in equality-promoting ways. When we shift attention to important burdens relating to climate change—the costs of funding mitigation, or adaptation, or developing green technologies, or protecting rainforests—this suggests that an ability-to-pay principle requiring greater sacrifices from those who are generally faring better has a strong role to play. Often the exposure of

3.5. INTERGENERATIONAL JUSTICE

Discussions of intergenerational justice are troubled by some difficult philosophical questions.[33] Many of us are prepared to believe that we act wrongly in avoidably causing future people to face worse prospects for wellbeing than we do ourselves. But the 'non-identity' problem suggests that, if our actions actually influence the identity of the particular people who will later come into existence, it is far from clear how we can be said to be harming them in making their lives go worse than they might. After all, if someone would not have existed had it not been for our actions, can we be said to act wrongly in causing him to lead a life which is tolerable but happens to be inferior in prospects to our own?[34]

If the non-identity objection is compelling, it may reduce the scope for egalitarian principles of intergenerational justice, however strongly some of us intuitively feel that what we owe those in the distant future is no different from what we owe to those who are distant from us in the present. Responding adequately to the non-identity problem would be a complex project; but perhaps there are ways of sidestepping it. One recent argument by Anca Gheaus suggests a way of defending a duty of sustainability—which might, for instance, demand that we grant future generations equal prospects for enjoying wellbeing—without assuming anything about the rights of, or our duties towards, people who are as yet unborn.[35] Her argument proceeds on the basis that humans have an important interest in being able to parent children, an interest that grounds a right to parent. The activity of parenting is valuable insofar as it allows us to enjoy a relationship with people who love and trust us (in the unique way which children can), and gives us the ability to develop as individuals, both personally and morally.[36] But if we have a right to parent, then so, presumably, do our children. Consider, though, a world in which a particular generation (G1) used up natural resources avariciously, so as to leave subsequent generations without enough resources to enjoy equal access to wellbeing. That would leave *its* children (G2) in a situation where they could not parent an equal number of children themselves without forcing on *those* children (G3) lives of inferior wellbeing. In effect, the children of G2 would face a terrible choice. Either they could choose to sacrifice, for at least some of their members, the ability to parent children—and hence become victims of injustice. Or they could—unjustly—continue to bear an equal number of children in the knowledge that *they* (G4) would then face the same tragic choice between being either victims or perpetrators of injustice. Although a number of generations could act unjustly and keep passing the buck down to the next (by producing equal numbers of children), at some point a generation would have to face up to its responsibilities and either restrict its consumption of natural resources to a sustainable level or else sacrifice, for perhaps large numbers of its members, the right to parent.

As Gheaus notes, the argument can be given a minimalist or egalitarian rendering. The minimalist rendering would specify that 'each generation must pass on to the next generation sufficient resources for sustaining adequate life prospects for human beings indefinitely'.[37] An egalitarian rendering, by contrast, would require each generation to pass on to the next the resources necessary to sustain *equal* life prospects for human beings indefinitely. But either way, the challenge posed by the non-identity problem is bypassed. For the duty of sustainability is owed, crucially, only to already existing people—our living children or grandchildren—but *concerns* all generations to come, and its demands extend into the distant future. It can therefore readily support a principle of intergenerational equality.

If we can indeed endorse an egalitarian account of intergenerational justice, what does it tell us we must leave behind for future generations? An egalitarian principle of intergenerational justice will demand that we ought not, if we can at all avoid it, impede the ability of future generations to lead lives for which the advantages and disadvantages relevant to distributive justice are as good as those we have enjoyed ourselves. But it does not appear to be a requirement of justice that generations across time ought to have equal shares of the benefits and burdens flowing from natural resources *in particular*. That is so for all of the familiar reasons we have rehearsed in previous sections: in contexts of multifaceted, countervailing inequalities, equal benefits will augment, rather than challenge, the broader inequalities we ought to care about. (Any equal shares view would, note, be even more implausible in the case of non-renewable resources. For the distinguishing feature of non-renewable resources is of course that once used they cannot be used again. If we presume that there may be very many generations living successively in the future, the view that each should consume equal shares of non-renewable resources would appear to place an embargo on current generations using any appreciable amount of them. Indeed, the same would be true for any future generation. If we imagined enough future generations, the likely practical implication would be that non-renewables could never be used by anyone.[38])

On the view I am defending, there is no particular reason why we should endorse such a 'narrow' constraint on resource use, because what future generations must face, once more, is a world in which their prospects for wellbeing are equal. This need not demand equal shares of natural resources (and it certainly need not mean equal shares of particular classes of resources such as non-renewables). To be sure, in assessing the implications for intergenerational justice of our current practices we face formidable epistemic challenges. In the case of the current generation, we have some information—albeit imperfect—about the role that natural resources play in sustaining the wellbeing of people across the world. We also have a good deal of information about other aspects of advantage and disadvantage: we know a lot about global gulfs in life expectancy, in literacy levels, income levels, and so on. When we shift our attention to future generations our information about both of these things becomes radically less secure. We do not know just how future generations will convert natural resources into wellbeing: it might well be that their industries will be greatly more efficient than ours, and hence that much smaller shares of resources will be sufficient to serve their interests equally as well as ours. And it is a widespread view that future generations will be much better off than us in financial terms, that they will live longer and healthier lives, and that they will generally benefit from a host of technological advancements unavailable to us; if so, leaving future generations a share of benefits equal to our own appears unnecessary. Alternatively, it may be that we are, through our reckless pursuit of economic growth, consigning future generations to relatively impoverished lives. On such empirical questions we are irredeemably in the domain of informed conjecture.

But we are not *morally* rudderless in our contemplation of intergenerational justice. For one thing the basic rights constraint should remain in place with regard to future generations. Even if we know little about how natural resources will serve the wellbeing of future generations, we can be reasonably sure that future generations will be similar enough to us to need clean water, air, and so on just as we do. We should therefore leave future generations enough resources to meet what can reasonably be foreseen to be their basic rights (even if the duty in question is only held with regard to existing generations). This is not to say, to be clear, that we ought to be egalitarian about present generations, and sufficientarian about future generations. The point is the same as for current generations: *as egalitarians*, we have no good reason to favour strictly equal shares of resources, assuming that we care about wellbeing broadly construed. But we do have good reasons for endorsing a basic rights constraint, and endorsing equalizing shares of resource benefits. We should apply the same principles in the case of future generations.

For another thing, even in the face of a good deal of indeterminacy it may be plausible to adhere to some kind of precautionary principle.[39] It is not baseless to ask whether we are leaving behind us a world in which future generations will have fewer opportunities than us to enjoy biodiversity, or breathe clean air. Even if we cannot know for sure just what their overall levels of wellbeing will be, it is obvious that many current practices are seriously degrading various conditions that we can reasonably expect will be required for decent lives in the future. Moreover, we might well believe that it is wrong if present generations unilaterally determine which natural resources—or which species—future generations will be able to interact with. Furthermore, if it is true that 'nature' represents an important independent setting for meaningful lives,[40] we must ensure that the ecosystems we leave behind are not so small or fragile as to be unsustainable. This might involve avoiding tipping-points whereby biological diversity becomes too small to guarantee healthy populations of natural organisms, or actively protecting keystone species crucial to wider ecosystems.

We can also make judgements about the costliness of our present patterns of consumption. Some patterns of consumption may not be prohibited by our equality-promoting view, but if we properly factored in the costs of maintaining them *and* leaving behind a world offering equal prospects for wellbeing to future generations we would surely rapidly desist from them. Consider our current reliance on non-renewable sources of energy such as coal and oil. Equality places no absolute embargo on the use of non-renewables, so long as we can provide other opportunities for future generations which would offset any negative consequences of our addiction to fossil fuels. But if we properly calculated the *costs* of achieving such an offsetting—and, indeed, properly calculated the costs of the damage fossil fuels will cause to *existing* generations—then the use of fossil fuels will come to look like a very expensive and wasteful choice.[41] It is only because we neglect the costs of that consumption that their use is appealing in the first place. At present, political policy subsidizes the fossil fuel industry and refuses to make either consumers or producers internalize the costs of fossil fuel use, even though we have good grounds for believing that a sensible policy would both remove that subsidy and increase the price of fossil fuels to recognize the true costs of their use, using the revenue gained to spread green technologies in the developing world.[42] Such a policy may not strictly be required by egalitarian principles: we could go on harming, and expensively compensating, the poor of the world, and future generations. But considering equality and utility together, such a policy would be very ill-advised.

3.6. EQUALITY, WELLBEING, AND RESPONSIBILITY

This chapter has argued against various forms of natural resource exceptionalism. In a slogan, the egalitarian's attitude to natural resources should be: *tremendously important, but nothing special*. Although some accounts have devoted considerable—and sometimes exclusive—attention to sharing the benefits and burdens they bestow upon us, natural resources truly are not special—in providing a currency for equality, in the arbitrariness of their distribution, or in the invidiousness of unequal holdings in them. Important as they are, they are not all that matters; and because they are not, an egalitarian account which grants them their rightful place will not call for equal shares of the benefits and burdens flowing from them. That position, much-beloved though it has been down the history of modern political thought, is not egalitarian enough. The pursuit of equality would be better served by sharing benefits and burdens in such a way as to best advance equal access to wellbeing as a whole. Likewise, insofar as an egalitarian proviso should govern the appropriation of resources—whether we think of this as appropriation now, or appropriation vis-à-vis future generations—it should be a 'broad' egalitarian proviso calling for similarly equality-promoting—but not equal—shares of benefits. There may be much to be gained from focusing on natural resources as an entry point for global egalitarian arguments, perhaps because taxes on natural resources would be relatively easy to administer, or relatively likely to command support (see Chapter 8). But identifying that possible strategic advantage does not provide any direction on how the proceeds of any such taxes should be used. Here the likelihood remains—especially if targeting natural resources is going to be one of the more navigable routes towards global justice—that carefully targeted and equality-promoting shares of benefits should be our goal. I address some of the implications of that argument in the remaining chapters of this book.

* * *

I want to conclude this chapter, though, by considering one final thorny issue, which is the relationship between equality and the value of choice or responsibility. One of the foremost currents within egalitarian thought suggests that these are in fact one and the same value, and that the pursuit of equality simply consists in the eradication of the impact of unequal circumstance, whilst simultaneously tailoring distribution to the choices which people actually make.[43]

That view has been the subject of considerable controversy. Now, in some ways it appears unobjectionable that distribution should be tailored to choice. For one thing, it might be thought that those endorsing a welfarist metric should not object to situations in which the distribution of concrete goods is guided by different preferences, so long as individuals still have the same degree of access to wellbeing. When people enjoy 'a comparable aggregate enjoyment of life', the egalitarian may be satisfied if one person ends up consuming apples and the other oranges, or one income and the other leisure, so long as those distributions reflect genuine preferences.[44] For another thing, welfare egalitarians have to recognize that we cannot, in fact, distribute wellbeing itself. We cannot take happiness, or a sense of success, or personal fulfilment, or a successful relationship, for example, from one person and give it to another. All that we can distribute are various concrete *drivers* of wellbeing, such as social goods, natural resources, or other opportunities. But we cannot guarantee that the people we give these opportunities to will actually derive wellbeing from them: we can lead people to water, but we cannot make them enjoy their drink (and even if we could, to do so would be incompatible with treating them as agents, as opposed to factories for producing particular mental states). We can act on our hunches about what tends to make a person's life go better or worse, but we cannot finally ensure that they do go better. Giving people the chance to enjoy equal levels of wellbeing may be worthwhile and important. But when people freely choose not to enjoy wellbeing, the egalitarian should accept that outcome. This thought, of course, is compatible with the idea that as far as equality goes, equal wellbeing should be our ideal, even if distributing the various fuels for wellbeing so that equal wellbeing *could* ensue is the closest we can get to that ideal. I call the resulting conception—which offers people the fuels to achieve equivalent levels of wellbeing, whether they choose to take them up or not—*equal access to wellbeing*.

But many would accord choice or responsibility a much greater role than this. The luck egalitarian might argue that what we should distribute to people are not the concrete goods capable of fuelling equal wellbeing, but *equal chances to achieve* those goods. If we give people equal chances to obtain those fuels for wellbeing, and some of them do so and others do not, equality might still be satisfied, because equality means tailoring distribution to reward the differential exercise of effort or ambition. Addressing this idea fully would probably demand a book in its own right, and this is not the place to settle debates about the correct relationship between the ideals of equality and responsibility. I will restrict myself to noting five reasons for scepticism about the scope for choice or responsibility to further justify inequalities in wellbeing:

First, defenders of equality of opportunity for wellbeing sometimes argue that unequal outcomes are only justifiable when they emanate under conditions in which the initial option-sets individuals face are equal, and that inequalities arising from unequal starting points are to be considered suspect.[45] Since this is a counterfactual which is rarely going to be satisfied, this alone would suffice to impugn most real-world inequalities in access to wellbeing.

Second, consider the issues that arise from the fact of overlapping generations. Imagine that an agent makes a bad decision for which we consider it appropriate to hold him responsible. Even if we are content that he remains worse off in future as a result, we should not consider it fair that his children will be worse off too. But people are nested in formal or informal families and social networks which have significant distributive impacts upon their own lives, and if we want to preserve equal opportunities for children, this may practically restrict the extent to which we are able to hold parents responsible for their choices. A parallel issue arises with regard to nation-states. Some theorists of global justice hold that it is just for nation-states to fare worse as a result of poor decision-making—and unjust, by contrast, to disregard that poor decision-making by continually redistributing resources to restore some version of equality.[46] But if we believe that individuals coming into the world (some of them into nation-states whose leaders, or indeed citizens, have made bad choices, and others into nation-states which have made good choices) should face equal opportunities, the scope for ensuring that good and bad decisions are rewarded is attenuated, lest the mistakes of the parents again be visited upon their children.

Third, consider the time-frame over which a choice-sensitive conception of equality is meant to extend. A purely 'starting-gate' view would demand that individuals face equal prospects for achieving wellbeing at one cardinal moment of their lives—such as the onset of adulthood. But that idea is often, and rightly, considered unappealing. Someone who made a single bad decision shortly after this cardinal moment could, on such a view, justly be consigned to a much worse life in terms of access to wellbeing. But why, if equal prospects is such an important value, should we be content with a situation in which people were presented with equal prospects *once*? We might, rather, want to restore equal chances to attain the sources of wellbeing at a variety of points of an individual's life. But doing so would move us much closer to pure equality of access to wellbeing.[47]

Fourth, even someone who believes that tailoring distribution to choice is important need not consider it to be all that matters to egalitarians. Consider a world in which the rewards associated with various social positions differ greatly. One way to advance equality might be to ensure equal opportunities to fill those different positions. Imagine, then, a competition in which the hardest-working entrant will be rewarded with the goods sufficient to drive 100 units of wellbeing, and everyone else will achieve goods sufficient to drive 10 units. In that sense, for the choice-sensitive egalitarian, equal prospects might well be secured. But the egalitarian might—and should—remain uneasy, and want to reduce the differential rewards attached to the outcomes in the competition, so that wherever people ended up was less consequential from the distributive point of view. That view, though, cannot be arrived at by focusing on the value of choice alone.[48]

Finally, even if we held that at the bar of distributive justice the exercise of free choice justified unequal outcomes, that need not commit us to accepting those unequal outcomes all-things-considered. If our egalitarianism appeared to sanction large inequalities which would sit ill with a conception of society as a community of equals, then we could respond that we ought to care about equality of status and social interaction uncontaminated by hierarchy and stigma too, so that the value of social equality forbids some of the harsher conclusions of our egalitarianism.[49] There is an important debate about whether a concern for relationships uncontaminated by hierarchy is properly viewed as internal or external to our distributive egalitarianism, but the important point is that either way we move closer to equality of condition when we place value on such relationships.[50]

I find each of these five moves compelling, and taken together they suggest a healthy scepticism about the ability of choice to justify unequal access to wellbeing. The first two objections suggest that the scope for holding people responsible is smaller than we might suppose, whereas the final three suggest that even if people can be held responsible for some of their choices, an egalitarian theory should exercise caution in endorsing the unequal outcomes which might result. But I will not attempt to settle positively the role that choice should play in an egalitarian theory. Insofar as I aim in this book to make various interventions into current debates on global justice and natural resources, some more modest claims will suffice. In Chapter 2 I noted that some sceptics about global egalitarianism have suggested that we ought to reject that view because it fails to acknowledge the responsibility which nations or states bear for the existence, or value, of the natural resources in their territories, and in response I provided some reasons for scepticism about those attributions of responsibility. In Chapter 4 I examine what we shall call improvement-based special claims over natural resources, and the key to those special claims—or at least the key to the version on which I will focus—turns out to be a claim that improvers are responsible for the existence of the additional economic value which an improved resource comes to have. Once more I will provide reasons for scepticism about such a view: whereas I acknowledge the possibility that good special claims from improvement might be made, I question both whether improvers can plausibly be held responsible for all of the additional value in question, and whether these claims, insofar as they are good, might in any case add up to a serious constraint on our ability to promote equality at the global level. But those objections are negative in character, and do not commit me to any positive view about the extent to which choice or responsibility might justify otherwise intolerable inequalities.

We can, however, usefully discuss here one other way in which choice or responsibility might intervene to generate scepticism about the egalitarian redistributive project at the global level. Perhaps the best-known objection to welfarist versions of egalitarianism is the so-called 'expensive tastes' objection. The objection would impugn the goal of providing individuals with the goods sufficient to drive equal degrees of wellbeing (or what I have called equal access to wellbeing), on the basis that, at least sometimes, individuals can appropriately be held responsible for holding tastes or preferences which prove more 'expensive' to fulfil. The objection is chiefly identified with defenders of a resourcist metric. Even if the various versions of equality of resources fail to sufficiently protect the interests of people who are not responsible for their own capacities to convert resources into wellbeing—such as the seriously disabled—the idea of equality of wellbeing is, it is said, *too* concessive to people who *are* sometimes responsible for the ways in which they convert resources into wellbeing. For instance, someone whose freely chosen hobbies just happened to be more expensive should, according to the defender of equality of wellbeing, be provided with more goods with which to pursue those hobbies.[51] But the resourcist considers this an unpalatable implication. One influential way of responding to the objection is to reassert the importance to the egalitarian of *control* or choice, and attempt to demarcate a category of factors for which agents clearly should be held responsible, and a category for which they clearly should not. Perhaps deliberately cultivated tastes should be placed in the first category, for instance, whereas addictions are in the second category.[52]

Although the expensive tastes debate is important, from the point of view of debates on natural resources and global justice what looks to me to be more significant is a slightly different question about individuals' putative responsibility for the ways in which concrete goods are converted into wellbeing *across different countries*. Consider, to begin with, that, as an empirical matter, allocating the same per capita portions of natural resources to different communities will predictably give rise to different levels of wellbeing for the individuals living in them. We noted in section 3.1 some 'micro' ways in which the same set of resources can drive different levels of wellbeing, as a result of divergent internal capacities or disabilities; but we can also predict 'macro' differences at the cross-societal level. The way in which individuals in different societies will derive wellbeing from natural resources may depend, amongst other things, upon the local property rules, conventions about how resources are to be used, and levels of technology. For instance, giving a quantity of oil to two communities will drive wellbeing differently if one of those communities possesses the internal combustion engine and the other does not, or if one has invested in roads and the other has not. Giving the same per capita carbon emission rights to two different communities will result in divergent wellbeing, other things being equal, if one community has better-insulated houses, more efficient public transport, and more recycling than the other. Let us call features which influence how much wellbeing can be driven by a given quantity of natural resources 'conversion factors'. Crucially, whilst we might be able to identify factors for which it is relatively clear that we should not hold individual communities responsible, there may be other factors where it is more contentious whether we should consider communities (or individuals in them) responsible.

One approach the welfarist might take here is to stipulate that (from the point of view of natural resource justice) equality simply requires giving communities the resources which could, with the best available conditions, drive equal wellbeing. Alternatively, we might stipulate that it consists in giving them resources that would drive equal levels of wellbeing given average conditions. Either way, we would not therefore tailor the allocation of resources to local conditions. But we could easily imagine cases in which taking either approach would seem unfair: a given community might be provided with resources notionally capable of driving a given quantity of wellbeing, but only assuming they are used in a way in which they are not in fact able to be used. And it might not be the fault of the community concerned that its technology is less efficient, or its infrastructure less developed (it may, for instance, be seriously impoverished because of unjust trade rules, or the impact of colonialism or a war of aggression). Alternatively, then, the welfarist might argue that the standard for judging whether equality obtained should track how resources will *actually* be used in each society. Thus we would keep feeding communities natural resources until such a point that their access to wellbeing became equal. But we can imagine cases in which this too would appear unfair: a community which has saved so as to invest in expensive technology allowing it to use resources more efficiently than another would end up being given less. And we might *sometimes* be prepared to hold a country with less efficient technology responsible for that fact (quite aside from the incentive effects involved).

Like the expensive tastes objection, this problem seems to demand a way of distinguishing conversion factors for which agents can plausibly be held responsible from those for which they cannot, and again the degree of control appears to be salient. But in attempting to impute that control, we face complications which make the attribution of responsibility more difficult than in individual cases of expensive tastes. Specifically, in attributing responsibility for a given conversion factor we would not only need to be confident about the degree of control over that factor which a given society possesses. We also ought to be interested in the degree of control which *individuals* in each community possess over whatever overall control their society possesses. This will be a live issue in, for instance, communities which are undemocratic, and where economic or environmental policy decisions have been made without consulting individual subjects. It would be perverse, for example, to hold that from the point of view of individual subjects equality is served when dictators have equal shares of resources but squander them to advance vainglorious and unsuccessful infrastructure projects. Positive attributions of responsibility on the part of individuals are undercut, too, by the recognition that (unlike individuals in the expensive tastes case) nation-states are trans-generational communities.[53] For even if a country has culpably developed inferior infrastructure, or culpably failed to invest in more environmentally efficient technologies, it would be implausible to attribute any responsibility for that to an individual who was born after those decisions had been made.

These complications reduce the scope for holding individuals in diverse communities responsible for their society's quality of conversion *even if* we hold that control over those qualities is normatively significant. It suggests we maintain a degree of scepticism about holding individuals responsible for society-level conversion factors, and that individual responsibility for the ability to convert natural resources into wellbeing needs to be demonstrated rather than assumed. What, though, are the conclusions if we decide that individuals—or some individuals, at least—are *not* responsible for these conversion factors? Is the implication that we should carry on providing individuals in those communities with disproportionately large shares of natural resources, so that they can maintain access to the same degree of wellbeing as outsiders? The welfarist argument certainly seems to point in that direction. But we should recognize that this is decidedly not the only option. Consider once more the parallel with the individual expensive tastes case. There is—though this is relatively infrequently discussed—an alternative to providing people with expensive tastes with disproportionately large shares of resources: we could act so as to change those tastes. It might be pointed out, here, that it would be illiberal to intervene so as to change someone's expensive tastes or preferences once they have been formed. That might, plausibly, depend upon how we sought to change them. We might attempt to foster an egalitarian ethos which sought to make the development of some expensive tastes less likely, or, more controversially, try to persuade those who had developed such tastes to relinquish them.[54]

But the crucial point is that in the societal case more options are open to us. Without intervening to change people's preferences, we could improve a society's conversion function simply by providing it with better technology, or providing assistance in developing its infrastructure. That is precisely the goal of the 'duty of assistance' supported by some minimalists about global justice. The key point is that such moves can also be endorsed as an element of an egalitarian programme, if the aim is to move us closer to equal access to wellbeing. In debates about climate justice, for instance, it is often argued that richer societies should fund the roll-out of green energy to the developing world, so that developing countries can escape poverty without endangering the global environment.[55] Alternatively, if we cared about local water shortages one option would be to transport fresh water to communities experiencing scarcity. But another option—likely a *better* option—would be to enhance those communities' ability to capture rainwater, and to encourage forms of irrigation in agriculture which were more efficient and less environmentally destructive.[56] If our goal is to improve the wellbeing of the world's least advantaged, shifting resources—or even the value of resources—to poor countries is certainly one option. But enhancing the capacity of those countries to use resources effectively can be important too. Even if this option may not occur to those who see natural resources as the equalisandum and distribuendum for justice, it is certainly available to those who want to promote equality in access to wellbeing in general. This apparently esoteric foray into 'conversion factors' will have been worthwhile if it reminds us of this important fact.

ENDNOTES

1. Paine 1835: 402 405.
2. George 2005.
3. Beitz 1979. Beitz was reticent about the role such a principle could play in a fully developed account of global justice, and ultimately embraced a much broader-based global difference principle, the implications of which for resources would likely be quite different (and, as it happens, much closer to those defended in this chapter). In a later piece reflecting on his book's immense impact, Beitz (2005) nevertheless suggested that a principle of equal entitlement to natural resources could still play a useful role in a broader egalitarian account. But on my argument here that is doubtful.
4. Barry 1982; see also Barry 1981; Mazor 2010; and Luper-Foy 1992. Vanderheiden (2009) defends equal rights to use the world's natural resources. Steiner (2005) defends a similar right, though not, as we will see on the basis of an argument about arbitrariness. Other left-libertarians who endorse equal shares of the value of the world's resources include Roark 2013 and Tideman 2000.
5. Amartya Sen's famous critique of resourcist versions of equality accused them of fetishism, or the view that the distribution of resources mattered in and of itself regardless of what those resources actually do for people, or allow them to do for themselves. More pressingly perhaps, resourcist views are held to neglect—or at least, even on their more sophisticated versions, to not properly account for—people's very different capacities to use resources to allow them to *do* or *be* the things which actually matter to their lives (Sen 1980). Strictly speaking, this important critique leaves open the possibility that either welfare or capabilities might furnish the correct metric; Sen argues for the latter. For a good assessment of Sen's criticisms of welfarism, see Moore and Crisp (1996: section III).
6. Steiner 1994.
7. He would not, however, block voluntary in-life transfers, which might have equally responsibility-violating distributive effects.
8. Steiner 2011a: 112.
9. Steiner 2009: 4.
10. As Ian Carter has suggested to me, there is no reason why Steiner must be bound by the common usage of the words 'natural resources', and hence it is not an objection to his theory per se that his definition diverges from it. Thus Steiner could stipulate that natural resources simply means 'whatever no living person owns', or 'the things no one has a special claim over', by contrast, perhaps, to the products of one's own labour. It would then be perfectly intelligible to describe one's dead parents' Beatles records, for instance, as natural resources. However, it is hard to reconcile such a conception with a definition Steiner *does* provide. As he puts it, 'By natural resources, I mean, at its broadest, portions of physical space. This compendiously includes all global surface areas and the supra- and sub-terranean spaces contiguous to them, as well as the natural objects they contain' (Steiner 2011b: 330). It is difficult to read such a definition as excluding the products of one's labour but including one's parents' Beatles records.
11. Steiner 1994: 279

12. If a parent pays a tax on apparently valuable genes at T^1, what if the economy changes so that at T^2 the talents they support are no longer valuable? Or what if an apparently non-valuable talent at T^1 happens to become scarce at T^2? Is it in any case genes that (arbitrarily) determine earning power, or genes in combination with upbringing and the (equally arbitrary) vicissitudes of the market?
13. Steiner 1994: 280.
14. Otsuka 2003; Vallentyne 2012.
15. Tideman and Vallentyne 2001.
16. Note that Otsuka (2003) argues for a heavy tax on inheritance and so he must, like Steiner, define the content of bequests too as natural resources regardless of their actual content. He suggests that we can also add to the redistributive pot by raising revenue from criminal fines. But even with those additions his theory will not equalize opportunities for welfare. In the case of the disabled, Otsuka suggests that his theory would (merely) give them sufficient opportunities for minimal economic independence.
17. Segal 2011. We can make a similar observation about national wealth: the World Bank estimates that 'natural capital' represents on average 4 per cent of a country's wealth, compared to the much more significant 'produced' and 'intangible' capital shares. World Bank 2006: 4.
18. Hayward (2006) has argued for equal shares of 'ecological space' (which implies equal opportunities to utilize the world's *renewable* natural resources). Some of the criticisms I have levelled at left-libertarianism would also apply to such a view. However, in more recent work Hayward (2013) has suggested that he does not advance ecological space as a currency for equality.
19. Beitz 1979: 137.
20. The claim is made by Pevnick 2008 and Cafaro 2008.
21. Risse 2008: 258–9.
22. Casal (2011: 312) cites as an advantage of natural resource taxes the relatively low likelihood that they will disincentivize productive activites.
23. Casal 2011: 312.
24. A defender of equal shares might, of course, point to the costliness of calibrating the appropriate disbursements if individual wellbeing is what matters, and press the relative cheapness of universal flat-rate benefits. I doubt very much that this advantage outweighs the injustice of redistributing resource value from the generally poor to the generally rich. But even if it did, intermediate proposals could be imagined which would be fairer and still virtually as efficient (such as a regime of flat-rate disbursements targeted exclusively at inhabitants of poor countries; cf. Thomas Pogge's arguments for a Global Resources Dividend aimed at the developing world (Pogge 2008, chapter 8)).
25. See Caney 2012, for an excellent discussion and defence of broad substitutability between categories of advantage, with particular reference to emissions rights. Note that my argument here does not actually depend on a general claim that different categories of goods ought to be considered perfectly substitutable, and therefore that particular deficits ought to be seen as morally compensable by way of other goods. Rather, my more moderate argument depends upon two precise claims: first, *even if* there are special reasons for resisting substitutability with

regards to some goods, these scarcely apply (except in cases which I discuss later in this section) to natural resources. And second, there are *at least some* disadvantages which are compensable by way of other goods. As such, deficits in natural resource holdings will often be compensable by way of greater shares in other goods and, on the reverse side, greater shares of natural resources can sometimes be used to offset inequalities in other goods. Regardless of the plausibility of general substitutability across the board, that is sufficient to make the argument of this section significant.

26. See Brighouse and Swift 2006a.
27. This is what Caney (2012: 273–4) calls the 'equal rights' argument.
28. It might be that we can identify still further fuels for wellbeing which cannot be adequately substituted for by shifting other goods around. Gheaus (2009) argues that love and companionship are one such good, for instance. To repeat, my focus here is not on how many such goods we can identify or, accordingly, with the general strength of the constraints on moral substitutability which then arise. My focus is on whether we have good reason to consider natural resources as a non-substitutable fuel for wellbeing.
29. For information on the efforts of the United Nations (UN) to advance women's land ownership, see for instance Office of the High Commissioner for Human Rights 2013.
30. Singer 2002: 35.
31. Caney 2012.
32. In this I therefore concur with Axel Gosseries's suggestion that we should pursue an 'opportunist' approach to climate justice: 'A climate regime should be seized as an opportunity to contribute to the improvement of the situation of the least well off, beyond merely making sure that climate change does not hurt them.' In any negotiation, our fundamental consideration should be 'the general redistributive goal' of mitigating overall inequalities in wellbeing (Gosseries 2014: 101).
33. Many of which I cannot even discuss here. One is whether reflection on inter-generational justice produces distinctive problems for a welfarist egalitarian metric. For a very good treatment of that issue, see Lippert-Rasmussen 2012.
34. Parfit 1984.
35. Gheaus 2016. For another argument for a duty of justice to conserve natural resources for future people based solely on duties which present people owe to each other, see Mazor 2010.
36. For an influential defence of an important interest in parenting children (which is distinct, note, from any purported right to physically produce children) see Brighouse and Swift 2006b.
37. Gheaus 2016: 20.
38. This point is noted by Barry 1989; and by Collier 2014.
39. For a careful defence of a precautionary principle in the context of climate change, see Gardiner 2005.
40. Goodin 1992.
41. That we do not realize this has much to do with the political influence of the petrochemical lobby. For a valuable counterpoint, see the arguments of the Carbon Tracker Initiative 2014.
42. Shue 2014.

43. For influential defences of that 'luck egalitarian' view, see Dworkin 2000 and Cohen 1989. The term 'luck egalitarianism' was actually coined by a critic of that view, in Anderson 1999.
44. Cohen 2009: 19.
45. See e.g. Barry 2005.
46. See for instance Rawls 1999; Miller 2007.
47. For scepticism about 'cardinal moment' views, see Arneson 1999; Chambers 2009. For a defence of a 'fresh start' view which would seek, under certain circumstances, to restore equal opportunities at various stages during a person's life, see Fleurbaey 2005.
48. See Baker 1988.
49. Lippert-Rasmussen 2013.
50. For contrasting views on the relationship between social and distributive equality, see Fourie, Schuppert, and Wallimann-Helmer 2015.
51. See Dworkin 2000.
52. For the debate about just when expensive tastes should be subsidized, see Cohen 2004 and Dworkin 2004. For a good retrospective account of that debate from a welfarist perspective, see Lippert-Rasmussen 2013.
53. There might, in fact, be grounds for holding that our conclusions about the moral salience of control in *individual* expensive tastes cases should also be attenuated, if we conceive of individual identity as dynamic rather than static over time. For a discussion of the possible implications for luck egalitarianism of viewing identity as dynamic, see Tomlin 2013.
54. For an argument to the effect that influencing the preferences of future generations so as to make them less expensive may be not only permissible but morally required, see Lippert-Rasmussen 2012.
55. See for instance Shue 2014.
56. Often this will mean shifting irrigation technologies away from under-pressure 'blue-water' sources (rivers and aquifers) and towards 'green-water' sources (rainfall). For a fascinating account of the pitfalls and opportunities for effective use of global water resources, see Hoekstra and Chapagain 2008.

4

Rewarding Improvement

> [I]t is the value of improvement, only, and not the earth itself, that is individual property.[1]

Chapters 2 and 3 defended an egalitarian approach to the world's natural resources, and illustrated some of its implications. But what of the special claims people might have over specific resources? Might these claims circumscribe or qualify the degree to which we can redirect the benefits flowing from natural resources so as to promote global equality? To date egalitarians have had relatively little to say about such claims. It has often been argued that the distribution of natural resources is morally arbitrary, with the apparent implication that the pattern of (unequal) advantage and disadvantage attaching to those resources has nothing to be said for it from the point of view of justice. If some prosper while others struggle as a result of the haphazard distribution of resources, this is a clear instance of injustice—perhaps the clearest and most undeniable instance, according to many.[2]

It is true that no one created natural resources, or put them where they are. So-called 'flow' resources occur naturally, as part of natural processes over which humans have little or no control (the global hydrological cycle, or the swirling of the atmosphere, or the moon-driven power of the waves). 'Stock' resources are the result of processes (mineral formation, or the prehistoric plant growth and decay which created petrochemical deposits) which took place before humans even existed. These facts—that no one created natural resources, or put them where they are—explain why we call them 'natural' resources. The potential they have to serve particular human interests over time may turn out to be socially contingent, but still, we might say, these two facts are natural enough.

Are these facts sufficient, though, to justify the argument from arbitrariness? In this chapter and Chapter 5 I examine two kinds of special claim, from improvement and from attachment. Take attachment first. If the claim is that the current distribution of natural resources tracks nothing of any moral significance, adherents of attachment-based special claims would beg to differ. There could be a notional time in prehistory—the dawn of the human species, say—at which people came into a world where nobody was already attached to one resource rather than another. But since then many people have become deeply attached to particular resources, such that continued access to them becomes key to some of their most central life-plans. On many accounts of justice, this ought to matter. If so, we have at least a *pro tanto* reason to prefer an allocation of rights over resources which maps onto existing patterns of attachments over a distribution which does not. As I will suggest in Chapter 5, recognizing this does not require us to sacrifice the pursuit of equality because properly understood attachment-based special claims are not claims about *how much* advantage people are entitled to, but rather about *which* goods, compatibly with justice, people ought to be able to maintain access to or control over. Still, attachment-based claims embarrass any argument that the current distribution of natural resources is morally arbitrary *if* that argument is taken to mean that there is nothing to be said in favour of leaving particular resources where they are.

But perhaps that argument is not the significant one in any case. Perhaps the key point is that it is the pattern of *unequal* advantage and disadvantage attaching to the distribution of resources which is arbitrary. No one, after all, is responsible for *that*. This claim has a degree of initial plausibility. But it remains to be seen whether it is in fact true in any given set of circumstances. Again, if we could imagine the first genetic human beings popping into existence at some time in the very distant past, it would be by definition true that no humans had any degree of (positive or negative) responsibility for the pattern of advantage and disadvantage attaching to natural resources. It is impossible to imagine, however, that this would continue to be the case once any significant period of time had come to pass. Humans have a variety of impacts on their environment: they adjust their lives to fit their environments but also, as the years pass, adjust their environments to fit their lives. Marx viewed that process as a great dialectic of 'man' and 'nature' which drove history itself, but the point is a very simple one—and from our point of view the key factor to take account of is the impact which humans have on natural resources. Over time we begin to consume them, destroy them, tend them, or protect them to a far higher degree than any other species does, which is why some commentators have suggested that we call the current era the 'anthropocene': an age which will see our activities impacting upon the very geological record of our world.[3] These actions will shift both the actual distribution of resources—as people move them around, interfere with the natural flow of some of them, and destroy still others—and (partly as a result) the pattern of advantages which will flow from those resources. Plausibly these actions might at least sometimes—when they are intentional, say, and/or where there are reasonable alternatives—allow us to attribute responsibility to human beings for the outcomes. It would then still be true that individuals coming into existence at any point in time bore no retrospective responsibility for those outcomes. But during their lives they may well come to bear such responsibility, and the distribution of benefits would then have to be seen as at least partly a social, as opposed to purely natural, fact.

How should we talk about this new situation—descriptive of the present, and of any period of human history we can name—in which the distribution of unequal advantages attaching to natural resources is actually influenced by human actions? It seems now that even the revised claim—that the distribution of advantages and disadvantages attached to natural resources is morally arbitrary (because no one is responsible for it)—is troubled. To be specific the claim becomes either irrelevant (if we acknowledge that it only applies to some pristine world before agents began to engage with resources) or false (because it must claim, implausibly, that none of the things agents have subsequently done with resources can generate any degree of moral responsibility over the pattern of advantages attached to them).

This responsibility might conceivably take a variety of forms. Consider for instance a resource which was necessary for everyone's wellbeing—such as the trees of the rainforests, whose ability to sequester carbon dioxide is hugely important in a world devoted to using fossil fuels to meet 85 per cent of its energy demands, and which already contain huge quantities of CO_2 which would produce a climate catastrophe if released (see Chapter 10). If an agent controlling a sizeable swathe of the world's forests wilfully destroyed them or through negligence allowed them to be destroyed, we might hold them morally responsible.[4] Or, as in this chapter, we might consider more positive attributions of responsibility, which suggest that because agents have increased the value of (some) natural resources they are entitled to something in return. This, in a very general form, suggests what I call a special claim from improvement. This chapter investigates, in particular, arguments to the effect that nations, or perhaps states, have improvement-based claims over the natural resources within their territories. If such claims can be defended they would limit the scope for the egalitarian redistribution of the benefits flowing from natural resources, and egalitarians would need to find a way of accommodating those claims. But whether and how those claims can be defended, and what their content is, remains to be seen.

The structure of the chapter is as follows: section 4.1 examines some competing accounts of how it is that agents come to gain rights over specific resources, and identifies the responsibility-catering account that will be the focus of my enquiry. Section 4.2 scrutinizes the claim that nations or states have good improvement-based claims over the value of the natural resources in their territories. Section 4.3 examines more closely the responsibility-catering principle that national special claims appear to be based upon, and provides some reasons for caution about its desired conclusions. Section 4.4 demonstrates some of the implications of the arguments of the chapter so far for our theorizing about natural resource justice. Section 4.5 concludes by returning to the question of how egalitarians ought to respond to improvement-based special claims.

4.1. CAPTURING IMPROVEMENT

It is a very widespread view that those who have improved specific assets have also thereby generated some claims over them: that those who make things out of other things have a claim over those new things; that those who have picked up a resource and transformed it into something more valuable are mistreated when we hand that resource on to someone else as if the transforming agent had no claim over it. Such ideas are most famously associated with liberal views on private property and particularly with the contribution of Locke. But the very general idea has been picked up repeatedly, within a wide range of philosophical traditions.[5]

The political consequences of the view will depend, among other things, on whether we hold that improvement is the *sole* ground upon which we can generate special claims over external objects. Locke's argument was exclusive in this way and as such is often identified with the dispossession of the indigenous populations of the Americas who, on his view, inhabited the land without improving it.[6] But the very same (exclusive) idea has often been turned against the rich and powerful. Thomas Paine's suggestion that improvement, and improvement alone, generates claims to particular external assets underpinned his criticisms of the unfairness of actual distributions of land and property in eighteenth-century England,[7] and his lambasting of the 'idle rich' is a familiar move within the leftist tradition. The idea continues to find resonance in the claims of Brazil's Movimento Sem Terra, for instance, whose members argue that the landless and unemployed have a right to inhabit land which is not being used by Brazil's rich landed class, because titles over land and resources cannot endure unless they are accompanied by improving labour.[8] The resonance of similar ideas in the work of Marx is also familiar: his critique of exploitation depends upon the view that what the labourer creates is his own, and apparently upon the exclusive claim that it is only by labouring on objects that we generate claims over them. The labour theory of value holds that when given objects become more valuable, that increase in (exchange) value must be attributable to the input of labour; hence Marx is able to say that when the capitalist appropriates some of this value he steals from the labourer what is his or hers.[9]

Notably, improvement-based claims have even commanded support from those who believe that property claims are based upon convention or social utility. Consider John Stuart Mill's claim that:

Nothing is implied in [the idea of] property but the right of each to his (or her) own faculties, to what he can produce by them, and to whatever he can get for them in a fair market...The essential principle of property [is] to assure all persons what they have produced by their labour.[10]

Improvement-based claims might garner two kinds of support. On the one hand we might support them for *direct* reasons. For instance we might hold that justice is served better whenever improvers are able to keep what they have improved, simply because it is morally fitting that the improver retains his product. On the other hand we might support those claims for *instrumental* reasons. We might believe that, regardless of whether it is fitting in and of itself for improvers to retain their product, broader ends of justice can be served by allowing them to do so. Perhaps allowing improvers to retain the value they 'create' is a necessary spur to socially useful labour, or a stimulus to economic life which is capable of generating wealth for redistributive purposes. The two supports have often existed side by side. We saw in Chapter 2 that Locke, like Nozick, introduced both direct and instrumental justifications for a right to privately appropriate resources. Mill's defence would, we might expect, lean largely on instrumental (and specifically utilitarian) considerations—but the argument cited might also be read as a direct argument, or at least as suggesting that Mill held improvement-based claims to have some force independent of their social utility.[11] But in principle the two kinds of justification can come apart: even those sceptical of (either the normative force or the practical actionability of) direct justifications have tended to endorse instrumental ones. In what follows we will consider direct arguments for improvement-based claims first, and instrumental claims later.

This widespread endorsement of what I am calling improvement-based claims masks, unsurprisingly, deep contestation of the precise nature of the claims involved. Take the most famous argument for the genesis of private property, to be found in the work of Locke. Locke clearly believed there was a strong direct justification for the claims of those who take up and use natural resources. But not even Locke's defenders have been able to agree on what, if anything, can be salvaged from his view. The claim that we wrong someone when we remove from them a resource which they have improved because they have 'mixed' their labour with it turns out to be highly obscure and, when it becomes clear, impossible to defend. We might try to reformulate the general idea in the language of desert, so that those who work hard *deserve* special rights over the objects they labour on. But even that principle could not support the conclusions Locke wanted, not least since there seems to be no close connection between the quantity or intensity of labour expended upon an object and any resulting claims over it.[12] Nor, finally, could the even more suspicious claim that labourers *create* natural resources when they labour on them and hence have 'makers' rights' over them.[13]

Some have tried to rehabilitate the Lockean defence of private property in natural resources by insisting that the normatively significant event which occurs when we mix our labour with them—or, indeed, interact with them in any way—is that we integrate control over them into our 'purposive projects'.[14] When we interact with resources we come to form expectations that we will continue to maintain control over them, and those expectations can become crucial to many of the personal projects that give our lives meaning and structure. But this argument no longer depends upon any change occurring to a resource, such as might be accompanied by an increase in its economic value. Such claims can be made even if the resource in question is wholly unaltered; all that may have changed is a particular agent's attitude towards it. The weight of any claims therefore derives entirely from the (increased) significance that particular resources come to have *for those who seek to control them*. If so, I would claim that they are not properly claims about improvement at all, but about what I call attachment; and the strength of those claims is determined not by the degree to which agents are responsible for the (additional) value they now have, but by the degree to which we have reason to care about projects which are central to people's lives. In Chapter 5 I suggest that we should often care about such attachments, and that other things being equal we have reason to favour a situation where people are able to maintain control over the particular resources they are attached to. But what is not obvious, on this account, is why people with attachments should be entitled to a greater share of natural resources than others. Whereas claims from improvement seek to answer that question by suggesting that agents have a degree of responsibility for the existence of (at least some of) a resource's value, attachment-based arguments can make no such suggestion.

The critical discussion of Locke's theory has engendered scrutiny not only of the justification of special claims over resources, but also of the important question of their content. Even if improvement-based claims can be vindicated, just what would improvers have a claim *to*? Locke's answer to that question is no less contentious. He assumed that the target of special claims must be something akin to full liberal ownership over resources; but this is too quick, because whenever an agent has improved a resource several alternative responses are possible: most prominently, why not grant a claim precisely over the additional economic value which has now come into existence, rather than over the resource as a whole? Why must we assume that bestowing ownership is the only way of responding to improvement-based claims?[15]

A key alternative to full ownership over an improved object emerges on what I will call the *added value principle*. It states (as did Paine in the epigraph to this chapter) that it is (only) the extra value which comes into being when an object is improved that the improving agent has a claim over. Whereas 'unimproved' value may be wholly subject to general claims—and hence to redistributive taxation—the principle dictates that the difference between the value which a resource has when unimproved, and when later improved, is something over which the improving agent has a special claim.[16] And this claim, on its strongest version, is to retain that added value in full. The principle gains appeal in many quarters, it seems to me, because it connects with the value of responsibility: if the reason a resource moves from a value of $10 at T^1 to $15 at T^2 is that an agent has intervened to change its properties, then responsibility-catering views on justice will prefer a situation in which that agent is able to retain the difference between the two values over one in which she is not. Endorsement of something akin to the added value principle is widespread—including within debates on global justice—and it will be the focus of the discussion that follows. In particular, I will investigate whether the principle is capable of justifying special claims over natural resources on the part of nations or states, and if so whether this requires us to delimit the scope for egalitarian redistribution in light of it.

Before we can answer that question adequately, some necessary ground-clearing. We will construe the improvement of a natural resource as the altering of its chemical and/or physical properties in such a direction as to make it more economically useful. These chemical and physical properties include ductility, porosity, conductivity, flammability, opacity, reflectivity, brittleness, elasticity, hardness, and so on. Industrial processes will value resources principally as carriers of these properties, and shifts along each property-continuum (as a resource becomes harder, or more ductile, or more elastic) will make them more valuable than rival resources bearing similar properties.[17] To count as an improvement these changes must be perceptible *as* improvements by others. As a working assumption, we can expect those changes to be accompanied by increases in exchange value.[18]

4.2. NATIONAL AND STATIST CLAIMS FROM IMPROVEMENT

There are both nationalist and statist variants of the idea that political communities have compelling improvement-based claims over the natural resources inside their territories. On the nationalist version the relevant conjecture is that the present value natural resources have is in no small part attributable to the improving actions of individual national communities. Through actions such as clearing land, irrigating, and cultivating, communities increase the bountifulness of their land and other resources, and these represent improvements which are identifiable on some reasonably universal standard.[19] It may not be the case that the entire value of a nation's resources is attributable to improvement, to be sure; some unimproved portion of value could in principle be identified. Now, it might be thought that there is reason to doubt whether the cut between the two portions could reliably be made, and perhaps this casts doubt in turn on the enterprise of redistributing unimproved values which global egalitarians are sometimes committed to.[20] We might respond that if the cut cannot be made, that fact no more supports the claim that we should leave all value where it is than it does the rival claim that we should redistribute all of it. But let that pass. The significant point is that epistemic difficulties aside, on this view the principled claim nations can make is to the added value they are responsible for and not to the improved resource as a whole.[21] On the statist version, the crucial event is not that states directly intervene to improve resources (which presumably they rarely do), but rather the way in which they provide a context wherein their members can improve resources securely and efficiently.[22]

On either the nationalist or statist version, though, claims to retain the added value of natural resources on the back of direct improvement will have limited scope. For the degree of 'cultivation' of the various resources in a given territory will be very variable.[23] Some resources will be undiscovered, and hence unimproved. Unless we adhere to the dubious idea that those who discover resources thereby create them,[24] eventual discovery would not change that fact either. Still others will, like fresh water, literally fall from the sky, or else flow from sources in other countries (or from the oceans or the atmosphere). Others, though discovered, will lie dormant and unimproved. Some of these will eventually be sold in unimproved form—and although communities might then justly recoup the costs of discovery, extraction, and transportation, the resources in question will be otherwise untransformed. In still other cases, nation-states will sell exploration or extraction rights to outside actors such as multinational corporations, and neglect to engage directly with the resources in question at all. In each of these cases, improvement-based claims on the part of local nations or states will be notable only by their absence.

Even when the direct improvement of resources does occur, of course, it is not obvious that it makes sense to attribute it to the state or to the nation as a whole. Nations, for instance, will not collectively labour on individual resources in any direct fashion; such acts of improvement will be the preserve of individuals or corporations. We cannot immediately assume that any added value therefore belongs to the community: a libertarian might ask why individuals' claims devolve up to the nation or state in which they belong, rather than being held against them, for instance.

At least some of these problems are contingent, and leave open the possibility that the added value principle might apply to *some* of the natural resources within a territory, thereby reducing the scope for egalitarian redistribution. But the added value principle turns out to face more fundamental, and less tractable, challenges.

4.3. INTERROGATING THE ADDED VALUE PRINCIPLE

Consider the added value principle again. It appears to suggest that when an agent changes the properties of a resource, with the result that its market value increases from, say, $10 to $15, that agent is entitled to retain the additional $5 *on the grounds that he or she is responsible for its coming into being*. But that view faces a number of familiar objections which unsettle the claim that the agent is in fact responsible for (or fully responsible for) the emergence of the additional economic value. One familiar charge points us towards influences on value for which others are responsible. Perhaps a given improvement could not have occurred unless a particular technology had been developed (by others), or a transport system put in place (via public taxation), and so on. If the creation of value requires the presence of public goods, or infrastructure, which has been bankrolled by others, then the improvers' claim to retain the full added value may be weakened. Another charge, with its own very considerable philosophical pedigree, points out that even if the improving agent is responsible for the existence of an improvement (at least in the sense that their action was a necessary condition of its coming into being, even if not a sufficient one), that does not establish that they are responsible for the *value* which that improvement then commands on the market. Prices after all are an artefact of supply and demand, and in a complex economy prices may escalate or decline as a result of factors for which individual improvers are not responsible. For instance, the market price of crude oil increased more than fivefold between 1998 and 2008, and it is difficult to see how we might credit oil producers with that increase in exchange value.[25] Though the causes are complex, the political reforms initiated by Deng Xiaoping in the 1980s were probably as important a factor as any.[26] An influential strand in theorizing about natural resources has diagnosed the prevalence of 'scarcity rents' in real-world markets, and argued that their widespread existence must undermine any responsibility-based claim to retain the full added value which improvements garner.[27] The 'rent theorists' of the early twentieth century also frequently argued that differential returns to labour, just like returns to land, are the product of contingencies—such as scarcity—for which individual labourers can hardly be considered responsible.[28] The price of a given product—such as an improved resource—can in that sense be seen as a deeply social fact, and moreover one which contains a large slice of what egalitarians sometimes call brute luck. When we distribute natural resources themselves, we distribute something which nobody has played any part in creating. But when we assign natural resources' economic value to one agent or another, on the other hand, we distribute something which is a *social* product; and it is not clear why improvers should have unlimited title to added value if its existence—and extent—also depends upon the actions of others.

Some such objection underpinned Rawls's famous scepticism about market returns to labour. A Rawlsian will distinguish questions about individuals' rights to employ (or not employ) their talents from questions about the same individuals' rights to retain the full market returns from selling their talents. Even if we knew that an individual was responsible for the existence of a talent (which Rawls also cast doubt on), she surely has no strong claim on the market value of that talent at any point in time, since that value is determined by many factors—including its scarcity—which are properly outside her control. Given his lack of faith in the prospects of disentangling the 'value' of individual contribution once the various contingencies of the natural and social lotteries involved are accounted for, Rawls appeared to believe that the justification for any inequalities tracking individual contributions must be instrumental in character—and hence his difference principle treats unequal returns to labour as justified (whether 'deserved' or not) only insofar as they are necessary to improve the position of the worst off in society.[29] As far as the irreducible contingency of exchange values goes, a parallel point can be made about returns to any improvements to natural resources. Even if agents are responsible for developing or exercising their different capacities to improve resources (which is open to question), given that they bear no responsibility for, say, the level of technological development which influences demand for those improved resources (and indeed determines which changes to a resource's properties will *count* as improvements), or the overall level of supply or scarcity, then they surely cannot make a sound responsibility-based claim to all of the additional exchange value which comes into being when they exercise those capacities.[30]

One way of expressing this challenge to the added value principle, as I have suggested, is to argue that at least some portion of the market value of improved assets can be construed as 'rent', and that this rent, depending as it does on factors outside the control of improving individuals, can be considered an asset which is not owned by improving individuals but is rather available for equality-promoting causes. There are many ways of calibrating the rent which arises in market contexts. One would depict rent as any market value over and above the 'reservation price' for improved goods, where the reservation price simply represents the lowest price which would still persuade an individual improver to bring her improved goods to market. An individual who would in principle be prepared to sell her refined oil for $12—because that allows her to recoup the costs of discovery, extraction, and processing—but nevertheless holds out for a price of $18 is engaging in rent-seeking behaviour, and has no moral claim over the extra $6. Alternatively, we could construe rents in terms of market value over and above the 'clearance price', defined as the lowest price which would still, in a competitive market, see *all* goods sold.[31] The clearance price would, in a multi-seller market, designate a smaller proportion of exchange value as rent than would the reservation price approach, and would therefore produce more modest funds for egalitarian redistribution. But whichever method we chose, the rent approach challenges any simple view that, whereas the unimproved portion of a resource's value might justly be treated as a social asset, the improved portion is an asset that rightly belongs to the improver.

How might a defender of collective claims over added value respond to these challenges? At least some defenders of collective claims are likely to concur on the social character of market prices. Though the economic value of a resource can increase or decline in relation to shifts on various property-continua, the value of a resource is of course not wholly determined by changes to its properties. These properties become valuable insofar as economic processes exist which can make use of them, inasmuch as those processes serve human ends more or less well in relation to the costs associated with them, and in relation to the cost of alternatives. Technological developments which do not alter the physical or chemical properties of properties can nevertheless stimulate increasing (or declining) demand for them; developments in socio-economic infrastructure can have the same kind of impact. So, both statists and nationalists remind us, can developments in social rules governing the use of resources. If the use of a given resource is (effectively) prohibited by law, its economic value can be expected to be lower; its legalization will tend to increase that value, assuming that human wants exist which it can satisfy more cheaply than alternatives. In that way, we might say, the actual economic value of resources is crucially dependent upon prevailing political and economic structures.[32]

Crucially, though, in order to sustain the conclusion that he or she is after, the nationalist or the statist would need to claim that the context within which prices come to be determined is something for which individual nations or states are also responsible. Hence the claim could be that although direct improvers are not responsible for the full value of their improvements, in *combination* the individual improver and the context-determining national community (or state) *are* responsible. If successful, this argument might once again support the conclusion that redistributing resource values would do a serious injustice to particular communities.

Now even if this argument could succeed, it is interesting to note that nationalists would themselves be saddled with the problem of how to distinguish the portion of value for which improvers are responsible from the portion for which context-determining national communities are responsible. A parallel problem will also arise for statists. This is because even if they are correct that nations or states determine the context in which improvements come to have one value rather than another, we would still need a way of dealing with cases where a resource is directly improved by an outsider, albeit within a social context putatively determined largely by insiders. Unless we chose to revert to an economy in which outsiders—such as multinational corporations—were prohibited from improving natural resources, this problem will not go away—however intractable nationalists believe the epistemic problem involved to be.

But nationalists and statists face still deeper problems. Their emphasis on the collective determination of the context within which resources come to have one value rather than another addresses the claim that social context influences market price. But to achieve their aim they need to establish that the social context in question is national rather than global. Once more, if nationalists were committed to a world in which natural resources could not be sold on global commodity markets, this problem might be made to disappear. But that is unlikely to be an attractive option. To the contrary, a major reason why nation-states make claims to resources in or around their territories is *because* they can be sold on global markets, and they would be worth far less to individual nations if they could not. But any claim that it is domestic demand and supply which determines market prices for natural resources appears to be plainly false. Note that this is distinct from the (vexed) question whether domestic economic growth is essentially endogenous or exogenous. Regardless of our answer to *that* question, the market prices of natural resources is, in a reasonably well-integrated global economy, unquestionably an artefact of *global* demand and supply. Miller himself once made this point very directly, arguing that 'the value of the resources available within the territorial boundaries of any one state depend on global institutions such as the international commodity market', and that 'states are enriched and impoverished in seemingly arbitrary ways by such institutions'.[33] He was of course right about that: if the US or China tomorrow discovers a new use for resource X, then the value of resource X *everywhere* can be expected to increase as a result. If a large supply of one nation's supply of resource Y was destroyed tomorrow in a freak explosion, the value of resource Y everywhere can be expected to increase. If a nation tomorrow discovered an effective and usable way of harvesting energy from nuclear fusion, world prices for coal, oil, and gas would plummet. In each case the market price of a resource would rise and fall in ways which enriched and impoverished particular communities in ways for which they could not plausibly be held responsible. Moreover, goods produced in a domestic economy will command higher prices if they can be exported to overseas markets in which the infrastructure to deliver them to final consumers exists, and in which property rights are robustly protected. Their value will also fluctuate as such overseas governments legally enable or constrain the use of the goods in question, or lay on or withdraw other goods which enable their use (such as education, or electricity, or access to the internet). In short, all of the things a domestic government might do to influence the value of particular resources also have their extra-domestic counterparts.

The nationalist might now content himself with the thought that his view would nevertheless apply in a world which was genuinely autarkic. But that is actually not obvious either. Recall Beitz's thought-experiment of a world in which nation-states were hermetically sealed, and made use of their own natural resources alone.[34] In *that* world, there would be no supra-national influence on natural resource prices, and those prices, we might suppose, would reflect only factors for which individual nations were responsible. The first claim is true by definition; but we cannot infer the second claim from it. Even a hermetically sealed nation cannot automatically claim responsibility for everything that goes on within it. First, when comparing the respective fates of autarkic nations we might still impugn any inequalities that arose on the back of unequal initial endowments in natural resources (and we might say the same for climate or geography, which are similarly unchosen). Second, other contingencies might intervene for which nations cannot be held responsible. Perhaps shares of particular resources in *combination* turn out to be useful (think of the significance of fast-running water, coal, and iron in England's industrial revolution). Perhaps one nation rather than another produces an engineering genius, transforming the ways in which its resources can be used. Can the nation as a whole claim full responsibility for that? Why, and in what circumstances? Third and perhaps most importantly, if the nationalist position is going to justify intergenerational inequalities, then it will depend upon the view that the advantages or disadvantages which any nation builds up are *heritable*. But that view may be hard to justify. How can it be explained, from the point of view of children coming into the world, that their prospects can permissibly diverge so much simply because of the labour or political decisions of their ancestors? If it cannot, then facts about what different nations or states make of their natural resources may not suffice to justify inequalities even in an autarkic world.

These counterfactual conjectures aside, the point remains that nations or states appear to have, in a global economy (and possibly in a non-globalized economy too), weak claims to the market value of the improvements which take place in their territories. The added value principle, or something like it, has attracted considerable support because it appears to tie rewards to the exercise of responsibility, and in particular to the bringing into the world of additional economic value. But it faces serious problems which undermine the nationalist or statist attempt to argue for the collective determination of value. This has important consequences for debates on natural resources and global justice. Nationalists have, sometimes, been prepared to countenance—at least in theory—the idea that the unimproved portion of natural resource values is something over which individual communities have weak or non-existent claims. But if the arguments of this section are compelling, claims to the improved portion of value too are not immune to calls for equality-promoting redistribution.

4.4. IMPLICATIONS

The argument in section 4.3 about the social determination of natural resource values has important consequences for the way we should think about natural resource justice. It reaffirms the conclusion (defended in Chapter 3) that natural resources are less distinctive or 'special', from an egalitarian point of view, than is sometimes assumed. Many have been attracted to the idea of redistributing natural resources because the argument for doing so appears, on the face of it, simpler than in the case of any other goods. After all, natural resources are 'natural': no one created them, or put them where they are. In selecting them as candidates for redistribution, we take from no one what is properly theirs. However, if our goal is (as it usually turns out to be) to equalize the *value of*, or the *benefits and burdens flowing from*, natural resources, then we must face the fact that this value, or those benefits and burdens, are deeply social.

The claim to redistribute that value therefore cannot rest on the argument that it is itself 'natural'. It can still rest, though, on the argument that nobody has any strong special claim over that value—such as the kind of claim that might arise, on some theories, from the exercise of responsible choice. Here it is significant that it is not only the unimproved portion of natural resource values which is liable to equality-promoting redistribution. At least some portion of improved values, too, is immune from any plausible claim from responsibility. It is immune because, though 'social' in an important sense, no individual (or non-global community) can be fully credited with the coming into existence of that value. When we focus properly on the social character of natural resource values we see once more how natural resources are much like the other things we come into the world facing unequal shares of. Society is, in Van Parijs's brilliant phrase, 'a massive gift distribution machine',[35] and so is the world at large. When individuals come into the world one of the things they bear no responsibility for—and as a result of which their lives should not go better or worse—is the distribution of natural resource values. But that is one (albeit significant) item on a long list.

What flows, though, from the recognition that the value of natural resources is social in the sense I have specified? It is important to note that this view of natural resource value—including improved portions of value—as a 'social' artefact does not commit us to the limiting view that the task of a theory of justice is to distribute the 'social product' or 'social surplus', and hence that where there is no such product, those theories must remain silent. Relationists do sometimes argue that the social surplus is a common asset, *and* that the sole task of a theory of justice is to divide this surplus between participants in the practice that gives rise to it. But non-relationists can accept the former claim without endorsing the latter. For non-relationists there may indeed be no good individual claims on the social surplus, and that surplus may therefore be liable for equality-promoting redistribution. But the social character of that surplus is a sufficient but not a necessary condition for its liability to redistribution. It merely identifies, for the non-relationist, the absence of compelling special claims. Yet even in a divided world with no common practices—and hence no global social product—the argument for redistribution of resource values remains open; and so too does the argument for redistributing any advantages over which individuals have no good special claims, whether their origin is social or 'cosmic'. Revisit for a moment the idea of society as a massive gift-distributing machine. For relationists, the egalitarian will care about the unequal outcomes insofar as a *machine* (society) is doing the distributing. For non-relationists, it is enough to trigger egalitarian concern that it is *gifts*—that is, unearned but consequential advantages and disadvantages—which are being distributed.

A final implication of the arguments of this chapter is that we ought to reject any simple view that the distinction between unimproved and improved portions of value is of fundamental normative significance, such that redistributive claims can arise over the former, but not over the latter. I have already argued that the added portions of value attendant on improvement ought not to be seen as immune to redistribution. But the converse is also true. There could, potentially, be responsibility-catering claims on unimproved values, if it were the case that some agent (whether individual or collective) had increased the value of unimproved resources by some action of theirs. For that reason, the insistence that an especially 'pure' or uncontroversial egalitarian argument can be made for redistributing natural resource value suffers a final setback. Just as both unimproved and improved portions of value can be assets for egalitarian redistribution, so both portions can conceivably be the subject of special claims. Still, even if it were true that some collective agent had increased the value of a natural resource, it would remain likely that this increase in value itself contained some portion of economic rent. These facts reduce, I suspect, the salience (if not the intelligibility) of the much-beloved distinction between unimproved and improved natural resources. Special claims could intelligibly arise, but will also be vulnerable to equality-promoting redistributive claims, on both sides of the unimproved/improved divide.

Just like for attachment claims

4.5. CONCLUSIONS

What appears to be the most prima facie plausible basis for improvement-based special claims—and which I have called the added value principle—is still vulnerable to the rejoinder that market values comprise a portion of unearned income, or rent. It is not easy to distinguish the rents in question.

The various proposals, however, converge on the general idea that value over and above that necessary to ensure that improvement in fact occurs should be seen as liable to redistribution.

On this point, we can begin to observe what looks like an important and interesting convergence between direct and instrumental arguments. Rawls's view, recall, was that there is no straightforward way to disentangle the portion of returns to labour over which an individual can register a plausible desert-based claim from the portion over which he cannot. Rawls sliced through the Gordian knot by describing the idea of reliably rewarding desert as impracticable. Rather, the normatively best solution is to limit any inequalities in returns to labour to those necessary to improve the absolute position of the worst-off. Even if the institutions endorsed by the difference principle allow some agents to accrue rewards over and above what they might deserve, such unequal returns to labour are acceptable when they lead to improvements in the lot of the deprived among us. Since then, much attention has focused on the question of how we identify when unequal returns are genuinely *necessary* to improve the position of the worst-off. There is a world of (moral) difference, Rawls's critics have pointed out, between paying an individual an amount sufficient to compensate him for the costs he has incurred in delivering a good or service—so that delivering it is perfectly rational—and paying him an amount sufficient to encourage him to deliver it in a context where he knows he can hold out for a price over and above the former.[36] Though the critique of those 'excess' rewards has employed different moral language (targeting hypocrisy in a society supposedly committed to equality), it is, in essence, a critique of rent-seeking behaviour. The upshot of the criticism is not that there should be no unequal rewards to improvement (or labour), but rather than such rewards ought to be as low as is compatible with continued improvement (or labour). This would appear to be the gist of the direct view also, or at least the direct view once it has encountered the rentist critique.

The apparent convergence between the most modest rendering of the direct view—or what is left of the direct view once it has conceded the contextual determination of exchange values—and the modified instrumental view is interesting, and worthy of further exploration. But it could also be overstated, because two potentially important differences remain between the two views.

First, the direct view interprets the correct reward for improvement in terms of the retention of (some portion of) the economic value of the improved resource. There is something morally fitting, on this view, about leaving (some portion of) added value where it falls, which is in the hands of the improver. The rentist critique queries how large that portion is, but not whether it exists. But the instrumental view is not committed to this conclusion. The instrumental view assumes that improvement must be brought about (see below), and insofar as that is true it then becomes an interesting empirical question just which, if any, incentives would need to be in place in order to bring it about. But there is no logical reason why these incentives should take the form of retaining value in improved objects. Other incentives are imaginable, in both market and non-market settings. Individuals might be given material incentives to improve resources which remained common property, for example, so that improvement could be encouraged without granting special rights over—never mind ownership of—improved resources. Alternatively, socialists might place their hopes in the efficacy of moral incentives which would reduce or remove the necessity of material incentives.[37] We might say, then, that the marriage between instrumental egalitarian arguments and special claims from improvement is at best a marriage of convenience, and perhaps no more than a dalliance until something better comes along.

Second, the instrumental view will—or should—be much more circumspect about *when* to issue rewards to improvement than the direct view. I spoke in the last paragraph as if instrumental egalitarians are committed to the view that improvement needs to occur, because insofar as it does we can advance materially and free up resources for egalitarian redistribution. But the instrumental view is less firmly committed to that view than we might think.[38] We need to distinguish between a general contention that some improvement of natural resources is necessary for pursuing justice (and therefore ought to be rewarded) and the implausible assumption that any and all acts of improvement advance justice (and hence always ought to be rewarded). If we are being instrumental about justice, a principle rewarding improvement should be discriminating, rather than rewarding any and all improvement which occurs. In one sense direct arguments usually internalize a parallel kind of conditionality: picking up and scratching an object before putting it down is not usually held to generate improvement-based claims (although Locke suggests that just such actions do justify special claims; what is doing the work, if he is right in the individual case, is likely to be attachment rather than improvement). Rather, the advocate of the direct argument wants to ask questions about whether the act can be considered an improvement by others, and will suggest some benchmark (such as exchange value) for assessing when this is so. But after ascertaining answers to those questions the direct argument becomes rather undiscriminating: the very fact that an improved object commands a higher market reward is enough to justify a claim over (some portion of) that reward. There is no reason why we should be so undiscriminating, however, because there is no reason to suppose that the fact that a market can be found for an improvement establishes that justice is served by that improvement. If the logic of the instrumental argument is that improvement should be rewarded because it can advance other goals of justice, we need to know *when* it will advance those justice goals, rather than assuming that all improvements serve justice simply *qua* improvements.

And there are, surely, no grounds for assuming that justice will be served by an unlimited rush to improve. Climate justice, and intergenerational justice, may demand that some resources are *not* transformed, because the effects of transforming them would be to damage, rather than to maximally advance, the interests of the worst-off in the world. Consider, for instance, fossil fuels. It is not immediately obvious how any instrumental argument could justify improvement-based claims concerning the extraction or refining of fossil fuels, simply because it is not immediately obvious that justice is served by their extraction or improvement. To the contrary, perhaps those serious about justice should consider measures to make the extraction or improvement of fossil fuels positively uneconomical (see Chapter 8).[39] This might be a radical political result. But it also has radical implications for the way we think about rewarding improvement. Instrumental arguments for improvement-based special claims may not recommend any rewards whatsoever for many acts of improvement. The same could be true of other natural resources whose extraction or use produces negative externalities which are all too rarely recognized in market price. Whilst improvement can serve justice, there is no reason for assuming that it always will. On this basis, too, egalitarians' endorsement of improvement-based special claims should be highly circumspect.

ENDNOTES

1. Paine 1835 [1795]: 403.
2. Beitz 1979: 136–43; Jones 2001; and Barry 1982.
3. See for instance Crutzen 2003.
4. We might hold them morally responsible even if we believe that outsiders have defaulted on their own duty to share in the costs of rainforest conservation. See Chapter 10.
5. Simmons 1994: 223.
6. Locke 1960, chapter 5.
7. Paine 1835.
8. For a discussion of the movement's broader aims, see http://www.mst.org.br/.
9. Marx 1993.
10. Mill 2000: 159, 161.
11. Mill would not be unusual in this. As Waldron (1988: 174–5) notes, 'Even positivistic philosophers like Hobbes and Bentham, who maintain that property rights are entirely a matter of convention justified if at all by their utility, drop their guard from time to time and say that the natural function of positive law is to secure to every man the fruits of his labour.'
12. This does not exhaust possible arguments from desert, because desert claims are sometimes held to be grounded on the effort one invests in an activity, and sometimes on the *output* of that activity. The 'added value' principle which I discuss in section 4.1 captures the latter idea, and might be redescribed using the language of desert.

13. For a well-known discussion of these various formulations, and their pitfalls, see Waldron 1988: 197–204.
14. Simmons 1994: 272.
15. Locke's response might have been that there is no interesting difference between a claim to ownership of a resource, and a claim to the increased portion of value which is attributable to an act of improvement. He famously suggested that labour is responsible for a very large part of the (use) value of a resource, and if some residual portion of its value is still 'natural' it would be a very small part. Waldron (1988: 193) suggests that this claim is more plausible in the case of land than other natural resources. But either way, it appears to suffer from intractable problems. See the discussion in Cohen 1995, chapter 7.
16. There is still potential for cross-purposes regarding important questions about control and alienation. If I improve an apple tree, making it more bountiful, do I gain the right to sell the additional apples, and retain their value (whereas the unimproved value—the value of the apples which would have existed anyway—is pooled)? Or do I merely have a right to retain the added value *if* the resource is sold, whoever happens to have rights to alienation? For the purposes of the chapter I will assume the latter, more modest conclusion is the target. Certainly arguments exist which seek to ground a more extensive set of rights on the back of a claim to the added value contained in improved resources, including a reasonably full set of territorial rights. But a discussion of those arguments must wait until Chapter 6.
17. We might say the same about location, a physical property changes in which can be accompanied by increases in the value of a resource (as when someone brings an ore closer to a factory). Such actions might also count as direct improvements even if the 'internal' properties of a resource remain unchanged.
18. David Miller (1996), whose work I discuss in section 4.3, has argued that the basis for desert claims is best understood in terms of one's productive contribution, and best measured in terms of exchange value.
19. Miller 2012: 259. See also Meisels 2009.
20. Miller 2007; Moore 2012.
21. Miller 2007: 218.
22. Cara Nine (2012: 142) has suggested that states can make desert-based claims to the resources in their territories. As she puts it, 'Because the collective has caused a change in the resource, that change is attributable to the collective, and they come to deserve a claim to those goods because of this causal connection.' Actually, on Nine's view it appears to be the case that states' actions justify not property rights, but jurisdictional rights, and that they do so because they provide a context in which *individuals* can more effectively improve resources. I consider the argument for states' jurisdictional rights over the resources in their territories in Chapter 6. Still, since individual improvements create a presumption against global redistribution of resource values, the conclusions of Nine's view might, in the right conditions, coincide with those of the nationalist account.
23. Miller 2007: 219.
24. Miller (1995: 106, n. 34) repudiates that idea—which he associates with Israel Kirzner.

25. Energy Information Administration, World Crude Oil Prices, 2008. See http://www.eia.gov/petroleum/.
26. For a much more nuanced account of the influence of Chinese political and economic developments on world commodity markets than its title implies, see Economy and Levi 2014.
27. See e.g. Spencer 1851.
28. For a discussion see Fried 2002, especially chapter 4.
29. Rawls 1971: 100–8.
30. For a good discussion of the problems with such claims, see Fried 1995: 226–45.
31. For a discussion of the reservation price approach to economic rents (and other approaches) see Fried 2002, chapter 4. For a defence of the clearance price approach to natural resource rents, see Van Parijs 1995, chapter 4.
32. Miller 2007, chapter 3. Risse 2005.
33. Miller 1995: 105.
34. Beitz 1979: 136–43.
35. Van Parijs 2009: 160.
36. Cohen 2000, chapters 8–10.
37. Carens 1981; Cohen 2009.
38. Notably, the instrumentalist should be in the business of endorsing rewards (of whatever variety) *when* resources are improved, and not *in the hope* that resources will be improved. Compare this with Rawls's very different argument in *The Law of Peoples*, in which he suggested that peoples should be considered owners of the resources within their territories because if they were, they would be more likely to tend those resources rather than wasting or neglecting them (see Chapter 6). Rawls 1999: 8. This view errs in sanctioning claims far in excess of those necessary to encourage improvement, and in sanctioning full ownership as the requisite incentive; but most importantly, it puts the cart before the horse.
39. This is a little quick: as I note in Chapters 8 and 10, it might be that justice allows, or even requires, that poor communities retain access to fossil fuels for some time, especially if they lack access to alternative means of escaping poverty.

5

Accommodating Attachment

This chapter investigates the significance, from the point of view of egalitarian justice, of patterns of attachment to natural resources. Section 5.1 introduces the idea of attachment as a source of special claims over resources. Section 5.2 shows why attachment over natural resources should be taken seriously. It is often supposed that egalitarians must be hostile—or at the very least indifferent—to such attachments, and that their redistributive schemes would ride roughshod over them. I will argue that this is not the case. But even if egalitarians should take attachment seriously, it must be demonstrated just how they can accommodate it whilst also holding firm to their egalitarian commitments. Section 5.3 therefore provides an account of how we might accommodate attachment-based special claims, and spells out the implications for global justice. Finally, section 5.4 considers but rejects an alternative account of how we should accommodate attachments. By the end, we will have established that egalitarianism contains far greater capacity for taking attachment seriously than we might suppose, and that this capacity should be put to good use.

5.1. ATTACHMENT-BASED SPECIAL CLAIMS

When it comes to the sources of special claims over natural resources, attention to date has overwhelmingly focused upon improvement. But the exclusive claim that *only* the productive use of land and other resources can generate claims has had an often ignoble history. It has been used, for instance, to justify dispossessing indigenous peoples from land which they have inhabited or interacted with, but not used 'productively'.[1] Assuming that an account which only considered special claims based on improvement would be an impoverished one, this chapter will examine a second source of such claims, in this case premised upon 'attachment'. Attachment-based claims seek to ground rights over resources on the close relationship which some agents have formed with specific resources, such that continued access to them, for instance, comes to be significant to their wellbeing. For this project to be worthwhile we do not need to assume that claims from attachment and improvement will always be entirely separate. We may be able to identify many cases where in practice the same agent has both improved and become attached to a specific natural resource, thereby generating overlapping special claims over it. But this will not always be true. A poor miner might work hard to extract coal from a coal-seam—thereby generating a special claim based on improvement—but feel no attachment to that coal, and indeed disdain his career as a miner and wish to change job at the earliest opportunity. On the other hand someone might become attached to a resource without improving it. A Hindu might place great store upon the expectation that on his death his ashes will be scattered on the Ganges; a Christian might place great store by her ability to baptize her children in the water of the Jordan. Neither act will improve a river from an economic point of view. If there are cases where improvement-based claims are weak or non-existent but significant attachment to a resource nevertheless exists, we need to know whether separate moral claims can derive from such attachment, and what force those claims have. If we can identify such claims, it will thereby become more obvious why, for instance, the dispossession of indigenous peoples was (and is) objectionable.

If the conventional account which focuses solely on economic improvement—often associated with Locke—appears unduly restrictive in its implications for judging resource claims, the Kantian account provides little guidance on when claims are compelling. On Kant's account of 'provisional right', we can obtain a provisional claim over an object simply by declaring our will to control it, at the same time as declaring our willingness to submit that claim to the adjudication of a civil (and, ultimately, cosmopolitan) political authority. The account does not place any further conditions on what constitutes a valid claim over an object. Lea Ypi has recently suggested that the Kantian account can afford to be 'ecumenical with regard to how groups of people end up occupying specific geographical areas'—or, perhaps, controlling particular objects; Kantians can accept improvement-based criteria, or attachment-based ones, or indeed any criteria so long as the claims arising under the various accounts share the crucial commitment to binding authority.[2] But Kant's account is able to be ecumenical precisely because it is so undemanding. The emphasis on the need to generate political authority means that Kant's account will grant claims just wherever the declared will to control an object exists, along with the willingness to commend that claim to final adjudication by a higher political authority, and independent of any relationship of attachment or improvement.

Moreover, whilst this Kantian account provides some guidance on how to treat claims generated prior to the establishment of civil authority, it does not aim to settle the basis on which good claims might be registered once a civil authority actually exists. The account tells us that 'provisional' claims are to be confirmed, but also possibly constrained, by the rightful civil authority. But it does not tell us on what grounds that authority (whether cosmopolitan or otherwise) will adjudicate between good and bad claims. In the meantime (that is, prior to the establishment of the civil authority), the criterion for assigning provisional right appears *too* permissive. If we assume that the transition to a civil condition is morally required, then it is certainly plausible to consider it a necessary qualification for any valid claim over an object that the claimant in question expresses a willingness for his or her claim to be bound by some future civil authority. What is simply not obvious is why we should consider that willingness to be bound by civil authority a *sufficient* condition (or, to be more precise, a condition which, alongside the will to control an object, is jointly sufficient) for judging a claim to be sound. The importance of elucidating submission to a binding authority does not prevent us from qualifying such claims in *further* ways.

On this latter score, it is not obvious why the declaration of one's will to control an object provides a sufficiently weighty basis for allocating even provisional rights over it, given that these rights will serve as a basis for the justified exclusion of others. For one thing, it is not immediately obvious why the desire to control possesses independent normative significance in the first place, not least if it is to justify the exclusion of others who may presumably wish to interact with an object too. At the very least, we surely require some principled basis for assessing how *much* land and other resources I can rightly control. (For instance, if I declare a wish to control the oil buried under the ground on the island where I live, ought we to place any weight on that claim? Does it not matter how much I stake a claim to?) Now, one interpretation of the Kantian position would maintain that what is normatively significant is not the mere act of willing control over an object, but the actual achievement of bringing that object under one's control.³ But it is not clear why the achievement of control per se should make a difference in justifying claims either. It may be instead that if control has normative significance it lies in the fact that as a consequence of controlling objects we come to develop expectations of continued access, and to begin to orient our life-plans around those objects (see section 5.2). But if so, control ceases to be significant in itself; what matters here is what can ensue when people are permitted to control objects. Moreover, once we shift our focus to the significance of life-plans per se, we must recognize that people can develop plans around objects they do *not* control, and it is not obvious why those plans should be judged to lack any normative weight. We must be wary of showing concern only for the plans of those who control objects, and disregarding the claims of those who seek to access or control them. (Recall, for instance, the scenario in which someone is deeply attached to the river Ganges, and wishes to scatter his relatives' ashes there. Placing normative weight only on the attachments of those who control the Ganges now means, in effect, that India can prevent people who are deeply attached to the river from interacting with it. Whilst such a settlement has international law on its side, it clearly places normative store by the plans of some but not others.[4]) That would introduce a regrettable status quo bias. Moreover, it would threaten to render the justification of special claims circular, so that the right to control came to be grounded upon the fact of control.

A more compelling foundation for special claims, then, may be one which focuses directly upon the significance of individual life-plans, and not on the achievement of control in and of itself. Any plausible account of justice will consider it important that we are able to see ourselves as at least jointly directing our own lives, making plans for those lives which we in turn have some prospect of achieving. On Rawls's account that will require justified confidence in our ability to develop our talents and to exercise them, so that one's ends fall within the realm of the reasonably attainable.[5] It will require, in addition, the basic liberties necessary for pursuing our various projects. And it will also have material preconditions: at the very least, we will need secure access to the objects of our basic rights. An egalitarian account will specify still more demanding material prerequisites, constraining tolerable material inequalities in a variety of ways. If we accept that, we have grounds for specifying general claims to various material resources, including natural resources. These will be general in the sense that we all possess such claims simply as human beings, and insofar as we are all capable of generating life-plans that ought to matter.

But what of special claims? An attachment-based justification for special claims over natural resources will emphasize the way in which *particular* people sometimes form life-plans which depend upon their continued access to *specific* resources. If they are to be weighty, attachment-based claims will be claims which cannot be met, at least without significant loss, merely by providing equivalent shares of other resources. Such claims should interest not only Rawlsians but advocates of many theories of justice. Consider two possible worlds, where in the first natural resources are distributed in accordance with pre-existing attachments, such that everyone is equally attached to some resource, and everyone is allowed to maintain secure access to that resource. In the second world, by contrast, although everyone is attached to some object, some mechanism ensures that no one is able to securely access the resource that matters to them individually. Equality, I take it, counts equally in favour of either world, offering no reason to choose one over the other. Nevertheless many of us would favour the first world, whether because of considerations of efficiency (that is, because aggregate wellbeing is higher), or because in that world people are better able to advance the projects that matter to them distinctively and so exercise their distinctive human agency. Indeed, any plausible theory of justice will probably find some reason for favouring the first distribution. Egalitarians who are pluralists will likely find such reasons, although they may not, strictly speaking, be egalitarian reasons. A welfarist egalitarian will care about resources precisely insofar as they fuel human wellbeing, in their various ways; resources can come to matter, derivatively in that sense, inasmuch as they are important to the success of the various pursuits that matter to us. But if so, he or she has good reason to pay heed to any information we might have about how *particular* resources are important to us, as paying heed to that information can potentially leave us able to secure greater aggregate wellbeing. A capability egalitarian may care about people's ability to exercise some control over their environment, or to develop a meaningful relationship with nature, and those abilities will be developed further, other things being equal, if people are able to maintain relationships with the resources that matter to them.

Notably, some Locke scholars have offered support for such a view, arguing for a move away from a focus on improvement as the only basis for special claims over resources, and suggesting instead (or in addition) that special claims can be granted wherever an individual integrates an object into what Simmons calls her 'purposive projects'.[6] Given the central role that objects can come to play in our life-plans, we have a prima facie reason not to reallocate those objects lightly. Some contemporary Kantians have also given support to this kind of account. In her (ostensibly Kantian) defence of rights of 'occupancy' over land, Anna Stilz suggests that there is a good prima facie claim for someone to continue to occupy land whenever that person has incorporated access to that land into his life-plans, such that occupancy becomes 'fundamental to the integrity of his structure of personal relationships, goals, and pursuits'.[7] Individuals may have used land to advance their central projects, projects which give their life meaning and make it valuable to them. In particular we ought to care about those life-plans which are 'comprehensive' rather than 'peripheral'—which 'structure many of our goals and choices, and are fundamental to our sense of ourselves as self-determining authors of our lives'.[8]

Indeed, we might suspect that our conception of attachment ought to be broader than this, such that we could recognize attachment-based special claims even when they are not accompanied by specific life-plans.[9] An individual might derive considerable satisfaction from visiting a forest even if she has no firm objective of visiting it with a certain regularity. Indeed, she might derive satisfaction simply from knowing it exists, whether she is able to visit it or not. An individual might love, or at least feel deep affection towards, a river or a mountain, and even if she has formulated no particular plan with regard to it, she might be devastated if the river were diverted by a dam, or the mountain despoiled by, say, mountaintop-removal mining. People's identities can also be bound up with an object (such as a river, or a mountain) such that its disappearance would cause them to feel an enormous sense of dislocation and loss. Razing a forest or removing the top of a mountain might therefore count as a setback to someone's wellbeing even if she had no discernible plan with regard to it. Plausibly, these facts ought to be reckoned with whenever decisions are made about whether a particular resource is used (or indeed destroyed). Now undoubtedly assessing the degree to which individuals derive pleasure, or satisfaction, or solace, from the existence of particular resources will be difficult; but it will also often be difficult to assess the extent to which individuals' central life-plans hinge upon continued access to them. There seems to be no principled reason for focusing on plan-related manifestations of attachment alone, to the exclusion of non-plan-related versions. To the contrary, to give weight only to the wellbeing which accrues when we formulate life-plans and see them through to fruition would be to introduce an 'intellectual bias' into our assessment of the attachments that matter. In what remains of this chapter I will for the most part examine cases in which individuals have developed life-plans dependent upon secure access to particular resources. But I will also discuss some examples in which individuals simply love, cherish, or identify with particular resources. Both facts, it seems to me, can be normatively significant.

One clarification is necessary before we proceed. To date, defences of what I am calling attachment-based special claims have usually focused on control over territory, rather than natural resources in particular. Stilz's account, for instance, focuses on the wrong of removing people from the places they inhabit, and does not apply the argument directly to natural resources. But although in practice this can be difficult, expensive, and destructive, natural resources such as metals, petrochemicals, and minerals can in principle be removed and transported away from the territories in, on, or above which they lie. This means that we can intelligibly ask questions about whether rights over such resources should be allocated separately. There is increasing recognition, accordingly, that rights over resources cannot simply be 'read off' from the territorial right to police a particular geographical jurisdiction, and that the standard justifications for rights of jurisdiction or border control cannot simply and immediately be extended to produce a justification for rights over resources.[10] As a result it is desirable to distinguish between direct and indirect claims to natural resources. A *direct* claim to a resource is a claim which states that a specified agent has a prima facie claim to control, securely access, or constrain others' access to a specified resource simply because of some feature of her relationship with that resource (for instance, because secure access to that resource is in itself necessary to her ability to pursue her central life-plans). An *indirect* claim to a resource is one which states that a specified agent has a claim to control, securely access, or place constraints on others' access to a resource but derives that claim purely from other, prior claims such as claims to exercise control over territory or over borders. Thus a person might say: I must be allowed to control resource X, or to be allowed to exclude others from accessing it, because use of resource X by others will involve the violation of my (putative) right to regulate access to a territory. Such indirect claims are rather a weak basis on which to ground claims to natural resources. For one thing, many natural resources (such as fresh water, fish, wild animals, and possibly even oil) are not tied to a particular piece of territory but are rather 'fugacious'. On the other hand, even claims to resources which are not fugacious are vulnerable to the challenge that if resource X *could* be removed without entering a territory (for instance, by some high-tech horizontal mining technology), any resource claims would then dissipate. By contrast, a direct claim to a resource would remain intact regardless of whether and how others might access or extract it, and does not depend upon a close connection between resources and specific geographical sites. This chapter will therefore investigate whether an attachment-based account can be extended to produce direct claims over natural resources, and on finding that it can, will investigate how we should integrate those claims within a broader account of resource justice.

5.2. TAKING ATTACHMENT SERIOUSLY

There are many cases in which individuals have formulated life-plans which are dependent upon secure access to particular natural resources. The most compelling instances are probably those in which members of certain relatively small-scale groups have formed a close and enduring relationship with resources that have become key to central and enduring practices,[11] and where that relationship is sustainable, and the resources non-substitutable in the way they support individual life-plans. Where access to specific resources is integral to one's way of life and indeed one's sense of self, it is plausible to say that this generates a prima facie—but defeasible—claim to continuing access. The resources in question must be specifically valuable, though, such that they are not straightforwardly substitutable as supports for life-plans. For a good claim to exist over *these* trees, it should not be the case that other trees would serve the purposes of a given individual without discernible shortfall. It must be the case that in carrying out his life-plans access to anything other than these trees would be, to him, (a possibly very poor) second best.

Some might still find attachment implausible, by itself, as an independent source of special claims. If no improvement has occurred, why grant claims over resources? Why should I be able to ground a claim over a resource simply as a result of developing an expectation that I will be able to access it, and then developing life-plans to match? We need to give serious attention to the suspicion that attachment to a resource is too weak a normative consideration to generate a claim to exercise rights over it. In his discussion of the moral arbitrariness of resource distribution, Beitz suggested grounds for just such suspicion. He alleged that the argument from attachment to resources to rights over them was even more tenuous than the argument from the possession of talents to a right to the economic rewards attendant on such talents which Rawls had earlier done so much to unsettle. Specifically, he claimed that:

> It would be inappropriate to take the sort of pride in the diamond deposits in one's back yard that one takes in the ability to play the Appassionata ... talents, in some sense, are what the self is; they help constitute personality. The resources under one's feet, because they lack this natural connection with the self, seem more like contingent than necessary elements in the development of personality.[12]

The reason that pride in the diamond deposits in one's back yard is inappropriate, to be clear, is that pride is (something like) a justified satisfaction with one's character or abilities, given that character and ability are elements of the self which we often deserve (some) credit for cultivating. By contrast natural resources—such as the diamonds in one's back yard—'lack [a] natural connection with the self'.[13] Or, to put it another way, when the Rector in George Eliot's *Middlemarch* asserts that 'It is a very good quality in a man to have a trout stream', we ought to take this as one of Eliot's many jokes.[14] The connection between personality and the possession of diamonds or trout streams is simply too weak for concern with the former to justify rights over the latter. The suggestion, then, is that if we are at all persuaded by the argument that talent is a morally arbitrary basis for distribution, we ought to apply that argument *a fortiori* to natural resources.

But Beitz's claim repays closer attention. He is suggesting that, by contrast to the kind of pride it is appropriate to take in playing the *Appassionata*, it would be inappropriate to take pride in one's relationship with natural resources—given that one has, by hypothesis, done little or nothing to actively nurture them, and given that they are not, unlike talents, actually 'constitutive of the self'. Now that first clause is too quick, for of course a particular resource may well have been developed and improved, even in the autarkic world Beitz supposes in that part of his argument. But the second clause initially appears more secure. It does look to be a distinctive feature of talents that they are internal to the self, or constitutive of the self as Beitz puts it.

However, consider again the *Appassionata* example. Imagine that Sophie has invested her whole being in playing that piece, and that now she can do it she thinks about herself in a different way—she appraises herself more positively as a person capable of cultivating her abilities and sensibilities, she has a real sense of living within a musical tradition, and so on. Now the ability to exercise that talent is always going to be vulnerable in certain ways. Sophie might injure her hands, and be unable to play any longer. Likewise if Sophie's piano was taken from her—or if she was forbidden from playing *any* piano— she would be unable to exercise her talent. Whilst not directly deprived of her talent, she would be deprived of a crucial object for its exercise, and we would also expect her talent itself to suffer in time. If so, the loss to her sense of self, and her sense that she had skilfully brought her life-plans closer to fruition, could be just as acute as if she had injured her hands. Her control over her talent and her control over her piano—or, failing that, a substitute piano—are both crucial to her continuing to experience her sense of agency, and to the fulfilment of a project which is central to her life. Although there are some talents which do not obviously depend on control over external objects for their expression (like dancing, or singing), there are many talents which are dependent for their exercise on secure access to objects such as musical instruments, sports equipment, vehicles, and so on.

But if control over a piano—an external artefact, which she has done nothing to create or improve—is crucial to Sophie's pursuit of her life-plans and even to her sense of self, then we have a reason to ensure she can continue to access it. And we can say the same thing, in many cases, about natural resources. Imagine that Ken, a fisherman, has oriented his life around fishing—developing his talents, his ability to work out where the fish are, what they want to eat at any given time, and so on. Here it seems that Ken's sense of pride in the performance of fishing is no more misplaced than Sophie's pride in her ability to play the *Appassionata*. But again Ken's pursuit of his life-plan is vulnerable: we could remove his rod, or we could take the fish from the river he fishes, or ban him from fishing. If we did so, we would be directly interfering with his central life-plan. Indeed, removing an object necessary to someone's performance of his central life-plans without a very compelling reason for doing so will likely be construed (often correctly) as evidence that we do not consider those life-plans valuable, and may be interpreted as a sign of deep disrespect. Assuming that Ken's life-plan is very valuable to him, we have a strong reason not to do so.

Are real-world cases available in which individual identity is bound up in individuals' ability to securely interact with a specific resource, so that removing that ability would present them with a situation where they did not even believe themselves to be the same people any more? A good example might be the Saami people of Scandinavia: roughly sixty thousand members of an indigenous community which has sustained itself for more than a thousand years by herding reindeer.[15] The task of feeding and herding reindeer dictates the movements of *Siidas*—small groups composed of several families—across the seasons. It provides an economic foundation, but more than that it provides a shared life-plan, deeply wrapped up in a specific mode of existence in relation to the physical environment. What we have in this case is a situation where there is an intimate and profound connection between an individual's identity and her ability to securely interact with a specific natural resource. Whilst all of us will have life-plans dependent on the availability of some natural resources (including the objects of our basic rights), some of our life-plans demand secure access to specific natural resources. We don't understand ourselves *as fishermen* or *as hunters* if there are no fish to fish, or no prey to hunt. And we may not understand ourselves as Sioux or Tlingit fishermen or hunters unless certain species—or even certain populations—of fish or prey are available to us. To believe this represents a loss, from the point of view of justice, we do not need to think that cultures are in themselves valuable, or that their 'essential characters' ought to be preserved. The present account makes no such claim. We merely need to take seriously the idea that it matters to individuals that they are able to act on plans which are central to their lives, and that in order to act on such plans secure access to certain resources may be required.

As a matter of legal reality, the various governments of the Scandinavian countries have recognized this in their individual enactments of Saami-specific rights over reindeer herds.[16] These do not typically extend to land ownership, but rather to rights to continue to herd reindeer. Similar accommodations have been made in Canada.[17] Although international law protecting indigenous peoples' lifestyles is weak in many respects, it does clearly purport to defend access to resources where those resources are important to specific ways of life. Elaborating on the 'right to culture'—potentially, for the sake of our argument, a misleading term—defended in Article 27 of the Covenant of Civil and Political Rights, for instance, General Comment 23 suggests that:

> (c)ulture manifests itself in many forms, including a particular way of life associated with the use of land resources, especially in the case of indigenous peoples. [Thus cultural] right might include such traditional activities as fishing or hunting and the right to live in reserves protected by law. The enjoyment of these rights may require positive measures of protection and measures to ensure the effective participation of members of minority communities in decisions which affect them.[18]

The reference to 'culture' here ought not to mislead us into believing that what is at stake are rights to use natural resources for exclusively cultural or symbolic purposes. Rather the Covenant has been used to protect uses of a resource—whether 'economic' or 'cultural' or otherwise—which are essential to the way of life of a particular party.[19]

The connection between specific resources and our life-plans and even identities does not always appear to be as tenuous as Beitz suggests, then. In many cases Beitz may be right that the connection between (individual or national) personality and the mineral deposits buried beneath one's feet is weak. Some natural resources will not even have been discovered, and others will be largely untouched, and will not feature in our projects to any significant degree. It may be that at the level of nation-states the connection will typically be weak (see Chapter 6). But we should not rule out just any attachment-based claims. We can identify particular natural resources which are hugely significant to particular people's sense of agency, and to their ability to carry out projects to which they are deeply wedded. Moreover, it is does not appear difficult to identify cases in which particular resources matter deeply to people, and their identities, even in the absence of discrete projects to make use of them.

5.3. ACCOMMODATING ATTACHMENT

Attachment-based claims will be ill met by undifferentiated redistribution—such as a principle distributing equal, or equality-promoting, shares of natural resource value—since what they typically demand in the real world are rights over *specific resources*.[20] What is at stake is the right to insist that *these* trees should not be cut down, or that *this* agent should continue to be able to herd *those* reindeer. But on the other hand, attachment-based claims cannot be unconstrained by broader considerations of distributive justice. They surely must not, that is, ground unlimited rights over unlimited portions of natural resources. Just how stark a challenge, then, do they pose for conventional theories of natural resource justice?

To make any progress in answering that question we need to be clear about the precise content of attachment-based special claims. Specifically we need to be clear about which rights over natural resources are being claimed, and whether those rights are necessarily exclusive—a move that is, regrettably, not often explicitly made. I distinguished in Chapter 1 a number of rights which an agent might enjoy over a given natural resource, including the right to *access* and non-subtractively use a resource, to *withdraw* and consume resource units, to *manage* a resource, to *exclude* others from its use, to *alienate* it, to *derive income* from it, to *regulate income*, and to *regulate alienation*. Special claims over natural resources will be much more demanding—and will be much harder to justify—if we assume that the only intelligible special claim is a claim to 'full liberal ownership' of a resource, or a full complement of jurisdiction-type rights, comprising an extensive rather than narrow set of rights.

But this is certainly not the only intelligible claim, and indeed it probably does not reflect the spirit of most indigenous resource claims. If my life-plans centrally include an ability to walk in the woods near my home, for instance, that does not require that I own the woods, or that I am able to prevent others from walking in the woods, or that I can derive any or all of the income from the woods. It demands precisely that I can walk in the woods without disruption (it may also be dependent upon the woods being sustainably managed, whether by me or someone else). Likewise, as we saw in section 5.2, someone's ability to live in a rainforest unmolested is compatible with granting outsiders the right to emit greenhouse gases, and hence sharing that rainforest's

124   Justice and Natural Resources

absorptive capacity. Continued and unmolested access, in many such cases, is what is at stake in attachment-based claims. Such claims can therefore be granted without jeopardizing anyone else's claim to share the income or ecosystem benefits arising from the resources in question.

In the case of the Saami, the secure pursuit of central life-plans will require rights beyond mere access. Here the demand seems to be to rights of access (including, notably, a right to traverse Scandinavian national borders which is as old as those borders themselves[21]), but also a share in management, some (limited and sustainable) rights of withdrawal, and the right to derive some income from selling meat, jewellery, and clothing produced from reindeer. But the demand is not to ownership of reindeer, and even so far as it extends it is not necessarily a claim to *exclusive* rights. Management rights over reindeer herds can plausibly be shared, access to the reindeer need not be exclusive so long as access by outsiders does not disrupt herding practices significantly, and so on. Meanwhile the income derived from selling meat, jewellery, and clothing offers a rather basic standard of living to the Saami herders, and is unlikely to trouble those with egalitarian sentiments.[22] Overall, the cluster of rights claimed appears to pose no special obstacle to those who would seek to distribute the benefits and burdens flowing from the world's resources in order to advance equality. Indeed, more than one variety of egalitarianism has grounds for treating our knowledge of the depth of attachment to reindeer or to walks in the woods as a valuable source of information about how wellbeing can be advanced. That point can be made *a fortiori* in cases where the attachment in question does not involve a specific plan to access or use a resource, but rather comprises a feeling of affection towards, or identification with, it. For in these cases the attachment in question is likely to be best respected simply by allowing the resource in question to continue to exist, rather than according agents exclusive rights of ownership. In short, unpacking the precise content of the rights claims implicit in many special claims from attachment immediately renders the question of how they can be accommodated much more tractable, and reveals the potential compatibility of many special claims with protecting access for others, enjoying the benefits of shared management, using some share of income in the broader interests of justice, and so forth.

We ought not, though, to imagine this move is a panacea. Special claims from attachment could conceivably be much more expansive than in the Saami or woods-walking cases. How should we think about the appropriate limits to special claims, then? One obvious constraint is supplied by the injunction that no one ought to be deprived, or deprive others, of natural resources (such as fresh water, or air) which are essential for meeting their basic human rights. If one party's attachment-based claim to control a river has the inevitable consequence that others will imminently face dehydration then it ought to be rejected. It might be objected here, of course, that we should understand the right to control or to securely access particular resource tokens as *itself* a basic human right. I do not believe that we should. It is plausible to suggest that as humans we all have an entitlement to the objects of our basic right to subsistence and in some cases this will imply a (general) right to specific *kinds* of natural resources (i.e. fresh water and clean air). But it is not clear that the same can be said for specific *instances* or tokens of natural resources. No one, I suggest, has a basic human right to continued access to or control over this tree, or that river. There may, to be sure, be good pragmatic reasons for allowing people to meet their basic rights by way of the specific resource tokens they already control and are attached to; if we believe that attachment is important in the way in which I am suggesting then there may be good principled reasons for preferring them to. But this does not take us very far, and in any case those reasons have to be seen as defeasible when the basic rights of others are at stake.

Aside from a basic rights constraint, does egalitarianism place further constraints on the extent to which we should grant special claims from attachment? I believe that it does, but not in the way which is usually suggested. A very common view on the demands of equality with regard to natural resources suggests, roughly speaking, that the distribution of such resources is morally arbitrary, that it wrongly advantages and disadvantages people according to accidents of birth, and that we all have an equal entitlement to share in the benefits and burdens arising from the world's natural resources. That view itself is often linked with what I have called a 'narrow' egalitarian constraint on appropriation which holds that we ought to cease appropriating resources once our share reaches the maximum level which could be symmetrically held by everyone else.

I argued in Chapter 3 that egalitarians ought to reject such a view. There are two general reasons why. First, we should not neglect the divergent ways in which natural resources serve human interests. Why insist on equal shares when those benefits drive wellbeing in unequal ways across persons? Second, the egalitarian ought to be unsatisfied with a situation in which natural resource benefits were equalized in isolation, and without regard to the impact of 'internal resources' or endowments—or, indeed, other social goods which ought to matter to the egalitarian, such as income, inherited wealth, healthcare, or education. In the face of widespread and multifaceted inequalities in important social goods, equal shares of natural resource benefits become unattractive. This renders any narrow proviso on appropriation unattractive too. When we ask the question what quantity of natural resources (or benefits and burdens) individuals ought to be allowed to appropriate, we ought to recognize the utility of allowing agents to appropriate *greater* than equal shares of natural resource benefits insofar as this usefully offsets inequalities in other areas or where it usefully offsets their unequal capacity to convert resources into whatever broader category of advantage we care about. I have called the resulting principle a 'broad' egalitarian proviso.

As with the recognition of the diverse set of rights which attachment claims might in practice target, this theoretical move also establishes that egalitarians are able to be more accommodating towards attachment-based special claims than we might suppose. In cases where an agent is attached to particular resources equality can condone allowing him or her to control a greater than equal share of resources (or resource benefits), or indeed to block the use of a greater than equal share of resources where the attachment in question would be disrupted by their use (see below).[23] This renders the case of indigenous claims to justice more tractable. Such claims often target secure access to large swathes of resources, but they are also, typically, accompanied by substantial inequalities in other goods—by the general poverty and exclusion of indigenous peoples, for instance. There are limits to the degree to which we should embrace substitutability with regard to the goods relevant to egalitarian justice, and if we have a commitment to equal citizenship then we ought not to be wholly content with a situation in which large shares of natural resources 'compensated' for political exclusion. But if indigenous peoples do indeed turn out to have a strong preference for greater than equal resource shares at the expense of, say, income, granting such attachment-based claims is compatible with equality.

* * *

I have suggested so far in this section that quite substantial attachment-based claims to natural resources are compatible with egalitarian justice, and that egalitarians often have good reason to endorse such claims. But this is not to suggest that attachment-based claims will *never* conflict with equality. Indeed, if that were the case my argument would be uninteresting. It is *because* conflicts can occur that we need to know exactly how far egalitarians can go in accommodating such claims. I have suggested that we can go much further than we might at first suspect, if we are prepared to carefully unpick the precise rights targeted by special claims rather than assuming that 'ownership' is the only option on the table, and if we are prepared to apply a broad egalitarian proviso.

But there will still be cases which ask more than egalitarians can, in their capacity as egalitarians, accede to. Even if special claims from attachment do not directly target control over an expansive set of resources, the costs of meeting them could still potentially be very high. In many contentious cases in the real world a claim to exercise control over resource X is contentious not because X describes a large or valuable set of resources, but because control over resource X proves to be incompatible with exploitation of resource Y by others. In legal practice many indigenous land and resource claims appear to take precisely this form, being in essence defensive or 'blocking' claims against logging and oil-extraction activities, for instance, where those activities would seriously disrupt indigenous practices.[24] What is claimed in such cases is that secure access to these trees is incompatible with clearing the forests for agricultural use, or that the enjoyment of traditional fishing practices in these waters is incompatible with exploiting the oil shales of such a stretch of the coastline for petrochemical production. Whilst the claim to those trees or those fish is not in itself especially expansive—and, as such, not directly worrying to egalitarians—the opportunity costs of respecting the claims are high because respecting them will place a block on local or global economic development (development which might itself advance wider goals of justice).

We can imagine, then, a case where there is a definite global interest in the development of the resources contained in a region,[25] but where agent A would prefer such development not to take place because he or she is attached to a particular resource which would be destroyed if development occurred. Such blocking claims, I suggest, should be treated in the same way as direct claims, and as such should also be subject to a broad egalitarian proviso. This has the implication that development of a set of natural resources *can* be blocked by indigenous communities where the benefits and burdens associated with those resources are not so great that no plausible direct claim could be granted over them; and in a context of countervailing disadvantage indigenous communities may be able to make quite large blocking claims. But it is hard to see on what grounds egalitarians could endorse blocking claims which violated even a broad egalitarian proviso. If the block on development has the result that outsiders inevitably become or remain worse off—across the whole range of goods relevant to distributive justice—than agent A, granting such claims would demand, in effect, that we treat the projects of agent A as more important than the projects of outsiders. Even if reasons can be produced for accepting such a result—whether reasons of justice or reasons beyond justice—it is hard to see how egalitarians, *as egalitarians*, could endorse them.

5.4. ATTACHMENT AND JUSTICE

This chapter has suggested that if egalitarians care about people and their diverse interests, then a range of egalitarian accounts also have reason to care about the way in which people form projects which often crucially rely on secure access to specific external objects such as natural resources, or indeed become attached to them more generally. Existing defences of rights over territory, I have suggested, do not automatically extend to and settle the issue of rights over natural resources. But if a number of territorial rights theorists have recently endeavoured to take seriously the desire of many people to maintain access or 'occupancy' over particular sites which have come to matter deeply to them, I have pursued a parallel project with regard to resources, with one qualification: it is the fact of attachment, I suggest, and not the achievement of occupancy or control which commands our attention, and in that sense accommodating attachment can be a transformative rather than a conservative project. But proceeding with that (large) caveat in mind, we can say that, rather than assuming that since the distribution of natural resources is arbitrary there must be nothing to be said, from a moral point of view, in favour of people maintaining (or achieving) access to the resources they are attached to, we ought to care when such attachments persist and seek, within the proper constraints of an egalitarian account, to accommodate them.

But although I have shown that egalitarians both can and should make much more room for attachment-based special claims than has often been recognized, it might be thought that my account still leaves some agents' access to precious resources too vulnerable to the general claims of outsiders. Perhaps where attachment exists we should say something stronger, to the effect that the resources to which an agent is attached should not actually be considered natural resources from the point of view of justice, and hence ought to be entirely immune from programmes of global redistribution. In that way justice—egalitarian or otherwise—would cease to constrain attachment-based special claims at all. Attachment would then become, in fact, grounds for wholesale exclusion.

As I noted in Chapter 1, Avery Kolers has recently defended such a view,[26] but I believe that it is deeply mistaken.[27] On his account, once we recognize the right kind of relationship between a resource and the community which controls it, questions about outsiders' claims on that resource simply do not arise—no matter how vital the countervailing interests of outsiders happen to be. When we recognize these crucial relationships, what we are doing, in effect, is accepting that communities invested in particular resources are entitled to say that they are *not natural resources*. But how do we determine when the requisite relationship exists? We should cease to consider something as a natural resource, from the point of view of justice, whenever the controlling community does not treat it as a mere substitutable good to be traded as a commodity.[28] Whenever a good is not considered (by the community controlling it) to be non-substitutable either across types *or* across tokens—that is, when it cannot be substituted, without loss, with another resource of the same type, or indeed with a resource of a different type—external claims simply become irrelevant. Interestingly, special claims here do not gain force from the intensive use of resources (as, perhaps, in the case of improvement-based special claims), but from their *non*-intensive use. Where a resource is being used non-intensively—and not treated simply as an economic asset to be sold on open markets—this is likely to indicate a depth of attachment which overrides merely economic uses.[29]

But non-intensive use looks likely to be a poor proxy for the existence of morally significant relationships between people and resources, or the significance of specific resources to their wellbeing. It might, after all, simply mean that a given agent is utterly uninterested in a resource, or that they have such a great quantity of natural resources that they could not possibly use them all. It is also unclear how the fact that a given agent considers a natural resource not to be substitutable across *types* suffices to ground a claim to particular *tokens* of a resource (the fact that I have a project dependent on access to water in general does not suffice, surely, to justify a claim over the precise water I currently control, and certainly not over all of it). But most significantly, Kolers's account simply draws the wrong type of conclusion from the existence of attachment to some natural resources. It stipulates that where there is a good claim based on non-intensive use, any broader questions about how to share access to a particular resource are simply voided. That resource (now a non-resource) becomes, in Kolers's words, 'immune to resource justice considerations'.[30] This is a repugnant conclusion, especially in the face of possibly urgent claims from outsiders whose basic rights might be under threat. A more plausible account would seek to accommodate the different claims over resources, and endorse special claims where this is compatible with equality—and where that does not infringe on the basic rights of others—and not simply where we identify the mere *existence* of a certain kind of claim which immediately trumps other claims. Deciding on such cases is not easy, but I have suggested that we will find the task easier if we are prepared to explore more complex ways of sharing rights over resources, and if we are prepared to endorse a broad rather than narrow egalitarian constraint.

I hope to have shown that it is possible to take attachment-based special claims over natural resources seriously without simply disregarding the claims of outsiders. Recognizing a resource's usefulness to others is compatible with recognizing—and, when appropriate, defending—its special significance to some people in particular. If so, we can provide reasons *of* justice to take attachment seriously, rather than immediately seeking to place attachment-based claims *beyond* justice. If we are prepared to advance reasons why we should take attachment seriously from the point of view of justice, then, it seems to me, we can also enhance our understanding of just why colonialism and the forced dispossession of indigenous peoples was so wrong.

ENDNOTES

1. See e.g. Tully 1993.
2. Ypi 2014: 303.
3. This interpretation was suggested to me by Annie Stilz.
4. Margaret Moore's account of territorial rights, for instance, emphasizes the significance of plans which depend upon control over particular objects or places; but it appears only to reckon with the plans of those who are already *in situ*, as opposed to those who seek to access them but are currently unable to. See Moore 2015.

5. See e.g. Rawls 1971: 440 (on confidence in one's abilities); Rawls 2001: 60 (on the 'social bases of self-respect').
6. Simmons 1994, chapter 5. As noted in Chapter 4 of this volume, Simmons considers this focus on purposive projects a development of the labour-mixing view. It is not obvious to me how labour in any meaningful sense is crucial to the view.
7. Stilz 2009: 585.
8. Stilz 2013: 336–7. Though sceptical of attachment-based arguments, in motivating her defence of a Kantian account of provisional claims Ypi (2014: 292) also reaches out to examples whereby a claim promotes a sufficiently important end of agents, or where people unable to stake such claims have their ability to form and act on life-plans undermined.
9. For discussion of the issues addressed in this paragraph, and the possible intellectual bias of some accounts of attachment, I am indebted to Anca Gheaus.
10. Miller 2012: 254; Stilz 2009. A. John Simmons (2012: 5–6) also observes that the 'connection between territorial rights and rights over all resources in the relevant territory is not in any way (morally, physically, conceptually) necessary'.
11. As explained later in section 5.2, the argument I am making does not depend upon attributing value to 'cultures' or to collective identities; the argument from attachment can be persuasively made, I believe, solely with reference to important individual interests.
12. Beitz 1979: 139.
13. Beitz 1979: 138.
14. Eliot 1994: 70.
15. As I noted in Chapter 1, there is ongoing controversy—quite distinct from the question of whether animals can have rights—about whether humans can have rights over wild animals. If the reader thinks not, he or she can imagine examples where the attachment is to rocks or rivers instead.
16. For some useful discussions of the recent history of these rights, see Jentoft, Minde, and Nilsen 2003, chapters 5, 12, and 14.
17. Anaya and Williams 2001: 51.
18. Office of the High Commissioner for Human Rights, General Comment 23 (1994): The Rights of Minorities (Article 27). See: http://www.unhchr.ch/tbs/doc.nsf/0/fb7fb12c2fb8bb21c12563ed004df111?Opendocument.
19. Anaya and Williams 2001: 52.
20. Simmons (2000: 241) claims that denying this 'means denying the actual arguments made by Native American tribes [for instance] for historical rights to particular lands and resources have any moral force at all, or any appeal beyond ungrounded emotionalism'. Typically these claims are claims to the *actual* lands the Native Americans 'lived, hunted, and worked on'.
21. Korsmo 1988.
22. I suspect, in fact, that the attachment-based argument for a right to derive income is less secure than the argument for, for instance, rights to access or manage resources. Specifically, I agree with Simon Green (1989: 18) that if the ability to securely pursue one's own life-plans is what is at stake, then a right to the 'deployment of one's talents' as an artist (to use Green's example) is not obviously intimately tied to, and does not obviously demand, the right to also sell one's

paintings on an open market and keep the proceeds. Thus it might be that a Saami herder could enjoy her life as a herder without being able to sell reindeer goods, so long as she otherwise had the income to get by. That said, we might have other grounds for granting those rights (such as improvement-based claims, or a belief that it would be more efficient, infringe her liberty less, or respect her autonomy more, if we allowed her to earn her own income rather than depending on handouts from others).

23. As Jeremy Waldron (1992: 16) suggests in another context, any such claims cannot of course be granted once and for all and without being subject to future revision. Changes in population, or the scarcity of resources, may affect whether a holding should be considered just.
24. Anaya and Williams 2001.
25. This will not be true in many important cases, including the rainforest case briefly mentioned earlier in section 5.3. In such cases there may be a national interest in 'developing' the forests, but global interests are actually aligned in favour of preservation. Where this is the case, there may be an argument for outsiders sharing the opportunity costs of preservation with locals. See Chapter 10.
26. Kolers 2012.
27. See also Armstrong 2014c.
28. Kolers 2012: 279.
29. Margaret Moore (2012: 88) also argues that 'the capacity to "count" something as a resource is important to collective self-determination'. However, later in the same paper she appears to repudiate the claim that local communities should get to decide whether something counts as a resource or not (2012: 103–4, n. 9).
30. Kolers 2012: 282.

6

Against Permanent Sovereignty

Early in Per Petterson's novel *Out Stealing Horses*, the young protagonist stands looking down into a river running from Sweden into his native Norway and back over the border again. Having grown up in a conservative area in the rural east of Norway, and now craving adventure, the 'foreign' water flowing out of Sweden and then back over the border seems to him to evoke the possibility of escape. Later in his life he recalls looking down into that water and wondering 'whether in some way or other it was possible to see or feel or taste that the water was really Swedish and was only on loan this side of the border'. Of course, he decides, it was not. 'I was so much younger then and didn't know much about the world,' he tells us, 'and after all it was just a fancy.'[1]

Now in one sense it certainly is fanciful to suppose that water flowing from Sweden tastes somehow Swedish. But though we can be sure that the water, or tin, or copper found in Sweden are no different in their properties from the water, or tin, or copper found in Norway, there is one sense in which they are 'Swedish'. They are Swedish in the sense that international law defines them as the preserve of the Swedish people. A number of instruments of international law stipulate clearly and unambiguously that natural resources are at the 'disposal' of the nation-states 'in' or 'under' which they exist. The United Nations' (UN's) (1966) International Covenant on Civil and Political Rights, for instance, states that 'All peoples may, for their own ends, freely dispose of their natural wealth and resources.'[2]

This doctrine, which has come to be known as the doctrine of 'permanent sovereignty' over natural resources, is a powerful organizing principle within world politics. Although we might make the mistake of assuming it to be a natural fact of a world of states, the principle only came to be elaborated and enshrined within international law during the 1950s and 1960s, when it was a highly controversial part of the struggle for decolonization. Whilst many newly independent countries were keen to institute a strong doctrine of permanent sovereignty into international law, major world powers were keen to restrict permanent sovereignty with a set of provisos ensuring that natural resources were used for the wider good, and in the interests of global economic cooperation (for more on these debates, see Chapter 7). Still, the principle continues to have a major effect in constituting what we might call the status quo of the contemporary world order. Individual nation-states enjoy an extensive and often exclusive set of rights over the resources within their territories, albeit with exceptions to that rule arising through voluntary treaty-making.

In a pragmatic sense, then, permanent sovereignty is the default position: any argument for a particular distribution of resource rights will have to contend with the fact that states possess those rights as a matter of legal reality, and are unlikely to give them up easily. It makes sense therefore to engage in a serious critical examination of the doctrine. Even if the world has been made in the image of permanent sovereignty, ought it to be seen as the default position from the *moral* point of view? What, if anything, is its normative basis? Can it be justified? This chapter will identify the best arguments that might be made in favour of the doctrine, and assess whether they are adequate to the task of justifying it. Despite its huge significance within world politics, permanent sovereignty is not often explicitly justified within either international law or political philosophy.[3] As such, the method will partly be one of extrapolation, involving an investigation whether various defences of territorial rights *could* generate a compelling defence of permanent sovereignty.

Four arguments which might potentially support permanent sovereignty will be drawn out—and each, ultimately, will be found to be insufficient to the task. Section 6.1 examines whether nation-states have plausible improvement- or attachment-based special claims over 'their' resources. These would underpin what we called, in Chapter 5, direct arguments for vesting resource rights with nation-states. These two arguments turn out to be of very limited value to the defender of permanent sovereignty. Even if some improvement-based special claims could be made at the level of nation-states, these would apply to some resources and not to others, and moreover are best responded to by granting not full and exclusive rights over all of the natural resources within a territory, but an appropriate share of the income from the relevant resources. In the case of attachment, whilst there are again some plausible special claims within nation-states, these likewise fail to justify granting full and exclusive resource rights to them; they apply to some resources and not to others, do not in any case demand the full set of resource rights, and in the strongest cases actually challenge, rather than support, the brute fact of permanent sovereignty.

Sections 6.2 and 6.3 examine two instrumental arguments, each of which suggests that the doctrine of permanent sovereignty serves an important good which would not be served without it—with the candidates being the good of effective custodianship of resources (section 6.2), and of self-determination (6.3). These arguments also fail; they are compatible with a regime of dispersed control over resources, and do not require or even recommend thoroughgoing

6.1. SPECIAL CLAIMS FROM IMPROVEMENT AND ATTACHMENT

In recent decades rather more attention has been paid to the justification of territorial rights over land than over natural resources more broadly. But whilst not all defenders of territorial rights over land explicitly set out their stall to defend rights over the resources on or under it, it is possible that they provide the conceptual tools for doing so. A variety of nationalist theorists have placed their faith in a justification of national control over land which focuses on the way in which nations or nation-states come to enjoy a particular kind of relationship with it.[4] A first argument draws on improvement-based special claims, and suggests that national communities may have invested a good deal of care and work on the land or on resources more broadly, and as such earned rights over them. A second argument relies on the significance of attachment, and suggests that the attachment which national communities come to form with land (or resources more broadly) is significant from a normative point of view, and that it justifies granting nation-states extensive resource rights. These arguments ground claims on the way the people and the land (and perhaps its resources) have become adapted to each other in a deep way. One variant emphasizes the generation of economic value whereas the other emphasizes the centrality of land and resources to national projects or identities; some nationalist accounts advance a combination of both arguments. We will enquire whether these nationalist accounts could provide the required justification for permanent sovereignty. I will show that they can not.

6.1.1. Improvement-Based National Claims

Perhaps a special claim from 'improvement' might provide us with a reason why nations are entitled to control the resources within their territories. The argument will suggest that nations add value to natural resources over time, and that justice is secured if we therefore place control over those resources in the hands of the nation in question. To get such an argument off the ground we first need to be able to say that a nation has done things to improve land and resources which can be appreciated as improvements according to some universal criteria of material value; examples might include cultivating land, digging wells, draining malarial swamps, making land more productive, and so on.[5] And second, we need to show why (and which) resource rights are an appropriate response.

The argument, though, cannot provide solid backing for anything like the doctrine of permanent sovereignty. First, as we saw in Chapter 4, any argument for permanent sovereignty will be troubled by the fact that the degree of 'cultivation' of resources is very variable. Some resources have been improved but others have not. As a result, improvement-based claims will not support rights over just whatever resources fall within a given territory, but over some subset which have been improved.

Second, when the improvement of resources does occur we have again seen that it is not obvious that it makes sense to attribute this to the national community itself. China has pursued a thoroughgoing policy of buying the natural resources of many African countries, many of which were previously unappropriated. What improvement-based claims could those African countries then make over these resources? They have certainly sold exploration rights to Chinese companies, but pointing to that fact to justify their possession of resource rights in the first place can only beg the question. In a global economy the extraction and refining of natural resources are frequently the preserve of multinational corporations which employ people in many countries, may pay taxes in another country and dividends to shareholders in still further countries. In very few countries is ownership of natural resources by foreigners forbidden, and in the rest the overlap between improvement and national membership will be patchy at best. (We have also seen that, although nationalists might turn to arguments about the way in which nations determine the context in which improvements come to have one exchange value rather than another, those arguments are also undermined to the extent that value is globally determined.)

The third and most significant problem is that even if the improvement-based argument generates a plausible national special claim over resources, it is insufficient to justify allocating exclusive and full resource rights to nation-states. As we have seen, even if we accept the argument from the creation of value through to some kind of national entitlement, we could respond by simply giving nations a right to derive income reflecting that added value (and even here, I suggested, the argument for retaining all of that added value can be embarrassed). Justifying broader property rights on the need to reward improvers—whether we resort to direct or instrumental arguments about the aptness of those rewards—is not easy.

Moreover, consider that the argument under discussion seems to target property-type rights. Even if it was successful (and it seems to be plagued with problems), we would need additional arguments why a regime of individual national *jurisdiction* was also required. One such argument would suggest that granting only property rights to a national community would not allow its members to securely reap the benefits of their labours, since the receipt of these benefits would be left to the whim of whoever held jurisdictional rights. Miller has argued along these lines. 'If a group has added value to territory,' he writes, 'its continued enjoyment of the value it has created will always be insecure unless the territory is controlled by political institutions that represent the group.'[6] If an outside actor can potentially change and change again the rules determining how, when, and under what constraints income from resources will flow back to the rightful recipients, eventual receipt of that income will be highly precarious, and the incentive to improve will diminish.

But the argument from insecurity does not quite establish that a nation ought to enjoy exclusive jurisdictional rights over 'its' natural resources. It merely stipulates that *some* agent should have stable jurisdiction over resources, and that we should be able to construe this agent as a *representative* of the nation with a property-like claim. But why should this be a single agent, and if so why should it be the nation in question? A Kantian might retort that rights over objects such as natural resources are never *ultimately* secure until the civil authority of states is nested within a cosmopolitan international order. If what we are after are stable and just rules of property, then perhaps we ought to commit ourselves to the emergence of such an order.[7] Or we could argue for a layered and multi-level regime of resource governance, by way of which jurisdictional authority was nested across a variety of institutional locations. If that regime upheld stable rules on resources, and adequately represented agents who had created value, that would satisfy the nationalist's claim. In light of those possibilities the case for exclusive national control has not been made.[8]

Indeed, we can turn the insecurity argument on itself: if the point is that for an agent to reliably benefit from its productive efforts it must also exercise a share in jurisdiction over any resources it has improved, then once we acknowledge that the national community is only *one* of the agents capable of increasing the value of a particular resource it is obscure why this jurisdiction should be *exclusively* national. If the value of a given resource is the product of the efforts of nationals, non-nationals, multinational corporations, and so on, then we face the question of how to render secure streams of income to which outsiders could also be entitled. Exclusive national jurisdiction would itself render outsiders' claims vulnerable to national whims.[9] A regime of shared jurisdiction over resources, in which each party was appropriately represented, would likely serve justice better.

6.1.2. Attachment-Based National Claims

Perhaps nations should be given rights over local resources because they (or the individuals who make them up) have integrated control over them into their collective life-plans, and come to understand themselves, as communities, as collections of people who live in a close relationship with this forest or that gold-seam. I suggested in Chapter 5 that the attachment-based argument for resource rights is often credible. Rather than question the validity of attachment-based special claims, I will cast doubt here on whether they can generate a plausible claim for exclusive national control over all the natural resources within a given territory.

First, the kind of strong and enduring attachment we have discussed typically applies to a limited subset of resources, rather than to all resources within a territory. National attachment will be patchy and uneven, and there will be many other resources which simply do not figure in the national imagination in any significant way, and which are in fact relatively neglected. The logic of the attachment-based argument suggests that claims over such resources will be lacking.

Second, strong and enduring attachment appears to be a quality of rather small-scale communities, rather than nations themselves. Consider again the Saami people of Scandinavia: I suggested that here we may have an instance of intimate and profound connection between an individual's identity and his or her ability to securely interact with a specific natural resource. To be sure, it is an open question to what extent any special claims are weakened by the recent 'modernization' of the semi-nomadic Saami existence (with reindeer-herding being transformed by the introduction of two-way radios, snow-scooters, and cross-country motorbikes), or by the gradual 'Scandinavianization' of the Saami (with only an estimated 10 per cent of the community now engaged in herding, or dependent upon it for their upkeep). But in principle the case could provide a plausible basis for attachment-based special claims over some resources. When we shift our focus to nations, though, it does not seem possible to produce examples where a majority of the members of a given nation genuinely identify as part of that nation as a result of their direct relationship with specific natural resources.

Both reasons suggest that although attachment appears capable of generating good special claims over some resources, it is highly unlikely to give us the argument for permanent sovereignty which is being sought. In fact it is worth returning to the concrete political implications of the case, for it is not only true that the specifics of the Saami case fail to transfer substantially to the national case; the case actually challenges the argument for exclusive national control over resources. The rights of the Saami people—like the rights of indigenous peoples in many other parts of the world—are claimed *against* nation-states. The Saami community—like many indigenous communities (or 'non-state peoples') in the Americas—fail to map onto national boundaries. Rather, the Saami land—*Sapmi*—spans Norway, Sweden, Finland, and Russia (as do the reindeer herds themselves, given their seasonal movements). Although the logic of international law has often channelled the claims of indigenous peoples as though they were claims for something like permanent sovereignty over resources, their actual character has often been very different (and frequently much more limited).[10] Through forums such as the Saami Council,[11] the Saami people are able to campaign for equitable treatment across several countries, and during the Council's membership of the World Council of Indigenous Peoples they were able to voice an indigenous challenge to the principle of exclusive national control. In this context, rather than each country granting the Saami control over 'its' reindeer, in granting rights over reindeer and then allowing the Saami to move their herds freely across national borders it may be more accurate to say that each country has, often reluctantly, *relinquished* control over these herds.

So even if the example of indigenous communities supplies cases where plausible claims for resource rights can be made, it does not, typically, bolster the case for national resource rights. Indeed, it appears to undercut it[12] (likewise, we have noted that anyone outside the national community who has developed a symbolic attachment to a given resource—a Canadian Hindu wishing to perform *puja* at the Ganges, for example—can, under the regime of permanent sovereignty, be barred from accessing it at the whim of the local nation-state). The best hope for defenders of national control would presumably be to point towards truly national cases where the same very intense relationship between resources and communal identity can be identified. But it is not clear that such examples can be provided (and it is certainly the case that they have not yet *been* provided by defenders of national control). Rather, it appears likely that insofar as genuinely national attachment to resources exists, it will be both specific to particular resources, and also potentially satisfied by way of limited resource rights. Typical cases may include ones where there is a close connection between specific resources and parts of the landscape—where a specific kind of extractive industry, for instance, has played a key role in a nation's socio-economic development, and where that development has clearly left its mark on the landscape. But such attachments could be respected by granting rights to access such sites, and perhaps rights to continue to derive some income from traditional industries of extraction or husbandry. It is not clear why they would demand a full complement of resource rights, and it is far from clear that such arguments extend to *all* of the natural resources to be found within each national community. In sum, the attachment-based argument appears supremely unlikely to deliver good grounds for full resource rights over all of the resources within a nation-state. It will be partial in both scope and content, and it will deliver conclusions which should give nationalists pause for thought.

6.2 EFFECTIVE STATES

The nationalist arguments canvassed in section 6.1 will not justify permanent sovereignty, but we might try to defend the doctrine on other grounds. An alternative is to focus on the value of effective *states*. Perhaps states secure important goods for individuals, and perhaps it is the case that they are unable to secure those goods unless they are able to exercise effective ownership or jurisdiction (or both) over the resources within their territories. If we can demonstrate that states advance important ends of justice, and that their ability to advance those ends depends upon their having such rights, we will have derived an instrumental argument for states' resource rights. I will examine two such arguments here. The first, which I examine in this section, suggests that giving resource rights to states produces the best outcomes in terms of the conservation and effective use of resources. The second argument, which I examine in section 6.3, suggests that self-determination is valuable, and that insofar as self-determination requires that states retain rights over the resources in their territories, we should allow them to do so.

* * *

Our first instrumental argument focuses on the way in which resources are used—efficiently or otherwise—and suggests that states ought to have rights over resources because this will produce an optimal pattern of resource use. Such an argument might lean on the commonplace claim that assets will deteriorate in value unless they are 'owned' or controlled by a single, specified agent. Rawls drew on such an argument for territorial rights in *The Law of Peoples*, albeit briefly. He suggested that territorial rights might be justified via a parallel with property: much as an asset 'tends to deteriorate' 'unless a definite agent is given responsibility for maintaining it', so a government ought to take responsibility for a territory and for 'maintaining the land's environmental integrity'.[13] By contrast we might endure a 'tragedy of the commons' unless specified parties are allocated an interest in conserving resources and their value. Perhaps this is the reason states ought to possess resource rights: because they will then act as good custodians for those resources, ensuring that they are improved or, where appropriate, conserved.

Rawls's instrumental argument is scant and underdeveloped. But even as it stands, there are three points that need to be borne in mind. First, it is not obvious why we would take Rawls's argument to support extending *all* resource rights to individual states. Elinor Ostrom's pioneering work established that there are many examples of communal 'proprietorship' rather than ownership over natural resources in which resources are effectively and sustainably used and managed. Proprietors enjoy rights to access and manage resources, along with some rights to withdraw from the common stock, but do not enjoy rights to alienate them or even necessarily to derive income from them. Nevertheless, granting agents these more limited rights is often sufficient to provide an incentive for effective, sustainable use.[14] Likewise, Rawls's argument appears to suggest that states ought to have *an interest* in safeguarding the future of local resources. But it does not pause to establish that this must comprise full ownership, say, as opposed to more limited income rights. Moreover, even if there was a sound argument for granting some income rights to states, it is unclear why they must also be accompanied by exclusive jurisdictional rights. As we saw in section 6.1, the insecurity argument for exclusive national jurisdiction fails to show that states must have such rights in order to possess an incentive for improvement.

Second, note an odd reversal in Rawls's argument. The economic argument he picks up is actually an argument intended to establish the superiority of *individual* ownership over the inefficiency and wastefulness of state or communal control. This argument standardly suggests that individual ownership is necessary to provide an incentive for resources to be conserved or improved, whereas communally held assets will tend to deteriorate in value, at least relatively.[15] It is unclear just which conclusion Rawls is driving at, but it seems a fair interpretation to say that the goal is in fact some kind of communal ownership. Economists will be unconvinced, as their view is precisely that communal ownership is inefficient. What is important is that individual property rights are secure, which in principle would require some kind of regulation (whether by states or by some local or international authority). But state ownership of resources is not their target. None of this is to say that the economists are right; but it is to say that it is far from obvious how Rawls can support his own argument by leaning on evidence which is usually held to serve the opposite conclusion.

Third and most importantly, the claim that the optimal custodianship of resources will come once we grant exclusive rights over them to individual states is ill-considered both in light of the shared nature of some important resources, and in light of common global challenges centring on the exploitation or conservation of natural resources. Consider, for instance, that many important pools of resources span state borders. Important examples include the oceans, watercourses such as rivers and aquifers, and populations of migratory species of birds, mammals, and fish. Managing those resources is a significant challenge. But any response to that challenge which emphasizes untrammelled state control is destined to failure.[16] A wealth of literature on environmental governance has investigated the prospects for managing natural resources so as to secure efficiency, sustainability, and equity. In that literature the dominant view is that management serves these ends best when there is a close 'fit' between resource sets or ecosystems on the one hand, and systems of human governance on the other; this is the substance of the much-discussed 'matching principle' within environmental governance.[17] Ostrom also suggested that governance tends to be more successful when the set of users of a particular resource coincides with the set who can exercise accountable decision-making over its use.[18]

In light of resource governance challenges, then, there is no particular reason why settings such as the nation-state should be seen as superior. It is true, of course, that nation-states often possess the political power to make and enforce binding agreements. But it is also true, contrary to Rawls's hope, that they have tended to exercise that power very ineffectively when it comes to resource governance. One reason is that ecosystems simply do not coincide with national boundaries. Indeed, considered from the point of view of ecosystems, the 'national' level is hardly an intelligible level of governance at all: 'nation-states' encompass tiny states with human populations of under a million, and vast states with populations of over a billion. In terms of their resources and ecosystems they run from the small and homogeneous to the huge and highly diverse.[19]

None of this is to deny that effectively managing resources beyond the state is a formidable undertaking, not least in the absence of binding global authority. Nevertheless, Ostrom demonstrated that cooperation to manage precious resources has frequently emerged in circumstances in which a strong and binding authority—a precondition for the resolution of social dilemmas according to conventional theory—is lacking. Effective monitoring, conflict-resolution mechanisms, and systems for graduated sanctioning can generate positive outcomes even in the absence of strong authority. Considering large and urgent challenges—such as climate change—Ostrom suggested that, although the emergence of a strong and binding authority might be preferable, it should prove unnecessary for substantial progress to be made. In particular, she emphasized the salience of experiments in 'nested' or 'polycentric' governance under which apparently fragmented and overlapping systems of cooperation have nevertheless repeatedly proved capable of delivering effective outcomes.[20]

Fortunately, in response to a series of challenges, cross-border management schemes have proliferated in recent decades, resulting in a mosaic of transnational resource governance with overlapping jurisdiction and mixed—but nevertheless often significant—degrees of success. A key example in which transnational governance developed remarkably early is that of watercourses. Nearly half of the land surface of the planet can be considered as part of one international river basin or another, and the water from those basins accounts for roughly 60 per cent of global freshwater supply.[21] More than 220 nation-states share watercourses with a neighbouring country.[22] The de facto transnational sharing of water has been accompanied by a growing body of international law which has, since the 1920s and 1930s, eschewed any idea of exclusive national ownership of or jurisdiction over river water, and adopted instead a principle of 'equitable and reasonable utilization' which aims to adjudicate overlapping claims.[23] Unlimited state sovereignty has long been seen as a gross error in the case of precious water resources.[24]

But the growth in the transnational governance of water is far from unique. More broadly, perhaps the most sustained and coordinated programme of transnational resource governance has emerged under the auspices of the European Union (EU). The EU has been instrumental in resolving—or at least mitigating—a series of collective action problems over resource use. Even if individual states have little incentive to adopt expensive principles of environmental regulation, the knowledge that like rules will be applied to all EU member-states makes them much less costly.[25] More complex forms of global and transnational resource governance have already delivered results, and if humanity is to use scarce resources wisely, and respond effectively to major global problems such as climate change, surely these will be only the first of many experiments in resource governance beyond the state. Whatever the prospects for such institutional innovations, and whatever the prospects for developing any specific mechanism of enforcement and monitoring at the global level, it is already abundantly clear that resolution of a series of massive challenges concerning environmental integrity and sustainable resource use are not, as Rawls claimed, best met by leaving exclusive resource control in the hands of individual states. If Rawls's *Law of Peoples* was criticized as posing a set of rules for a 'vanished Westphalian world',[26] this little-inspected part of the argument forms an important exemplar. Fortunately, states themselves have begun to recognize this, and, in key cases such as freshwater management, have long since restricted their own permanent sovereignty in favour of transnational governance structures. Our success in meeting a series of environmental challenges depends upon such practices becoming much more widespread, with the likely result that the state level will be, at best, one level of resource governance amongst many.[27] Even if states have a role to play, then, the goal of ensuring the sustainable or effective use of resources will not be achieved under a regime of exclusive sovereignty over those resources. A proper concern for that goal is likely to undermine, rather than strengthen, support for permanent sovereignty as a practice.

6.3. RESOURCE RIGHTS, SELF-DETERMINATION, AND BASIC RIGHTS

Our second instrumental argument emphasizes the useful functions that self-determining states perform. On a 'functionalist' view, well-ordered states are required in order that the basic rights or needs of citizens can be met.[28] Specifically, on one version, states are necessary to 'provide a unitary and public interpretation of the rights of individuals and to enforce those rights in a way that is consistent with those individuals' continued freedom and independence from one another'.[29] If we did not have states, individuals' basic rights or needs would go without adequate protection. But their performance of key roles may require them to possess certain territorial rights. Specifically, protecting the basic rights of citizens might require them to exercise ownership or jurisdiction over the natural resources within their territories.

If we are to assess the prospects for such an argument underpinning something like permanent sovereignty, our critical focus must fall on the question whether states' ability to protect their citizens' basic needs actually depends upon the full and exclusive rights over the natural resources within their territories which permanent sovereignty bestows.[30] If we accept for the sake of argument that a state which secures its members' basic needs is (at least minimally) legitimate, we still need a precise account of just which rights over which resources are necessary to meet citizens' basic needs.

A very strong claim would hold that states simply require exclusive rights over all the natural resources within their borders in order to enjoy self-determination and hence be able to secure justice.[31] That claim would be impossible to sustain, however, in terms of either property rights or jurisdictional rights. We can easily imagine a regime of mixed individual (including foreign), common and state ownership in which the state regulated the extraction, exchange, and expatriation of resources, and perhaps taxed owners at each stage, without claiming for itself the status of owner; it would be much too strong to suggest that a state in this scenario would not enjoy self-determination, or that it would be unable to secure citizens' basic needs. Likewise, as we noted in section 6.1.1. in response to the argument from insecurity, there is no reason to suppose that exclusive jurisdiction is necessary for states to perform core functions. States have in fact placed many constraints upon their own authority by signing international instruments, and joining international organizations, governing the use of, for instance, fisheries, trans-boundary waterways, and hazardous chemicals.[32] We have also witnessed the gradual emergence in international law of a set of duties accompanying permanent sovereignty which, although at present rather weak, seeks to constrain the ways in which states exploit natural resources. Examples include the duty to respect the rights and interests of indigenous peoples, the duty to equitably share trans-boundary natural resources, and the duty to use resources sustainably, amongst others.[33] Sovereignty over natural resources has not therefore been a static and absolute phenomenon, but one which has been constrained by the partial sharing of sovereignty over resources between states and by the parallel growth in duties under international law.[34] But if those moves are compatible with states meeting the basic rights of their members—which they appear to be—the strong claim fails. Protecting basic rights might be facilitated by granting states some resource rights, but it does not appear to demand a full and unqualified set of rights.

A further difficulty is as follows. If the basis of state claims under the functionalist view is the necessity of meeting basic rights, it is unclear why it would not support, for individual states, rights over precisely those resources necessary to meeting basic rights, as opposed to all of the resources within a territory. There could conceivably be communities in which the (rather meagre) quantity of natural resources available was precisely sufficient to meet basic needs. But in many communities there will be a surplus—and often a very considerable surplus—which is not necessary for meeting basic rights. Why grant rights over *these* resources to local states? The question becomes more pointed when we recognize that there may be some communities in which the resources available are *in*sufficient to meet basic rights. Here it is an interesting question whether the functionalist account might underpin claims on *other* states' resources, and in so doing limit the permanent sovereignty of those states, if transfers of resources were necessary for well-ordered states to exist elsewhere. The functionalist account, in the end, appears to demand relatively little in the way of resource rights. The one thing it certainly does demand is an entitlement to the natural resources needed to meet citizens' basic rights. But that is compatible with—and in cases of shortfalls in some states may *demand*—constraints on permanent sovereignty.

* * *

In recent years some defenders of self-determination have, in fact, presented more modest claims about which resource rights flow from a commitment to self-determination. In particular, some of them have suggested that self-determination does not require that states retain the income—or at least all of the income—derived from domestic resources. States' claims over income might turn out to be weak for just the kinds of reasons canvassed in section 6.1.1; and if so, defending self-determination is, according to some theorists, compatible with sharing income from domestic resources. Nevertheless *control* rights—including, roughly speaking, rights to determine whether and how resources are to be used—are allegedly closer to the heart of self-determination, and accordingly less negotiable. If global justice theorists would agree to leave control rights where they are, and defenders of self-determination relinquished national claims over income, a rapprochement appears possible.[35] In fact at least one global justice theorist has made a similar move. Thomas Pogge suggests that his Global Resources Dividend, while sharing income with the world's poor, 'confers no right to participate in decisions about whether or how natural resources are to be used and so does not interfere with national control over resources'. It does not, for instance, interfere with states' ability to decide whether particular resources should be extracted or consumed or not.[36]

The move by self-determination theorists to relinquish claims to full income rights is valuable, and suggests that global taxes on natural resources are not as inimical to self-determination as some critics of global egalitarianism have claimed.[37] Nevertheless egalitarians cannot in good conscience accept the attempted rapprochement between global justice and self-determination. This is because we should not, in fact, condone 'leaving' full control rights over natural resources with the states in which they fall. This is for three reasons. First, even if it is true that it is important, for the collective life of a state, that it is able to exercise some control over the way in which resources are used, it will plausibly be important for many sub-national (and sometimes transnational) communities to exercise such control too. Indeed, some defences of state control have actually traded on the centrality of some resources to the lives of national minorities or indigenous communities when arguing for a presumption of state control over resources. For instance, Margaret Moore has argued that attention to the significance of specific rules over resource use to communal ways of life generates a normative 'presumption in favour of state control'. But the examples Moore produces of communal connection to specific resources actually undermine rather than underpin claims to control on the part of nation-states. Those examples (the Lakota Sioux, and cultural minorities in New Zealand and Papua New Guinea) concern communities engaged in struggles to wrest control over resources *away* from the local state, and usually unsuccessfully at that.[38] This is ill-considered in light of the fact that state control—and permanent sovereignty more broadly—is a licence to disregard such claims (and a licence which has been exercised freely). We must therefore concede the possibility that taking the value of self-determination seriously speaks in favour of constraints on state authority, rather than a world in which states monopolize jurisdictional or meta-jurisdictional authority.

Second, I argued in section 6.2 that there are compelling reasons to favour a dispersal of management rights over a variety of resources to the transnational and even global level, rather than accepting a regime under which decisions whether and how to exploit resources are vested with nations or states. As I have suggested, the state level coincides poorly with the ecosystems which sustain many precious natural resources. Far from state control being a boon to efficient or effective use, granting states control over resources which correspond poorly at best with state boundaries has often intensified their exploitation. In such cases transnational and sometimes global resource management appears likely to deliver better consequences for sustainability and intergenerational justice (see Chapter 9).

Third and finally, states' ability to make decisions about how to exploit resources must be constrained in order to prevent unjustifiable harms to the interests of outsiders. We are only gradually realizing the many ways in which states' exploitation of natural resources can impact, sometimes very seriously, upon outsiders. In recent years key decisions and instruments of international law have therefore emphasized the need to balance the general principle of state control over resources with the interests of non-citizens and with the requirements of sustainability and intergenerational justice. One example would be the duty to equitably share resources which span the borders of more than one state; the greatest progress here has been made in the case of trans-boundary watercourses. But even the exploitation of resources which are not 'shared' in this sense can have a great impact upon outsiders. In Chapter 10 I will discuss cases in which the exploitation of natural resources in one state can cause significant harms in others. Although duties under international law to limit such harms are rather weak, it is again plausible that recognition of such harms recommends further qualification of any unconstrained right of states to make decisions about how and whether to exploit the resources within their territories.

6.4. CONCLUSIONS

In recent years discussion of the territorial rights of nation-states has come on in leaps and bounds. Several things have become obvious during this time. One is that defending states' territorial rights is not easy, not least in the face of the claims of outsiders. To the contrary, if defending the interests of individuals is what we care about, granting states strong territorial rights is a blunt instrument indeed. It may once have been assumed that defending the territorial rights of states was a rather simple enterprise, but whilst the sophistication of defences of territorial rights is increasing, so too are the challenges they have to face becoming more apparent.

A second conceptual advance has been the recognition that the traditional elements of a state's territorial rights—standardly comprising rights to exercise control of borders, to maintain jurisdiction over a territory, and to control resources—are not as tightly intertwined as was once thought. Each, potentially, requires a separate justification. This chapter has investigated the prospects for defending one element of a state's territorial rights, as understood within contemporary international law. It is now clear that defending permanent sovereignty over natural resources is fraught with difficulties. Although nations may possess some good claims over natural resources, the institution of permanent sovereignty is a legal sledgehammer sent to crack a moral nut. Nationalist arguments from attachment do not come close to justifying permanent sovereignty, and permanent sovereignty in effect gives states licence to disregard the attachment-based claims of sub- or transnational communities whose members may be deeply attached to some resources. Arguments from improvement appear ill-equipped to justify giving states either full ownership rights or full jurisdiction-type rights, and as we have seen, the need for stable property rules could in principle be met by way of a variety of institutions below or beyond the state. Functionalist arguments based on self-determination and basic rights cannot justify anything like permanent sovereignty either. Functionalist arguments from conservation and effective use, if taken seriously, would tend to support a dispersal of resource rights *away* from nation-states, across a variety of institutional settings. Meanwhile the claims of sub- or transnational communities to exercise some influence over decisions on resource use are ill-met in a regime which grants states such extensive powers. Each of these arguments is compatible with a world of multiple memberships and dispersed authority over resources. Indeed, such a dispersed regime of resource rights will likely serve justice better than the existing regime of permanent sovereignty.

Now consider a striking fact about the argument of this chapter so far. We have considered four arguments which appear to offer the best available justifications for permanent sovereignty, and found them wanting. Introducing special claims does not speak in favour of permanent sovereignty, but in favour of granting quite limited rights which in any case are at least partly orthogonal to any national claims. Similarly, taking citizens' basic rights, or conservation, seriously speaks in favour of distinctly limited rights for states, and suggests that constraints on states' permanent sovereignty are both allowable and, indeed, desirable.

The striking fact is that we have managed to undermine permanent sovereignty without even invoking general claims. I have *not* suggested that permanent sovereignty is unjustified because it denies individuals equal—or equalizing—shares of resources. Neither have I invoked the spectre of bloody history, and suggested that permanent sovereignty is undermined by the facts of colonialism, resource grabs, and the sheer historical brutality of the drawing of boundaries. Rather, I have examined each of the four arguments on their merits and shown, in each case, that following the logic of the argument leads us *away* from, rather than towards, exclusive permanent sovereignty over resources. Even without invoking wider claims of justice—even if improvement, attachment, the protection of citizens' basic rights, or the effective use of resources are all that we care about—permanent sovereignty is found wanting.

But if we relax this rather massive constraint on the argument and allow broader claims of justice their due weight, the sheer clumsiness of permanent sovereignty in serving justice becomes undeniable. If our question is whether permanent sovereignty offers the best possible integration of special and general claims over natural resources, the answer is resoundingly negative. For the regime of permanent sovereignty simply ignores the claims of outsiders, insofar as it restricts any benefits from resources to members of the nation-states in which they happen to lie. Moreover, as we shall see in Chapter 10, it localizes some important burdens even when doing so intensifies inequality. This familiar plank of the contemporary world order has to be seen as a considerable obstacle to the pursuit of justice.

ENDNOTES

1. Petterson 2006: 40.
2. For the full text, see http://ohchr.org/en/professionalinterest/pages/ccpr.aspx.
3. That is evident in the wording of the 1966 Covenant cited in note 2, for instance, which does not provide any reasons supporting permanent sovereignty. The only clue we have is the fact that the clause about permanent sovereignty is included in an article (Article 1) about self-determination. We consider the connection between permanent sovereignty and self-determination in section 6.4.
4. See for instance Moore 2015; Meisels 2003; and Miller 2007. For an account which is not ostensibly nationalist but nevertheless shares some features with that account, see Kolers 2009.
5. Miller 2012: 259.
6. Miller 2012: 263.
7. Ypi 2014.
8. For a useful critical discussion of Miller's insecurity-based argument, see Angell 2013.
9. As we will see in Chapter 7, this was precisely the heart of the debate about permanent sovereignty in the 1950s: colonial powers claimed that foreign investment—and the smooth functioning of the global economy—were incompatible with nations' ability to change the rules of the game at will (at least without significant compensation). I am not endorsing their position, which appears to have been largely self-serving. Rather, I am pointing out that *if* what we care about is the ability of agents to recoup the proceeds of improvement, then in a global economy this may count *against* unqualified national jurisdiction rather than for it.
10. For a good account of the way in which Saami claims have often failed to challenge the overwhelming fact of state sovereignty in Scandinavia, see Korsmo 1988.
11. See http://www.saamicouncil.net.
12. This fact has not been recognized by defenders of nation-states' claims. For example, as I note in section 6.4, in supporting what she calls a 'presumption of state control', Margaret Moore actually leans on examples of sub-national communities which exist in an often antagonistic relationship with local states, and have claimed resource rights against them (often unsuccessfully). Moore 2012.
13. Rawls 1999: 8; also Rawls 1999: 38–9. See also Moore 2012.
14. Ostrom 2003.
15. For an example of that kind of argument, see Smith 1981: 467: 'the only way to avoid the tragedy of the commons is to end the common property system by creating a system of private property rights' in natural resources such as wildlife.
16. For a good recent argument to that effect, with specific reference to migratory species, see Mancilla 2016.
17. See e.g. Butler and Macey 1996.
18. Ostrom 1990.
19. Young 2002.
20. Ostrom (2010: 552) notes that, within a domestic setting, polycentric systems in which a number of potentially overlapping authorities endeavour to deliver public

goods or other public services have tended to *outperform* more unified systems. According to Ostrom, such apparently chaotic (or non-hierarchical) systems 'tend to enhance innovation, learning, adaptation, trustworthiness, levels of cooperation of participants, and the achievement of more effective, equitable, and sustainable outcomes at multiple scales'.

21. Wolf 1998.
22. Gleick 1998b: 577.
23. McIntyre 2007; Dellapenna 2003.
24. Note also the UN's recent emphasis on developing policy frameworks for the management of what it designates Shared Natural Resources, such as water, which are held to be inadequately protected by a regime of primarily national control. See http://www.internationalwaterlaw.org/bibliography/UN/UNILC/. For an argument that proposals for shared sovereignty over rivers might be applied to other resources too, see Nine 2014.
25. For useful comparative studies, see Vig and Faure 2004. See also McCormick 2001, chapter 9.
26. Buchanan 2000.
27. This conclusion coincides with influential defences of 'cosmopolitan governance' in which decision-making power is dispersed across a variety of institutional locations, see for instance Held 1995; Caney 2005a, chapter 5.
28. For an influential statement of a functionalist view of legitimacy, see Buchanan 2003.
29. Stilz 2009: 580. Cara Nine (2012: 41) also claims that a state may acquire territorial rights if the acquisition 'is necessary for the provision of members' basic needs [and] does not prevent others from meeting their basic needs'.
30. Stilz (2009: 573) is not sure that it does (at least by itself), and suggests that by contrast to the right to territorial jurisdiction over land, any putative rights to control resources 'requires a more complex justification'.
31. Nine 2008: 272.
32. In the case of hazardous chemicals the most famous example of successful transnational regulation is probably the regime for the control of Chlorofluorocarbons (CFCs) which emerged in the late 1980s, beginning with the Montreal Protocol of 1987. For an historical account, see Morrisette 1989.
33. See Schrijver 1997, chapter 10.
34. For a more general account of the functional dispersal of sovereignty in the contemporary world, see Slaughter 2004. For some forceful objections to the idea that the sovereignty of the state cannot be either practically or conceptually shared across a variety of institutions, see Pogge 2002: 178–81.
35. Angeli 2015, chapter 5; Moore 2015.
36. Pogge 2001: 66.
37. See e.g. Miller 2012.
38. Moore 2012.

7

Perfecting Sovereignty?

The most likely principled defences of permanent sovereignty as an organizing principle within world politics are, I have argued, inadequate to the task of justifying it. In fact permanent sovereignty appears to be a serious obstacle to justice, insofar as it is ill-placed to respond to the challenge of effectively managing the world's resources, and inasmuch as it entrenches inequality. We might draw parallels here with other criticisms of states' territorial rights. In a world in which the advantages (including natural resources) available to people vary wildly in line with their political membership, the ability of states to exclude outsiders preserves inequality.[1] But permanent sovereignty plays a similar role. Whereas closed borders lock people out (at the discretion of the state), permanent sovereignty locks resources in (at the discretion of the state), helping to ensure that advantage tracks the facts of (political control over) geography.

Moreover, the mechanisms by which states achieve outward-facing authority over natural resources are morally undiscriminating; whilst states from time to time refuse to buy resources from one another, such refusals are comparatively rare. Even at the height of the Cold War, American citizens continued to drive automobiles fuelled by Soviet oil, propping up the economy of their great enemy in the process.[2] By and large the most valuable natural resources are traded as global commodities on a 'might makes right' basis. Just whoever controls a territory, no matter how just or how legitimate their rule, is legally entitled to sell the resources to be found within that territory, and this can open up enormous streams of income.[3] At the time of writing five of the world's nine highest-income countries (ranked by GDP per capita) are oil exporters with undemocratic and frequently abusive governments.[4]

Still, we might be forgiven for hesitating before embracing the bold conclusion that permanent sovereignty ought to be transcended. After all, it is not only the rich countries of the world which have supported state sovereignty over resources. In the wave of decolonization which reached its peak in the 1950s and 1960s, poor countries argued vociferously that gaining control over 'their' natural resources would be key to domestic economic development, and a linchpin for the establishment of a much-vaunted New International

Economic Order that would allow them to throw off the economic, and not just the political, shackles of the West. That fact has given some—including Thomas Pogge and Leif Wenar—pause for thought. Both suggest that, if reducing global injustice is our goal, we ought to focus on urgent reforms to the everyday practice of permanent sovereignty—reforms which fall far short, however, of abandoning it. Significantly neither Pogge nor Wenar explicitly reject global egalitarian principles. But they do suggest that, even if we accept those principles, our practical focus should be on certain urgent reforms to permanent sovereignty which do not fundamentally challenge it as an institution. Wenar's account, in particular, might be thought to pose a 'pragmatic' challenge to more ambitious reforms: our priority, he suggests, should *not* be to effect radical reforms to the prerogatives of sovereign states, but rather to ensure that a governing principle of world politics—that natural resources belong to 'the people', and ought to be used in their interests—is properly realized. Even if promoting some brand of global equality is our goal, we ought to work to more fully realize the potentially radical normative principle of popular resource sovereignty, rather than attempting more ambitious but less certain reforms. Our objective should be to make popular control over resources a reality.

Section 7.1 examines these more modest 'accountability' reforms, and shows that global egalitarians can offer conditional support to them, although we must necessarily see them as but one part of the picture in moving towards natural resource justice. As such they can supplement, but cannot replace, other reforms egalitarians have reason to support. Section 7.2 assesses the claim that accountability reforms are to be favoured because they score highly on grounds of political accessibility. We *could* respond to the claim that theorists ought to take accessibility seriously by asserting that political theorists need not pay attention to empirical facts when investigating the character of normative principles. If such facts matter they do so at the level of implementation, we might say, and working out the most appropriate steps to take towards their realization might best be left to social scientists. But that is not the move I make here. My response to the 'pragmatic' challenge has two parts. On the one hand, I agree that the urgency of tackling global poverty and inequality means that investigating what the next steps on the road to reform ought to be is a hugely important task that theorists can ill ignore (even if we might not possess all of the answers). Amongst the reforms I explore in Chapters 8, 9, and 10, a central role is therefore played by reforms which could be advanced by way of institutions which already exist. This is not to say that we should not also call for the creation of new institutions; to refuse to do so would objectionably tie our hands. Neither should we restrict our attention to reforms on which there is already substantial agreement and for which the requisite political will already exists: that would also be an abrogation of the job of the egalitarian theorist, who must be prepared to demand (and help engender) support for policies that can at present appear rather distant. But it is nevertheless well worthwhile showing that many reforms which would bring about a more equal world could be achieved by way of existing institutions; moreover, as I will demonstrate in the following chapters, we can also usefully show that substantial political support often does exist for them, not least in the developing world. In that sense part of my response to the pragmatic challenge is a positive one.

But part of my response to the pragmatic challenge will be more critical. It might be thought that even if egalitarians can identify promising reforms which would have welcome redistributive consequences, the accountability reforms proposed by Wenar in particular are far *more* accessible, in the sense that they only require us to act on principles which are already endorsed across the world, including within international law. Section 7.2, though, raises some doubts about the accessibility of these reforms, which suggest that the pragmatic advantage they enjoy over some egalitarian alternatives is not as great as we might suppose.

Section 7.3 then looks more closely at the political history of permanent sovereignty. Wenar performs a service in reminding us of the ambitions of countries fighting to overthrow colonial rule. Indeed, the suggestion is that his proposals would continue the struggle for popular control that these countries were engaged in. But this section shows that it would be a mistake to view the achievement of permanent sovereignty as an isolated goal for newly independent countries, because their goals were in fact both narrower and broader than that. Narrowly these countries wanted to establish, under international law, the supremacy of domestic law in determining the rights of overseas investors. More broadly these countries believed that the desired brand of permanent sovereignty would, *when nested in a broader set of global reforms*, allow them to make rapid economic advances. On both scores, as I show, they have been very sorely disappointed. Resurrecting some of these ambitions may well be a valuable project. But taken by themselves, accountability reforms will not do anything to promote them. Doing so will bring us beyond the goal of perfecting sovereignty and closer, in fact, to some of the erstwhile goals of global egalitarians. Section 7.4 draws together several conclusions.

7.1. THE SALIENCE OF ACCOUNTABILITY

When surveying the world around us, we seem to face a puzzle. On the one hand international law—including legal instruments ratified by most of the world's countries, from the US to Russia, Brazil to Ethiopia—seems to hold that natural resources belong to 'the people'. On the other hand resources are regularly sold from under the noses of those people by brutal and unaccountable dictators, after which they end up as components in the mobile phones used by Western citizens, or fuelling the cars driven by people in China, Canada, or Chad. It is a depressingly familiar story that in many cases natural resource rents barely touch the sides of state coffers before wending their way to Swiss bank accounts held in the names of family members of tyrants and despots.[5] Indeed, the very fact that we are so undiscriminating when we buy natural resources may incentivize coup attempts, since would-be dictators know that should they attain power, money will begin to flow which would allow them to recoup their costs and continue to arm themselves against challengers.[6] What then of the interests of the people?

Both Pogge and Wenar claim that if we want to make natural resource wealth work for the poor of the world, a priority should be to act so as to interrupt this depressing flight of resource rents, which flow from the world's consumers, via multinational corporations, into the hands of dictators in resource-rich countries, and frequently out of the country in turn. Specifically, we might simply stop buying natural resources from governments which do not meet certain standards of accountability to their citizens. After all, Wenar suggests, buying resources from those who we do not consider to be the rightful owners of natural resources is tantamount to receiving stolen goods. Refusing to buy such goods appears to be morally required if we consider them to belong to 'the people'. The details of their concrete proposals can be outlined very briefly. On Pogge's version, developing countries should pass constitutional amendments making clear that resources can only be sold by democratic governments, sending a clear signal to outside buyers to cease trade should non-democratic governments subsequently come to power.[7] On Wenar's version, we ought to cease purchasing resources from countries failing to meet minimal standards of accountability, by way of which citizens can obtain information about resource sales, openly discuss them, and, if appropriate, object to them.[8] Regimes which do not meet these basic standards should be barred from the resource trade. Should other countries continue to trade with them, we might place tariffs on imports from those third countries and hold the proceeds in a 'Clean Hands Trust' to be discharged to resource-exporting countries at such time as they meet the desired standards of public accountability over resources.[9] On either proposal, we would intervene powerfully to realign the incentives for good or bad governance within many developing countries. Coups and dictatorships would be less profitable not only for potential civil warriors, but also for multinational corporations, which would now have an incentive to do anything they could to encourage the emergence of accountable resource governance.

We might find a variety of reasons for supporting such reforms. We could endorse them because of their likely contribution to the alleviation of poverty or inequality, because they might promote accountable governance, or perhaps because the integrity of Western consumers demands that they should not buy resources from regimes they consider illegitimate representatives of their people.[10] Significantly, both theorists claim that support for their proposals does not require any deep acceptance of the idea of national ownership. Pogge indicates that his proposals for putting natural resources to work in alleviating poverty could be endorsed by global egalitarians, statists, libertarians, and others; their founding assumptions are relatively modest and capable of generating overlapping consensus at the theoretical level.[11] Wenar suggests that global egalitarians can and should endorse his proposal to entrench popular property rights and establish a Clean Hands Trust, because they 'will certainly condemn dictators and civil warriors seizing natural resources by force in underdeveloped countries. The approach here will push the highly unequal pattern of control over resources toward greater equality among individuals around the world.'[12]

Taken by itself, that judgement is plausible: *insofar* as accountability reforms push us towards greater intra-national equality, we have reason to support them. By the same token, global egalitarians should be sympathetic towards the many proposals for greater transparency in international resource sales, to the extent that they appear likely to promote greater sharing of resource rents.[13] The same can be said for proposals for greater public involvement in planning, and budgeting around, resource extraction.[14]

Still, there are reasons for caution. As a means of testing our judgements here, consider two ideal-types of regime. In the first a government fails to meet the relevant standards of public accountability over resources, but nevertheless shares resource rents fairly between citizens. In the second, by contrast, a government is properly accountable to its citizens but fails to share rents fairly. On the first example—the unaccountable but distributive regime—the proposals under review indicate that we should cease trade, even though resource revenues find their way fairly to all citizens. Is this the right judgement? The answer clearly depends on what we want the proposals to achieve. Are they proposals primarily aimed at advancing accountability, or at advancing distributive justice? If they are proposals aimed at advancing accountability, we might tolerate cessations of trade that actually set back the material interests of many citizens in developing countries, at least in the short to medium term. But if our concern is (at least partly) for the material prospects of citizens, this would be a worrisome conclusion.

The first ideal-type is too other-worldly. Although some dictatorships are reasonably distributive (here Brunei might be a good example), none of them are perfectly so. But even in mildly distributive dictatorships, the thoroughgoing cessation of resource trade could have regrettable effects. Scott Wisor has pointed out that placing an across-the-board embargo on resource imports from countries blighted by dictatorship would not only deprive dictators of income, but would have the same impact on many poor citizens—including people relying on small-scale mining operations for their subsistence, for example. We might do much better, in light of that fact, to pursue a more fine-grained sanctions policy rather than removing the right of societies with unaccountable rulers to trade in resources at all. If so, we would endorse not across-the-board cessation, but a system which could properly 'distinguish between resources based on their causal role in harming and/or benefiting the domestic population'.[15] Or we might explore alternatives, such as targeting rulers with travel bans, confiscating money held in Swiss bank accounts, and so on. Although removing dictators' access to the resource trade may induce pressure towards accountability, the short-term effect could be further setbacks to the interests of the global poor—and this would be quite something to ask of the world's poor if the outcome of these reforms was actually uncertain.[16] But whether we are able to endorse fine-grained policies—whereby some resource imports are avoided and others tolerated, so long as the poor in an exporting country continue to benefit—will depend upon why we support these reforms in the first place. Egalitarians might endorse such policies for instrumental reasons, and hence readily support a fine-grained approach according to which continuing the resource trade with people in countries whose governments are not accountable should sometimes be seen as permissible—or even required, if the likely damage to the interests of the worst-off is substantial enough. If our commitment to national ownership is deep, by contrast, we may be prepared to avoid imports even when doing so hurts the poor.[17]

Pogge and Wenar respond to this challenge in different ways. Pogge famously argues for a complementary Global Resources Dividend—a direct payment to the poor of the world, funded by way of a global tax on key natural resources, which is to be levied at the point of extraction at the relatively modest rate of 1 per cent of market value. Payments from that Dividend would target the poorest countries, and would be conditional on demonstrable progress in advancing the fight against poverty.[18] Such a move would do much to offset any negative impacts of the cessation of trade on the very poor. Wenar, by contrast, argues that we should pursue accountability reforms *rather* than global taxes. Though he does briefly address the possibility that cessation might harm the poor in exporting countries, his response is to reiterate that in the long run it will bring about better governance.[19] The problem, though, is that for some of the poor concerned there might not *be* a long run. We require further argument why we should pursue cessation even if it sets back the most basic interests of some of the people it is intended to help.[20]

Now consider our second example, the non-distributive but nevertheless accountable regime. So long as this set is not entirely empty, we are able to place pressure on the idea that cessation will in fact advance distributive fairness. For it to do so, two things must hold true. On the one hand, cessation must reliably engender accountability. On the other, accountability must then advance distributive fairness. If either link in the chain is weak, the egalitarian is left with little grounds for confidence that accountability reforms will advance the distributive goals that she cares about. How confident can we be, first, that cessation will engender accountability? Here it is striking that our reformists fail to seriously engage with the extensive empirical literature on the effectiveness of economic sanctions, and in particular on the success or otherwise of those sanctions in securing improvements in governance within non-democracies. One of the few points of agreement in that literature, as it turns out, is that sanctions—such as the cessation of trade—often have unpredictable and even counterproductive consequences. Whereas they are rarely effective as stand-alone policies,[21] they do often intensify the deprivation of the poor in target countries.[22] This intensified deprivation, however, does not regularly convert into effective pressure for political change. In many cases, in fact, sanctions are successfully presented by unaccountable leaders as illegitimate efforts to undermine popular self-determination. The nationalist backlashes which can ensue may then simply help despots to bolster their own power.[23] If the sanctions literature has any clear positive lesson, it is that effective sanctions are likely to be fine-grained and flexible rather than across-the-board and stable, and that they are best seen as one of a more complex set of policies seeking to encourage a transition towards good governance.[24] The problem here is that whereas those whose concern primarily lies with the wellbeing of the worst-off might readily endorse such flexibility, it is less obvious how those who claim that we ought to pursue cessation in deference to property rights can plausibly do so.

What, by contrast, of the idea that accountability (if cessation could only reliably secure it) would in turn deliver the more equitable sharing of resource rents? In assessing the evidence here we must pay proper heed to the fact that Pogge and Wenar operate with different standards of accountability. Whereas Pogge seeks to block the resource trade with non-democracies, Wenar aims to block trade with regimes which fail to guarantee that citizens are aware of resource sales, are able to stop them without incurring severe costs, and are not subject to extreme manipulation—conditions which many non-democratic regimes could meet.

As far as Pogge's proposal goes, there is certainly good evidence that democracy tends to promote distributive justice better than other forms of government. Amartya Sen's finding that democracy reduces the incidence of famine—because when the voices of the poor are heard, their interests are less likely to be brutally neglected—is well known, for example.[25] There is also fairly robust evidence that democracy reduces the incidence of serious human rights deficits more broadly.[26] Still, democracy does not appear to *guarantee* that the proceeds from resource sales will be fairly shared—whether our concern is with the promotion of equality or even with the easing of poverty. Consider, by way of example, the case of Iceland. Exports of fish account for

35 per cent of Iceland's foreign income, and are, along with the financial sector, a key source of the country's wealth. Iceland is also one of the world's more democratic countries. Nevertheless, rights to fish in Iceland are not shared equitably, or even auctioned to fund public good provision. Instead, under its system of Individual Tradable Quotas, the rights were given free of charge and in perpetuity to anyone who had a registered fishing boat in the period 1983 to 1986. Though it initially generated a more profitable industry, the system of tradable fishing quotas eventually led to an enormous concentration of wealth. Around twenty companies—the so-called 'Lords of the Sea'—now control the majority of quotas. Moreover, speculative sales and resales of quotas were a substantial factor in the financial collapse of 2008 which did so much damage to the interests of ordinary Icelanders (and outsiders). Iceland is, to be sure, much more egalitarian than most countries. Nonetheless years of agitation for a fairer and more egalitarian system have failed to disrupt the elite capture of resource wealth in particular.[27] We could make similar points in relation to the United States, which continues to grant rights to onshore mineral resources on a 'finders keepers' basis, without sharing the proceeds with citizens. Mineral resources 'are essentially given away to the mining companies'—which are major contributors to party funds—and a move from President Clinton to establish auctions for mining rights was abandoned after protests from lobbyists.[28] Far from resource revenues being equitably shared, studies have shown that revenues from extraction have typically failed to drive poverty reduction even in resource-rich US counties.[29] In at least some cases, then, the presence of at least minimal democracy fails to secure justice. My claim, to be clear, is not that democracy does not *promote* the equitable sharing of resource rents at all; that remains a subject of dispute.[30] But it certainly does not guarantee it, and for as long as this is so, further measures to promote equitable sharing retain interest.[31]

What of Wenar's more modest standards of accountability? Here it is again striking that, although we have good evidence that minimally democratic governments are much less likely to infringe basic human rights or tolerate severe poverty, for instance, we lack evidence for such positive effects in the case of countries whose citizens possess only what Wenar calls 'bare-bones civil liberties and basic political rights'.[32] Even amongst very poor countries, democracies outperform non-democracies on a variety of human development indices as well as on economic growth.[33] But as far as we can tell, improvements in accountability below the threshold of minimal democracy make little or no difference.[34] If there is evidence that minimally accountable governments share resource revenues more fairly, Wenar certainly does not produce it. His hope might be, of course, that providing an effective veto to the poor over resource sales will guarantee that revenues are shared fairly. But this too appears uncertain: even if they were given the right to veto resource sales, in light of their current desperate position the poor in such countries might well settle for very small gains over the status quo, not least since if it comes down to negotiation between elites and citizens, dictators with millions in Swiss bank accounts may be better able to drive a hard bargain than those who are teetering on the brink of starvation. Even in the absence of extreme manipulation, simple bargaining power surely matters.

David Wiens has usefully made a similar argument more formally. On his model, citizens' bargaining power is determined by both the availability of procedures of accountability, and the credibility of exit threats, where the latter is constituted by citizens' options to withdraw from cooperation with rulers without incurring severe costs to themselves. As Wiens points out, Wenar's accountability reforms would promote the former but not the latter. As such, the bargaining power of the poor may remain very weak. How, then, might we promote plausible exit options? Doing so is difficult, but could involve broader reforms such as changes to the immigration policies of rich states, or shifts in international trade rules to reduce dependency on resource extraction.[35] Though Wiens does not develop the argument in detail, the point about trade rules can usefully be drawn out. Industries such as oil are typically very easily 'captured' by a few large producers, and, in some countries, by governments themselves. They then secure very large economic gains for a relatively small number of people, and do little to sustain local employment or develop local infrastructure or training (see section 7.3). By contrast, other sectors of the economy hold considerably more promise. Agriculture, for instance, is a much 'flatter' sector, typically involving many more producers, a more even distribution of gains, and a much higher degree of local employment. For decades the prevailing system of international trade (which has witnessed a de-escalation of subsidies and tariffs in many sectors, but not in the foodstuff and textiles trade) has made it very difficult for African countries, for instance, to develop their comparative advantage here. Were they to be given an opportunity to export on a level playing field to developed states, the economic consequences could be dramatic. More specifically—and this, I take it, is Wiens's point—a diversification of developing country economies into such fields could sow the seeds of greater economic security, and hence independence, for (greater numbers of) citizens vis-à-vis their rulers. Of course, we have abundant reasons to pursue reforms to international trade. The fact that they could engender greater responsiveness of leaders to citizens, though, is a relatively neglected reason. Conceivably, the boost to the bargaining power of the poor which arose from redrawing international trade rules to favour developing-economy diversification could be just as significant, and quite possibly more significant, than the accountability reforms Wenar proposes.

If we are interested in boosting the relative economic power of citizens vis-à-vis rulers, we might also usefully investigate global tax proposals which seek to place income directly into the hands of citizens in poor countries (see

Chapter 8). These too might engender a significant shift in the relative power of ordinary citizens. In short, accountability reforms are likely to be part of the picture in promoting responsive governance, but they cannot be the whole story. The argument here is not intended by any means to be an argument against pursuing accountability reforms. But it does suggest that we should not pursue accountability reforms to the exclusion of a range of other policies which would seek to alter the power relationships between governors and governed in resource-exporting countries.

The conclusion towards which I have been building in this section is as follows: even if there are grounds for expecting some success in pushing distribution in an egalitarian direction, global egalitarians cannot see accountability reforms as a replacement for more ambitious reforms. This is the case for at least three reasons. First, these proposals likely would not suffice to ensure even intra-national equality. In fact both links in the causal chain appear quite weak: on the one hand, cessation does not ensure accountability in the first place; on the other, accountability does not in turn guarantee the fair sharing of rents.

If we want to promote equality, my view is that the worst-off should be the overwhelming beneficiaries of resource rents. But even if our goal was merely to share resource rents equally per capita, it is not obvious why we would expect accountability-promoting reforms to guarantee such an outcome (especially if our goal is to secure minimal accountability, rather than democracy). The egalitarian will want to ask why a better solution would not be something more direct, such as a requirement to make substantial individual payments from resource rents.[36] On this point Wenar and Pogge part company. Although Wenar does, in his most recent work, discuss proposals to share resource rents intra-nationally, he appears to be interested in those proposals primarily insofar as they might advance accountability and not inasmuch as they spread wealth.[37] By contrast Pogge's accountability reform is proposed as *one* policy we ought to pursue to advance natural resource justice, but which would not be sufficient to achieve justice by itself. As I noted earlier in this section, his Global Resources Dividend would simultaneously redistribute (some) resource rents directly to poor countries, on condition that the poor benefit. Such a belt-and-braces approach offers better prospects for the world's poor.

Second, as I have suggested, the cessation of resource trade with dictators (or with non-democracies) could conceivably have negative—even devastating— short-term effects on the world's poorest. Even if the poorest benefit only to a very small extent from the sale of their country's natural resources, cutting off that flow of income (even if cutting it off is in their long-term interest) may be very painful (and may mean that some of them do not even survive into the long term). Pogge's Dividend would do much to offset any negative short-term effects of a cessation of trade—although we might still ask why our sights ought not to be set higher. Wenar's argument, by contrast, is suggested as an *alternative* to schemes for global resource taxation (which he claims are troubled by the lack of global institutions with the requisite coercive power to enforce them, and by the lack of international agreement on even broad distributive principles[38]). But it is hard to see how it could be.

Third, even if accountability reforms sufficed to achieve intra-national equality (which appears unlikely), we must recall that they would have no immediate impact upon international inequalities. Even within countries, the impact they had would depend upon initial shares of natural resources, and as such the equalizing effects would be very uneven. Intra-national equalization of resource rents would do little, in particular, for poor countries which are also resource-poor. Some countries have negligible resource rents in the first place, and sharing those rents equally would make a minuscule dent in their levels of poverty.[39] Whilst the distributive impact would be very large in some countries—transforming countries such as Indonesia, Iran, Nigeria, and Russia into much more egalitarian countries at one fell stroke—the impact on Sub-Saharan Africa would be smallest.[40]

Despite these reservations about whether they are sufficient to achieve justice, accountability reforms have considerable promise. The discussion about how we could, within the constraints of permanent sovereignty, begin to make resource wealth work more reliably for ordinary citizens is an important one.[41] But they would not achieve justice in one fell swoop, and therefore it would be a mistake to view these proposals as a replacement for the egalitarian reforms we will discuss in Chapters 8, 9, and 10.

7.2. POPULAR SOVEREIGNTY AND INTERNATIONAL LAW

Egalitarian calls for redistribution, however, run directly into Wenar's pragmatic challenge. Such proposals might be thought to perform poorly on the criterion of feasibility, especially if they require coercive institutions which we do not yet possess.[42] By contrast the ideal of popular resource sovereignty—that the citizens of each country own its resources and are entitled at the very least to a say in how those resources are used, and whether and when they are sold—is already a basic principle of the contemporary international order. Popular sovereignty and property rights over resources 'are not ideas that the world needs to be converted to; these are the world's stated principles'.[43] As Wenar puts it, the principle of popular resource sovereignty holds that 'the people must authorise the regime's management of its resources', including decisions to sell those resources.[44] Since 'popular resource sovereignty ... has

Perfecting Sovereignty? 161

pride of place within international legal documents to which almost all nations have committed',[45] our task is simply to put those ideas into practice more consistently.

In this section I will look more closely at the international legal doctrine of permanent sovereignty, and its connection with the ideas of popular resource sovereignty and public accountability. We examined the doctrine of permanent sovereignty in Chapter 6, and saw that it reserves a broad set of rights over the resources contained in a territory to the local state. But when it does so, does it reserve these rights for 'the state' generally, or does it further reserve them for the citizenry as *distinct* from their government? That question is key: when the 1966 Covenants, for instance, declare that 'All peoples may, for their own ends, freely dispose of their natural wealth and resources', what is meant by invoking 'peoples' in this context? If 'people' here simply meant 'state', leaning on it as a critical principle would deliver no obvious gains for ordinary citizens. But if international law dictates that ordinary citizens hold resource rights *against* their governments, by contrast, we have a practical critical lever to work with in advancing their interests.

Wenar's claim is that we should interpret documents such as the 1966 Covenants on the basis of the plain meaning of the terms they use, and in light of the objects and purposes of their authors.[46] And though he accepts that their meaning is to a degree unsettled, he also claims that the repeated references to 'peoples' as agents of permanent sovereignty indicates that these instruments should be read as reserving resource sovereignty to ordinary citizens. But that is far from clear. Invoking 'peoples' as rights-holders, when it comes to permanent sovereignty, allows of two quite distinct interpretations. The first holds that a 'people' is a society or community as distinguished from *other* societies or communities. What it means to say that the resources of Kenya belong to the Kenyan 'people' is that they do not belong to the people of Germany, or Australia, or Kazakhstan. The second interpretation holds that reference to the 'people' is (or is *also*) meant to reserve ownership rights for the populace of a territory as distinct from their own government—to make clear, that is, that it is the national community—the citizenry—who are the ultimate owners of resources. On this view the government at best acts as the trustee of those resources.[47] We might say that the first interpretation externally differentiates the people from outsiders, whereas the second internally differentiates them, as rights-holders, from their rulers.

The ideal of 'popular resource sovereignty' on which Wenar leans reflects the second, internal interpretation. This is an ideal, however, which appeared to play no role in the long-running debates which eventually gave rise to the key international instruments proclaiming permanent sovereignty. The clear sense from discussions at the time was that reference to 'peoples', in these instruments, was understood to distinguish locals from metropolitan powers as owners of natural resources, instead of selecting 'citizens' rather than 'rulers' as owners (hence the claim, in all of these instruments, that resources belong to 'peoples' and not *the* people'). In fact the references to 'peoples' as the subjects of self-determination in the third quarter of the twentieth century are explicable simply by pointing to the fact that many of the communities in question were not yet independent states, but rather communities seeking independent statehood (and the various proclamations of permanent sovereignty occur precisely in articles proclaiming that such communities ought to enjoy such self-determination). All of the instruments which reference the rights of 'peoples' date from the 1950s and 1960s, at which point some societies struggling for independence were precisely *peoples but not yet states*.

As Nico Schrijver has succinctly put it, 'It can be inferred from relevant permanent-sovereignty-related UN debates that the term "peoples" was originally meant to refer to those peoples who had not yet been able to exercise their right to political self-determination...Once most of the former colonial peoples had gained independence, emphasis shifted back to States as the main subjects invested with the right to permanent sovereignty.'[48] That shift was abrupt and complete. After the 1960s, both 'hard' and 'soft' international law sources revert, uniformly, to the language of 'states' in discussing claims under permanent sovereignty and make no references to 'peoples' at all. Take for instance the 1974 General Assembly Resolution 3281 (XXIX), Article 2 of which simply declares that 'Every State has and shall freely exercise full permanent sovereignty, including possession, use and disposal, over all its wealth, natural resources and economic activities.' Later instruments—including the 1992 Convention on Biological Diversity, the 1994 Convention on the Law of the Sea, and the 1994 United Nations Framework Convention on Climate Change—follow the same trend of referring to states, and never to 'peoples', as holders of the right to permanent sovereignty. The same goes for 'soft law' documents such as the 1972 Stockholm Declaration on the Human Environment, the 1972 Resolution on the Permanent Sovereignty over Natural Resources of Developing Countries, the 1974 Declaration on the Establishment of a New International Economic Order, and the 1992 Rio Declaration on Environment and Development.[49]

Moreover, of the instruments from the 1950s and 1960s which do reference 'peoples' as the subjects of permanent sovereignty, none of them explicitly delineates any purported rights of citizens vis-à-vis their rulers, or mentions any mechanisms, or indeed criteria, of 'public accountability'. Any discussion of the idea that citizens have resource rights which demand protection against their governments, or indeed of possible constraints such an idea might place on resource utilization, is entirely absent from these instruments. Moreover, it was, as far as I can tell, absent even from the discussions which gave rise to them.[50] It is true that some instruments, including the 1962 Declaration on

Permanent Sovereignty over Natural Resources, declare that 'natural wealth and resources must be exercised in the interest of... national development and of the well-being of the state concerned'.[51] This has provided encouragement to those who favour the citizen-versus-state interpretation. But we can note two things in response. First, the history of negotiations over the instruments in question suggests that the use of resources to foster *national* development is being opposed here not to the enrichment of local leaders, but to the enrichment of *foreign* corporations or colonial powers who claimed continuing title over some of those resources (see section 7.3). This does nothing to enshrine any rights of citizens against their rulers. Second, if those who drafted the relevant instruments did intend to exhort states to use resources in the broader interests of their citizens, it is striking that no provision is made for the protection of those interests. This forms a stark contrast to the explicit protection of the interests of foreign investors—where, as I show in section 7.3, both mechanisms for redress, and sanctions, proliferate, and have been reiterated within numerous arbitrations and declarations. Nor, as far as I can tell, was there any discussion of such mechanisms. Absent any firm rules, or any mechanisms, for making resource governance responsive to the will of the people, the situation under international law is that the degree to which the people of any given geographical area are entitled to benefit from resource exploitation is considered 'in principle a matter of domestic politics'.[52] The fleeting emergence of 'peoples' as subjects of international law addressed a transitional problem in the shift from colonial to post-colonial statehood. Their brief legal life did not represent a deeper victory for the rights of citizens against states. Any such victories in this period were won, as we will see in section 7.3, on behalf of corporations and not citizens.

This pessimistic conclusion reflects the general status of self-determination under international law, in which proclamations of the right to self-determination of 'peoples' have emphasized 'external' self-determination—that is, freedom from external rule—but failed to enshrine any formal rules on the right of 'internal' self-determination—that is, rights of citizens to direct their own governments.[53] It remains the case, in particular, that 'no right has yet been conferred by general international norms on the whole population of sovereign States freely to decide by whom they should be ruled: "consent of the governed", a continuing right that peoples might have exercised against the government of the State where they live, has been perceived as too dangerous for the present fabric of the world community'.[54]

All of this matters considerably when we come to appraise the pragmatic challenge. In light of this, just what could it mean to say that popular resource sovereignty—which is said in turn to require public accountability over resources—is already a basic principle of the international legal order? If the claim were that the letter of international law enshrines the ideal of public accountability over resources, that claim would be, however regrettably, false.

Whilst the African Commission on Human Rights has published (non-binding) Resolutions which give some support to the ideal of public participation in resource decision-making,[55] no such moves have been made in Asia, Europe, or the Americas; and within the major global instruments I have discussed, no discussion of public accountability can be found. An alternative claim might be that public accountability is nevertheless hardwired into the *spirit* of the principle of permanent sovereignty, albeit that it has not yet adequately found its way into legal reality. Such a claim is harder to appraise. But certainly it must fail if construed as a simple 'originalist' claim about the ideas that *actually* inspired the authors of these instruments. For as we have seen, public accountability was never even raised as an issue among the voluminous and lengthy negotiations leading up to the documents' creation, and the trend within international law has actually been to replace 'peoples' as agents of resource sovereignty with 'states', rather than the reverse.

Where does this leave the argument for accountability reforms? I have suggested that international law has done little—if anything—to enshrine the ideal of popular sovereignty more broadly, or public accountability over resources more narrowly. If so, it does not appear to be the case that international law precludes states from trading resources with autocrats. Instead our job is presumably to *persuade* them to desist by way of moral argument. Despite his extended forays into international law, Wenar's description of the situation each state is presented with in relation to oil-exporting autocracies suggests precisely that states are *not* bound by international law to cease trade with those states. As he notes, property is inherently 'local' in the sense that each state determines for its own citizens, by way of its own legal codes, which states they will be permitted to buy resources from.[56] Now if a sovereign state can decide *not* to trade with an autocrat, it can also decide to *continue* doing so. And its freedom of action in that regard is clearly incompatible with international law *requiring* states not to allow their citizens to buy resources from dictators. The argument that states are free to decide whether they can do so opens up space precisely for the possibility that critics might persuade states not to allow us. When we do so, we seek to persuade each of them to pass into *domestic* law a prohibition on trade which is *not* required by international law.

But on this basis, it makes much less sense to describe popular resource sovereignty, still less any specific standard of public accountability, as a principle of the modern international *legal* order. Rather, it is perhaps an idea which is present in the global public political culture—or, more likely, in the domestic public cultures of many states—which we ought to make a part of the *domestic* legal order. As a result, the pragmatic advantage which accountability reforms are supposed to hold over egalitarian alternatives is much less certain. To a large extent the initial pragmatic credentials of the argument appeared to rest on a claim that it works up what is already present in law.

Now of course we can make *moral* arguments that countries such as the US or the UK *should not* buy resources from dictators, or that it would be hypocritical, in light of their own domestic commitments, for them to do so. But if when we do so we no longer lean on the (supposedly incontrovertible) 'facts on the ground' of international law, but rather on interpretations of the (presumably somewhat looser) shared ideals of citizens within many states, we are on much less solid ground. Moreover, proposals in each state to pass laws forbidding trade with dictators will presumably face powerful opposition from vested economic interests—interests which have so far successfully resisted efforts to even require them to make public the payments they make to dictators, for instance, citing the national sovereignty of exporting countries as their rationale for doing so[57]—and which will ask governments why they ought to act in such a way as to set back their economic interests when international law does not require it, and when other states may not do the same. If so, a powerful coalition of states acting in unison would probably be required to make real progress.[58] Many egalitarian reforms appear to be in rather the same boat. I do not mean to claim that the accountability project is doomed by any means, or that it might not deliver positive outcomes (I have already suggested that it could). I simply claim that, if we are in the business of persuading states to pass laws rather than implementing them, and to act on principles which they are not in fact required to act upon but which we believe they *ought* to uphold, then it may turn out that at least some of the proposals of global egalitarians begin to look somewhat less distant and other-worldly by comparison.

7.3. SOVEREIGNTY, COLONIALISM, AND GLOBAL REFORM

Let us recall something else that Wenar's argument usefully emphasizes. Permanent sovereignty was not imposed upon the poor of the world. It was, to the contrary, keenly fought for by former colonial subjects. People living in newly independent countries had to fight for legal control over resources, he reminds us, 'through violence and at the cost of many thousand lives'. On Wenar's view their eventual success represents 'the great triumph' of the twentieth century as far as poorer countries are concerned.[59] But it is worth examining precisely *what* newly independent countries were fighting for under the guise of 'permanent sovereignty'. Doing so drives home the extent to which the ambitions newly independent countries had for permanent sovereignty were not, in fact, met. In this section I identify the narrow and the broader goals behind the struggle for permanent sovereignty. Reflecting on their success is valuable when appraising permanent sovereignty as a legal and political reality. But it also reveals how little accountability reforms would do to advance many of the (still unmet) ambitions newly independent countries actually had for permanent sovereignty.

Narrowly, a key aim of newly independent countries was to win the right to determine compensation domestically when they cancelled deeply unpopular resource concessions granted in the colonial period. Without that right, they argued, sovereignty would be a mere mirage. A second and much broader goal was to use their new-found control over resources to catch up economically with the developed world. During the 1960s this project was captured in the expression of hope for a New International Economic Order (NIEO), eventually enshrined in the 1974 Declaration of a New International Economic Order. The Declaration embraced permanent sovereignty, but at the same time it called for fairer trade rules which would redress massive global inequalities, provide a substantial boost to overseas assistance, and ensure debt cancellation and increased representation within international organizations (including a comprehensive overhaul of the Bretton Woods institutions). These measures would lead to 'accelerated development of all the developing countries', so that 'the prevailing disparities in the world may be banished and prosperity secured for all'.[60] Moreover, International Commodity Agreements would be established in order to stabilize global prices for natural resources, reducing the vulnerability of resource-exporting economies to dramatic fluctuations in income.[61] Thus permanent sovereignty was not a stand-alone strategy for the decolonization period, but a component of a broader package of reforms which would allow catch-up development and economic autonomy for newly independent countries.[62]

In retrospect, both struggles ended in comprehensive failure. Consider first the narrow goal concerning compensation. The emergence and eventual codification of the doctrine of permanent sovereignty was fraught with conflict between the developing world and the former colonial powers. France, Britain, and the US maintained many resource 'concessions' which, they claimed, retained legal force even if they were originally signed by colonial-era leaders who were deep in the pockets of the metropolitan powers. Newly independent countries were adamant that any brand of permanent sovereignty worth its name must include the right to cancel those concessions, nationalize the 'property' of overseas investors, and determine any compensation in their own courts. Permanent sovereignty, for developing countries, centrally involved the right to determine compensation domestically.[63] Former colonial powers, by contrast, insisted that expropriating the property of colonial investors, whilst permissible, must attract due compensation—and, crucially, compensation which should be determined not by the expropriating state but by international law.[64] Anything else would be iniquitous in itself, and discouraging to future investment.

Who was the ultimate victor in this lengthy struggle? As far as the legal instruments themselves are concerned, the former colonial powers professed themselves satisfied. As the US's legal adviser on the negotiations over the 1962 Declaration on Permanent Sovereignty drily noted, 'The fact that consensus includes positive recognition of the obligation to pay compensation where property is taken, to observe investment agreements and agreements to arbitrate and to abide by other requirements of international law should contribute to the enhancement of the international investment climate.'[65] The precise ramifications of permanent sovereignty for the legal relationship between newly independent countries and foreign investors were further worked out in a series of resolutions and tribunal decisions, and in the terms of regional trade agreements and bilateral investment agreements.

They have generally been disappointing, to say the least, for developing countries. First, a number of international arbitrations made clear that compensation is indeed owed, and should be calculated, according to international and not domestic law. The famous adjudication in the *Texaco/Calasiatic vs Libya* case of 1977 found that clauses in the Declaration of a New International Economic Order reserving the determination of compensation for domestic courts lacked legal effect, that compensation would be calculated internationally, and moreover declared, audaciously, that investing corporations had the 'legal personality' under international law to pursue claims for damages to their interests.[66] Second, whereas the defeat over compensation may now appear to be of largely historical interest, contemporary concessions signed by developing countries have themselves served to seriously constrain their self-determination. Concessions granted by exporting states to overseas corporations have been judged to constitute international agreements, and hence to possess the same status as treaty law (thus defeating exporting countries' claim that contracts with corporations are 'private', and that corporations cannot be considered to possess the same legal status as sovereign countries). This process has considerably increased the protection offered to investors, at the same time as circumscribing the jurisdiction of exporting states. Third, although states are generally apprehended as sovereign entities under international law, with the ability to make laws governing internal affairs, when it comes to attempting to *amend* resource contracts signed with corporations they are treated, by contrast, as private entities 'without any residual sovereign powers to amend the terms of the contract, whatever the demands of public welfare'.[67] In recent years investing corporations have regularly insisted upon 'stabilization clauses' which protect their commercial investments from uncertainty. Under those clauses an exporting state cannot subsequently pass laws which damage the interests of any corporation with which it has contracted. Such clauses can apply for decades, during which time 'companies limit the normal prerogatives of any legislature and government, such as their right to enact and issue protective environmental, labor, and other regulatory laws'.[68] These clauses are immune to domestic judicial challenge; the exporting state is simply taken, under international law, 'to have consented to suspend the exercise of its usual public functions, its legislative powers, to the extent that they affected the contract'.[69] The threat of legal action by investing corporations which perceive their interests to have been set back is not theoretical but real, and frequently enacted. Investment disputes between multinational corporations and developing countries can be so lucrative, for the former, that specialized investment companies have grown up to raise capital through them, treating claims against exporting countries as a new 'asset class'. As far as developing countries are concerned, by contrast, the threat of adverse arbitrations acts as a deterrent on policy-making on the environment or on labour standards: 'As the claims made by companies get bigger, it seems increasingly likely that the massive financial risks associated with investor-state arbitration will effectively grant foreign investors a veto over government decisions.'[70] Contracting with foreign investors to exploit resources can have, to put it mildly, dramatic implications for an exporting state's self-determination.

Meanwhile the broader goals of the NIEO, within which the struggle for permanent sovereignty was nested, also ended in failure. Trade rules were not renegotiated to favour developing countries. Whilst it had been hoped that the General Agreement on Tariffs and Trade, which governed world trade between 1948 and 1995, would overturn the pre-war system of elite trading-blocs which had heavily favoured industrialized countries, heavy tariffs on textiles and agricultural products (the principal hope for exports from the least developed countries) were maintained, and overall trade *only* increased between precisely the five countries which had dominated the pre-war system (the US, UK, Canada, Germany, and France).[71] International Commodity Agreements failed to guarantee stable prices to resource exporters, primarily because of the reluctance of importing countries to constrain their pursuit of profits, and commodity organizations either collapsed or turned their attention to research and marketing activities. Frustration at both the paucity of, and conditionalities attached to, lending from the World Bank and International Monetary Fund (IMF) saw many countries turn instead, in the 1970s, to private international lenders. But it was lending from these private banks which ultimately had to be restructured, at considerable economic and political expense, in the following two decades.[72] By the turn of the century one-fifth of the world's population lived in countries which were in arrears on, or had rescheduled, sovereign debts.[73] The late 1970s heralded a period of steeply increasing global economic inequality.[74] Africa ended the twentieth century with a lower share of global income than it started it with. Latin America's income, as a ratio of the global North's, diminished from 44.4 per cent to 25.8 per cent during the latter half of the century.[75]

Though in many cases the failure to escape poverty is in part explained by domestic political maladies—maladies carried over wholesale, often, from the colonial era—the near-forgotten dream of the NIEO throws into relief our failure to significantly shift the structural context in which developing countries operate. Consider, by way of illustration, the situation a resource-rich but generally poor developing country might now find itself in. Zambia is a country of 14 million people and has been, for the past two decades, a multi-party democracy with a degree of press freedom. As what the United Nations (UN) designates a 'least developed country', with a GDP per capita of $1,400 per year, Zambia faces a world in which its most accessible opportunity for economic growth is selling natural resources—and especially copper, a key ingredient for high-tech industries—to foreign investors. Refining such resources itself would be preferable since this is where most 'value' is added in the commodity chain, but extraction is highly capital-intensive; developing the required technology is expensive and time-consuming, and local levels of skills and infrastructure render this an unlikely prospect. Whilst, in 1989, developing countries established a Common Fund for Commodities which aimed to divert much-needed funds and technical assistance to countries like Zambia so that they might develop their own extractive infrastructure, it never did so in significant quantities. Instead extraction is typically performed by multinational corporations in isolated enclaves, reducing any positive impact of extraction on local education or employment—not least since the IMF has exerted considerable pressure to privatize resource extraction, and to grant contracts to the highest (domestic or international) bidder.[76] Meanwhile the World Bank has questioned the rationale for developing local copper manufacturing expertise, 'citing the landlocked country's distance from major markets, its poor infrastructure and high transportation costs'.[77]

For Zambia, these pressures from the IMF and World Bank are hard to ignore. Such is not the case for countries like Saudi Arabia or Norway which do not require development assistance, and which can afford to develop their own extractive infrastructure; both countries do in fact extract most of their own oil, to no obvious ill effect. But Zambia is in a very different structural position. In fact, its response to these injunctions has been unusually swift: it has been the most proactive amongst African countries in advancing privatization, and it secured the first of China's overseas Special Economic Zones. All of the major mines in Zambia are now owned either by subsidiaries of multinational corporations, or by Chinese state-owned enterprises. But as a result of extremely 'investor-friendly' development agreements signed in recent decades, tax revenue from copper as a proportion of Zambian government income plummeted from 59 per cent in the 1960s, to 5 per cent at the beginning of the twenty-first century.[78] Though in 2015 Zambia introduced a policy increasing government royalties from open-pit mining from 6 per cent to 20 per cent, a threat from mining companies to withhold capital and cut jobs quickly persuaded its President to repudiate it.[79]

Given its economic position, it is understandable that a country like Zambia has signed away resource concessions as a means of gaining revenue. Given its weak bargaining position, allied with a relative lack of legal and economic expertise (producing what economists like to call 'asymmetric information'), it is also depressingly comprehensible that Zambia's government has made deals in which the distribution of benefits is very highly skewed against them.[80] Whereas Norway, via the state-owned company Statoil, retains on average 70 per cent of all revenues from oil extraction, Zambia retains an estimated 5 per cent of the proceeds of mineral exploitation.[81] As well as differences in legal and economic expertise, these disparities, of course, also reflect the relative bargaining power of countries situated in very different locations within the global economy. In developing countries revenue from concessions often ends up being more meagre, and slower to materialize, than envisaged. Still, if Zambia decided simply to cancel the relevant concessions, it would owe potentially massive compensation for damage to investors' commercial interests—which according to international law must be both full *and prompt*. The reliance of these countries upon natural resource exports, meanwhile, may present them with vulnerability rather than security. As globally traded commodities, the prices of point-source resources fluctuate wildly, making expenditure planning difficult, potentially creating severe difficulties for such countries in lean years. Boom years often witness massive government spending which is later maintained only at the cost of incurring large debts—debts which can be serviced in many cases only by accelerating extraction.[82]

Many developing countries have, then, failed to fundamentally shift their status as cheap suppliers of natural resources to more developed economies, and are locked out of genuine opportunities for catch-up development.[83] Accessing markets other than natural resource exports might be preferable, but richer countries continue to make it extremely difficult for African states to profitably export agricultural products, and accessing export markets for higher-end consumer goods involves enormous start-up costs. If we were to wonder whether a country like Zambia might be better off simply exploiting its resources for its own ends and refusing to sell them at all to foreigners,[84] we should note that its membership of the World Trade Organization (WTO) would forbid such a move. Witness for instance the recent WTO judgement against China's policy of restricting the supply of rare earth metals to international investors—a judgement after which the European Union's (EU's) trade commissioner pithily declared that 'Today's ruling by the WTO on rare earths shows that no one country can hoard its raw materials from the global marketplace at the expense of other WTO partners.'[85] This, then, has been the reality of permanent sovereignty for many newly independent countries: vulnerability to the dictates of foreign investors; vulnerability to the vicissitudes of the resource market; and the continued failure to access lucrative markets which might fundamentally shift their status as cheap sources of primary materials for the world market.

The actual ambitions which these countries had for permanent sovereignty in the post-war period, then, were not met. This is not to say, though, that such goals were not worthwhile. Indeed, I believe that many of them are. But two points can be made. First, it seems certain that accountability reforms, though potentially valuable, would do little to advance those ambitions or to upset the structural context in which permanent sovereignty has come to be 'enjoyed' by the world's poorest countries. Second, these broader, systemic goals—to redraw the rules of international trade, to reschedule debts, to redress the bargaining asymmetries between developing countries and foreign corporations—take us closer to the vision of global justice defended by many egalitarians. Egalitarians can probably learn much by studying the avowed goals of newly independent countries. Doing so can also throw new light on the claim that global egalitarian reforms would have to be coercively imposed, by the West, on other countries which would reject them if they could.[86]

7.4. CONCLUSIONS

This chapter has covered a good deal of ground, but we are now in a position to collect together several conclusions. Section 7.1 examined some proposals for urgent reforms to the way in which we trade natural resources with dictators. It suggested that egalitarians can offer conditional support to these accountability reforms, insofar as they do indeed promise to move us closer to equality. But they will likely produce limited progress in that direction, and it was therefore suggested that such reforms cannot be a replacement for further or more ambitious egalitarian reforms. Section 7.2 examined a pragmatic challenge which suggested that whilst more ambitious egalitarian reforms may have very limited chances of success, international law does provide a ready-made set of tools for advancing the interests of the world's poor. Here I showed that although we might well argue that importing states should defer to the interests of poor citizens in exporting countries, international law does not require them to do so. Once we are clear about the extent to which popular sovereignty and public accountability are already 'facts on the ground' within our world, the pragmatic advantages of the reforming strategy recede.

Section 7.3 then looked more closely at the way in which permanent sovereignty figured in the ambitions of countries escaping colonial rule in the 1950s and 1960s. These countries sought to defend the rights of states to make decisions about resource use over and above the claims of foreign investors, and as such to definitively break the power inequalities typical of the colonial period. They also wished to achieve a new international economic order in which selling resources cheaply would not be their only route out of poverty. They sought a major overhaul of prevailing practices on trade, debt, overseas assistance, and the determination of commodity prices. In such a context resource-exporting countries might gain more from selling resources, but at the same time—as new markets opened up—become less dependent on resource sales. All of these hopes were definitively crushed. This matters, I would suggest, for the way in which we evaluate proposals to reform or to transcend permanent sovereignty as a practice. Permanent sovereignty over natural resources has not offered the expected advances to the poor of the world. Moreover, accountability reforms would not deliver on those goals, or shift the structural context in which exporting countries operate. Even if accountability reforms have some promise, rejecting global egalitarian reforms on the basis that the poor will benefit from more permanent sovereignty rather than less would be a mistake. The remaining chapters of this book examine some reforms which may allow us to do better.

ENDNOTES

1. Carens 2013.
2. Wenar 2016a: 83.
3. Pogge 2002; Wenar 2016a.
4. The countries in question are Qatar, Kuwait, Brunei, United Arab Emirates, and Saudi Arabia. For the figures: http://data.worldbank.org/indicator/NY.GDP.PCAP.PP.CD?order=wbapi_data_value_2013±wbapi_data_value+wbapi_data_value-last&sort=desc.
5. This is especially true of 'point-source' resources which can readily be removed from one physical location and traded as commodities. The most important case is oil, which comprises over half of global resource-as-commodity sales by value. For detailed analysis see Ross 2012.
6. Pogge 2002. In fact some empirical scholars have expressed scepticism about the claim that resource abundance truly incentivizes civil war, acting as a 'honeypot' for potential insurgents. See e.g. Ross 2012: 161.
7. Pogge 2002: 163.
8. Wenar 2016a: 228.
9. Wenar 2016a: 288–91.
10. Shmuel Nili (2011b) presents a variant of the proposal to cease trading with dictators which emphasizes liberal democracies' integrity as the reason for ceasing trade.
11. Pogge (2002, chapter 8) makes this case most clearly in the case of his proposal for a Global Resources Dividend, but it seems likely that he would suggest that

broad-based support for his proposed constitutional amendment could also be forthcoming.
12. Wenar 2008: 12, n. 28.
13. A number of non-governmental organizations (NGOs) are campaigning to increase transparency at all points of the resource trade, so that corporations publish detailed information about how much they have paid for resource contracts, resource-exporting governments provide information about where revenues have been spent, and so on. See for instance the Extractive Industries Transparency Initiative (https://eiti.org) and the Publish What You Pay coalition (http://www.publishwhatyoupay.org/). For a discussion of their objectives, see Karl 2007. Wenar (2016a, chapter 17) offers support to similar policies.
14. Slack 2004.
15. Wisor 2012: 191.
16. Wisor (2012: 193) in fact suggests that trade sanctions might *undermine*, rather than promote, the emergence of accountable institutions. As I note later in section 7.1, David Wiens (2015) has also provided reasons for doubt about whether Wenar's reforms would, by themselves, be sufficient to engineer a move towards genuinely responsive government.
17. Shmuel Nili's position is that we have a duty not to collaborate with thieves, and that our reasons for not buying resources from non-democracies hold regardless of the consequences of cessation for the victims of theft. As such, maintaining liberal integrity could justify serious setbacks for some of the world's poorest. Nili 2011a.
18. Pogge 2001.
19. Wenar 2016a: 293–9.
20. See also Wisor 2016: 13.
21. Krasner and Weinstein 2014.
22. Kerr and Gaigord 1994.
23. Snyder 2000.
24. Kerr and Gaigord 1994; Marinov and Nili 2015; Wisor 2016.
25. Sen 1999.
26. See for instance Davenport and Armstrong 2004. For a very good overview of evidence to that effect, see Christiano 2011.
27. For a good overview of the Icelandic case emphasizing the themes of elite capture and financial speculation, see Knight 2011.
28. Stiglitz 2006: 138.
29. James and Adland (2011) find that resource-extracting counties in Maine and Wyoming experience lower levels of growth than close neighbours which do not extract. Douglas and Walker (2015) reach a similar conclusion with regard to Appalachian coal counties, noting that most of the 'economically distressed' counties in the region are coal-exporters.
30. See Ross 2006 for a sceptical view on democracy's tendency to promote the welfare of the poor more broadly.
31. Note that Pogge's Dividend would not obviously promote equality either, in these two cases, since Icelandic or American citizens are unlikely to be recipients.
32. Wenar 2016a: 228.

33. Halperin, Siegle, and Weinstein 2010.
34. Christiano 2011: 153.
35. Wiens 2015. See also Wiens 2014.
36. This is Segal's proposal (Segal 2011). It is also endorsed, with specific reference to Nigeria, by Sala-i-Martin and Subramanian 2003, and with specific reference to Iraq by Palley 2003.
37. Wenar 2016a: 320.
38. Wenar 2016a, chapter 18.
39. Wiens 2015 estimates that, of the 1,400,000,000 people who live below the World Bank's $1.25-per-day poverty line, 300,000,000 live within countries which would conventionally be considered 'resource-cursed'.
40. Segal 2011: 480–1.
41. Note that those debates need not be of concern only to adherents of permanent sovereignty: even in a world in which communities controlled equal per-capita shares of resources, say, then on the reasonable assumption that such communities would sometimes wish to trade such resources we would still need mechanisms by way of which to determine that those trades were appropriately authorized by members.
42. As Wenar (2016b: 209) puts it, 'All the important questions surround the agency that will implement the cosmopolitan ideal. What is the nature of this agency's coercive power? Will anyone suggest that it be backed by armed force?'
43. Wenar 2016a: 267.
44. Wenar 2016a: 225.
45. Wenar 2016a: 207.
46. Wenar 2016a: 401, n. 21.
47. That interpretation is defended by Duruigbo 2006: 37.
48. Schrijver 1997: 9, 20. See also Anghie (2007: 218), who argues that rather than bestowing rights upon citizens against their governments, 'The use of the term "people"...suggests, then, that even those colonised peoples who had not yet become independent were granted certain rights that could protect their resources.'
49. When it comes to instruments such as the 1966 Covenants, Wenar (2016a: 214) claims that to interpret 'peoples' to mean 'states' (or proto-states) 'would contradict the object and purpose of these treaties and so would violate the prime directive of interpretation'. But then how, consistently with that directive, could one argue that the authors of these later documents replaced the word 'peoples' with 'states' but still meant the former?
50. Neither the contemporaneous accounts of Stephen Schwebel (1963) (legal adviser for the US in negotiations over the 1962 Declaration on Permanent Sovereignty over Natural Resources), nor the blow-by-blow account of Karol Gess (1964) (the Special Consultant to the Office of Legal Affairs of the UN), nor the detailed narratives of Halperin (1967–8) or Schrijver (1997) so much as mention the idea of citizens' rights against their states as an issue in the intense negotiations over either the 1962 Declaration or the 1966 Covenants.
51. United Nations General Assembly Resolution 1803 (XVII) of 1962, paragraph I.

52. Schrijver 1997: 20. A partial exception is the International Labour Organization's Convention 169 (1989), which specifies a right of indigenous peoples to be consulted on resource utilization where this directly affects their livelihoods (note that specifying this right would appear rather superfluous if all citizens already possessed it *qua* citizens). But the right does not protect the interests of citizens in general, and moreover does not appear, in practice, to have acted as either a brake on resource extraction or a spur to revenue-sharing. Moreover, it has only been ratified by twenty countries in its first quarter-century. For discussion, see Falk 1988; Schrijver 2008.
53. Cassese 1995: 320.
54. Cassese 1995: 334.
55. See for instance the Commission's Resolution 224 on a Human Rights-Based Approach to Natural Resources Governance of 2012.
56. Wenar 2016a: 106–8.
57. Considerable pressure has recently been placed upon Western corporations to detail the payments they make to resource-exporting countries. But their typical response has been that this is a matter for each individual country to make policy on, and that unilateral transparency on the part of corporations would infringe the sovereignty of exporting countries (which includes, by implication, perfect freedom whether to publish information on revenues or not). In the words of the International Association of Oil and Gas Producers, 'transparency should allow for the protection of proprietary information and be within the laws of host countries... The sovereign right of host governments to limit or prohibit disclosure of financial information is recognised, as is the obligation by companies to comply with any such restrictions' (cited in Gillies 2010: 119). In this case sovereignty over resources appears to act as a brake on moves to achieve binding global standards of transparency rather than a stimulus.
58. Wisor 2012.
59. Wenar 2010: 130.
60. United Nations General Assembly Resolution 3201(S-VI). Declaration on the Foundation of a New International Economic Order (1 May 1974), paragraph 4. For a discussion of hopes for the NIEO at the time, see Bhagwati (1977).
61. Chimni 1987.
62. 'The principle of permanent sovereignty over natural resources, economic activities and wealth is the substratum of the legal philosophy for the establishment of a new international economic order.' Chowdhury 1988: 59.
63. According to the renowned jurist and legal consultant to the UN Georges Abi-Saab (1984: 47), this was the very meaning of the term, at least as it was debated in the 1950s and 1960s: permanent sovereignty 'addresses the question of the limits imposed by international law on States regarding alien economic interests within their national jurisdiction'. Or as Hossain (1980: 35) put it, 'For developing countries the principle of permanent sovereignty was important because it provided a basis on which they could claim to alter "inequitable" legal arrangements under which foreign investors enjoyed rights to exploit natural resources found within their territories.' See also Cassese 1995: 50, 56.

64. Schwebel's account emphasizes that the key issue for the US was the protection of overseas investors by *international* law, and the paying of full and prompt compensation in case of nationalization. Schwebel 1963.
65. Schwebel 1963: 469.
66. See Cantegreil 2011.
67. Radon 2007: 96.
68. Radon 2007: 96.
69. Anghie 2007: 234.
70. Provost and Kennard 2015.
71. Gowa and Kim 2005.
72. Herman 2007: 17.
73. International Monetary Fund 2006: 182.
74. Milanovic 2007: 29–30.
75. Sutcliffe 2007: 56, 58.
76. Stiglitz 2006: 142. Piketty (2014: 47) estimates that the proportion of Africa's manufacturing capital (including extractive technology) owned by outsiders may exceed 40–50 per cent.
77. Lee 2014: 40.
78. Lee 2014: 32.
79. Stevens, Lahn, and Kooroshy 2015: 25.
80. As Radon (2007: 90) observes, the least developed countries are particularly affected by the lack of skilled negotiators. In the case of extractive industries, for instance, major foreign corporations 'often possess greater financial resources, superior knowledge of the oil or mining fields, and more experience in negotiating contracts. Indeed, most countries where oil companies operate have far fewer resources than the oil companies themselves.'
81. Feichtner 2015; Lee 2014. Of course, part of this difference might be explained by the greater extraction costs of minerals compared to oil. Nevertheless, enormous differences are present in the oil economy too. Karl reports that although some 'mature' oil-exporting countries retain approximately 90 per cent of revenues, Chad, for instance, retained a mere 7 per cent of oil revenues, at least in its early contracts. Karl 2007: 262. See also Gary and Karl 2003.
82. Slack 2004: 49.
83. In response to such fears, critics often point out that many East Asian economies have managed to grow rapidly in recent decades. But it is significant here that their growth was prompted by forms of state intervention and protectionist policies that have since been comprehensively prohibited by WTO agreements such as the Agreement on Trade-Related Investment Measures, and the General Agreement on Trade in Services. For an influential discussion, see Wade 2003.
84. An alternative would be to continue to sell resources but refuse to sign bilateral trade agreements, and/or tear up existing agreements and pay the financial penalty. But though some Latin American countries have discussed adopting such an approach, to date only Brazil, an 'upper middle-income country' according to the World Bank, has consistently pursued it.
85. Quoted in Donnan and Politi 2014.
86. Wenar 2006.

How to address the problem of ecological refugees?

8

Resource Taxes

Proposals for resource taxes have played a very prominent role in contemporary debates about global justice, from Beitz's 'resource redistribution principle', to Steiner's Global Fund, to Pogge's Global Resources Dividend.[1] This chapter investigates the role they could play in promoting greater equality at the global level. Section 8.1 establishes taxes as one amongst many policies capable of advancing equality. Section 8.2 further prepares the ground by sketching an account of when, and why, we might levy taxes. Section 8.3 then discusses proposals for taxing natural resources in particular. It defends resource taxes from some important objections, and in so doing clarifies the role they should play in an egalitarian project. Section 8.4 enquires what the precise tax base should be if we ought indeed to adopt at least some natural resource taxes. Amongst other things, I suggest that a single undifferentiated global tax on natural resources is unlikely to best promote justice. Section 8.5 therefore examines several proposals for some more specific resource taxes.

8.1. TAXES AS ONE POLICY AMONGST MANY

Our world is characterized by massive inequalities across a number of dimensions. At present, patterns of access to natural resources frequently reflect and reinforce, rather than challenge, these inequalities. I have suggested that egalitarians should not restrict their ambitions to shifting the pattern of benefits and burdens flowing from natural resources because, while important, they are not all that matters. Promoting equal access to wellbeing broadly considered would require a more expansive set of policies. These could include redrawing trade rules to better promote pro-poor development, and slashing developed-world tariffs and subsidies; reducing international tax competition and promoting the sharing of fiscal information across borders in order that existing taxes can be better collected; increasing technical assistance aimed at improving developing countries' ability to gather and spend tax revenues; and further writing down odious debts. Such policies are by no means unfamiliar: most of them played a central role in the unrealized project for a New International Economic Order (NIEO) which we discussed in Chapter 7. But they continue to demand the attention of anyone who wishes to reduce the brutal gulfs in life prospects that our world offers those born into it.

It would be a mistake to see these reforms as disconnected from issues of natural resource justice, in fact, because they could in themselves enable the poor to benefit more substantially from natural resource wealth. Writing down debts would reduce the dependence of some developing countries on a resource trade in which they are often weakly positioned and which all too often generates vulnerability (to fluctuating prices, to the whims of multinational corporations and arbitrators, to the dictates of international organizations) rather than stability. Increased tax cooperation and support for domestic tax-raising capacity would allow the world's poor to enjoy a greater share of often massive resource rents. Finally, pro-development trade rules would open up alternative routes out of poverty, easing the diversification of developing economies away from primary resource exports by offering them access to the markets in which most 'value' is added to—and income derived from—those resources. At the same time they would augment the bargaining power of citizens vis-à-vis often unaccountable rulers.

We have identified other important reforms too. In chapter 7 we saw that transparency reforms (which would open up information about the resource trade, and particularly about the size and destination of resource rents) have some potential to promote greater intra-national sharing of resource revenues. The cessation of trading relations with regimes which are not even minimally accountable can also be a useful strategy, although the support egalitarians offer to this policy must be circumspect. There are good reasons to doubt whether transparency and accountability reforms would secure the equitable sharing of resource rents even within states, and they would leave international inequalities undisturbed. But they nevertheless deserve serious attention.

Proposals to increase South–North migration may also hold some promise in reducing global injustice.[2] Closed borders preserve inequalities in access to natural resources and other sources of advantage too. Increasing South–North migration, by contrast, represents one means of evening out access to those advantages. In practice, increasing migration flows is probably a limited strategy for reducing global inequality or even ameliorating severe poverty. It might, to be sure, be more effective in this regard than political theorists have sometimes assumed; but it would also come with significant moral costs. Any reduction in poverty or inequality which it generated would be contingent upon people in developing countries leaving behind their friends and families and moving to places where the locals may not share their language, culture, or religion. If we take seriously the interests people have in being able to lead decent lives without such wrenching change, this would be a lot to ask of the world's poor.³ So it may well be that wealthy states should open their borders to more migrants from poor countries; indeed if they refuse to share their advantages with the poor of the world, illegal immigration might well be morally permissible.⁴ Certainly the ability to emigrate is an important protection against serious injustices; it is also, on some views, an important human freedom. But as a solution to global injustice migration is limited. Direct measures to spread access to the benefits and burdens arising from natural resources (and other sources of advantage) should also be pursued.

All of these reforms are important, and moreover they are relatively well understood. It has been suggested that greater global equality will only be achieved at the inception of some global Leviathan capable of bringing it about by *force majeure*.⁵ But most of these reforms do not even require the creation of new institutions. Significant progress could be achieved by the lights of institutions which already exist. It has also been suggested that the cross-cultural consensus needed to pursue greater global equality is not apparent, and that promoting equality would require us to foist upon people in other countries reforms which they could reasonably reject.⁶ But significant and lively political constituencies exist for many of these reforms, especially within the developing world. As the fate of the NIEO illustrates, their failure to materialize probably owes a good deal more to the intransigence of the privileged North than it does to the reticence of the global South. But citizens of the North can, and should, support these proposals and call their leaders to account when they obstruct or fail to deliver on them.

Though these reforms would achieve a very great deal, it is also well worth investigating more direct ways of equalizing the benefits and burdens flowing from natural resources, and that is the task of this and the final two, Chapters 9 and 10, of this book. In this chapter, I examine proposals for natural resource taxes. Such proposals have received considerable attention from theorists of global justice, who have suggested they possess the potential to contribute significantly to redressing injustice. Such schemes do not merit our *exclusive* attention, because there are many other ways in which we might push the distribution of those benefits in a more egalitarian direction; some of them have already been discussed in this section, and the Chapters 9 and 10 will discuss still more options at our disposal. But tax-and-transfer schemes are undoubtedly an important weapon in the egalitarian arsenal.

8.2. THE ROLE OF TAXES

This section will clear some ground by addressing several broad starting questions for any tax-and-transfer scheme: why should we levy taxes on agents, when, and on what?

8.2.1. Why Tax?

The objectives of tax-and-transfer schemes exhibit some diversity. We can usefully distinguish four general goals. First, we might tax agents in order to discourage activities which generate harmful consequences. Surcharges on air fares, for example, can reduce the attractiveness of air travel and hence its attendant harms—such as air pollution or the emission of greenhouse gases—by forcing travellers to bear the true social and environmental costs of air travel. Second, we might levy taxes in order to reduce inequality. This might simply mean removing assets from those who have no, or weak, claims upon them. We might levy progressive income taxes or wealth taxes, for instance, if we believed that the income or wealth in question was in substantial part unearned. Such measures might also be desirable inasmuch as they reduced the undesirable consequences of inequality, including the elite capture of political power, the monopolization of key positional goods, or the production of hierarchies of status and esteem. Third, levying taxes can raise revenues for a variety of justice goals. For instance we might use tax revenues to bankroll the provision of education or healthcare, or to directly distribute income and wealth to the poorest. Fourth, we can envisage some taxes as a kind of user charge. We might tax people when they consume public goods, for example, so as to fund their production or protection. Alternatively we might charge people for using or appropriating assets which, while they can be consumed as private goods, are properly considered common property. Water charges or fees for exploiting mineral resources under publicly owned land might fall into that category.

Noting this diversity of objectives is important for the discussion which ensues. This is because different taxes (or so I will argue) will likely score higher or lower in advancing these various goals, and it may well be that no single tax will securely advance all of them. If that turns out to be the case, a plausible conclusion is that the optimal tax regime will comprise a variety of different taxes.

8.2.2. When to Tax?

I have suggested that taxation is but one of many ways of bringing about greater equality, and therefore ought not to monopolize our attention. We can illustrate that in a more fine-grained way: once we have identified our four goals of taxation, we can readily see that taxation will not always be the only means of advancing each of them, and neither will it always be the best means. Consider, for example, the generation of harms. Some harms are so serious, or so difficult to compensate for, that the correct policy will be to forbid them and to impose significant penalties upon those who continue to generate them. A policy of damaging people's most basic interests, and then compensating them, is usually the occasion of some moral loss, including perhaps to the self-respect or autonomy of the victims. Setting back people's projects and then compensating them is more acceptable when those projects are entirely substitutable sources of wellbeing, or relatively peripheral to their overall life goals, and less so to the extent that this is not true. In some cases, then, tax-and-transfer will not be an appropriate response to the generation of harms.

Second, consider the objective of reducing inequality, for instance by removing assets from those who have no, or weak, claims over them. If an agent refuses to relinquish an asset which he has no moral claim over, and which someone else desperately needs, then the correct response may be confiscation. By contrast, taxation makes sense if we believe either that agents have *some* claim over the goods they control, or that there is some value in giving those who currently control assets the choice whether to relinquish them or give up something else of equivalent value. Taxation is more autonomy-preserving (at least for those who control the goods in question) than confiscation,[7] and this may be a reason for favouring it. But what we should do will also hinge upon the urgency of the claims of the excluded. In some cases taxation will be the appropriate response and in other cases it will not.

Third, consider the raising of funds for justice goals such as the bankrolling of public good production, or the equalization of income and wealth. Taxation frequently commands overwhelming attention as a source of funding, but it is not the only source. Some governments engage in commercial activities which secure direct income, or earn interest on state assets or loans. Criminal fines or penalties can also contribute to the public coffers. In many countries the sale of oil or minerals reduces the need to tax the populace (though there may be gains to good governance and accountability when authorities do resort to public taxation). Taxation is not the only tool in the armoury when it comes to generating funds for promoting justice goals.

Consider, finally, fees or user charges. Imagine a resource from which users cannot or should not be excluded. In some cases we will believe that we should forbid the private appropriation of such a resource. It would be inappropriate to charge people for carving up portions of national parks for commercial exploitation; rather we should forbid them from doing so, because in designating a national park we simultaneously describe it as a place worthy of protection for the common good. In other cases private appropriation will be less troubling. Allowing agents to draw water from a commonly owned and open-access reservoir would be perfectly defensible: people need water to drink. But charging them when they withdraw water could also be defensible. User charges can contribute to the costs of upkeep and limit excessive or wasteful consumption. Charges for using shared water resources can be combined with discounts or fee-waivers for small-scale or less well-off consumers, but still discourage industrial users from withdrawing too much. When we consider assets held in common, then, three distinct options can be plausible depending on the nature of the case, ranging from forbidding withdrawal, to allowing free withdrawal, perhaps within prescribed limits, to allowing withdrawal but charging for it—that is, levying a kind of tax.

8.2.3. What to Tax?

In contemporary societies taxes are levied on a considerable variety of activities, including the generation of income, the ownership of wealth, pollution, consumption, investment, or savings. In light of the diverse goals that taxes are meant to serve, this diversity should not be surprising. No single 'tax base' is likely to secure, by itself, all four of the objectives delineated. Indeed, each tax base appears to possess its own shortcomings. Income taxes are very widespread at the domestic level, and egalitarians often support them on the basis that unequal rewards to talent in a market are in large part undeserved; but economists suggest that they serve as a disincentive to productive activity, and that we ought to prefer taxes on wealth or consumption instead. Taxes on consumption can usefully discourage environmentally or socially harmful activities; but they are often criticized on the basis that they may hit the poor hardest.[8] Moreover, taxing consumption can lead people to hoard their income, effectively converting it into wealth. Now accumulating wealth (that is, saving) is desirable inasmuch as it secures valuable investment for the future; but excessive saving means that scarce resources are not available for investment now. By contrast, economists often see taxes on land and natural resources as a useful spur to economic activity, when compared to the deadening effects of other taxes.[9] But as we will see in section 8.4, justice is not always best served if those who control resources have incentives to develop them. In practice, policy-makers tend to show some flexibility, taxing each of these bases but shifting the relative burden between them as economic conditions and political priorities evolve. A multi-pronged approach, with some tax bases advancing some of our justice goals and further bases advancing others, is widespread. Theorists of global justice should be open to such an approach too.

We can draw two principal conclusions from the arguments of this section. First, while taxes do not exhaust the egalitarian armoury, they can be an important weapon within it; and second, given that taxes advance several important ends, it is very likely that a plurality of taxes will be desirable, and that these taxes will plausibly cover a variety of tax bases.

8.3. ARE RESOURCE TAXES IRRELEVANT OR REGRESSIVE?

Taxes are an important mechanism for altering the distribution of advantages and disadvantages. But what role is there for taxes on natural resources in particular? There is a great diversity of positions on this question, ranging from the view that it is only resources that should be taxed, to the view that taxes on natural resources should be avoided entirely. Henry George believed that we could abolish all other taxes if only we levied a 'single tax' recouping the unimproved portion of the value of land and its resources,[10] and some contemporary left-libertarians lean towards the same conclusion. But we should reject such a view. If we should also be concerned about unequal market rewards to talent, or inequalities in inherited artefacts or capital, say—as I have suggested we should—then the potential of natural resource taxes to mitigate those inequalities will be limited. Moreover, recall that George and some of the other intellectual progenitors of left-libertarianism wrote at a time when a society's wealth was much more strongly grounded on (skewed) ownership of land and other natural resources than it is now. Viewed in that light the insistence that a single tax would combat all injustice is more intelligible (though still flawed). But in the ensuing centuries the basis of economic production shifted fundamentally. For most countries national income is now much more dependent upon shares of capital, including some quite 'abstract' forms of capital, than it is upon resource rents (which, recall, make up on average 4 per cent of a country's GDP). Global taxes on capital have accordingly captured greater political attention in recent years.[11] Given that, from the perspective of children born into the world's societies, unequal shares of capital are just as undeserved as resource deficits, and given that the effects of accumulated capital inequalities can be very significant, this is a welcome development.

This shift in the basis of economic production—for most countries—does not, however, mean that calls for natural resource taxes are now unsupported or irrelevant, despite some claims to the contrary. Joseph Heath, for instance, has argued that the salience of capital for development renders resource taxes largely irrelevant.[12] Alternatively, it might be thought that what matters for economic development is the quality of institutions, and that resources matter, if at all, insofar as they improve the quality of institutions. Though distinct, we might conceivably infer from this view too that global resource taxes are unmotivated. Reaching the same conclusion as Heath on slightly different grounds, we saw in Chapter 2 that Shmuel Nili, Mathias Risse, and John Rawls have each suggested that the argument for resource taxes falters on the grounds of the (relatively modest or even negligible) role that resources actually play in sustaining economic development.[13] Three responses can be made to claims of that kind.

First, insofar as the claim that taxes on natural resources are irrelevant or unmotivated leans on the idea that shares of natural resources make no contribution to development, its foundation is weak (as I showed in Chapter 2). Meanwhile the weaker claim that resources are *less* important to development than other factors provides no grounds for exempting them from taxation.

Second, we need to clearly distinguish claims about the impact of resources on national economic development from claims about the potential impact of resource taxes on individual wellbeing. Even if it were true that unequal resource endowments made no difference to development, this does not establish that resource taxes could not make a positive contribution to the wellbeing of the poor. Shmuel Nili makes just such an argument, claiming that a weak correlation between poverty and resource abundance establishes that there is no reason 'to believe that a redistribution of natural resource wealth will achieve significant poverty gains'.[14] But this is simply a *non sequitur*. The claim that taxes and transfers cannot help the poor cannot rest upon (purported) evidence that resource rents, channelled through often unaccountable governments, *at present* do little for the poor. Rather it must rely on a demonstration (which Nili does not provide) that there is *nothing* we can do with the proceeds of resource taxes to improve the position of the poor. I will investigate later in this section a series of measures which would do just that, including direct transfers to the poor. Moreover, taxing 'resource-cursed' societies and sharing the revenues with the poor might allow us to short-circuit some of the apparent institutional pathologies that ordinarily prevent resource wealth benefiting citizens—and thereby enhance development prospects more broadly.[15] If these or similar policies can be effective, it is simply a mistake to extrapolate from our (purported) knowledge about the erstwhile effect of resources on development to the claim that resource taxes cannot themselves have valuable consequences.

Third, we should reject the assumption that we must choose between taxes on capital and on natural resources. States, after all, tax a wide array of assets and activities, and there is no reason why advocates of global taxes should be any less flexible. To put it another way, if at the domestic level there is no single tax base which will advance all of the goals we have for taxes, there is no obvious reason why we should expect there to be one at the global level. Furthermore, it is likely that pursuing a more pluralistic tax base will have pragmatic advantages. For instance, a broader tax base may reduce the overall incidence of tax avoidance. Capital is highly mobile in our world, and relatively easy to conceal. This is a contingent political fact rather than a necessary one, but it nevertheless presents formidable practical challenges.[16] By contrast many resources (including, but not restricted to, land) are much less mobile. They, and their consumption, are also often much harder to hide. Both facts render taxes on them harder to avoid, and a more pluralistic tax base more attractive even if taxes on capital ought to be pursued too.

Natural resource taxes will not be sufficient to achieve global justice, therefore. But they may well be highly desirable. Including at least some natural resources in the tax base will have significant benefits. Global taxes on income or wealth could raise considerable funds for egalitarian redistribution. But they would leave other justice goals unfulfilled. For instance, they would not by themselves (or not sufficiently) discourage the production of negative externalities such as pollution or climate change; for that we would likely require dedicated taxes on the consumption of at least some resources. And they would not see users being charged for the consumption of shared resources, even though we often consider such charges to be appropriate. Even if we could achieve a much more egalitarian distribution of income and wealth, then, it is likely that at least some natural resource taxes would be an invaluable part of a just overall package.

The recognition that natural resource taxes ought to be pursued as one part of a more complex tax regime is significant when it comes to addressing criticisms which have sometimes been levelled at them. I am particularly interested here in the claim that, pursued on their own, resource taxes would have a regressive impact. According to Heath, for instance, taxes on natural resources would shift funds from poor but resource-rich countries and in the direction of resource-poor wealthy countries, and in so doing unjustifiably set back the interests of the former.[17] It seems to me that this claim stands in an uneasy relationship with his erstwhile argument that resource revenues do not matter for economic growth[18] (because if those revenues do not make poor countries better off, why would removing them make them worse off?). But leave that to one side. The significant point is that even if it *were* true that natural resource taxes made some poor countries worse off, the fact that natural resource taxes were accompanied by taxes targeting for instance income or capital—or, perhaps, financial transactions[19]—would mean the overall impact would likely be progressive rather than regressive.

Even if this response is correct, of course, it might merely raise an important question of its own. It would be a disappointing conclusion if we had to wait until other taxes were in place before we levied taxes on natural resources (so that the possible regressive effects of natural resource taxes considered on their own could be offset as part of a broader package of transfers). According to some commentators taxes on natural resources are a more immediate political prospect than many of the alternatives.[20] Delaying their introduction until after an effective global tax on capital is secured, say, might be to kick resource taxes into the very long grass. In my view, we need not wait. But in order to see why, we cannot avoid tackling the claim that natural resource taxes pursued alone would have regressive effects—and in particular that they would set back the interests of the worst-off. Five responses can be made to that suggestion.

First, much will depend upon precisely how the relevant tax base is determined. As we will see in section 8.4, those who would levy taxes on natural resources have several options. For instance, they might tax those who own natural resources. Such a policy could place a considerable burden on many developing countries *if* they are properly considered resource-rich.[21] On the other hand, taxing the consumption of natural resources could have a dramatically different effect. Though both live in oil-rich countries, the average Norwegian consumes more than forty times as much electricity as the average Nigerian.[22] Though they both require a couple of litres of water per day to survive, the average Malian citizen consumes four litres of water per day, whereas the average American consumes over two hundred.[23] Moreover, even if rich countries had more meagre resource endowments (and we have seen that this is not obvious, in fact), their activities might turn out to be highly dependent on the consumption of some natural resources such as the absorptive capacity of the atmosphere. Taxes on consumption—especially if they were pitched progressively, and included appropriate thresholds—need not penalize the worst-off. They might, to the contrary, lead to large transfers in the direction of the world's least advantaged. Though I will address the precise tax base later, it should already be obvious that the claim that resource taxes per se will have regressive effects is too blunt.

Second, it may well be that not all valuable resources should attract taxes in any case. Here I do not simply mean that some resources should not attract, say, ownership taxes (see section 8.5). Perhaps, in a just world, some agents—or countries—might actually *attract* transfers aimed at offsetting or pooling the financial burdens of conserving valuable natural resources—in cases, for instance, when those resources deliver important ecosystem services to many people. I develop this argument in Chapter 10, and argue that it also complicates considerably the conventional view of resource revenues flowing from resource-rich towards resource-poor countries. In at least some cases justice recommends that funds flow towards the 'resource-rich'.

Third, when speculating on the likely impact of a given tax scheme we must show proper consideration not only to who pays a tax, but also to who receives revenues from it. Criticisms of the supposedly regressive effects of resource taxes sometimes focus on the former to the neglect of the latter. To be sure, if revenues from resource taxes were disbursed equally to the world's inhabitants, regardless of countervailing inequalities, then there might well be cases in which the effects of resource taxes, pursued in isolation, were regressive (in the sense that some poor countries would end up being net contributors, as opposed to net beneficiaries). That, in my view, provides one reason why we should favour a more broadly equality-promoting view rather than pursuing equal shares of resource values in isolation. But if we disbursed revenues with an eye to all of the multifarious advantages and disadvantages relevant to justice, the outcome would be very different: we would end up shifting funds *to* countries which were doing badly overall, even if they were relatively resource-rich. It is not immediately obvious that we would disburse any income at all to inhabitants of the world's most wealthy countries.

Fourth, reflection on the effects of resource taxes should not focus solely on the question of who pays taxes, and who receives the revenues, because the distributive effects can be broader still. One important effect of natural resource taxes might be to reduce the generation of environmental harms. Such harms often hit the worst-off hardest, whereas the advantaged—who generate most of them—are much less vulnerable to their effects. For example, resource taxes which discouraged the use of fossil fuels would diminish the effects of climate change and avoid serious damage to the interests of many of the world's most vulnerable people (see section 8.5.2). That fact too needs to be borne in mind when assessing the charge of regressivity.

Fifth and finally, we should return to the important distinction between the current effects of resource revenues on national development, and the potential effects of taxes and transfers on individual wellbeing. Imagine a resource-rich but otherwise poor country which does a very bad job of sharing resource revenues with citizens. Income gained from exporting resources might be enormous, but rather than funding redistribution, or the development of infrastructure, say, rulers squander it on vainglorious projects or on kickbacks to a small clique. Imagine now that we taxed this income, and shared the proceeds directly with individual citizens. Even if the overall distributive impact on the country was neutral, such a policy would place resource revenues in the hands of many poor people for the first time. That would be a very welcome result. If we can identify governments which do a very bad job of sharing resource revenues with their subjects, then, resource taxes could produce welcome results simply by short-circuiting the flight of those revenues away from the poor of the world. Moreover, we noted in Chapter 2 that directly sharing resource rents can be effective in ameliorating the institutional maladies *sometimes* associated with great resource wealth in weak states.[24] At the same time they possess great potential to reduce poverty and inequality. If resource taxes were genuinely global—and if revenues were pooled and disbursed in line with overall levels of wellbeing—the results could be even more substantial.

Any such policy would of course require some mechanism for sharing tax revenues with impoverished individuals across the world. Pogge's suggestion is that we collect tax revenues into a global fund and make payments to poor countries' governments, but render those payments conditional upon concrete progress towards poverty alleviation—so that revenues only flowed to countries which could show measurable improvements in the living standards of the poor.[25] A second option would be to distribute revenues directly to poor citizens, bypassing corrupt or ineffective governments entirely. Direct payments would redress widespread gender inequalities in the receipt of resource rents, as well as inequalities based upon ethnicity or religion. They would also leave recipients with the choice of what to spend their money on. Making direct transfers is administratively challenging; but our ability to move money around the world, even to very poor people, is rapidly accelerating, principally as a result of the spread of satellite and mobile phone technology, and there is substantial evidence that direct transfers can be more efficient than conventional forms of either aid or government spending. Around 170 million people in the developing world already receive direct transfers from their governments,[26] and non-governmental organizations (NGOs) have begun to explore their potential to shift resources across borders. Thus far, these experiments have not borne out the concerns of some economists—or some representatives of the established aid hierarchy—that direct transfers would be squandered.[27] To the contrary, money has most often been spent to develop better opportunities to earn income,[28] and direct transfer programmes have been shown to boost school enrolment of both boys and girls.[29] If pursued more systematically the effects of direct transfers on poverty could be dramatic. Even if such experiments for some reason could not be scaled up, a third option would be to use funds to support infrastructure projects or public good provision which would disproportionately benefit the worst-off.[30] Some of these projects might promote better access to natural resources. For instance, money could be spent on developing the greater capacity of communities in the developing world to harness rainwater and hence to reduce dependence on unsustainable forms of irrigation in agriculture; or it could be spent on developing and rolling out green technologies in order to reduce the dependence of emerging economies on fossil fuels. But there is no reason in principle why our focus should be on equalizing the benefits flowing from natural resources as opposed to any other category of advantage. The funds generated could be spent on incentivizing research into tropical diseases which disproportionately affect the world's worst-off but which at present attract a relatively small share of the global spend on research and development.[31] Or they could fund Marine Protected Areas on the high seas, in light of the dependence of many millions of people in the developing world on the employment, and sustenance, provided by the ocean's living resources (see Chapter 9).

To conclude: there are good arguments for pursuing taxes on at least some natural resources as part of a broader package of global taxes. Although these would be insufficient to achieve justice, they would nevertheless play an important and possibly vital role in advancing it. The allegedly regressive effects of resource taxes would be avoided if we followed such an approach. Indeed, when we assess the distributive consequences that resource taxes could have in a suitably broad manner, those regressive effects are far from certain in any case.

8.4. THE TAX BASE

Still, 'resource taxes' is a crude term of art insofar as it does not yet specify the precise tax base that should be employed. Should taxes be used to redistribute some of the income when resources are extracted and sold? Or to levy charges when they are consumed? Or should we tax the ownership of resources, whether they are actually used or not? Left-libertarians have typically favoured ownership taxes, on the basis that it is through ownership that we exclude others from the benefits resources deliver. But taxes on use have also received considerable attention. Pogge's Dividend would involve a tax on the extraction of (some) resources. Alternatively, Tim Hayward has suggested that the consumption of (some) resources should be taxed.[32] Each policy would likely have quite different distributive consequences.

Adopting any of these proposals as an exclusive base for resource taxation would, however, be unsatisfying. This is because it is unlikely that any of them will allow us to advance all of the goals we might want taxes to serve. Specifying ownership as the right tax base makes sense, for instance, if our priority is to shift resources—or resource value—away from agents who have weak claims over them. Such taxes could substantially widen access to the benefits that resources provide, if levied at a sufficiently high rate. They could also generate substantial funds for redistribution or the funding of other justice goals (on Steiner's account, the proceeds would bankroll equal capital grants or a global basic income). But taxes on ownership would not (sufficiently) discourage the generation of harms. Indeed, they might have the opposite effect. If owners pay taxes on the resources they own, this will incentivize their exploitation. As the tax rate rises, many will come to the conclusion that it is only economically 'rational' to hold resources when they are producing a flow of income. Now in some cases incentivizing the exploitation of resources will generate perfectly acceptable results, insofar as it prevents agents from hogging resources which others could benefit from (perhaps waiting for future increases in price, and ignoring the potential benefits to others of the resources they control). But an across-the-board incentive to exploit would not be desirable. As Pogge argues, in at least some cases 'A levy on natural resource endowments penalizes exactly what we ought to encourage: the preservation of (esp. non-renewable) resources for the benefit of the environment and future generations.'[33]

By contrast, taxes on extraction can deliver important environmental benefits, in discouraging the exploitation of resources whose use has harmful consequences. However, in some cases taxes on extraction would themselves produce unwelcome results. Whereas ownership taxes would dissuade agents from hogging resources, extraction taxes would allow them to do so. In many cases this too will be objectionable. In the face of rising global food prices, for people to control—but not use—fertile agricultural land will become increasingly costly for others. In such a scenario ownership taxes which encouraged them to put it to use might be desirable.[34] Indeed, an ideal package will likely include consumption taxes too. Extraction taxes would require those who currently control resources to pick up the tab even if they are eventually used by others—even if, as in the contemporary world, relatively poor countries end up extracting resources which are subsequently used by rich consumers overseas. Whereas we might hope that the costs will eventually be passed onto final consumers, this will not always be the case.[35] If not, the case for direct taxes on consumption is strengthened. Consumption taxes could contribute significantly to reducing some important harms, and also generate considerable income for promoting justice goals.

The pursuit of greater global equality does not, then, furnish an exclusive preference for any of these tax bases, but is rather likely to be served by a combination of them. The use of some resources should be discouraged, and in these cases taxes on either extraction or consumption can be a valuable tool. But conceivably, the use of some resources should be encouraged, and in these cases taxes on ownership can be valuable. In light of this diversity, we must be prepared to adopt a fine-grained approach.[36] This means that a single, undifferentiated tax on natural resources would therefore serve justice poorly.

Pragmatic considerations, it seems to me, point in much the same direction. Any proposal for a single, widely encompassing global tax on natural resources would encounter formidable resistance. The likelihood of resistance does not mean such taxes should not be pursued. But the chances of achieving a tax on a relatively circumscribed set of resources are likely much better, and such taxes could still deliver important progress. That progress might over time undermine some of the criticisms often levelled at resource taxes, and help to engender greater political support. If so, we might profitably attempt to broaden the tax base over time. By the same token, it may make pragmatic sense to introduce a relatively modest tax with the goal of increasing the tax rate over time. Political history suggests that the taxes which dominate the contemporary domestic scene had rather humble beginnings. Relatively targeted and modest resource taxes can prepare the ground for more radical policies.

8.5. PROPOSALS FOR SPECIFIC RESOURCE TAXES

In this section I will investigate some proposals for more specific resource taxes. Taxes on specific resources, or specific uses of them, sometimes attract the charge of arbitrariness. Brian Barry, for instance, declared that the idea of taxes on fossil fuel use was so obviously arbitrary that it was a mystery why anyone should have seriously considered it.[37] Why, after all, should the use of some resources be taxed when the use of others is not? We should indeed recognize that such proposals are arbitrary, in the sense that many other environmental impacts may require taxation too. But that does not mean we should not pursue such proposals as an urgent priority. The use of fossil fuels generates enormous environmental harms, and if taxes reduce those harms they will have achieved something important. But more importantly, we should be clear that broader-based taxes on the use of other resources could and should be pursued whenever this is politically possible. The suggestions in this section represent starting points rather than end points.

8.5.1. Taxes on the Use of Common-Pool Resources

Many valuable resources are not legally owned by anyone, but nevertheless deliver enormous benefits to those who consume them. Taxes on this consumption can be justified on two grounds. First, since these resources do not belong to anyone in particular, it is fitting that the consumption of the benefits they deliver is to the advantage of all, as opposed to merely advancing the interests of those who happen to possess the capacity to harvest them first. User charges could generate considerable revenues for promoting the interests of the world's worst-off. Second, taxes on consumption can discourage wasteful or inefficient consumption, and help ensure that these resources are also available to future generations of people. This consideration is particularly relevant to the case of renewable resources produced by ecosystems that are capable of exhaustion if they are over-exploited. In some cases (such as fees for catching the ocean's fish), user charges might therefore be justified in light of their pro-conservation effects even if their revenue-raising capacity is distinctly limited.

In Chapter 9 I will analyse in some detail a variety of proposals for charging people for using the resources of the world's oceans. The oceans contain hugely valuable resources, which fall outside the geographical borders of any state. In many cases it remains an open question, within international law, just how, if at all, their consumption or use should be regulated. Should they be available to all on a first-come-first-served basis? Should states be able to extend their jurisdiction over these resources, and thereby monopolize the benefits they deliver? Or should we favour a regime under which their use is licensed by a common global authority, and users are charged fees in order that use benefits all of us—including those who do not yet possess the capacity to harvest these resources themselves? I will argue that egalitarians have strong reasons for favouring the latter approach, and illustrate the argument with reference to important categories of resources such as the oceans' fish, and seabed minerals. I will also show that important progress has already been made towards making egalitarian benefit-sharing schemes a reality. The challenge is to extend such schemes to further categories of resources.

But it is not only the ocean's riches to which such schemes could be applied. We might conceive of the globe's freshwater supplies as a common resource, circulating through a complex and global hydrological system, and largely untouched by any special claims on the part of states. If so, proposals for levying a small charge on the use of water, with the proceeds going to enhance water-harvesting technology in developing countries, may gain traction.[38] The capacity of the atmosphere to absorb greenhouse gases might be treated in a similar fashion—and to that extent proposals for carbon taxes (on which see section 8.5.2) could also be described as a user charge for the use of a non-excludable resource. We might also extend such an approach to the spectrum-space of the world's atmosphere. The International Telecommunications Union (ITU) long ago established a principle of equitable sharing of the radio spectrum among all of the world's states, and has been successful in managing conflict over its use. It also allocates the geostationary orbits far above the surface of the earth which are crucial for much modern communication.[39] But at present rights to use these resources come free of charge, rather than being used to raise revenue for the amelioration of injustice. Perhaps this represents a missed opportunity. In Britain alone, a 2013 auction of the right to use 4G mobile phone frequencies raised £2.4 billion for government coffers, and auction revenues are expected to rise in future rounds.[40] There is no reason why such spectrum-space should not be globally auctioned by an organization like the ITU. Doing so would ease potential conflicts over their exploitation, and release considerable funds for the promotion of global justice.

8.5.2. A Carbon Tax

The use of fossil fuels generates very significant harms, from the relatively localized air pollution associated with coal use, to much more dispersed climatic effects associated with fossil fuels in general. These harms are by no means randomly distributed: vulnerability to airborne pollution correlates strongly with poverty, both domestically and globally. Meanwhile those most vulnerable to climate change are likely to include people living in low-lying island and coastal deltas, people immediately dependent upon agriculture for their subsistence, and those with the poorest protection from diseases such as malaria, dengue fever, and cholera.[41]

Carbon taxes—or taxes on greenhouse gas emissions more generally—are often advocated on the basis that they would oblige those who consume carbon to internalize at least some of the costs its use imposes. In light of the very serious harms which may be involved, taxes may not be the *only* appropriate measure for reducing carbon emissions. But they may well play an important role within an overall package of policies aimed at reducing those harms.[42] Carbon taxes would in the first instance be employed to discourage fossil fuel use, though they would also produce revenues by way of which to compensate those forced to adapt to climate change. Alternatively, revenue might be used to fund the transfer of low-carbon technology to developing countries in order that their development is rendered compatible with climate stability. But although in the short or medium term they could raise substantial revenues for such purposes, their ultimate objective must be to suppress demand for carbon-intensive products, and, as such, diminishing revenues would be a sign of success.

Carbon taxes are best considered as part of a package of policies which would also include the removal of a variety of subsidies. These take a variety of forms. First, oil, coal, and gas companies have benefited from enormous tax breaks, which have proven durable even in light of political turnover, and in spite of the fact that their effects are deeply inegalitarian. Second, many countries grant direct consumer subsidies which reduce the market price of fuels. These are especially common in the Middle East and North Africa, though they are also present in Indonesia and Venezuela (home to the world's cheapest oil).[43] Now even if policy-makers wish to reduce the overall consumption of fossil fuels, there may be a continuing role for direct subsidies for the poorest consumers, who have vital energy needs but very limited access to renewable technologies. Until that access improves, the world's poorest have a good claim to consume whatever portion of the world's fossil fuels the use of which is compatible with climate stabilization.[44] But existing fuel subsidies do very little for the poorest; typically most of the benefits are instead captured by higher-income groups.[45] Even if *some* direct subsidies are compatible with justice, then, the existing pattern of subsidies has little to recommend it.

Third, we might consider the everyday consumption of consumers to be indirectly subsidized. When the true social and environmental costs of consumption exceed its market price, we have what economists call a post-tax subsidy. But here the people funding the subsidy are not governments hungry for domestic support, but those who suffer the effects of pollution or climate change. Subtracting the price paid to use carbon from its true social and environmental cost, one study estimates that these subsidies totalled $4.9 trillion in 2013, or fully 6.5 per cent of total global income.[46] Coal, rather than oil or gas, accounts for by far the greatest subsidies because it is much the dirtiest fuel, associated as it is with many premature deaths from pollution. Post-tax subsidies on coal use alone were expected to account for 3.9 per cent of global income in 2015.[47] In this sense carbon taxes could themselves be described as removing a subsidy.

How close are we to effectively taxing carbon? Domestic fuel taxes are certainly very widespread. Moreover, in many places they have undoubtedly had an effect on consumption levels.[48] But the pattern of carbon taxes is patchy in three senses. First, some uses of carbon are taxed to the detriment of others (for instance, whereas individuals often pay heavy taxes on petrol, corporations often pay proportionately lower taxes on their carbon-intensive activities). Second, the pattern of taxation between countries is very uneven.

Globally, only about 12 per cent of global emissions are currently covered by carbon-pricing programmes.[49] Third, in many countries the 'shadow price' of carbon is set too low for taxes to make a sizeable difference to consumption. Perhaps only in Scandinavia is the shadow price of carbon pitched high enough to make a serious dent in emissions.

For carbon taxes to be truly effective, some degree of global coordination would be optimal. After all, if heavy domestic carbon taxes are introduced, local producers may respond by relocating to countries which do not impose carbon taxes, or where carbon taxes are lower. This generates what analysts call 'leakage'.[50] The immediate result may be that locals avoid some of the negative effects of fossil fuel use (including air pollution). But others, most likely in developing countries, may simply be exposed to more of them—and the overall global effect on carbon emissions may be minimal. A globally coordinated regime of carbon taxes would mitigate the problem of leakage, and could in principle provide a mechanism by way of which the burdens of decarbonization could be spread fairly. Still, even in the absence of such coordination, countries which are 'first-movers' towards carbon taxation need not be at a disadvantage. The unevenness of a playing field in which one country places a carbon tax on domestic producers but others do not can be eased by way of trade measures, and in particular the imposition of so-called 'border carbon adjustments'. These adjustments would allow a country which *did* have an effective carbon tax to levy tariffs on imports from countries which did not. At the same time, domestic companies exporting to non-compliant countries could receive rebates, allowing them to compete on a level playing field with goods from those countries.

Because of their distributional impact—which might place too great a share of the burden of mitigation on the shoulders of developing countries—border carbon adjustments are a second-best solution when compared to a regime of global carbon taxes.[51] But even when it comes to carbon taxes it is important to note that progress need not depend upon a truly global taxation regime. Aside from border carbon adjustments, progress could be secured by way of sufficient *coordination between* tax-levying institutions such as states. Proposals for greater international tax coordination typically aim to sanction defaulters which provide tax havens for those wishing to avoid domestic taxes, producing a 'race to the bottom' in the taxation of income or corporate revenues. The challenges faced in taxing carbon emissions are rather similar: when some countries do not tax carbon at all, they create 'emissions havens' for corporations (and, indirectly, for the consumers who buy their products). Since the emissions will happen regardless, their behaviour represents a form of free-riding, and reduces the likelihood of climate stabilization. But coordination of tax levels could minimize these effects even if the revenues were not pooled globally. Ultimately the effective coordination of carbon taxes—or any other taxes—would still require meaningful sanctions. Organizations such as the World Trade Organization (WTO) could help by 'linking' participation in international trade to active measures to suitably price, and hence minimize, carbon emissions.

A second form of coordination may also be required. Insofar as they raise revenues (for instance for spreading renewable technologies, or assisting those harmed by climate change), some mechanism for diverting funds across jurisdictions is in order. Once again, new institutions are not necessarily required. Institutions already exist which could collect and deploy the funds in question. Examples include the United Nations (UN) Adaptation Fund, the Global Environmental Facility (which aims at protecting key ecosystem resources such as rainforests—see Chapter 10), and the UN's Green Climate Fund (under the auspices of which the developed world has committed to funding the spread of non-polluting technologies throughout the developing world).

8.5.3. A Sovereign Wealth Tax

Since the turn of the century, dozens of countries have established Sovereign Wealth Funds (SWFs) in order to manage revenues gained from selling resources such as oil and gas on a tide of rapidly climbing commodity prices. Those revenues are invested on international stock and real estate markets. Returns on those overseas investments will increasingly supplement—and eventually replace—dwindling resource revenues, which are in any case highly vulnerable to fluctuation in exchange rates and commodity prices. Such Funds are the retirement plan of many oil-rich countries and regions. The wealth contained in them is sometimes vast. At the top of the pile sit the Abu Dhabi Investment Authority and Norway's aptly titled Government Pension Fund (Global). Each is swelled by billions of dollars of petroleum revenues every year. Whilst the Abu Dhabi Fund does not publish financial information, the value of its current investments is estimated at $772 billion—or $840,000 for each of Abu Dhabi's citizens.[52] About 60 per cent of Norway's petroleum revenues are diverted into its Fund, and as of 2015 its value was $866 billion.[53]

Given the enormous wealth of these funds, it is surprising how little discussion there has been of how their contents should eventually be spent, and in whose interests. Even within a relatively open country such as Norway successive governments have rarely been pressed about their plans for these assets—beyond viewing them as a huge pension pot, capable of maintaining living standards once the oil is gone. Recent years have witnessed the beginnings of a discussion within political theory about how their wealth might be shared.[54] Within that discussion, the assumption that their wealth should be used to raise the living standards of citizens, as opposed to outsiders, has so far gone untroubled. Theorists of global justice have not addressed these funds at all.⁵⁵ One reason this neglect is surprising is that national claims over the contents of these funds appear very weak. Consider Norway's Fund, for example. Its wealth has two sources. Some of it is generated when Norway sells exploration rights over crude oil buried under the North Sea; and the rest is raised by taxing the very large profits made by Norwegian oil companies. In the first case, the Norwegian state or the Norwegian people have done nothing to improve the oil or gas concerned; rather, they have simply sold pieces of paper allowing others to extract that oil. In the second case, the fact that the Norwegian government levies a substantial tax on corporate profits amply illustrates its own view that the large profits made by the companies concerned are essentially economic rents. Even after the costs of exploration, extraction, and transportation have been recouped, enormous sums are left over which the Norwegian state clearly views as liable for redistribution. But if these rents are unearned, it is not obvious why the beneficiaries of a tax on the windfalls involved should be the Norwegian people as opposed to anyone else.

Recall, moreover, that whereas oil rents are the initial source of these funds' *wealth*, the *income* they then generate arises solely from the performance of foreign investments. The Abu Dhabi Fund's overseas investments have attracted real returns of around 7 per cent per year⁵⁶—a rate of growth which would see its overall value doubling every decade. Even if no more oil rents were added to the Fund, such financial returns could bankroll an affluent lifestyle for each of its citizens in perpetuity. Abu Dhabi's citizens are already unusual among the world's peoples in paying no tax. Their Fund now generates an annual income of roughly fifty thousand US dollars for each one of them too. Moreover, as the Fund's stocks are appreciating in value at a rate faster than the growth of the world economy as a whole, it can be expected to control a larger and larger proportion of total global capital. As a result of such investments, it and many other Gulf states are fast becoming 'rentier' societies. Although they have invested some of their wealth in domestic industries and human capital (notwithstanding their well-known reliance on cheap expatriate labour), their livelihood is based to an increasing degree upon renting out capital to the rest of the world in order that citizens can live off the interest. That capital derives entirely from oil rents. Despite its impressive levels of education and its high-tech economy, Norway may be on a similar trajectory. The Norwegian Fund holds fully 1 per cent of total global equity, and is also growing faster than the global economy as a whole. New generations in Norway and the Gulf will inherit this burgeoning wealth even as others experience the terrible climatic effects associated with burning fossil fuels. In total, SWFs now hold approximately 5 per cent of all financial assets worldwide, and on Thomas Piketty's projections that proportion could increase tenfold in the next few decades.⁵⁷

A tax on resource-based SWFs could raise significant revenues for the fight against global inequality. The SWFs of Norway and Abu Dhabi alone contain more than five times the amount Thomas Pogge claims is needed annually to lift everyone in the world out of severe poverty.[58] They contain 250 times the amount of money needed to finance a minimally effective Health Impact Fund (HIF) which could ease the global disease burden and save millions of lives in the developing world.[59] Without even touching their capital, the income earned by those two funds alone could bankroll the HIF fifteen times over. Alternatively, the revenues from a tax on resource-based SWFs could be used to compensate those harmed by fossil fuel use, or to promote the spread of green technologies. A Sovereign Wealth Tax would also help mitigate burgeoning global inequalities in wealth and income. As Piketty's recent work has done much to remind us, without concerted political intervention those with great wealth are capable of locking in their advantages across many generations, and capable too of capturing political power to further defend and entrench their privileges. A tax on SWFs could play a part in interrupting that cycle.

The primary target of such a tax would plausibly be those funds operated by countries with high per-capita incomes and whose citizens would remain comparatively wealthy even if the oil (or a market for it) dried up. It is less immediately obvious what is to be gained by taxing the SWFs of poorer countries. But such measures could still be worthwhile. Positive outcomes can ensue when the governments of poor resource-exporting countries divert resource rents into SWFs. But they will be little solace to the poor so long as the eventual purpose of those funds remains ambiguous, or so long as leaders continue to bankroll vanity projects or squander their income on elite patronage. If some mechanism existed for sharing the income generated by these funds with the wider populace, and if the governance of such funds were sufficiently transparent and accountable, then there might be relatively little to gain by taxing them. But for so long as this is not the case, a tax on SWFs can be a progressive option.

ENDNOTES

1. Beitz 1979; Steiner 2005; Pogge 2002. Other proposals for global resource taxes are made in Barry 1982; Casal 2011; and Kymlicka 2001.
2. Carens 2013, chapter 11.
3. Oberman 2015.
4. This is an implication of Mathias Risse's account—although he also suggests that wealthy countries can justly exclude people trying to cross borders to gain access to land and resources. Risse 2012, chapter 8. In principle, many other forms of direct (and illegal) action might be justifiable in a context of deep global injustice, including theft, piracy, and counterfeiting. For an important discussion, see

Caney (forthcoming). For a more modest approach to the so-called 'right of necessity' (which focuses on actions to ease poverty), see Mancilla 2015a.
5. Nagel 2005. See also Wenar 2016b.
6. Wenar 2006.
7. This may depend partly on the tax rate. As a tax on ownership, say, approaches 100 per cent, the effects might be thought to approach those of confiscation. But even a tax at 100 per cent may leave agents with the option of paying the tax but retaining the asset, whereas confiscation does not.
8. Though much depends here on whether they target luxuries or more basic goods. Their impact also depends upon which other measures are adopted alongside them. Taxes can be accompanied by thresholds which protect the poor, or side-payments which offset any undesirable effects. When appraising fiscal regimes we should evaluate their overall effects, which may be pro-egalitarian even if individual elements are not (see section 8.3).
9. See e.g. Smith 1999, Book V.
10. George 2005.
11. Most famously in Piketty 2014, chapter 15.
12. Heath 2005: 214–17.
13. Nili 2016a; Risse 2005; Rawls 1999.
14. Nili 2016b: 7.
15. Moss 2011; Sandbu 2006; Sala-i-Martin and Subramanian 2003; Palley 2003.
16. For a recent study of the challenges of taxing capital in a world of states, see Dietsch 2015.
17. The claim is made in response to Pogge's proposal in particular: '[T]he global resource dividend... would penalize underdeveloped countries and benefit richer ones.' As a result, 'At worst, it would become a tax on poverty.' Heath 2005: 214–15.
18. Heath 2005: 214–15.
19. Originally intended to reduce the generation of a harm (market instability), a tax on financial or currency transactions has since often been endorsed on the basis of its potential to raise revenue for redistribution. See Tobin 1996. For a more wide-ranging discussion of proposals for global taxes, see Brock 2008. See also Armstrong 2014b.
20. See e.g. Pogge 2002. I do not endorse that claim here. It might be, for instance, that the prospects for a financial transactions tax are at least as good. But I examine what would follow if the claim were true.
21. That will depend upon our measure of resource endowments. As I noted in Chapter 2, within the 'resource curse' literature countries are often labelled resource-rich whenever a high degree of their income comes from resource sales. But this is not a compelling metric when it comes to allocating tax burdens.
22. http://data.worldbank.org/indicator/EG.USE.ELEC.KH.PC.
23. http://www.unwater.org/downloads/Water_facts_and_trends.pdf.
24. E.g. Moss 2011; Sandbu 2006; Palley 2003.
25. Pogge 2002.
26. Moss 2011: 13.

27. Blattman and Niehaus 2014; Kendall and Voorhies 2014. In any case, as Sandbu (2006: 1162) notes, 'what matters is not whether individuals would behave wastefully, but whether they would behave more wastefully than the government [in resource-rich developing countries]. There is evidence that the opposite is the case.'
28. Hanlon, Barrientos, and Hulme 2010: 7–9.
29. Of course, some transfers are conditional on school enrolment. But Moss (2011: 6) suggests that the boost holds independently of, and indeed in the absence of, such conditionality.
30. See also Pogge 2011: 347; Casal 2011.
31. Pogge 2008, chapter 9.
32. Hayward 2005.
33. Pogge 2011: 340.
34. Pogge 2011: 342–3.
35. Haubrich 2004.
36. See also Casal 2011: 320.
37. Barry 1982, section 2. Barry's fear was in part that fossil fuel taxes would harm the interests of fossil fuel exporters in poor countries. In Chapter 10 I discuss some ways in which this worry could be eased.
38. For a proposal for such a levy, and a brief discussion of some local innovations in that direction, see Armstrong 2012: 158–61.
39. The ITU was founded as the International Telegraph Union in 1865, but took its present name in 1934 and became an organ of the UN in 1947. See http://www.itu.int.
40. http://www.nao.org.uk/report/4g-radio-spectrum-auction-lessons-learned-2/.
41. Intergovernmental Panel on Climate Change 2007.
42. Goodin (2010) rejects what he calls an 'economistic' view which depicts carbon taxes as a cure-all for environmental injustice, allowing the market to determine the overall level of emissions and then using tax revenues to compensate for harms. But he agrees they can play an important role in reducing emissions.
43. Davis 2014.
44. See e.g. Shue 2014.
45. Arze del Granado et al. 2010.
46. Coady et al. 2015.
47. Coady et al. 2015: 20.
48. For instance, it is estimated that if fuel taxes were as low in the European Union (EU) as they are in the US, European demand for oil would be double its current levels. Sterner 2007.
49. World Bank 2014.
50. For a discussion of leakage effects see e.g. Sovacool and Brown 2009.
51. Böhringer et al. 2012.
52. http://www.swfinstitute.org/swfs/abu-dhabi-investment-authority/.
53. According to the Norges Bank's own calculations: see http://www.nbim.no/en/the-fund.
54. See especially Cummine 2016, and Widerquist and Howard 2012.

55. Cf. Armstrong 2013, and the critical responses by Andreas Føllesdal, Angela Cummine, Oliviero Angeli, and Paul Segal: http://www.ethicsandinternationalaffairs.org/2014/norways-sovereign-wealth-fund-and-global-justice-an-exchange/.
56. Piketty 2014, chapter 12.
57. Piketty 2014, chapter 12.
58. Pogge 2002.
59. The HIF would award money to anyone who succeeded in delivering treatments reducing the global disease burden. Its supporters (including Thomas Pogge) claim that it would powerfully realign incentives to engage in pharmaceutical innovation, making the development of treatments for serious diseases affecting many millions of people (often in the developing world) more attractive. The HIF estimates that $6 billion per year is a 'reasonable minimum' for the approach to be effective. http://healthimpactfund.org/financing-the-health-impact-fund/.

9

The Ocean's Riches

I have cast doubt upon the strength and scope of the special claims nation-states can make over the resources in their territories. But many important resources do not fall within individual states in the first place, and it is an important question how the benefits and burdens they secure should be distributed. This chapter will focus upon the resources of the world's oceans. Political theorists have in recent years paid precious little sustained attention to these marine resources. That neglect is regrettable, since some of them are hugely valuable, and the precise nature of the rules governing their exploitation will be enormously consequential. Left unchecked, exploitation is likely to track—and indeed to intensify—existing inequalities, as the agents possessed of the technology necessary to harvest them rapidly gather the spoils. On the other hand, if they were collectively managed, and their exploitation rendered conditional upon a scheme of benefit-sharing, their use could promote greater equality. Indeed, such policies, as we will see, are by no means a far-fetched prospect. Notwithstanding scepticism about the feasibility or accessibility of egalitarian reforms at the global level, we are able to point towards real progress which has already been made, and which furnishes a model which could be extended to further valuable resources.

The structure of the chapter is as follows. Section 9.1 briefly sketches the political struggle that has been waged over ocean resources in recent decades, in which the protagonists have locked horns over whether these resources should be brought under the control of individual states, left largely unregulated, or else globally managed as part of humankind's 'common heritage', and exploited in such a way as to ameliorate, rather than intensify, existing global inequalities. It details the uneasy compromise reached between these alternative ideals under the auspices of the United Nations Convention on the Law of the Sea (UNCLOS). Section 9.2 discusses the case of fishing rights, in which we have witnessed a mixture of extended state control and unconstrained exploitation in the area beyond any state's jurisdiction. It shows that this approach has comprehensively failed to deliver on either intra-generational justice or sustainability, and sketches some alternative proposals which would serve justice better. Section 9.3 discusses the mineral resources contained in the portions of the seabed which still fall beyond state control. Under the UNCLOS settlement these are treated very differently to the ocean's fish stocks. Agreement has been reached, under the auspices of the International Seabed Authority (ISA), to harness the exploitation of these potentially valuable minerals to promote global equality. Though challenges remain, section 9.4 welcomes this development and identifies some wider lessons we might draw from it. Section 9.5 briefly concludes.

9.1. THE STRUGGLE OVER OCEAN RESOURCES

In recent decades states have extended their powers far beyond their geographical borders. In particular, states have come to enjoy resource rights over broad swathes of the seas adjacent to their coasts. States have, to be sure, long claimed a kind of dominion over immediate coastal waters. From the late eighteenth century onwards many countries asserted the right to exclude foreign vessels from the sea within 3 nautical miles of their coastlines. By the 1960s and 1970s some states were beginning to claim 'territorial waters' of up to 12 nautical miles.

But those claims were fairly modest, and their significance for access to resources relatively minimal. Their standing under international law also remained uncertain. A global legal framework would be required to resolve the proper reach of state authority over the oceans. After many years of fraught negotiation, 1982 witnessed the emergence of UNCLOS. This treaty confirmed states' rights to 12-mile territorial waters—but its ramifications were far greater than that. Much more sweepingly, and in a distributive sense much more significantly, it also authorized states to designate Exclusive Economic Zones (EEZs) extending up to 200 nautical miles from their coasts. Within those EEZs each state would be entitled to the exclusive exploitation of living and non-living resources, including fish, the oil and gas deposits found beneath the seabed, and potentially valuable mineral deposits. Still more expansively it provided a framework by way of which states could lodge claims over non-living resources contained within 'extended continental shelves' reaching out up to 350 nautical miles from some countries' shores—although, in the latter case, exploitation was conditional upon acceptance of a revenue-sharing scheme designed to spread the ensuing benefits globally (see section 9.3). Over these areas—EEZs and extended continental shelves—states now exercise a novel form of quasi-sovereignty.[1]

UNCLOS represented a radical extension of state prerogative, providing legal cover for a rapid resource-grab—by some states, if not all—of historically unparalleled scale. Before UNCLOS, individual states monopolized withdrawal rights over less than 30 per cent of the earth's surface. After the treaty the figure was in excess of 50 per cent. From the distributive point of view, that move has been enormously consequential. The newly created EEZs, along with extended continental shelves, contain the vast majority of the known oil and gas reserves contained under the seabed. Norway's new-found control over North Sea oil allowed it to rapidly surpass its neighbours in economic growth, and channel resource revenues into what is now the world's largest Sovereign Wealth Fund (SWF). As its land-based oil reserves dwindle, the United States is increasingly satisfying consumers' thirst by drilling for offshore oil, to the extent that it may soon regain from Saudi Arabia its former status as the world's largest oil producer.[2] EEZs also contain nine-tenths of the world's fish catch.[3] Iceland has enriched *some* of its citizens by claiming control over rich fishing zones; other countries have followed suit. Meanwhile many states are turning their attention further afield. Some of them have developed a new-found interest in previously obscure overseas territories under the banner of which they can register claims to even larger EEZs. Britain, for instance, now has one of the largest EEZs in the world by total area, and the vast majority of it is claimed on the basis of dominion over colonial-era possessions such as the Falkland Islands, South Georgia, and the (barely inhabited) Tristan da Cunha archipelago. China is currently constructing a series of artificial islands hundreds of miles from its coast which, while of dubious legal standing, are presumably intended to bolster its ambitious claims over much of the huge South and East China Seas (as well as enhancing its armed presence in the region). Elsewhere, it is suspected that there could be as many as 90 billion barrels-worth of oil underneath the Arctic ice-cap, and as the sea warms, the retreating ice has, in a terrible irony, rendered that oil more readily exploitable. A tangle of claims has been registered over the region by Russia, Canada, Norway, and Denmark, on the basis of the extent of 'their' continental shelves.[4]

These trends have followed hot on the heels of technological change. The fish of the seas were once seen as being practically inexhaustible, and their consumption therefore non-subtractive. But harvesting technology developed rapidly in the twentieth century, and as it became apparent that stocks were distinctly limited, the question of how withdrawal rights should be allocated became politically salient. The ability to exploit offshore oil and gas is also a relatively recent phenomenon, and the technology necessary to exploit many seabed resources is only now coming to fruition (see section 9.3). Technical advances have given a sense of immediacy to the efforts, especially on the part of developed states, to carve out sections of the oceans for their own exclusive exploitation. The race to benefit from these resources is very much on.

At the level of principle, however, it is difficult to see quite how this huge and rapid resource-grab can be justified. Its effects are certainly deeply inegalitarian. Of the world's states, only around 170 even *have* coastlines; those which do not (including countries such as Ethiopia, Rwanda, Afghanistan, and Nepal) are unable to make claims over these valuable resources. The EEZ which Britain claims as a result of its sovereignty over South Georgia and the South Sandwich Islands—an inhospitable archipelago in the Southern Atlantic with no permanent population—is larger than that of China, with its population of over a billion people. The rules on extended shelves further deepen the distributive inequities associated with the UNCLOS settlement. Of those states with coastlines, only around 80 'possess' continental shelves extending beyond 200 nautical miles.[5] Those which are lucky enough to do so can register enormous claims over seabed resources (and the United Nations (UN) has received many of these). But it is hard to see how the fact that one's territory is on a swathe of rock that extends for more than 200 miles under the sea before dropping off to the deep seabed, rather than less, is an achievement intelligibly deserving of reward, or indeed that it has any moral relevance to the question of who ought to benefit from resources that are hundreds of miles away from any state's borders. That it should underpin claims which other states are, through no fault of their own, excluded from making appears to be a reflection of realpolitik rather than any recognizable moral principle.

We saw in Chapter 6 that the reach of the most promising defences of communities' rights over the resources within their territories is actually weak and patchy. They are certainly no stronger, and are plausibly weaker still, in the case of these marine or submarine resources. Even defenders of resource sovereignty have rarely argued otherwise.[6] States cannot claim to have improved the fish of the ocean, or the oil, gas, or minerals of the seabed: those resources are wholly untouched by human hand until the moment they are scooped up. Though exploiting agents might have a claim that the costs of discovery and extraction are recouped, the remaining value is simply a vast windfall. Attachment-based claims over these extra-territorial resources also look highly tenuous. Rights over oil, gas, and minerals are being claimed so that they can be extracted and sold on global markets; rather than these resources being prized cultural assets, they represent sources of ready cash. The fishing trade might appear to sit somewhat differently on this score. Some countries have fishing practices running back through many generations and which are undoubtedly identity-conferring. But it is hard to see how those practices can be used to justify newly *extending* (quasi-) sovereignty over greater and greater areas of the sea, and thereby newly excluding others from them. In any case, the highly capital-intensive and technological nature of fishing many miles out to sea should dispel any rosy visions we might have of fishing as a traditional subsistence practice (see section 9.2). Fish, too, are sources of revenue for highly mechanized and ruthlessly competitive industries, and, as in Iceland, fishing rights within many EEZs are highly tradable commodities.

The prospect of making sound instrumental arguments for state control over these resources also appears bleak. As some defenders of state sovereignty over resources themselves attest, control over these resources is not necessary for any particular state's self-determination.[7] The legal invention of EEZs and extended shelves has no implications for security or border control; it is a regime for allocating resource rights alone. But insofar as it does so, it does nothing for the self-determination of communities which are not lucky enough to have coastlines or extended shelves in the first place. Insofar as the generation of quasi-sovereignty over EEZs and extended shelves had any intellectual foundation at all, it probably lay principally with the other variety of instrumental claim we have discussed—that is, with the claim that granting each state exclusive control would secure the effective custodianship of limited resources. But in the case of renewable resources such as fish, the claim that extending state control would secure sustainability faces, as we will see in section 9.2, an embarrassment of evidence to the contrary. The solution to the collapse of global fish stocks lies in global coordination, and not in a regime under which each state is given autonomous control over fish which often do not respect jurisdictional boundaries in any case. In the case of non-renewable resources, EEZs and extended shelves have simply enabled states to find still further supplies of fossil fuels to exploit at a frenetic rate, and thereby to postpone the transition to a post-carbon future. Whatever other goals this has served, it is difficult to see that effective custodianship has been among them.

* * *

International law, does not, however, extend to individual states control over *all* of the resources contained within the oceans. To the contrary, it declares some resources to be part of the 'common heritage of humankind'.[8] This is a notoriously elusive phrase—which is another way of saying that labelling a resource as part of the common heritage has often postponed, rather than resolved, questions about exactly how rights over it are to be allocated. Certainly, though, labelling a resource as part of our common heritage has signified that it is considered to fall outside the jurisdiction of any state. Appropriation of such resources may be either forbidden outright or, when permitted, required to be conducive to the common good of both current and future generations. In some important cases—which I discuss in section 9.3—exclusion rights in common heritage resources are vested with the international community such that withdrawal can only occur when authorized by the community or by some agent representing it. And when permission is given to exploit common heritage resources, the idea is that such exploitation should be to the benefit of all. Specifically, we can identify important cases in which exploitation is conditional upon the acceptance of a benefit-sharing scheme which seeks to harness revenues in order to ameliorate global inequalities.

Something akin to the common heritage idea was implicit in the pioneering Antarctic Treaty of 1959, which proclaimed Antarctica to be 'a natural reserve, devoted to peace and science'. Signatories to the Treaty agree to use the region for exclusively peaceful purposes; later provisions under the Treaty regime have enjoined member-states to limit their environmental impacts, to protect wildlife, and to facilitate international scientific cooperation. Perhaps most significantly, the Treaty regime witnessed a suspension of territorial claims over Antarctica, and banned prospecting for minerals in that vast region. That regime has been very successful, and the prohibition on mineral exploitation will not be up for discussion until 2048.[9] Until that date, the resources of the Antarctic cannot legally be exploited. If their exploitation is to be authorized post-2048, it is likely that signatories to the Treaty will only allow it under some kind of collective licensing scheme with an associated benefit-sharing mechanism.

The idea of common heritage gained fully explicit currency, though, during the late 1960s. In a famous speech before the United Nations General Assembly in November of 1967, the Maltese diplomat Arvid Pardo declared that the resources of the oceans should be protected from a resource-grab by states possessed of superior harvesting technology, and instead considered as part of the common heritage of mankind—and that revenues from exploiting these resources should be used to narrow the gap between rich and poor countries and not to widen it.[10] Though, as we have seen, the UNCLOS settlement did extend state prerogative into new areas, it simultaneously designated the mineral resources contained under the high seas—that is, the oceans beyond the reach of EEZs and extended shelves—as part of the common heritage of humanity.

Since that time the scope of the common heritage idea has been extended further. Notably it has been applied to the resources contained in space.[11] And whereas the 1992 Convention on Biological Diversity describes the terms under which biological diversity, including the genomes of particular species, can be considered the property of individual states, the human genome was explicitly exempted and as a result cannot be patented by anyone.[12] Support for the idea that some resources should be considered part of the common heritage of mankind has, to be sure, been somewhat precarious, especially when it has been explicitly accompanied by specific benefit-sharing schemes.[13] But it still plays a significant role in international law, where it represents a valuable bulwark against the inequity associated with creeping state prerogative. Sections 9.2 and 9.3 address two classes of extra-territorial resources in greater depth; the first has not been declared to be part of our common heritage, whereas the second has.

9.2. FISH

In the view of seventeenth-century philosophers such as Vattel and Locke, our activities on the high seas could hardly set back anyone else's interests, since the resources of the sea (and its navigable space) appeared to be inexhaustible.

But when it comes to fish, it is now apparent that if this empirical assumption was ever tenable, it is no longer. What our ancestors treated as a pure public good is in fact a collective good. The fish of the oceans are in distinctly limited supply, and a situation in which each agent is able to scoop up as many fish as he or she likes has guaranteed short-term gains for those with advanced fishing industries, but has brought about the long-term collapse of fish stocks. The response of UNCLOS was to extend the reach of state prerogative under the auspices of EEZs, inside of which states would enjoy exclusive fishing rights.[14] The rationale was that giving each state exclusive property rights over 'local' fish would see them being harvested more sustainably and efficiently, in contrast to the collection action problem represented by a fishing free-for-all. Extending state control over coastal regions (in which most of the world's seafish live) would secure an interest in long-term stability, given that fish harvests are worth over a hundred billion dollars per year. States, it was assumed, would be loath to lose such income.

The results of the EEZ experiment have been, to put it mildly, extremely disappointing. The proportion of the world's fish stocks which are considered depleted has not declined, but rather increased—from 10 per cent in 1974 to 32 per cent in 2008.[15] A situation whereby individual states determine what constitutes a sustainable catch has had very mixed results. In some instances— in which given fish stocks live wholly within particular EEZs—states have limited catches and thereby secured upturns in fish populations. But large fishing companies have continually lobbied for increases in quota size, and many states have not set quotas at all. Moreover, fish do not, by and large, recognize the borders of EEZs. Many fish species migrate across their boundaries, and intense inter-state competition to harvest those mobile stocks has seriously damaged their sustainability. At current rates of fishing it is projected that stocks of *all* species which are currently fished for food will have collapsed by 2048, with very serious implications for ocean ecosystems more broadly.[16]

Beyond the reach of EEZs, UNCLOS does not constrain fishing activities at all. Despite the hopes of many developing countries, fish have never been brought under the common heritage principle. The United Nations Fishing Stocks Agreement of 1995 sought to constrain high-seas fishing activities, but has largely failed to do so (and to date only a minority of UNCLOS memberstates have ratified it). Whereas a series of regional agreements have emerged to regulate fishing activities, the effect has been piecemeal and conservation is rarely even an explicit objective of such agreements.[17] In the meantime, largescale and increasingly high-tech fishing corporations scoop up the fish of the high seas in industrial quantities, often doing irreparable damage to marine environments and marine mammals in the process. High-seas fishing is the preserve of very few countries, and 50 per cent of revenues are earned by the US, Spain, Japan, South Korea, and Taiwan.[18] But rather than turning a net profit, high-seas fishing is heavily subsidized by home states, to an estimated global total of $35 billion per year—and without these subsidies, it would actually be uneconomic.[19] Domestic lobbying has resulted in these fleets being paid to destroy an important global resource. The fleets which roam the world's oceans have even invaded the coastal waters of poorer states which lack the capacity to effectively exclude them, destroying domestic fishing industries in the process (as they did, famously, off the coast of Somalia, after which many fishermen who had tried and failed to exclude them turned instead to piracy).

UNCLOS has not, then, delivered appreciable benefits. In the words of one commentator, 'all that resulted was the expansion of domestic fishing efforts to fill the gaps left by foreign fishermen... Thus the tragedy of the commons was perpetuated by domestic fishermen in the EEZ, and intensified on the high seas by foreign fishing fleets dislocated from traditional fishing grounds.'[20] Indeed, the UNCLOS fishing regime—a combination of state control over EEZs and a free-for-all over the high seas—has been modelled in one recent economic study as virtually the worst-case scenario for both profitability and sustainability.[21] In the medium to long term, intensive fishing in EEZs—particularly of migratory stocks—might be sustainable if fish had refuges in which populations could recover; but unconstrained (and economically unproductive, but subsidized) fishing on the high seas means that the reverse is true. Closing the high seas to fishing entirely would likely lead to large increases in stocks—and profits—in the world's EEZs. The optimal policy, though, would be to manage the high seas collectively, with an independent global agency setting catch quotas for individual species.[22] Such an agency could also establish marine reserves in which vulnerable stocks could recover over time.

To be sure, progress in this direction would require the cooperation of the five states which currently dominate high-seas fishing, and in which fishing lobbies exert a powerful pull on policy. A key step—probably best managed under the auspices of the World Trade Organization (WTO)—would be to orchestrate the de-escalation of fishing subsidies.[23] Despite the political strength of fishing lobbies in many countries, it makes no kind of sense to pay fishing fleets to hunt fishing stocks to extinction, in the process destroying their own livelihoods and a valuable source of nutrition for many of the world's communities. The money saved could be invested in Marine Protected Areas on the high seas or in other conservation efforts. But more broadly the ultimate goal must be for a global agency to determine sustainable yields in the high seas and to publicly auction fishing rights. A global agency charged with securing a stream of revenue for marine protection would have an incentive to ensure that the revenue-stream—and hence fish stocks themselves—were sustainable.[24]

Of course the proposal to charge for fishing rights might be objected to on the basis that some communities currently depend upon subsistence harvesting, and indeed that their fishing activities are traditional, identity-conferring pursuits which would be threatened under such a scheme. The requirement to bid for quota space might place undue pressure on communities which are finding it hard enough to hold their heads above water as it is. In response, we could propose that—as with other charges for resource use in the real world, such as water charges—the system could provide free quota-space for small-scale artisanal users, and particularly those in developing countries. But in addition, and more fundamentally, we should observe that the objection is point-missing. The threat to traditional subsistence fishing is not global regulation, but the lack of it. Unregulated big-business fishing is fast crowding out traditional fishing fleets, cutting away the livelihoods of some of the poorest communities of the world, and destroying the fish stocks themselves and hence the *raison d'être* of traditional fishing industries. Ninety-seven per cent of the world's fishermen and -women live in developing countries, but their employment is increasingly precarious in a world in which large vessels employing only 4 per cent of fishers catch 65 per cent of the oceans' fish.[25]

If a levy on fishing can be seen as a kind of global resource tax, it is worth being clear about its objectives. It would, in all likelihood, release relatively meagre funds for global redistribution, though it could certainly support valuable conservation efforts in the world's oceans; it could also fund efforts to reduce illegal fishing on the high seas and, perhaps, within the EEZs of poor states lacking the capacity to do so themselves. As fish stocks recover, and pressure on agricultural land becomes more intense, the value of fish stocks is likely to increase significantly; as a result the revenue-raising effects of a fishing levy would then become more substantial. But in the first instance a global levy on fishing would represent a user charge on a limited resource which would serve to discourage wasteful and unsustainable (and often uneconomic) exploitation of a limited resource. Its immediate goal would be to stabilize fish stocks. In doing so it would secure the livelihoods of many people in the developing world. Globally, 35 million people work in fishing—the vast majority within artisanal fishing in developing countries—and an estimated 520 million people's livelihoods depend upon their efforts, whether directly or indirectly.[26] Many people depend upon the access to relatively cheap protein that fish provide, and indeed the health of ocean ecosystems more broadly has been shown to be crucially dependent upon healthy populations of marine animals.[27] A global fishing-rights auction would protect the interests of many of the worst-off people in the world, which are currently threatened by ruthless competition from subsidized industrial fleets, and at the same time it would protect vital ecosystems for future generations.

9.3. SEABED MINERALS

The seabed is home to resources of potentially vast economic value. Many are already being exploited: countries harvest oil and gas, gold, diamonds, tin, sand, and gravel from the sea. Approximately 30 per cent of global oil production, and 50 per cent of gas production, now takes place offshore, and the figure is rising as land-based reserves dwindle. By the beginning of the present century these activities were already generating over a trillion US dollars in revenues each year.[28]

There are further resources on or under the seabed which are not yet exploited on an industrial scale but which soon might be. Most of the world's tectonic plate boundaries lie under the oceans. Submarine volcanoes at these seams are the location for chemical exchanges between magma, hot rock, and seawater. These exchanges produce vents of 'black smoke' around which sulphide mineral deposits accumulate, and which are often rich in copper, tin, lead, gold, and other elements crucial to high-tech industries. Enormous hydrothermal exchanges within the world's oceans also lead to the concentration of large quantities of manganese and iron upon the ocean floor. Over millions of years complex compounds precipitate into polymetallic nodules or polymetallic crusts, which contain significant supplies of copper, cobalt, manganese, nickel, and rare earth elements. These processes are present-day incarnations of the forces by which terrestrial mineral resources were once accreted. But the results are spread across all of the world's oceans, and many of them lie under the 'high seas'—that is, beyond the legal reach of any state.

Although many marine minerals are already exploited on a colossal scale, there is disagreement about how soon we should expect these polymetallic resources to be commercially recoverable. Whilst many commentators believe that mining will commence within a decade, some are more sceptical. But commercial availability is a moveable feast. Technology can develop in leaps and bounds. Moreover, not only technological but also geopolitical changes can convert plain 'resources' into lucrative 'reserves' very quickly. Countries which place a premium on security of supply may exploit resources even when others would not consider it economic to do so.[29] We should also remember that as well as producing insecurity of supply, buying minerals from other states can lock buyers into relationships with actors who brutalize their subjects, and disregard labour or environmental standards. Reticence about supporting human rights abuses abroad can make the resources of the oceans, where no one lives, more attractive. In any event, many countries, universities, and corporations are currently spending considerable sums of money researching how these resources might be accessed.

Before it becomes commercially viable to exploit these resources, we must address the question of how any benefits arising from their exploitation should be shared. Political theorists have rarely tackled that question explicitly. Notably, Cara Nine has repudiated any claim on the part of states to exercise jurisdiction over these resources, and suggested that mere geographical proximity is no basis upon which to allocate access to them. But the absence of compelling special claims does not mean that they must go unexploited. Instead she sketches a framework under which states could arrive at a multilateral agreement allocating property rights over these resources. But Nine's concern is to determine who ought to be included in such an agreement, and not to determine which constraints ought to finally apply to appropriation. In principle, a number of different constraints might emanate from such an agreement.[30]

On this question, the various normative approaches sketched in Chapter 2 would provide their own distinct answers. But most of the leading answers appear uncompelling. A right-libertarian approach would recommend either no constraint on private appropriation of these resources, or (on Nozick's version) a weak constraint under which appropriation is permissible so long as the wellbeing of others is not actually set back. But we have seen that much hangs on how exactly we specify any 'worsening' in someone's condition. Appropriation can seriously restrict the opportunities of others even if it does not make them materially worse off. If this is to count as a worsening of others' position then we will arrive at an egalitarian constraint on appropriation, or something very much like it. If it is not to count as a worsening, then the right-libertarian 'constraint' is implausibly lax. If exploitation is only objectionable if it makes others materially worse off by some absolute standard, this standard likely counsels no constraint at all upon the exploitation of seabed resources. As a result it will allow enormous rewards to go to the fast, the strong, or the lucky—and in this case, it would deliver major gains to technologically advanced states which already possessed (or were closest to developing) the means of harvesting these minerals. On the lax interpretation we appear to be back with precisely the outcome Pardo wanted to avoid, in which technologically advanced countries are able to exploit these resources without sharing any of the proceeds with the poor of the world. A minimalist approach, by contrast, would sanction appropriation whenever it does not deprive others of the objects of their basic rights. But since no community currently depends for its subsistence on the mineral resources contained under the seabed, this proviso looks unlikely to be violated in practice–and therefore it is uncertain that it has any practical implications. The minimalist position too appears to grant license to the resource scramble on the part of the wealthy of which Pardo was so afraid.

An equality-promoting approach provides a more compelling answer to this question. There is no reason in principle why these seabed resources should not be exploited, so long as care is taken to limit the associated environmental damage, and provided the arising benefits are utilized in a way compatible with intergenerational justice. But these benefits should be shared in such a way as to ameliorate, rather than intensify, broader global inequalities. Once exploiters have recouped their costs, substantial revenues will remain. They should be pooled, and disbursed largely in favour of the poor inhabitants of developing countries. In addition, rather than allowing countries which possess the technology required to exploit these resources to monopolize their extraction, we might usefully employ some of the revenues gained to engage in technology transfer, so as to help poorer countries to develop the ability to participate in that exploitation too.

A critic might object, at this point, that such an approach sounds attractive in theory, but is unlikely to be put into practice. One objection to the egalitarian view, for instance, is that given current inequalities in wealth and power we can hardly expect rich countries to agree to share the proceeds of exploitation in this way. But we should not accept this counsel of despair, because the set of normative principles which *have* been agreed upon internationally is encouraging. By contrast to EEZs or extended shelves, the seabed under the high seas is designated, under UNCLOS, as part of the common heritage of humankind. In contrast to the case of the fish of the high seas, any exploitation of its resources must, legally speaking, be licensed by the international community as a whole. In fact, here we have what political theorists would recognize as a form of joint ownership. Moreover, a share of the proceeds must be remitted to an international agency charged with disbursing funds with a particular emphasis on the claims of poorer countries.

Indeed, the same goes for the resources contained in the extended continental shelves between 200 and 350 nautical miles from the shores of some states, exploitation of which may well precede that of any resources contained under the high seas (because the seabed, in many of these cases, is closer to the ocean surface). These, too, are the subject of international agreement. Whilst some states—and predominantly, not surprisingly, so-called 'broad margin' states such as the United States which *have* shelves extending beyond 200 miles—argued in the run-up to UNCLOS that local states should have unconstrained rights to exploit resources within those peripheral areas, others—including many developing countries—argued that they should be considered part of our common heritage. A compromise was reached. Article 82 of UNCLOS authorized the creation of the ISA, which was eventually established by way of an Implementation Agreement in 1994, and now has 167 member-states (including the UK, France, Germany, Japan, China, India, and the vast majority of developing countries).[31] The Authority allows states to exploit mineral resources within extended shelves. But as with high-seas resources, any state doing so is required to make royalty payments to the Authority.[32] The funds accruing are to be allocated 'on the basis of equitable sharing criteria, taking into account the interests and needs of developing States, particularly the least developed and land-locked among them'.[33] In addition, Article 144 of UNCLOS envisages a process of technology transfer whereby parties exploiting seabed resources are required to share technology, or technical or scientific knowledge, with states that do not currently possess the wherewithal to engage in exploitation. To that end the ISA has established an endowment fund aimed at 'supporting the participation of qualified scientists and technical personnel from developing countries in marine scientific research programmes and providing them with opportunities to participate in international technical and scientific cooperation'.[34] Supporting (and funding) that participation is a necessary part of any contract for exploration signed under the ISA framework.

The realization of these goals still faces some obstacles. Notably, the United States signed the 1994 Implementation Agreement but both Democratic and Republican administrations have repeatedly failed to steer ratification through a hostile Senate. Indeed, the US has not yet ratified UNCLOS itself—though insofar as it recognizes it as a codification of customary international law, its intransigence is not fatal. It is clear, for instance, that under international law claims over continental margins can only be registered if a claimant accepts that payments arising from exploitation must be made to the ISA;[35] as a result, commercial interests in the US have long attempted to persuade sceptical Republican Senators that ratification is desirable. A further issue is that the Agreement leaves much unsaid, and not least how, when, and by whom funds arising from exploitation should be disbursed. One suggestion made by several of the least-developed states is that a Common Heritage Fund should be established to distribute revenues. Alternatively, it has been suggested that they could be administered by the United Nations Development Programme.[36] Progress on that issue is required, but there is no reason why it should not be attainable. Finally, there is not yet agreement on a precise formula for sharing revenues which would weigh various factors such as GDP per capita, access to the sea, and so on. This is an important question to which political theorists could make a valuable contribution. But even in the absence of a settled principle, the general agreement on revenue-sharing is significant. In 2001, the ISA signed the first set of contracts with governments and private organizations seeking to commence exploration for polymetallic nodules. It has now signed over twenty such contracts with a variety of private and public sector concerns.[37] When that exploration comes to fruition, the revenues arising will be used to reduce global inequalities, by promoting the development of the poorest of our world.

9.4. LEARNING FROM THE CASE OF MINERALS

The example of the ISA is important both in itself, and in the broader conclusions it allows us to draw about the struggle for greater global equality. Notably, it represents a welcome counter-example to those who claim that cultural diversity, or indeed the intransigence of the powerful, means that we cannot expect international agreement on even broadly egalitarian principles.

Here is one concrete example in which international agreement has been reached both on the general principle that exploitation of extra-territorial resources must be globally sanctioned, and on a set of revenue-sharing principles which egalitarians should generally welcome. Despite the scepticism of some minimalists about global justice, the example of the ISA shows that progress in this direction is possible. In Chapter 7 we identified what might be called an 'accessibility challenge' to global egalitarianism, which suggests that egalitarian reforms on the global level are unlikely, and that we should therefore lower our sights and focus on more minimal, but more achievable, reforms. I did not endorse that challenge as a constraint on egalitarian theorizing; but I did claim in response that it is desirable for egalitarians to identify at least some reforms which are accessible by way of existing institutions. The example of seabed resources shows that egalitarian benefit-sharing schemes are not infeasible, and I will suggest below that they could be extended to further classes of resources. This forms an important counterpoint to scepticism about the prospects for agreeing common global rules to manage, and share benefits from, the ocean's resources. Margaret Moore, for instance, has recently suggested that while an international regime governing seabed resources would be ideal from a normative point of view, it is unlikely to emerge in reality.[38] But such an institution *has* emerged. The ISA has legal reality, and an egalitarian mandate, and its brief might well be extended in the coming years (see section 9.4).

There has also been some scepticism about whether the various communities of the world could agree on what progress towards global equality would even look like. Perhaps, to the contrary, progress towards greater global equality would require us to impose upon other countries policies which they could reasonably reject. But this view too appears to be embarrassed by the case of seabed resources. Though they are usually discussed separately, the common heritage principle which has been applied to them was a further element of the project for a New International Economic Order (NIEO), and should be understood in that context.[39] Its realization in the case of the ISA owed much to the voting power of the Group of 77 developing states.[40] If there is resistance to further progressive realization of the principle that exploitation of extra-territorial resources should be used to narrow global inequality, it lies largely with the reticence of several powerful developed countries. I have suggested in this chapter that this reticence is unjustified, however. No good moral grounds can be given for the resistance of developed countries to revenue-sharing schemes which would see the proceeds from exploiting these resources being shared globally. The resources in question are not the product of any state, and no state's self-determination depends upon control over them. Their effective use is not served by a resource-grab by individual states, but will likely be best served by coordinated global governance. Insofar as no developed state depends upon revenues from resources such as seabed minerals or ocean biodiversity, the requirement to share revenues from them does not unjustifiably set back their interests either. These resources currently represent sources of further enrichment for the already wealthy. All that is being asked of them is that if they are to access these ocean resources, they should share the spoils of doing so. As an element of a broader programme to narrow global inequality, user charges and benefit-sharing schemes applied to ocean resources have considerable promise.

I have argued that the relative neglect, by contemporary political theorists, of questions about rights over the resources of the oceans is regrettable because political struggles over these resources have such major distributive consequences, and because the rules on how those resources are to be exploited are right now being shaped, albeit largely beyond the notice of ordinary citizens of the world. A priority for egalitarians should be to fight to entrench egalitarian benefit-sharing principles, and to seek their extension to further classes of resources. Section 9.3 discussed fish, a case to which there has been reluctance to expend common heritage principles, and specifically to embrace global management and user charges. But there are further important classes of resources about which we can make the same argument. In the years since the UNCLOS Treaty it has only become more obvious just how precious the ocean's resources are. It is now understood, for instance, that the water column alone represents around 30 per cent of the global carbon sink, and that the oceans play an important role in regulating our climate. More than 90 per cent of the heat trapped by the greenhouse effect is stored within the oceans, and more than half of the oxygen that we breathe is produced by the oceans.[41] It has also become apparent that the deep seas contain potentially valuable biodiversity. Its genetic resources might turn out to be crucial to food production in decades to come, or they might hold the key to vital medical treatments. If so, we will face again the question of whether that biodiversity should be the object of unconstrained prospecting—as the fish of the high seas are at present—or designated as part of our common heritage, with an associated management and benefit-sharing scheme.

The battle-lines have been drawn in a familiar fashion. The argument of China and the other G77 developing countries has been that ocean biodiversity should be considered part of our common heritage, and its exploitation licensed under the competence of the ISA. The response of many developed states has been a good deal of foot-dragging. Initially efforts were made to bring the biodiversity of the oceans under the framework of the Convention on Biological Diversity. When those attempts failed, efforts were instead made to make progress under the auspices of a new treaty under the UNCLOS framework. For years these efforts were hampered by the reticence of a loose coalition of states including the US, Russia, Japan, Canada, and Iceland, all of which suggested that whereas an international agreement was perhaps desirable, it should not be legally binding (these countries are, not coincidentally, among those which stand to gain most from unregulated prospecting of the ocean's biological resources). But after several years of negotiation a breakthrough has recently been made. In June 2015, the United Nations General Assembly passed a resolution pledging to work towards a new (and binding) treaty under the UNCLOS regime, aimed at establishing an Implementing Agreement designed to protect, and to share benefits from, ocean biodiversity. Several states which had initially resisted a settlement (including, crucially, the US) in the end came to support this development.

The Agreement, of course, remains to be made, by a target date of 2018. But significantly, it has been agreed that the terms of reference for any Agreement will incorporate four key pillars. First, any eventual Agreement will designate Marine Protected Areas on the high seas. Protected areas would not only enable stocks of fish and marine mammals to recover, but would enhance food security more broadly, since the world's oceans carry a variety of nutrients to coastal areas which enable them to remain biologically productive. Although some states—including the UK—have designated Marine Protected Areas, under UNCLOS this is an activity voluntarily undertaken by some states within their own EEZs.[42] Second, an Agreement would spell out the circumstances in which states are required to carry out Environmental Impact Assessments with regard to their activities on the high seas. Third, it will develop a framework for regulating access to marine genetic resources, accompanied by an associated benefit-sharing scheme. Fourth and finally, it will develop a mechanism for 'capacity building' and the transfer of marine technology to developing countries, enabling them to protect, and where appropriate exploit, marine genetic resources on a more level playing field.

The precise contours of the Agreement which emerges from these negotiations will be hugely significant. It remains to be seen whether such a scheme would be administered by some new organization or, as many developing countries and non-governmental organizations (NGOs) would prefer, by the ISA itself. It also remains to be seen how robust and detailed any process of technology transfer will be, and what the relevant benefit-sharing mechanism will look like. There is, though, a sizeable constituency of support for an egalitarian benefit-sharing scheme, which is principally but not exclusively drawn from developing countries. Whilst some developed countries will lobby to water down the benefit-sharing and technology-transfer mechanisms under a new agreement, activists and concerned citizens of the more intransigent developed countries can lobby their governments to show greater openness to a more egalitarian solution.

9.5. CONCLUSIONS

The fate of the ocean's riches commands our attention because significant conflicts are currently being waged over their exploitation, and because the outcome of those struggles will be hugely significant from a distributive point of view. Those struggles will likely intensify rather than ease in the coming decades. The world's population is widely expected to hit 9 billion by the end of this century. If it does, the pressure placed on land resources to feed the world's hungry will become very intense, and it seems certain that increasing demands will be placed upon the ocean's resources too.

Whilst the ocean's resources are of the utmost importance, the task of managing these resources for the common good has been ill-met. The emergence of the UNCLOS settlement was without doubt one of the most significant developments in global resource politics of the twentieth century. But it left much to regret. The extension of resource rights to states under the EEZ experiment has certainly delivered great gains for many of them, albeit primarily those with extensive coastlines and the technology to avail themselves of their bounty. Indeed, one of its own intellectual architects, Arvid Pardo, was crushed by the eventual form UNCLOS took, describing it as 'probably the most inequitable treaty that has ever been signed'.[43] It has certainly not delivered sustainability or promoted equality.

But although the EEZ experiment has been a lamentable failure, other elements of the UNCLOS settlement provide grounds for hope. The enhanced capacity to harvest seabed minerals and ocean biodiversity prompts important questions about the terms under which their exploitation should be permitted, and the direction in which any benefits should flow. I have argued in this chapter against minimalist views on this question, and in favour of an equality-promoting view. I have also shown that the prospects of using these resources to promote equality are much better than theorists have sometimes assumed. Significant institutional progress has already been made towards the goal of making these resources work for the world as a whole, and especially its worst-off. I have argued that those innovations should be welcomed, and extended.

ENDNOTES

1. I say quasi-sovereignty because UNCLOS did not extend all the elements of state sovereignty to EEZs. Rather it created a *sui generis* legal regime in which states have a monopoly on exploiting living and non-living natural resources; but it has no implications for jurisdiction over persons and does not qualify, for instance, traditional rights of innocent passage. Orrego Vicuna 1989. A similar regime governs extended continental shelves, but in this case the monopoly extends only to non-living resources (i.e. it has no implications for fish or other biological resources).
2. Aside from a brief period at the turn of the twentieth century (during which it was supplanted by Russia), the US was the world's largest producer (and consumer) of oil between 1860 and the mid-1970s. Ross 2012: 52.

3. Independent World Commission on the Oceans 1998.
4. Borgerson 2008.
5. Swing 1976.
6. Partly, perhaps, because these resources have received so little attention from political theorists in the first place. An exception is Wenar (2016a: 203–4), who briefly claims that a resource situated a hundred miles from the US coast should 'of course' be considered the property of the United States.
7. Margaret Moore (2015: 169–70) argues that for this reason there can be no claim to state jurisdiction over resources in the oceans. Cara Nine (2013) makes the same claim with regard to the mineral and petrochemical resources of the high seas and the polar regions. She does, however, argue that states can turn these resources into property by agreement (see section 9.3).
8. The idea that some resources are part of our common heritage is distinct, note, from the (somewhat weaker) idea that some resources (potentially including resources *within* states) may be 'of common concern' to all of humanity.
9. See e.g. Stokke and Vidas (1996).
10. For a discussion, see Churchill and Lowe 1999, chapter 12.
11. Though the progress of the common heritage idea has not been smooth here. States which currently possess exploration technology have supported the 1967 'Space Treaty', which declares that the moon and other extra-terrestrial bodies cannot be brought under state sovereignty. But they have not supported the 1979 'Moon Treaty', which declares the moon to be part of the common heritage of humankind and calls for the 'equitable sharing' of benefits derived from the exploitation of its resources.
12. Limits on private profits from the human genome are also laid out in the 1997 Universal Declaration on the Human Genome and Human Rights, Article 1 of which declares our genome to be 'the heritage of humanity'.
13. Kiss 1985.
14. In the case of fishing rights, recall, extended continental shelves have no legal significance; UNCLOS divides the oceans into EEZs and the high seas alone.
15. Food and Agriculture Organization 2010.
16. Worm et al. 2006.
17. Ban et al. 2014.
18. Global Ocean Commission 2014: 41.
19. European Parliament Directorate General for Internal Policies 2013.
20. Barnes 2009: 5.
21. White and Costello 2014.
22. White and Costello 2014: 3.
23. Stone 1997; Collier 2010a: 164.
24. This is far from a new suggestion. It was suggested several decades ago that 'the ultimate solution [for preserving fish stocks] is to treat these resources as a giant commons managed as a trust by some international agency such as the United Nations'. Ciriacy-Wantrup and Bishop 1975.
25. Global Ocean Commission 2014: 13, 22.
26. Food and Agriculture Organization 2009.
27. Worm et al. 2006.

28. United Nations 2002: 6.
29. For instance Japan, which lacks domestic supplies of rare earth metals, has been close to the forefront in developing deep-sea mining technology.
30. Nine 2015.
31. http://www.isa.org.jm/member-states.
32. Payment is required after the first five years of production, and is to be levied at 1 per cent of the value of resources extracted, rising to a maximum of 7 per cent in the twelfth year.
33. United Nations Convention of the Law of the Sea, Article 82(4).
34. https://www.isa.org.jm/contractors/endowment-fund.
35. 'Acceptance of the right to an outer continental shelf is accompanied by the obligation to contribute, so the right and obligation are inseparable.' Lodge 2006: 327.
36. Lodge 2006: 327.
37. https://www.isa.org.jm/files/documents/EN/Newsletter/Issue1-2015.pdf.
38. Moore 2015: 170.
39. Notably the Preamble to UNCLOS suggests, in language strongly redolent of the Declaration of a New International Economic Order, that it would 'contribute to the realization of a just and equitable international economic order which takes into account the interests and needs of mankind as a whole and, in particular, the special interests and needs of developing countries'.
40. Vogler 2012: 66–7.
41. Global Ocean Commission 2014: 3.
42. Moves to designate marine protected areas on the high seas have largely failed to date. In 2013, for example, Russia vetoed efforts to create two large marine sanctuaries in the Antarctic region. At present, only 3 per cent of the world's oceans, and 1 per cent of the high seas, are protected. Global Ocean Commission 2014: 3.
43. Woo 1999.

10

The Burdens of Conservation

Natural resources have frequently been depicted as sources of advantage, with the key normative question therefore being how to share access to the benefits they provide. But they can also be sources of disadvantage. Entire communities can be endangered by volcanoes and hurricanes. The presence of stagnant ponds in which mosquito larvae grow may cause communities to be exposed to malaria, dengue, and yellow fever (mosquito-borne diseases are associated with over a million deaths per year, with most of them occurring in parts of the world which are already disadvantaged). Even life-giving resources such as fresh water can bring terrible burdens in tow. In one infamous case, Bangladeshis were for many years exposed to water-borne diseases via the surface water they relied upon for drinking and cooking. During the 1970s the national Department of Public Health, with the assistance of Unicef, engineered a wholesale shift towards the extraction of water from groundwater sources which were presumed to be safer. The result was that millions fell victim to the abnormally high levels of arsenic contained in the local groundwater. The largest mass-poisoning in history has left a brutal legacy of skin lesions, cardiovascular disease, and cancer.[1] Indeed, the human need for continual access to water all too often generates threats to people's (and especially women's) health, physical security, and access to education and labour-markets.[2] For all that we have tended to represent the world's resources as a cornucopia, the image of a poisoned chalice is sometimes more accurate.

I have suggested from the outset that a theory of natural resource justice should concern itself with the distribution of the benefits *and* burdens flowing from the world's resources, because each can have a significant impact upon human wellbeing. Since Beitz, egalitarians have often suggested that it is unjust if one community is able to live a life of comparative luxury because of the resources contained within its territory, whereas others must work hard to make the most of more meagre spoils. But on that logic, it must be no less objectionable if one community's children are systematically exposed to diseases and developmental disorders simply as a result of naturally occurring toxins or hazards, whereas others are not. Such facts can also have a significant impact upon overall levels of wellbeing.

The proper distribution of burdens is therefore an important element within a theory of resource justice, albeit one which has received rather less explicit attention than the proper distribution of benefits. Like the distribution of benefits, it promises to be a rather large topic. This chapter will not examine all of the burdens which can be associated with natural resources.[3] Instead it focuses upon one specific category, which we will call the burdens of conservation. Many (potentially overlapping) reasons might be supplied for conserving particular resources. We might, for instance, believe that given resources ought to be conserved on the grounds that they have intrinsic value; that their exploitation would give rise to unacceptable costs for distant others; that intergenerational justice requires us to ensure they are available to future people; that their exploitation would jeopardize the wellbeing of people currently attached to them; or that it would irreparably damage the ecosystems in which some resources play a central role. Many theories will be able to supply reasons for conserving some resources some of the time, whereas a theory which never counsels any restraint upon our exploitation of resources will surely be unattractive. But I do not aim to settle in any general sense which arguments count, and to what extent, in favour of conservation. All we must assume in order for the ensuing discussion to be interesting is that there are *some* resources which should, from the point of view of justice, be conserved. As the chapter proceeds, I will supply examples in which at least some, apparently powerful, grounds for conservation can be provided.

The general term conservation encompasses three types of action (or inaction).[4] *Protection* occurs when an agent takes steps to insulate a resource from some threat which would destroy or degrade it. *Restoration* occurs when an agent takes steps to repair damage done to a resource as a result of some such threat coming to fruition.[5] *Non-exploitation* occurs when some agent who owns or controls a resource refrains from destroying it or altering the properties which make it worthy of conservation.[6] In each case, the key issue I will address is this: if some resources are to be conserved, this will often produce burdens for agents (where burdens are understood as setbacks to their access to wellbeing). This will be true whether we have in mind conservation as protection, restoration, or non-exploitation.

This final chapter addresses the normative question of where such burdens ought to fall. It proceeds as follows. Section 10.1 clarifies some of the issues at stake and presents an argument against what we might call the *proximity principle*: the idea that those who own the land on which resources are to be found should pick up the tab for their conservation. Sections 10.2, 10.3, and 10.4 discuss three alternative principles which appear relevant to the allocation of the costs of conservation as protection and as restoration. These focus respectively on an agent's *contribution to* threats or damage to natural resources; her *ability to bear* the costs of protection or restoration; and the degree to which she *benefits from* acts of protection or restoration. Section 10.5

shifts our focus to the costs of conservation as non-exploitation, and examines the conditions in which justice might also require the mitigation of these costs (that is, the lifting of those costs from the shoulders of those who own or control the resources in question). Section 10.6 discusses some of the practical mechanisms available to us when we seek to share the burdens of conservation beyond borders, and section 10.7 briefly concludes.

10.1. AGAINST THE PROXIMITY PRINCIPLE

Whilst the question which resources ought to be conserved and why has rightly attracted considerable attention, the question I investigate here—of who ought to bear the *costs* of conservation—has received rather less. It has, for instance, been largely neglected by theorists writing on natural resource justice, who tend not to have developed the implications of their theories for this issue. But the question is a very significant one. When we get the allocation of these burdens wrong, it can constitute a considerable injustice. In this section and the next three (sections 10.2, 10.3, and 10.4) I will focus upon conservation as protection and as restoration—where justice requires that either particular resources are insulated against various threats which would destroy or degrade them, or that the damage done by such threats is repaired. To keep the exposition relatively simple, I will work up examples of protection alone. But whatever arguments properly apply to the burdens of protection, it appears likely the same arguments will apply to cases of restoration too. Imagine, for instance, that justice requires an agent to insulate a particular resource against a threat for which he is responsible. If that threat comes to pass—and the resource is therefore damaged or destroyed—it appears at least plausible that we should also ask him to pick up the tab for restoration too (if restoration is what justice requires). Likewise, we will sometimes need to distribute the costs of protection in cases where no responsible agent can be found (imagine, for instance, a threat which is not caused by humans at all). However we tackle *that* issue, there seems to be at least a prima facie case that the same principle(s) should regulate the costs of restoration too (if restoration is required by justice).

To get the discussion going, imagine, if you will, that justice requires the preservation of a particular species. Perhaps it is a 'keystone' species playing an indispensable role within an important ecosystem, such that its extinction would have drastic consequences for other species and ultimately for human beings. Imagine, if you like, a flying insect such as a bee, which performs a key 'ecosystem service' in pollinating plants upon which we depend for food. But imagine now that this species faces an existential threat. Whilst it can be protected from this threat, doing so will generate costs for whoever takes up the task. Who ought to bear the costs of heading off the threat in question?

One simple response would be to require locals, and more particularly those who own the land on which the species in question lives, to pick up the tab. We could say to those locals: these are your bees, and so you can protect them. Let us call this the proximity principle, because it localizes costs in line with facts about ownership. On further reflection we would, I hope, conclude that such a principle was a poor guide to the question at stake. On the one hand, it will fail to offer any useful guidance when it comes to the many resources which fall outside any community (such as the resources of the high seas, or the polar regions). It will also struggle to provide guidance in the case of resources which are fugacious or free-flowing (such as global freshwater supplies, or animal or bird species with regular migratory paths spanning many countries). We know that resources which fall outside any one national community have often gone unprotected, in part because although many people may benefit from their existence, it may be that no one community possesses a sufficient incentive to be a first-mover in securing, or more particularly funding, their protection. But even if international or global solutions could be reached, we would require normative principles by way of which to allocate the costs. And the proximity principle seems to offer limited guidance here.

On the other hand, the principle appears morally suspect even in the case of resources which do fall neatly within the boundaries of individual property holdings, or indeed of wider communities. For the principle is blind to considerations that plausibly *should* play a role in the allocation of costs. First, we might well note that the haphazard distribution of precious resources seems an arbitrary basis upon which to distribute the costs of their protection given that locals may have done nothing to determine that the bees live in their community, and perhaps more pertinently might have done nothing to generate the threat in question. Perhaps the threat emanates from some source wholly outside human control (imagine that the bees are afflicted by parasitic wasps). Or perhaps it arises from the actions of human beings who live outside the community in question (imagine that neighbours spray their crops with dangerous pesticides which are then dispersed, by wind or water, onto the land where the bees live). Such facts might well be relevant to the allocation of protection costs.

Second, the principle pays no heed to people's capacity to bear burdens. Perhaps the community where the bees live is very poor. Perhaps, therefore, requiring locals to meet the full costs of protection will only push them further into poverty. On the other hand, outsiders might possess much greater capacity to bear the costs of protection. This too might matter.

Third, obliging locals to bear the full costs of protection might appear egregious in cases where the resource in question delivers important benefits to outsiders. Perhaps the bees which live, and face a threat, in one area also pollinate plants in other areas, allowing food production to continue there too.

The distribution of these benefits will often be highly dispersed, and fail therefore to map neatly onto facts about ownership of or control over the resources they emanate from. It might, on reflection, appear unfair to ask one community to pick up the whole tab for protecting an ecosystem service which accrues to many other people.

In light of these considerations, the principle that locals should pay by now looks highly suspect. Proximity to, or ownership of, the threatened resources in and of itself seems to track nothing of moral significance. We might, alternatively, attempt to construct an instrumental justification for the proximity principle. Thus we might argue that ownership, benefits, and conservation burdens ought to be allocated to the same agents (such as states), because in so doing we will provide those agents with an incentive to ensure that resources are effectively used, or indeed conserved. I already cast doubt on that idea in Chapter 6, where I noted that state control has often led to comprehensive failure from the point of view of conservation. One problem is that the instrumental argument is blind to the differential capacity of states. Many states possess weak enforcement capacity, and indeed many states face such serious disadvantage that conservation in the interests of distant others, or of future generations, comes to be viewed as a luxury citizens can ill afford. We might, of course, wish such facts away at the level of ideal theory, and claim that the proximity principle would serve us well in a world in which all states were reasonably well ordered. But even in such a world the proximity principle would lead us astray, morally speaking. For the resources which are likely to require conservation are distributed in a haphazard fashion too. Proximity would therefore require some states to bear greater conservation burdens than others. Moreover, in cases where the benefits flowing from those resources accrued as global public goods, the proximity principle would—inappropriately—require local states to bear all of the burdens associated with sustaining those goods.

To be sure, just as a world of permanent sovereignty systematically localizes benefits, it is a stubborn political fact that in practice—barring a few underfunded international programmes, on which more later—it localizes the costs of protection too. But it is difficult to see how the fact of ownership, taken by itself, justifies leaving protection costs at the door of locals. To the contrary, we have identified three features (invoking contribution to threat or damage, ability to bear costs, and the distribution of benefits accruing from conservation) which do appear relevant to the allocation of costs but which appear likely to track ownership poorly. Each of these considerations has engendered a rich discussion within the literature on climate justice, and I suggest that advancing justice in allocating the costs of protection and restoration will involve giving a role to one or more of them. Sections 10.2, 10.3, and 10.4 examine them more closely.

10.2. ABILITY TO PAY

When judging where the burdens of protection and restoration should fall, an egalitarian will immediately feel the normative pull of the idea that agents ought to bear costs in proportion to their overall levels of advantage. In debates on climate justice the resulting principle is typically called the *ability to pay principle*.[7] I have suggested in this book that the benefits accruing from natural resources should—to the extent that they are untouched by special claims from improvement for instance—be distributed so as to promote equality. Natural resources are emphatically not all that matters, but they are an important fuel for wellbeing, and when possible we ought to seek to channel their benefits so as to promote more equal access to wellbeing for all the world's individuals. Given that burdens are normatively similar— they are, in effect, simply the reverse of benefits, and can have a significant impact on wellbeing in their own right—we should also favour an allocation of protection and restoration burdens which promotes equality broadly construed.

Moreover, there is no obvious reason for treating burdens and benefits separately. To the contrary we ought to distribute the benefits *and* burdens flowing from natural resources so as to promote equality, rather than applying different principles to the allocation of each. Simon Caney has argued powerfully that our allocation of any particular source of advantage or disadvantage should be considered not in isolation from other sources, but in combination with them. The proper distribution of rights to consume a resource such as the world's atmospheric sink capacity, for instance, should not be determined by focusing on the features of that one particular case, but should bend in light of the *other* (positive or negative) impacts an agent makes upon the global environment, and indeed in line with their share of advantage more broadly.[8] I presented an argument for a similar conclusion in Chapter 2, and it has been put to work in subsequent chapters. In Chapter 5, for instance, I showed that our concern with *overall* levels of wellbeing allows us to be more flexible than we might suppose when it comes to accommodating attachments to specific natural resources. In Chapters 8 and 9 I argued that the proceeds of resource taxes, and the benefits accruing from the exploitation of the ocean's resources, ought likewise to be distributed in an equality-promoting fashion.

This suggests a strong role for some version of the ability to pay principle in dealing with our question about conservation, so that contributions to protection and restoration are allocated with an eye to overall levels of access to wellbeing.[9] Consider the following case. As we noted in Chapter 9, there is a pressing need for the establishment of Marine Protected Areas on the high seas. These reserves would protect valuable forms of biodiversity from human exploitation. They would allow fish stocks, for instance, space to recover from aggressive overfishing; and they would allow forms of nutrient cycling crucial to humans and to many other species to continue unabated. But there will be costs associated with both designating and maintaining such reserves. These will include the costs of technical work to map the reserves in question, of the administrative work involved in declaring them protected areas, and probably most significantly the work of monitoring their ecological health and excluding those who would illicitly damage them. Protected areas might also be established in order to protect the world's coral reefs, currently threatened by ocean warming and acidification. Here additional costs might be generated by activities such as the establishment of coral nurseries (an act of restoration), or the removal of invasive species (an act of protection).

In such cases the ability to pay principle would suggest that costs should be allocated with an eye to background levels of advantage and disadvantage, broadly construed. Perhaps some index factoring in GDP per capita and levels of 'human development' could be constructed which could serve as a reasonable proxy for access to wellbeing, and thereby allow us to allocate costs to those most able to make the required sacrifices. The principle may appear particularly relevant in cases where laying burdens at one agent's door would compound existing disadvantage, preventing them from escaping poverty or pushing them further into it.[10] But even amongst agents far from the brink of poverty, ability to pay is usually taken to be relevant to the allocation of a wide variety of costs. States, for instance, typically fund their activities by way of taxes which are proportional or indeed progressive in their impact, and as such require greater sacrifices from those more able to bear them. In many states protection and restoration efforts are bankrolled with the resulting revenues.

10.3. CONTRIBUTION TO THREAT OR DAMAGE

Ability to pay may not, however, be the whole story. Recall that when I have discussed the benefits arising from natural resources my claim has not been that these benefits ought simply to be distributed in an equality-promoting way. Rather I have claimed that benefits ought to be allocated in an equality-promoting way once any special claims have been taken proper account of. If agents have accumulated good improvement-based special claims over resources, for instance, then such claims ought also to be respected, and the surplus allocated so as to promote equality. As I presented it in Chapter 4, a special claim from improvement looks plausible to the extent that an agent can be judged responsible for the coming into existence of (at least some portion of) a resource's value. But then we might also stake out an argument which looks rather symmetrical: perhaps agents who can be judged responsible for the *deterioration* of some resource, or its exposure to a threat which justice demands its protection from, stand in line to carry special burdens. Some such thought presumably underpins the *contributor pays principle*, which would place greater burdens upon the shoulders of those properly considered responsible for the generation of the threat in question, or the damage it has in fact done.

If the allocation of costs is to track agents' contributions to threat or damage, we must be satisfied that the appropriate conditions for holding agents responsible are met. I do not intend to closely specify those conditions here, but I will suggest that they might plausibly include knowledge of the possible adverse consequences of one's actions, and the presence of alternatives which would not unduly set back one's interests. Where those conditions are met, we have a prima facie case for placing greater burdens on the shoulders of those who have generated a threat or damage. For instance, if the principal reason that Marine Protected Areas have become necessary is that some communities have engaged in reckless overfishing, or refused to take reasonable measures to reduce pollution from ships, or avoidably continued to emit great quantities of greenhouse gases in the knowledge that this can contribute to the acidification of the oceans, it may well be appropriate to oblige those communities, or individuals in them, to bear protection or restoration burdens.

There will, however, remain several types of case in which the contributor pays principle struggles to offer adequate guidance.[11] Most obviously, in cases in which the threat is not attributable to human beings, the contributor pays principle remains silent. Nevertheless, even in cases where no human or group of humans is properly considered responsible for the threat, the consequences, if unabated, might still seriously set back the wellbeing of some of them. And given that the victims cannot be considered responsible for their own losses either, then, on a variety of egalitarian theories, the case for pooling the costs of responding to them can survive. In such cases some other principled basis must be found upon which to allocate costs. Moreover, the contribution principle's guidance will be limited to the extent that some threats, or instances of damage, are best understood as only partly (even if substantially) anthropogenic. Here there will be an unattributed remainder which the principle leaves untouched.

A second category in which guidance is lacking would comprise cases in which the threat or damage was engendered by people who are no longer alive. Whilst it might have been appropriate to oblige the culprits to bear a greater share of protection or restoration burdens during their lifetimes, that option is not now open to us. Now some might argue that their direct descendants should take on the unmet burdens of their ancestors. But the thought behind this argument cannot be that these later generations are responsible for the threat or damage. The argument must instead depend upon some other basis, such as the fact that the descendants of those who have caused the threat or damage are thereby better able to bear additional burdens. To the extent that these descendants are *not* better off than their peers, asking them to bear greater burdens appears groundless.

We can also easily imagine cases in which agents have caused some threat or damage, but the relevant conditions for holding them morally responsible are not met. A third category of problem cases would comprise instances where agents were excusably ignorant of the consequences of their actions for valuable natural resources. For instance, scientific knowledge about the impact of a particular pesticide on populations of flying insects might be relatively recent. In such cases although it may be reasonable to ask farmers to cease use now—at least when alternatives are available which will not threaten their most basic interests, for instance—it is much less obvious why it would be reasonable to hold farmers responsible for the consequences of their historical use.[12]

A fourth and final category would comprise at least some threats, or instances of damage, caused by the disadvantaged. Requiring people to bear the costs of some threat or damage their activities cause to vital resources is more appealing to the extent to which desisting from the threat- or damage-causing activities would not jeopardize their most basic interests. But making people pay for protection or restoration may be objectionable when doing so would leave them in poverty. For instance, within climate justice debates some have argued that whilst the consumption of fossil fuels must be phased out—and that such an end might be achieved by, for instance, mechanisms which render their consumption more expensive—such a policy would produce injustice if the result were that poor people who did not have access to renewable energy sources were therefore unable to gain access to energy.[13] Similarly, asking the fishing industry to phase out the use of a particular kind of net—because it endangers populations of dolphins or turtles, say—might be justified. But asking very poor communities to meet the costs of the transition may not be. If so, we could usefully uncouple the duty to cease causing a certain threat from the duty to bear the costs of doing so. In such cases the principle that contributors should bear greater burdens is overridden by considerations of ability to pay.

10.4. BENEFITS ARISING FROM CONSERVATION

The final principle for allocating protection or restoration burdens suggests that costs ought in some sense to track the benefits arising from conservation. Now, there can be no general principle that those who receive benefits ought to pay for them, or for the costs of their production (we do not, for instance, require people who receive prizes to meet their costs, or ask those who are smiled at to pay the smilers for their trouble). But once certain further conditions are in place, such a principle may begin to gain traction. Consider the claim that when we consume public goods, we ought to contribute to the costs of their production. Some such idea is widely accepted, with the result that those who consume public goods but refuse to make a contribution to the costs of producing them are often labelled as free-riders (think of people riding a public tram service without a ticket, taking advantage of the fact that ticket inspectors are thin on the ground).[14]

To be sure, some have claimed that we cannot reasonably be obliged to pay for benefits we have not solicited, and may not even want.[15] But either of two further conditions may render the claim that we should contribute to the costs of producing public goods whether we solicit them or not much less contentious. First, in some cases justice will plausibly require the production of public goods, for instance because they are vital to core interests of at least some human beings. Whereas obliging agents to pay for purely 'optional' or discretionary public goods might be difficult to justify, the argument appears more straightforward in cases in which goods *must* be produced, and someone *must* incur costs as a result.[16] Second, we can usefully point once more to the contrast between pure public goods and collective goods, where the former are non-excludable and non-subtractive and the latter are non-excludable and subtractive. When one additional person begins to consume a pure public good, the costs incurred by its producers do not increase, and no less is left for others. But when one additional person begins to consume a collective good, less is left for others by definition. In at least some cases, crucially, this will have the effect of driving up the costs of production (imagine that the costs of running a tram rise strictly in proportion to the number of passengers, so that the person riding without a ticket imposes greater costs for those who fund the service; or imagine that the more people consume a forest's carbon-sequestering capacity, the more trees must be planted or protected). In such cases to refuse to share in production costs is to require others to pay for one's consumption. When we exploit the difficulties of enforcement so as to avoid contributing to public goods whose provision is required by justice, and/or where our consumption of those goods increases the costs incurred by those who do pay, the charge of free-riding is robust.

In order to apply this argument to cases of protection, we must first identify cases in which protected resources deliver significant non-excludable goods to people. Such cases are in fact common. Our attention can sometimes be captured by a picture of natural resources in which they lie dormant until someone is able to dig them up and put them to use. But many of them provide significant benefits even if left untouched by human hand—or perhaps especially when untouched. Such benefits can be hugely significant, even vital, to the survival of human beings and the broader ecosystems in which we live. I have already mentioned the role of flying insects in pollination, a key 'ecosystem service' without which global food supplies would be seriously threatened. But we could also consider the role of trees in providing security against flooding and soil erosion; in helping to minimize pollution; in sustaining the global hydrological cycle through capillary action; and in supporting tremendous biodiversity. Or we might consider the role of the oceans which, as we saw in Chapter 9, act as a huge carbon sink, cycle nutrients, and regulate global temperatures. It should not be too controversial to suggest that the benefits some resources deliver can be so great that justice mandates their protection. After all, human life depends upon some of them.

We must also be prepared, second, to treat incurring costs in order to protect resources from threats as being morally equivalent to incurring costs in order to produce public goods. This extension of the public goods argument, it seems to me, presents no difficulty. What is morally significant in the case of public good production—and what potentially gets the debate about free-riding going—is that agents sink costs into securing benefits which then accrue to other agents (who are potentially able to avoid sharing those costs). But protection displays the same features: when a resource which provides important ecosystem services is protected against some threat which would diminish or destroy its capacity to provide those services, agents are once more sinking costs into securing greater benefits than would counterfactually exist, outsiders cannot be excluded from those benefits, and the same possibility of sharing or refusing to share in those costs emerges. If successful, an argument along these lines can open up a potentially productive line of argument for those who would see conservation costs pooled. If justice requires that a resource is protected from a threat, proximity once more fails to provide a satisfactory guide to where costs should fall. To the contrary, those who consume the public good which protection secures have a reason, other things being equal, to share in the costs of protection efforts.[17] And they have a reason, other things being equal, to contribute in proportion to their consumption. I assume that the same argument can be made in relation to the costs of restoration. Indeed, the parallel with public good production appears even more straightforward in cases of restoration, assuming that restoration *increases* the ability of a pool of resources to produce some public good.

Elsewhere I have sketched one important case in which there appears to be a sound argument for allocating protection costs at least partly in proportion to patterns of benefits.[18] The world's forests perform a vital climatic role in sequestering CO_2, whereas their destruction not only erodes that sequestering capacity but releases huge quantities of carbon back into the soil or the atmosphere, thereby potentially accelerating dangerous climate change. The world's rainforests, for instance, contain roughly 650 billion tonnes of carbon, the equivalent of 2,300 billion tonnes of carbon dioxide. This is, strikingly, more than four times the amount of CO_2 emitted by humanity since the beginning of the industrial revolution. When communities take steps to protect forests from various threats, they secure a non-excludable but subtractive good: the good of carbon sequestration. Whilst a transition to a low- or no-carbon economy will be required at some point in the near future, the existence of forests allows agents to emit more carbon dioxide than they otherwise could. If we lost the sequestering capacity of the forests, that transition would have to happen much faster and would likely be much more costly. If costs must be incurred in order to protect forests from various threats, it appears plausible that those who benefit from carbon-intensive activities ought to share in those costs, in proportion to their consumption of sequestering capacity. To refuse to do so, when forest protection will be required in any case, is to free-ride upon states with forests (I bracket, until section 10.5, the costs forest states might be said to incur when the need to conserve reduces their economic development opportunities; such losses might well outstrip any protection costs in scale).

I will conclude by noting two points about the argument I have made here. First, when assessing whether an agent who has protected or restored some natural resource ought to have their costs mitigated, we should look to that agent's *net* contribution to the public good in question. If an agent protects or restores a forest which then generates 100 units of carbon-sequestering capacity, the case for mitigating the costs he incurs in so doing is cancelled if we know that he also consumes 100 units of that capacity by way of his own economic activities. If the agent is responsible for the generation of 100 units but consumes 150, he might even be considered a net debtor when it comes to any duty to share in the costs of forest protection. If by contrast he is responsible for the generation of 100 units but only consumes 20, he may have a claim that others, who consume the other 80, share the costs of forest protection or restoration with him. The same will hold for other environmental public goods which agents might both protect and consume. In concrete terms, this implies that the case for mitigating protection or restoration costs will survive in cases of forest states which are low emitters (such as Peru or the Democratic Republic of Congo), but not in cases of countries (such as Canada or the United States) which are net consumers of sink capacity.

Note that my argument is one about the mitigation of costs. These costs might in principle be mitigated in various ways, and one possible method would be to grant states which protect forests higher emissions budgets in order to offset the burdens of protection. But we should be clear about the argument for that move. It has been suggested that those who consume the world's carbon-sequestering capacity might have the sequestering capacity of forests on their territories 'credited' to them when calculating their emissions budgets.[19] But merely *having* forests on one's territory is not enough to justify transfers (such as, here, higher emissions entitlements). On my account, claims for mitigation are generated (in the specified conditions) when communities incur morally significant *costs* in conserving resources,[20] whether that means the costs of protection or of restoration, or the costs of non-exploitation, in cases where this pushes a community into overall disadvantage (section 10.5). If a rich state had so many resources that it had never occurred to it to cut down its forests, or if forests did not require protection from any threats, it is not clear why that state should qualify for higher entitlements.

Second, the argument is distinct from, and does not depend upon, the 'beneficiary pays principle' as discussed in debates on climate justice. On one well-known version, this principle asks those who have benefited from injustices to compensate surviving victims even if the beneficiaries were not perpetrators of the injustices in question (call this the 'benefiting from injustice' principle). It has been suggested that such a principle might help plug the gap left by the contributor pays principle in cases where present harms have been caused by past generations.[21] The benefiting from injustice principle has been the target of some formidable criticisms.[22] Rather than engaging with those criticisms, we can usefully emphasize the differences between it and the public goods argument.[23] If it were applied to cases of protection, the benefiting from injustice principle would presumably allocate greater burdens to those who have benefited from any activities which have caused threats to a resource. The principle would invoke duties to compensate victims, moreover, rather than duties to share the costs with those who must engage in protection. These duties should, according to prominent defenders of the principle, be understood as duties of corrective or rectificatory justice.[24] This suggests, moreover, that the principle applies within the domain of non-ideal theory, and that it is a backward-facing rather than forward-facing principle.

The public goods argument, by contrast, places greater burdens on the shoulders of those who consume the public goods secured by way of conservation efforts, and not those who have made them necessary (these categories could, but will frequently not, overlap). It seeks not to compensate victims, but to fairly share costs with protectors (and again, these categories may not overlap). The public goods principle is a principle of distributive rather than rectificatory justice. It does not depend for its relevance on some act of injustice, and might therefore apply even in ideal cases. All we must assume for it to gain traction is that agents will sometimes be obliged to protect resources from threats (whether anthropogenic or not), and that the distribution of the burdens attendant on that protection maps imperfectly onto the benefits arising from it. And at least as I have presented it, the argument develops the forward-facing implications of benefiting from conservation efforts.

* * *

I will pause briefly to establish where the last three sections have taken us. I have endorsed the view that, where those who cause threats to natural resources can be identified, justice often requires those agents to bear the costs of protection. To be more specific, it does so when relevant conditions such as knowledge of consequences and availability of alternatives are satisfied. We can call these cases of 'attributed' threats. However, there will be many cases in which there were no contributors (because threats are non-anthropogenic), contributors have left the scene, or the relevant conditions for holding agents responsible are not met. In such cases of 'unattributed' threats we must turn to some other principle. On one view—at least when it comes to responding to climate change—in such cases we ought to turn to the ability to pay principle.[25] I have argued that egalitarians have good reason to grant a substantial role to the ability to pay principle, insofar as it will generate outcomes which promote equality better than the alternatives.

But I have suggested that facts about benefits can also be relevant. In particular, it seems appropriate to require those who consume the public goods secured by conservation to contribute more, in cases where conservation efforts are required by justice, and where the fact that an agent consumes drives up the costs for those tasked with protection. In cases of unattributed threats, the principle that those who consume public goods ought to share in the cost of their protection gains appeal. I will not present a detailed account of how to integrate the public goods argument with the ability to pay principle. It is plausible to me that the degree to which agents consume public goods which protection secures is much less relevant, if at all, in cases where those agents possess below-average access to wellbeing. As with many cases of public good provision within states, it makes moral sense to exempt the worst-off from the burdens of securing public goods from which we all benefit. Amongst agents with better-than-average access to wellbeing, by contrast, the case for requiring those who benefit to contribute in line with their consumption is much stronger. That argument will provide distinctive guidance in cases in which the degree of overall advantage and the degree to which agents benefit from protected resources diverge. In many cases, to be sure, consumption of benefits from protected resources will tend to track ability to pay fairly closely. There is probably a fairly strong correlation, for instance, between states' standards of living and their consumption of carbon-sink capacity.[26] In such cases the public goods argument may not provide much in the way of distinctive guidance. But even so, it may supply an additional *reason* why a contribution ought to be made to protection costs. It will often be wrong for the well-off to refuse to share in protection costs, where protection is required by justice. But when that protection actually secures an important source of their advantage, to do so appears even more egregious. The correlation between benefits and ability to pay may make their duty to mitigate the costs of protection still more stringent.

10.5. CONSERVATION AS NON-EXPLOITATION

Besides active protection or restoration, the term 'conservation' can also encompass cases in which agents simply refrain from exploiting resources.

Imagine that a community possesses a stock of valuable resources but justice requires its members to leave those resources untouched. Threats notwithstanding, those resources will therefore be available to humans in future and will, in many cases, continue to play a role in sustaining ecosystems or delivering important public goods. Such cases gain interest, from the point of view of justice, because those who refrain from exploiting a resource might also be considered to accrue a kind of cost. Indeed, on the surface of it, there seems to be no profound moral difference between the sacrifices an agent makes when justice requires her to actively protect a resource from a threat, and the sacrifice she makes when justice obliges her not to exploit a resource which she otherwise could. In both cases her interests are set back relative to a counterfactual world in which conservation was not required. In some instances the prohibition on exploiting resources could even leave a community mired in poverty. We face the question, therefore, of whether justice can also require the pooling of the (opportunity) costs of conservation as non-exploitation, or whether locals can fairly be required to bear those costs alone.[27]

This section will illustrate the issues involved by discussing an important and topical example: the non-exploitation of fossil fuels.[28] The role of the combustion of fossil fuels in increasing the 'radiative forcing' of our world's atmosphere, and thereby opening the door to rises in average temperature and the disruption of weather patterns, is well understood. The degree of warming humanity can expect to experience will depend upon the proportion (and type) of fossil fuels which are burned. In 2013 the Intergovernmental Panel on Climate Change modelled a 'business as usual' scenario which could be expected to trigger temperature rises between 2.6 and 4.8°C by the end of the century. Indeed, there is evidence that continuing on our current highly carbon-intensive path might prompt temperature rises of as much as 6°C.[29] Catastrophic consequences can be expected to ensue if such rapid warming comes to pass. Even temperature rises of 2°C would likely bring in train increased drought, desertification, food insecurity, and heightened vulnerability to water-borne diseases.[30] If still greater warming occurs, the most substantial impacts would be on future generations. But even amongst current generations, there would likely be a series of very grave threats to human rights the world over.[31]

It is surely plausible to suggest that avoiding such catastrophic outcomes is required by justice. That conclusion follows even if we adhere to a minimalist view of global justice which focuses solely on avoiding threats to basic human rights, whether of present or future people. I will not attempt to settle here the question of how great an increase in global temperatures we should tolerate. For my purposes it is enough to assume that on any of the acceptable scenarios *some* fossil fuels must go unburned. If the objective is to avoid temperature rises in excess of 2°C, for instance—the goal recently adopted by the Paris climate accord—it is estimated that two-thirds of proven fossil fuel reserves must go unused by 2050.³² More specifically, it has recently been suggested that a third of global oil reserves, half of global gas reserves, and four-fifths of coal reserves must go unburned to meet such a target.³³ Perhaps temperature rises slightly higher than that are tolerable, with the implication that the use of more of the world's stocks of fossil fuels is acceptable. But it seems as though any serious position on climate justice will recommend measures to ensure that at least a substantial portion of the world's fossil fuels are not burned.

Likewise, I need take no stance here on just how a transition away from fossil fuel use might be achieved. On one scenario, binding emissions targets would be agreed, with defaulters liable to sanctions via, for instance, the World Trade Organization (WTO). Perhaps carbon taxes would then be employed in order to suppress demand, making fossil fuels less attractive, or a cap-and-trade system agreed which would produce strict energy budgets.³⁴ Or perhaps some other body—such as an International Court of the Environment—might be required to effect an outright ban on the burning of (some) fossil fuels.³⁵ My focus is on the consequences for fossil fuel exporters *if* these resources are not used, whether through disincentives or outright prohibition.³⁶ Simply imagine, then, that some political intervention or combination of interventions sufficed to destroy or significantly reduce the market for these resources. Agents which 'left the oil in the soil'—or which, more expansively, left oil, gas, and coal deposits undisturbed—would lose out on opportunities for economic advancement. Whilst some of the countries which would be affected are already wealthy, the decarbonization of the global economy would also cut off income streams which play a central role in many developing economies. On the assumption that we should pursue the most efficient use of the usable reserves, for instance—in effect, that we should extract those reserves which are cheapest to extract³⁷—it has been calculated that 95 per cent of the extra-heavy oil in Venezuela would not be exploited, as well as 73 per cent of the coal found in Central and South America, and 90 per cent of the coal found in Africa.³⁸ Some key resource-trade developments of recent years—such as Sub-Saharan Africa's great oil boom—might be snuffed out in their infancy.

In this scenario our primary normative concern will not, in all likelihood, lie with the costs of protection, and not at all with the costs of restoration. Fossil fuel reserves can simply be left in the ground, and there is no reason to restore or replace what has been destroyed (if that were even possible). To be sure, we can imagine cases in which renegades or civil warriors still tried to extract fossil fuels whose use was prohibited (so that they could use them themselves, or sell them on the black market), and in which local communities either lacked the capacity, or found it very burdensome, to prevent them from doing so. In some such cases it could well make moral sense to share enforcement costs globally, rather than leaving them at the door of locals.

But our most pressing concern will very likely be with the opportunity costs of non-exploitation borne by communities with fossil fuel reserves. Would it be fair for these communities to lose out on the attendant development opportunities, or might there be an argument that outsiders should mitigate those costs?

At least some protagonists within the political debate have maintained that there is such an argument. Since the Rio Summit of 1992, Saudi Arabia has complained that a global shift away from fossil fuels will seriously set back the economic interests of oil-exporters. Its representatives have argued that, rather than placing the economic burden of climate mitigation onto the shoulders of citizens in exporting countries, the world ought to help ameliorate their losses. If not, they see no reason why they should cease pumping, and selling, the country's oil. Now, whether the Saudi demand is sincere, or a spoiling tactic aimed at derailing climate negotiations, has been much debated.[39] But that does not establish that the claim should be rejected out of hand. It is perfectly conceivable that justice could require transfers to at least some countries when justice requires them to leave resources unexploited.

How might we make out a case? We might begin by suggesting that whenever an agent is unable to exploit a resource, he has a claim to compensation. But this would be a false start, because it seems to me that there is no general principle to the effect that opportunity costs should be shared whenever agents are obliged not to exploit. On the contrary, it seems to me that if we have reason to mitigate the opportunity costs concerned, they lie with our general concern with some agents' disadvantage. A selective prohibition on the exploitation of some resources might be perfectly defensible, in light of the likely effects of that exploitation. But when that leaves some who are already faring badly even worse off, through no fault of their own, then the egalitarian can readily embrace mitigation measures—just as we have reason to try to improve the situation of individuals the world over who have never had access to valuable resources in the first place. Much therefore seems to depend upon how those agents are faring. In Chapter 3 I argued that the benefits flowing from natural resources ought to be distributed in an equality-promoting way. On that basis, some countries which are already relatively advantaged overall may simply be judged to possess greater shares of resources than justice requires. For such countries to lose out on opportunities for further economic development because using resources within their territories would turn out to harm others does not look morally troubling. On the other hand, for a country which is already faring badly in terms of overall wellbeing to lose out on opportunities to advance further does appear troubling, at least inasmuch as economic development can be expected to fuel improvements in wellbeing. In such cases the argument for mitigating those losses begins to look more compelling. We would mitigate their losses not because there is some general principle which suggests that all agents ought to be able to fully exploit the resources they control, and therefore ought to be compensated whenever they cannot. We would do so because the opportunities of people who were already faring badly had been set back still further.[40]

Recall also that on a welfarist view we do not care about the distribution of resources in and of itself, but insofar as (unequal) access to resources drives (unequal) access to wellbeing. On that basis we might find several reasons for doubting the claim that Saudi Arabia's economic losses, for instance, ought to be mitigated. First and foremost, Saudi citizens are very wealthy, and may be considered to have favourable access to wellbeing already. Second, we might have reason to doubt that still greater returns from selling oil will substantially increase citizens' wellbeing in any case, if it is true that there is an inelastic relationship between income and wellbeing once a community reaches very high levels of the former. Third, it appears that rich Gulf states such as Saudi Arabia already possess the 'human' and financial capital to engineer a successful post-carbon future, in which cases their losses appear much less significant. I suggested in Chapter 8, in fact, that some Gulf states have already secured their post-carbon future in recent decades, by way of investing oil revenues on international property and financial markets. Although some have been less proactive in this respect, they might nevertheless be thought to have had the opportunity to do so in the many years since processes of climate change were first understood.[41] For all these reasons, the case for mitigating Saudi Arabia's losses would be a very difficult one to make. Norway, too, could in all likelihood bear the loss of North Sea oil and gas revenues without giving the egalitarian cause for concern.

The situation faced by very poor oil-exporting countries (such as the Democratic Republic of the Congo, Cameroon, or Chad) is very different, however. First—judging by key indicators such as child mortality, literacy, access to primary and secondary education, access to healthcare, and life expectancy—the access to wellbeing of citizens in these countries is considerably more precarious. Second, it is reasonable to expect that the income generated from fossil fuel exports could make a substantial difference to the wellbeing of citizens.[42] Third, unlike Gulf states which have been earning massive oil revenues for several decades, the oil boom in Africa is a relatively recent (and in some cases very recent) phenomenon; if oil revenues were to dry up in the near future, in some instances they would have lasted only a few years. Fourth, opportunities to successfully diversify economies away from their present dependence upon natural resource exports appear to be rather poor for many of the least developed countries. Chapter 7 identified several obstacles facing poor countries wishing to diversify away from natural resource exports, and while there are some 'success stories', they are rather thin on the ground. All four facts suggest that the argument for mitigating the loss of development opportunities is a live one.

Though I have focused in this section on fossil fuels, there are many other cases in which a community's disadvantage is likely to be entrenched when justice requires the non-exploitation of particular resources. One of the most significant recalls an example discussed in section 10.4. If justice requires that the world's forests are preserved (or at least a substantial part of them), this may well generate protection costs. But it can also generate losses when the land on which those forests lie cannot be turned to other uses, including agriculture.[43] In many poor countries, the need to feed growing urban populations has driven extensive deforestation. Although the soil under the forests is typically of poor quality, and its nutrients exhausted after a few years, poverty has nevertheless driven both state-sanctioned and illicit clearing of the forests. It is in our collective interest that this deforestation is halted. But for so long as the losses associated with non-exploitation fall exclusively on the shoulders of the disadvantaged, conservation is unlikely to occur. Once more, egalitarians have reason to support proposals which would offset the losses in opportunities for economic advancement which poor countries experience when justice requires that forests, or the land or other resources under them, are not exploited. In section 10.6 I investigate the measures available to us when we seek to do so.

10.6. MECHANISMS FOR SHARING BURDENS MORE FAIRLY

This chapter has focused on cases in which conservation is required by justice, and has illustrated its arguments by way of several examples in which this appears highly plausible. I have argued that the costs of protection in the face of attributed threats (and restoration in light of attributed damage) ought to be allocated not in line with proximity, but in line with contribution to threat or damage. In cases of protection in the face of unattributed threats (and restoration in the face of unattributed damage), we must turn to other principles. Here I have argued for a central role for the ability to pay principle, according to which costs should be allocated so as to promote, rather than undermine, equality in access to wellbeing. But I have also identified a set of cases—in which protection or restoration secures important public goods—where the degree to which agents consume those goods can be salient. Given certain conditions—whereby the public goods in question must be secured, where someone must pick up the costs, and/or where the consumption of one agent drives up the costs for those who must protect or restore—there is a prima facie reason for allocating greater burdens to those who receive greater benefits.

I then shifted our focus to conservation construed as non-exploitation. When resources must not be exploited, this sets back the opportunities of any agents who would otherwise have been able to turn to them in order to secure economic development. I have not claimed such setbacks ought always to be mitigated. But they can compound injustice in cases where the agents concerned fare relatively badly already, and where non-exploitation removes a potential route out of that disadvantage. When this is the case, we have a reason to mitigate those costs. In cases of non-exploitation the proximity principle again turns out to be a poor guide to the proper allocation of burdens. Whilst it may sometimes be appropriate for owners to bear the losses associated with non-exploitation, often it will not be. Requiring owners to bear losses when they are already disadvantaged is to heap injustice on top of injustice. If the argument is correct—if there can be grounds for requiring outsiders to mitigate the losses associated with non-exploitation—we will require a principled basis upon which to allocate the costs of doing so. My suggestion, somewhat tentatively, is that the relevant considerations once more comprise ability to pay, and the pattern of consumption of the goods secured by non-exploitation. For the most part, it seems to me, the better-off should shoulder the burden when we have grounds of justice to offset the losses which poor communities face when they cannot exploit resources within their territories. But there will be cases in which the non-exploited resources will thereby continue to deliver important collective goods to outsiders (including, but not limited to, carbon sequestration). Here it is appropriate, other things being equal, to require those who benefit more to contribute more.

My focus in this section, though, will be the *mechanisms* available to those seeking to share the costs of conservation as protection, restoration, or non-exploitation. I will identify three distinct strategies here. The first appears particularly appropriate to losses from non-exploitation, whereas the second and third could in principle be employed to mitigate the costs of protection, restoration, or non-exploitation.

First, in cases where the duty not to exploit generates a normatively troubling loss of development opportunities, measures could be adopted which would reduce the scale of that loss in the first place. Consider again the example of disadvantaged countries which lose out on opportunities for economic advancement when resources such as fossil fuels must not be exploited. Recall that the loss of income from extracting fossil fuels will represent a significant blow precisely insofar as alternative means of escaping disadvantage are thin on the ground, or difficult or costly to pull off. The opportunity structure facing poor countries is not, however, a given; the advantaged could do much to alter that structure. Saudi Arabia has argued that the developed world should assist oil-exporting countries 'in achieving economic diversification'—that is, in opening up a viable economic path capable of securing citizens' wellbeing in a post-carbon future.[44] In the case of developing countries, one way to do just that would be to refashion international trade rules. A pro-development trade regime would reduce the dependence of poor countries upon exporting primary resources, and the diversification this would allow would soften the blow of any prohibition on resource exploitation. In addition, pro-development trade rules might allow countries to develop their comparative advantage in resources other than fossil fuels. Africa, for instance, is the site of huge expanses of very fertile agricultural land which could do much to feed a growing global population. But developed-world tariffs, and domestic subsidies, on foodstuffs and textiles have for too long scuppered the development opportunities the trade in food and textiles could offer. Cutting back those tariffs and subsidies would significantly reduce the costliness of a shift away from fossil fuel exports (indeed I suggested in Chapter 7 that the positive effects would likely be even wider: they might also promote the economic independence of individual citizens and, therefore, their bargaining power vis-à-vis their rulers).

Besides trade reform, many other measures could lighten any losses associated with non-exploitation. For instance, the drive to exploit resources is often intensified by indebtedness. Spending commitments made in boom years, when commodity prices are high, often leave governments overcommitted in fallow periods; rather than cut services (or scale back patronage), many developing countries then turn to international lending markets. Agreements which would restructure or cancel debts when resources are not exploited (so-called 'debt-for-nature swaps') therefore gain interest.[45] To take another example, measures to share technology with developing countries, and/or to moderate the developed world's jealous protection of intellectual property rights, could unlock broader economic opportunities which would mitigate the losses associated with non-exploitation. Finally, measures to unlock benefits from resources which are left *in situ* are worth exploring. We know that the world's rainforests, for instance, are the site of incredible biodiversity. Any means by which this biodiversity might be exploited whilst leaving the forests intact—for instance by funding developing-world programmes to harness the potential of plant or animal species to generate new medical treatments—would also reduce the losses associated with conservation. They would also reduce incentives for deforestation, turning the forests' precious resources into assets for locals as well as for the wider world.

Second, losses from non-exploitation could readily be mitigated in a world in which global taxes on natural resources were a reality. Consider again the non-exploitation of fossil fuels. Depending on the way in which fossil fuels were put beyond use, there are various ways in which the issue could be handled under a global tax-and-transfer regime. If a post-carbon transition occurred by way of an actual ban on the use of (all or some) fossil fuels for energy, or even a ban upon the extraction of (all or some of) these fuels, then the resources left *in situ* should be exempted from any global resource tax. Taxes would then target resources which could permissibly be used, and not resource holdings per se. If the transition was effected by way of measures which reduced or destroyed demand for fossil fuels, thereby decreasing their economic value, then this too would be accommodated by any tax-and-transfer system in which payments were calibrated to the economic value of resources. To destroy (or reduce) demand for fossil fuels is to destroy (or reduce) their economic value, and thereby make their owners proportionately less liable to taxes and, other things being equal, likely to receive proportionately greater transfers. Tax-and-transfer schemes therefore appear well placed to mitigate losses from non-exploitation. Indeed, in principle such schemes could also factor in contributions to protection or restoration when calculating tax liabilities. Taxes which charged users for using common-pool resources, for instance, could grant credits to users who engaged in the protection or restoration of some of those resources.

Of course global resource taxes may not be an immediate prospect. But even in their absence, third, other forms of transfer might be employed to mitigate the costs of conservation (as protection, restoration, or non-exploitation). International bodies already exist which are charged precisely with the task of channelling funds to countries which conserve important natural resources. Two key examples in this regard are the Global Environmental Facility (GEF) and the Green Climate Fund. The GEF was established by the World Bank in 1991, and is empowered to disburse funds for projects envisaged under the Convention on Biological Diversity, the UN Convention to Combat Desertification, and other protection schemes. When it comes to rainforests, the United Nations has established a framework for independently measuring reductions in emissions from deforestation and forest degradation (the REDD, or more latterly REDD+, programme). The GEF is the principal financial mechanism through which to channel funds from donor organizations and states towards forest countries. It has already made grants totalling over $14 billion, and claims to have been instrumental in avoiding billions of tonnes of carbon emissions, and in securing the protection of areas of forest equal to the total land mass of Brazil.[45] The GEF could also readily be charged with collecting and disbursing the funds required to maintain Marine Protected Areas on the high seas and other important conservation ventures.

The Green Climate Fund, for its part, was established under the UNFCCC framework in 2010, and charged with raising $100 billion in revenues per year by 2020. Its brief is to administer funding for environmental projects in developing countries, and at the time of writing it has achieved pledges (though not yet receipts) of $10 billion.[47] Though its focus is on the roll-out of green technology, it too could provide a vehicle not only for payments to enhance the protection or restoration of vital ecosystem resources, but also for transfers which would mitigate the losses associated with non-exploitation. Both these schemes are, to be sure, seriously underfunded. Contributor states appear to view the obligation to pay in to them as a purely charitable one, rather than a duty of justice which is required to spread the costs of conservation more fairly. That needs to change. But the problem here is one of motivation rather than a lack of institutional capacity per se. In light of the existence of these schemes, we can therefore usefully return to the 'accessibility' challenge to global egalitarianism, which claims that institutions or mechanisms for making substantial progress towards greater equality at the global level are lacking. This section has further undermined that challenge, by providing several important examples in which progress towards a more just sharing of global conservation burdens could be achieved by way of existing structures, whether this means direct transfers or structural measures taken to reduce the costs of conservation.

Potential strategies for mitigating conservation costs are, then, manifold. A global regime of natural resource taxes would offer an effective means of mitigating conservation costs. But such a regime may be some way off. In the meantime, the other two strategies gain in interest. One strategy would involve transfers to compensate for costs which have already been incurred, whereas the other would reduce the costliness of conservation measures in the first place. The question arises, therefore, whether we have any reason to favour one approach over the other. I will make two brief comments in response to that question. First, direct measures to reduce the costliness of conservation are in at least one respect more likely to generate effective conservation outcomes than schemes for *post-hoc* transfers. Post-hoc schemes involve an assurance problem: those who conserve resources must trust that others who are duty-bound to share in the costs will in fact do so, and that, should they fail to meet their obligations, sanctions will compel them to. Even if agents' compliance with their cost-sharing duties is quite good, measures which directly reduce the costliness of conservation enjoy an advantage here, and are therefore more likely to stimulate conservation. This appears to be an important consideration in a world in which many rich countries have made pledges to the Global Environmental Facility or Green Climate Fund but, regrettably, failed to deliver on them.

This suggests that we have at least one reason to favour measures to reduce the initial costliness of conservation. Nevertheless, I suggest that transfers will be an indispensable part of any regime promoting conservation justice. Indeed, they would appear to be an indispensable feature even in a much more equal world than ours. Even in a world in which people or communities possessed, say, shares of resources which were perfectly compatible with equality, two contingencies are still likely to arise (neither of which necessarily takes us into the domain of non-ideal theory). First, the distribution of the resources which happen to require preserving—whether this means non-exploitation or active protection—will likely be haphazard, and, as such, conservation will impose a greater burden on some than on others. Second, non-excludable and subtractive benefits will arise from some of those conserved resources. In such cases, justice will require some to conserve resources which deliver important public goods for others. On each contingency, there would be a case for transfers designed to restore justice. In this much more equal world the case for corrective transfers would, to be sure, be much less pressing. But transfers would still be required. In our massively unequal world, by contrast, the case for measures to mitigate the costs of conservation is far stronger.

10.7. TOWARDS CONSERVATION JUSTICE

The 1972 World Heritage Convention argued that the natural world 'constitutes a world heritage for whose protection it is the duty of the international community as a whole to co-operate'.[48] That is an admirable ideal. But notwithstanding some well-intentioned but chronically underfunded schemes to pool costs internationally, the default position, under our world of permanent sovereignty, is that the inhabitants of each state must pick up the tab for conserving the resources to be found within its borders. I have argued in this chapter that this is a source of serious injustice. The geographical location of conservation-worthy resources maps poorly onto the moral considerations which actually turn out to matter when we come to distribute the burdens of conservation: our ability to bear those burdens; our contribution to any threat or damage affecting precious resources; and the degree to which we consume the goods which their continued existence secures. Moreover, many significant resources do not fall within the boundary of any one state in the first place, and in such cases we require alternative principles for allocating the costs of conservation.

I have distinguished three forms of conservation and sketched a set of principles according to which the attendant costs should be allocated. Progress here is demanded by justice. That progress is also likely to slow the pace of large-scale environmental destruction. For as long as costs are localized, people mired in disadvantage will have an incentive to exploit local resources even if the impact on the environment, on distant others, or on future generations is hugely destructive. Those who burn down the forests do not necessarily consider them to be devoid of value. But even if they recognize that conservation is a noble goal, their own struggle for a better life is frequently a more pressing concern. A more just distribution of conservation burdens will reduce incentives to engage in environmentally destructive behaviour.

We have every reason to prefer a world in which duties to conserve resources do not fall exclusively on the states in which they exist. Perhaps we can imagine a world beyond permanent sovereignty in which they would not be. Key natural resources might then be managed transnationally, by way of some complex division of authority better suited to the complex distribution of valuable resources (see Chapter 6). I have not attempted to describe such a world here. My argument has been in a sense more modest: even in the world of states that we now inhabit, I have claimed, decoupling the duty to conserve from the duty to bear the costs of conservation must be a priority. The upshot of the argument is that a conventional picture of global resource justice—in which countries rich in resources are taxed in order to compensate those with fewer precious resources—is rendered more complex, but more satisfying. Justice does not only require that the resource-rich somehow compensate the resource-poor. We can identify many important cases in which the reverse may well be true—in which we ought to support supposedly resource-rich communities, that is, in conserving valuable resources.

ENDNOTES

1. Smith et al. 2000.
2. Inter-Agency Task Force on Gender and Water 2006.
3. One interesting class of burdens which I will not discuss, for example, would be those caused inadvertently to outsiders' interests by resources one controls. In 2010 a volcano on Iceland's territory spewed ash across Europe, disrupting industry and transportation in many countries. In such cases should the agent or community controlling the resource be held liable for the costs? It seems plausible that it should not. But for a discussion of the issues which arise in such cases, see Mancilla 2015b.
4. For a similar typology see del Corral 2015. Whilst she uses the term preservation rather than conservation, they appear to be equivalent for our purposes.
5. It might be clumsy to define restoration as a variety of conservation, given that conventional usage holds conservation to imply 'keeping things as they are'. But nothing substantive hangs on this. My focus is on who should bear the costs of the protection, restoration, and non-exploitation of natural resources, and I use conservation simply as a placeholder for those activities.
6. 'Non-interference' might therefore be a better term, since exploiting a resource is but one way in which we might destroy or degrade it (we might, for instance, destroy a resource out of sheer spite). I used the narrower term here simply because the real-world cases I have in mind are cases where an agent would like to transform or destroy a resource precisely in order to secure economic benefits, and because it is the loss of those benefits which generates the normative question I am interested in.
7. See e.g. Shue 2014, chapter 9.
8. See Caney 2012.
9. Caney (2010a) suggests a modified version of the ability to pay principle, according to which those whose present advantages emanate from unjust past emissions should, other things being equal, bear greater costs. If the underlying thought is plausible, we might still think that the argument casts its net too narrowly. For instance, we might think that those whose advantages emanate from *all* kinds of

injustice, and not only climate injustice, ought to bear greater burdens. Or we might think that those whose advantages are the result of good brute luck ought to bear greater burdens. If so, the modified principle presumably trades on some deeper and broader normative principle.

10. Moellendorf 2014, chapter 6.
11. For a fuller account of the cases in which what I am calling the contributor pays principle fails to provide adequate guidance, and on which I draw here, see Caney 2010a.
12. As Moellendorf (2014: 168–9) has usefully noted, whereas proclaiming a forward-looking principle of strict liability might be efficacious in eliciting 'incentives to act with a good deal of care', it is much less obvious that it is fair to place burdens on agents' shoulders retrospectively (that is, prior to such a proclamation).
13. Shue 2014; Moellendorf 2014; Caney 2010b: 212.
14. The argument is typically applied to cases where benefits are worth their costs, and costs are fairly shared. Arneson 1982. I endorse those constraints here.
15. Nozick 1974: 95; Simmons 2000. Note that both authors object especially to the argument that simply receiving public goods can generate political obligations (e.g. to cooperate with or obey the state). I make no claim about political obligation here.
16. Klosko (1992) has argued that the argument for sharing in the costs of 'presumptively beneficial' benefits is easier to make. I believe he means by this benefits which are indispensable *to the recipient*. In principle, though, I might be obliged to contribute to the costs of producing goods which are vital to the interests of others. I leave such cases aside here because costs would not then be allocated in line with my consumption of public goods, but presumably on some other basis such as ability to pay.
17. It is important to be clear that the focus of the public goods argument is precisely upon agents' consumption of public goods which are produced or protected. It does not obviously extend to cases where agents benefit more indirectly without consuming those goods, and still less to cases where they 'benefit' in the sense of not being harmed when those goods are consumed by others. The public goods argument requires those who ride trams to buy tickets. It does not require people to pay when *others* ride trams, even if they thereby avoid breathing polluted air, or being run over by cars. In the case of climate change, this means that those who consume sequestering capacity should pay for it. It does not mean that those who would otherwise be harmed by climate change must pay for others' consumption. See Page 2016 for a discussion of that counter-intuitive possibility.
18. Armstrong 2016.
19. See Blomfield 2013. Caney (2009: 131) has argued that states might be given higher emissions budgets, other things being equal, if they 'support' forests. 'Support' needs further specification, but if it is interpreted to mean incurring costs in order to protect or restore the claim is plausible.
20. See also Armstrong 2015.
21. Page 2012; Butt 2007.
22. See especially Huseby 2015; Caney 2006. For a response, see Barry and Kirby 2015.

23. In response to my application of the public goods argument to rainforests (in Armstrong 2016), Ed Page (2016) has suggested that I am allying myself with the beneficiary pays principle. I show here that the two arguments are quite different. It is also worth noting that in Armstrong 2016 I explicitly put to one side my global egalitarian commitments and investigate whether the public goods argument is capable of convincing even people committed to permanent sovereignty that protection costs ought to be pooled globally. Furthermore I do not suggest that the public goods argument can do all of the normative work in that case. Rather I suggest, as I do here, that it must be reconciled with considerations of ability to pay.
24. Page 2012: 306; Butt 2007: 135.
25. Caney (2005b) has presented an influential argument for a similar division of labour between considerations of contribution and ability to pay. Though there are important differences on the details, this is also the broad position adopted by Miller (2009).
26. Shue 2014, chapter 9.
27. For discussion of the arguments in this section, I am indebted to Henry Shue.
28. In what follows I will actually address the consequences if fossil fuels cannot be *burned* for energy, because it is this burning which is typically associated with the release of greenhouse gases into the atmosphere. There are alternative uses for oil—in the manufacture of lubricants and plastics for example—which do not have these consequences (or not to the same degree). But note that even if these other uses remained in play, the economic value of oil would be very significantly depressed if combustion were prohibited.
29. Intergovernmental Panel on Climate Change 2014. The various warming scenarios are discussed in more detail in Moellendorf 2014, chapter 3.
30. Intergovernmental Panel on Climate Change 2007.
31. Caney 2010b.
32. International Energy Agency 2012.
33. McGlade and Ekins 2015.
34. I do not pursue here the question of who ought to be able to use the fossil fuels which can permissibly be used, though I suggested in Chapter 8 that those who are disadvantaged, and who find access to alternative sources of energy most costly, have the best claim to do so. In principle carbon taxes or cap-and-trade schemes could be designed to protect access to energy for the worst-off.
35. For discussions of the role that such a Court might play in reducing environmental harms, see Schuppert 2014; and McCallion and Sharma 2000.
36. Can the approach recommended in this section also be applied to the losses incurred by companies or individuals holding investments in fossil fuels? So long as we avoid double-counting losses, there is no obvious reason why it should not. But it may be that companies are better placed to absorb losses than exporting countries. According to Stevens, Lahn, and Kooroshy (2015: 26), major oil and gas companies typically hold reserves of ten to fifteen years' worth of fossil fuels, and can fairly readily diversify their business activities without incurring losses beyond that point, whereas for countries the loss of income from fossil fuels looks more permanent, and diversification more fraught.

37. This is a questionable assumption. For instance, we might prefer that the reserves of the poorest countries should be used up first, in order to mitigate any distributive unfairness. Such a policy may have some promise, although I cannot calculate here whether it would neutralize the disadvantage we are discussing. But it is worth pointing out that such a solution, however creative, appears unlikely to arise from any of the scenarios for putting fossil fuels beyond use discussed earlier (a global fossil fuel tax is likely to make the consumption of fossil fuels less attractive irrespective of their origin, for instance, whereas a legal ruling which forbade extraction in light of its negative effects but condoned it in poor countries might be difficult to arrange). Moreover, there *may* be countervailing environmental reasons to prefer extraction from cheaper sources—for instance, continuing to extract oil from the enormous oil fields of Saudi Arabia may in one respect be preferable to digging new wells in countries which are relative latecomers to extraction.
38. McGlade and Ekins 2015: 189–90.
39. Mouawad and Revkin 2009.
40. This is an equality-promoting argument. But the minimalist could endorse the position too in cases where the prohibition left communities mired in poverty. For instance, Miller (2009) has argued that the costs of mitigating climate change should not fall upon communities with endemic poverty.
41. Saudi Arabia does have a Sovereign Wealth Fund (SWF)—called the Public Investment Fund—but its estimated holdings, at $5 billion, are dwarfed by those of Qatar or Abu Dhabi. It has faced much internal criticism for its tardiness in building up the Fund. In April 2016, however, Prince Mohammed bin Salman announced a plan to make the Fund the world's biggest, with a value of up to $2 trillion, by selling shares in Aramco (the world's leading oil-producing company). See Hubbard and Reed 2016.
42. We may well be able to identify cases, of course, in which oil income does not make a substantial contribution to the wellbeing of ordinary citizens *at present*. But as I argued in Chapter 8, we must not take this failure to be an immutable fact which in turn justifies indifference about access to resource rents. To the contrary, policies appear to be available which would allow resource rents to contribute much more effectively to citizens' wellbeing.
43. There are also cases in which other resources—such as oil—are contained under the forest and cannot be used if forests are conserved. I discuss the well-known case of Ecuador's Yasuni National Park in Armstrong 2016.
44. Mouawad and Revkin 2009.
45. Such swaps have been in operation for decades. For an early discussion, see Hansen 1989. For a useful note of caution about their potential, see Hassoun 2012.
46. https://www.thegef.org/gef/whatisgef.
47. Green Climate Fund press release, 9 December 2014, 'Green Climate Fund Reaches USD 10 Billion Threshold'.
48. United Nations Educational, Scientific and Cultural Organization (UNESCO) Convention Concerning the Protection of the World Cultural and Natural Heritage (1972), Article 6.

References

Abi-Saab, G. (1984). 'Progressive Development of the Principles and Norms of International Law Relating to The New International Economic Order.' United Nations Document A/39/504/Add. 1 (23 October).

Abizadeh, A. (2007). 'On the Scope (Not Site) of Distributive Justice.' *Philosophy and Public Affairs* 35/4: 318–58.

Alexeev, M. and R. Conrad (2009). 'The Elusive Curse of Oil.' *Review of Economics and Statistics* 91/3: 586–98.

Anaya, S. J. and R. Williams (2001). 'The Protection of Indigenous Peoples' Rights over Land and Natural Resources in the Inter-American Human Rights System.' *Harvard Human Rights Journal* 14: 33–86.

Anderson, E. (1999). 'What is the Point of Equality?' *Ethics* 109/2: 287–337.

Angeli, O. (2015). *Cosmopolitanism, Self-determination and Territory*. Basingstoke: Palgrave Macmillan.

Angell, K. (2013). 'Do Insecure Property Rights Ground Rights of Jurisdiction?' *Res Publica* 19/2: 183–92.

Anghie, A. (2007). *Imperialism, Sovereignty and the Making of International Law*. Cambridge: Cambridge University Press.

Armstrong, C. (2009a). 'Coercion, Reciprocity and Equality beyond the State.' *Journal of Social Philosophy* 40/3: 297–316.

Armstrong, C. (2009b). 'Defending the Duty of Assistance?' *Social Theory and Practice* 35/3: 461–82.

Armstrong, C. (2012). *Global Distributive Justice: An Introduction*. Cambridge: Cambridge University Press.

Armstrong, C. (2013). 'Sovereign Wealth Funds and Global Justice.' *Ethics and International Affairs* 27/4: 413–28.

Armstrong, C. (2014a). 'Global Justice between Minimalism and Egalitarianism.' *Political Theory* 44/1: 119–29.

Armstrong, C. (2014b). 'Distributive Institutions.' In D. Moellendorf and H. Widdows (eds) *Routledge Handbook of Global Ethics*. London: Routledge, 292–301.

Armstrong, C. (2014c). 'Resources, Rights and Global Justice: A Response to Kolers.' *Political Studies* 62/1: 216–22.

Armstrong, C. (2015). 'Climate Justice and Territorial Rights.' In J. Moss (ed.) *Climate Change and Justice*. Cambridge: Cambridge University Press, 59–72.

Armstrong, C. (2016). 'Fairness, Free-riding and Rainforest Protection.' *Political Theory* 44/1: 106–30.

Arneson, R. (1982). 'The Principle of Fairness and the Free-Rider Problem.' *Ethics* 92/4: 616–33.

Arneson, R. (1999). 'Equality of Opportunity for Welfare Defended and Recanted.' *Journal of Political Philosophy* 7/4: 488–97.

Arze del Granado, J. et al. (2010). *The Unequal Benefits of Fuel Subsidies: A Review of Evidence for Developing Countries*. Washington: International Monetary Fund. IMF Working Paper WP/10/202.

Axelsen, D. (2013). 'The State Made Me Do It: How Anti-Cosmopolitanism is Created by the State.' *Journal of Political Philosophy* 21/4: 451–72.
Baker, J. (1988). *Arguing for Equality*. London: Verso.
Ban, N. et al. (2014). 'Systematic Conservation Planning: A Better Recipe for Managing the High Seas for Biodiversity Conservation and Sustainable Use.' *Conservation Letters* 7/1: 41–54.
Barnaby, W. (2009). 'Do Nations Go to War over Water?' *Nature* 459/163: 282–3.
Barnes, R. (2009). *Property Rights and Natural Resources*. Oxford: Hart.
Barry, B. (1981). 'Do Countries Have Moral Obligations? The Case of World Poverty.' In S. McMurrin (ed.) *The Tanner Lectures on Human Values, Volume 2*. Cambridge: Cambridge University Press, 25–44.
Barry, B. (1982). 'Humanity and Justice in Global Perspective.' *Nomos XXIV: Ethics, Economics and the Law*: 219–52.
Barry, B. (1989). 'The Ethics of Resource Depletion.' In his *Democracy, Power and Justice: Essays in Political Theory*. Oxford: Clarendon Press, 511–25.
Barry, B. (2005). *Why Social Justice Matters*. Cambridge: Polity.
Barry, C. and R. Kirby (2015). 'Scepticism about Beneficiary Pays: A Response.' *Journal of Applied Philosophy*. doi: 10.1111/japp.12160.
Beitz, C. (1979). *Political Theory and International Relations*. Princeton: Princeton University Press.
Beitz, C. (2005). 'Reflections.' *Review of International Studies* 31/4: 409–23.
Bhagwati, J. (ed.) (1977). *The New International Economic Order: The North–South Debate*. London: MIT Press.
Blattman, C. and P. Niehaus (2014). 'Show them the Money: Why Giving Cash Helps Alleviate Poverty.' *Foreign Affairs* 93/3: 117–26.
Blomfield, M. (2013). 'Global Common Resources and the Just Distribution of Emissions Shares.' *Journal of Political Philosophy* 21/3: 283–304.
Böhringer, C. et al. (2012). 'The Role of Border Carbon Adjustments in Unilateral Climate Policy: Overview of an Energy Modelling Forum Study.' *Energy Economics* 34: S97–S110.
Borgerson, S. (2008). 'Arctic Meltdown.' *Foreign Affairs* 87/2: 63–77.
Brighouse, H. and A. Swift (2006a). 'Equality, Priority and Positional Goods.' *Ethics* 116/3: 471–97.
Brighouse, H. and A. Swift (2006b). 'Parents' Rights and the Value of the Family.' *Ethics* 117/1: 80–108.
Brock, G. (2008). 'Taxation and Global Justice: Closing the Gap between Theory and Practice.' *Journal of Social Philosophy* 39/2: 161–84.
Brunnschweiler, C. and E. Bulte (2008). 'The Resource Curse Revisited and Revised: A Tale of Paradoxes and Red Herrings.' *Journal of Environmental Economics and Management* 55: 248–64.
Buchanan, A. (2000) 'Rawls's Law of Peoples: Rules for a Vanished Westphalian World.' *Ethics* 110/4: 697–721.
Buchanan, A. (2003). *Justice, Legitimacy and Self-Determination*. Oxford: Oxford University Press.
Butler, H. and J. Macey (1996). 'Externalities and the Matching Principle: The Case for Reallocating Environmental Regulatory Authority.' *Yale Journal of Regulation* 14/1: 23–66.

Butt, D. (2007). 'On Benefiting from Injustice.' *Canadian Journal of Philosophy* 37/1: 129–52.
Cafaro, P. (2008). 'An Exchange: The Morality of Immigration.' *Ethics and International Affairs* 22/3: 241–59.
Caney, S. (2005a). *Justice Beyond Borders*. Oxford: Oxford University Press.
Caney, S. (2005b). 'Cosmopolitan Justice, Responsibility, and Global Climate Change.' *Leiden Journal of International Law* 18: 747–75.
Caney, S. (2006). 'Environmental Degradation, Reparations, and the Moral Significance of History.' *Journal of Social Philosophy* 37/3: 464–82.
Caney, S. (2008). 'Global Distributive Justice and the State.' *Political Studies* 56/3: 487–518.
Caney, S. (2009). 'Justice and the Distribution of Greenhouse Gas Emissions.' *Journal of Global Ethics* 5/2: 125–46.
Caney, S. (2010a). 'Climate Justice and the Duties of the Advantaged.' *Critical Review of International Social and Political Philosophy* 13/1: 203–28.
Caney, S. (2010b). 'Climate Change, Human Rights and Moral Thresholds.' In S. Gardiner et al. (eds) *Climate Ethics: Essential Readings*. Oxford: Oxford University Press, 161–77.
Caney, S. (2011). 'Humanity, Associations and Global Justice: In Defence of Humanity-Centered Cosmopolitan Egalitarianism.' *The Monist* 94/4: 506–34.
Caney, S. (2012). 'Just Emissions.' *Philosophy and Public Affairs* 40/4: 255–300.
Caney, S. (forthcoming). 'Responding to Global Injustice: Rehabilitating the Right of Necessity.' Unpublished manuscript.
Cantegreil, J. (2011). 'The Audacity of the Texaco/Calasiatic Award: René-Jean Dupuy and the Internationalization of Foreign Investment Law.' *European Journal of International Law* 22/2: 441–58.
Carbon Tracker Initiative (2014). *Unburnable Carbon: Are the World's Market Carrying a Carbon Bubble?* London: Carbon Tracker Initiative.
Carens, J. (1981). *Equality, Moral Incentives and the Market*. Chicago: University of Chicago Press.
Carens, J. (2013). *The Ethics of Immigration*. Oxford: Oxford University Press.
Carter, I. (2011). 'Respect and the Basis of Equality.' *Ethics* 121/3: 538–71.
Casal, P. (2006). 'Why Sufficiency is Not Enough.' *Ethics* 117/2: 296–326.
Casal, P. (2011). 'Global Taxes on Natural Resources.' *Journal of Moral Philosophy* 8/3: 307–27.
Cassese, A. (1995). *Self-determination of Peoples: A Legal Reappraisal*. Cambridge: Cambridge University Press.
Chambers, C. (2009). 'Each Outcome is Another Opportunity.' *Politics, Philosophy and Economics* 8/4: 374–400.
Chaudhry, K. (1989). 'The Price of Wealth: Business and State in Labor Remittance and Oil Economies.' *International Organization* 43/1: 101–45.
Chimni, B. (1987). *International Commodity Agreements: A Legal Study*. London: Croom Helm.
Chowdhury, S. R. (1988). 'Permanent Sovereignty over Natural Resources: Substratum of the Seoul Declaration.' In P. de Waart et al. (eds) *International Law and Development* 45. Dordrecht: Martinus Nijhoff, 59–85.
Christiano, T. (2011). 'An Instrumental Argument for a Human Right to Democracy.' *Philosophy and Public Affairs* 39/2: 142–76.

Christman, J. (1994). *The Myth of Property*. Oxford: Oxford University Press.
Churchill, R. R. and A. V. Lowe (1999). *The Law of the Sea*, third edition. Manchester: Manchester University Press.
Ciriacy-Wantrup, S. V. and R. Bishop (1975). '"Common Property" as a Concept in Natural Resources Policy.' *Natural Resources Journal* 15/4: 713–28.
Coady, D., I. Parry, L. Sears, and B. Shang (2015). *How Large are Global Energy Subsidies?* Washington: International Monetary Fund. IMF Working Paper WP/15/105.
Cohen, G. A. (1989). 'On the Currency of Egalitarian Justice.' *Ethics* 99/4: 906–44.
Cohen, G. A. (1995). *Self-Ownership, Freedom and Equality*. Cambridge: Cambridge University Press.
Cohen, G. A. (2000). *If You're An Egalitarian, How Come You're So Rich?* Cambridge, Mass.: Harvard University Press.
Cohen, G. A. (2004). 'Expensive Taste Rides Again.' In J. Burley (ed.) *Dworkin and His Critics*. Oxford: Blackwell, 3–29.
Cohen, G. A. (2009). *Why Not Socialism?* Princeton: Princeton University Press.
Collier, P. (2010a). *Plundered Planet*. London: Allen Lane.
Collier, P. (2010b). 'The Political Economy of Natural Resources.' *Social Research* 77/4: 1105–32.
Collier, P. (2014). 'The Ethics of Natural Assets.' *Journal of Global Ethics* 10/1: 45–52.
Collier, P. and A. Hoeffler (1998). 'On Economic Causes of Civil War.' *Oxford Economic Papers* 50: 563–73.
Cornes, R. and T. Sandler (1996). *The Theory of Externalities, Public Goods and Club Goods*, second edition. Cambridge: Cambridge University Press.
Crutzen, P. (2003). 'Geology of Mankind.' *Nature* 415: 23.
Cummine, A. (2016). *Citizen's Wealth*. London: Yale University Press.
Davenport, C. and D. Armstrong (2004). 'Democracy and the Violation of Human Rights: A Statistical Analysis from 1976 to 1996.' *American Journal of Political Science* 28: 538–54.
Davis, L. (2014). 'The Economic Cost of Global Fuel Subsidies.' *American Economic Review: Papers and Proceedings* 104/5: 581–5.
Del Corral, M. (2015). 'Respect, Protection and Restoration: Preservation as a Negative or a Positive Duty.' *Ethics, Policy & Environment* 18/3: 268–70.
Dellapenna, J. (2003). 'The Customary International Law of Transboundary Fresh Water.' In M. Fitzmaurice and M. Szuniewicz (eds) *Exploitation of Natural Resources in the 21st Century*. The Hague: Kluwer, 142–90.
Dietsch, P. (2015). *Catching Capital: The Ethics of Tax Competition*. Oxford: Oxford University Press.
Donnan, S. and J. Politi (2014). 'WTO Rules against China on Rare Earths Export Restrictions.' *Financial Times*, 26 March.
Douglas, S. and A. Walker (2015). 'Coal Mining and the Resource Curse in the Eastern United States.' Unpublished manuscript.
Duruigbo, E. (2006). 'Permanent Sovereignty and Peoples' Ownership of Natural Resources in International Law.' *George Washington International Law Review* 33: 33–100.
Dworkin, R. (2000). *Sovereign Virtue*. Cambridge, Mass.: Harvard University Press.
Dworkin, R. (2004). 'Replies.' In Justine Burley (ed.) *Dworkin and His Critics*. Oxford: Blackwell, 339–95.

Economy, E. and M. Levi (2014). *By All Means Necessary: How China's Resource Quest is Changing the World*. Oxford: Oxford University Press.
Eliot, G. (1994). *Middlemarch* [1871–2]. London: Penguin.
European Parliament Directorate General for Internal Policies (2013). *Global Fishing Subsidies*. Brussels: European Parliament.
Falk, R. (1988). 'The Rights of Peoples (in Particular Indigenous Peoples).' In James Crawford (ed.) *The Rights of Peoples*. Oxford: Clarendon, 17–38.
Fearon, J. (2005). 'Primary Commodity Exports and Civil War.' *Journal of Conflict Resolution* 49/4: 483–507.
Feichtner, I. (2015). 'International Investment Law and Distribution Conflicts over Natural Resources.' In W. Schill, C. Tams, and R. Hofmann (eds) *International Investment Law and Development*. Cheltenham: Edward Elgar, 256–84.
Fleurbaey, M. (2005). 'Freedom with Forgiveness.' *Politics, Philosophy and Economics* 4/1: 29–67.
Food and Agriculture Organization (2009). *The State of World Fisheries and Aquaculture 2008*. Rome: Food and Agriculture Organization.
Food and Agriculture Organization (2010). *World Review of Fisheries and Agriculture*. Rome: Food and Agriculture Organization.
Fourie, C., F. Schuppert, and I. Wallimann-Helmer (eds) (2015). *Social Equality: On What it Means to be Equals*. Oxford: Oxford University Press.
Fried, B. (1995). 'Wilt Chamberlain Revisited: Nozick's "Justice in Transfer" and the Problem of Market-Based Distribution.' *Philosophy and Public Affairs* 24/3: 226–45.
Fried, B. (2002). *The Progressive Assault on Laissez Faire: Robert Hale and the First Law of Economics Movement*. Cambridge, Mass.: Harvard University Press.
Fried, B. (2004). 'Left-Libertarianism: A Review Essay.' *Philosophy and Public Affairs* 32/1: 66–92.
Gardiner, S. (2006). 'A Core Precautionary Principle.' *Journal of Political Philosophy* 14/1: 33–60.
Gary, I. and T. L. Karl (2003). *Bottom of the Barrel: Africa's Oil Boom and the Poor*. Baltimore, Md.: Catholic Relief Services.
George, H. (2005). *Progress and Poverty* [1879]. New York: Cosimo.
Gess, K. (1964). 'Permanent Sovereignty over Natural Resources: An Analytical Review of the United Nations Declaration and Its Genesis.' *International and Comparative Law Quarterly* 13/2: 398–449.
Gheaus, A. (2009). 'How Much of What Matters Can We Redistribute? Love, Justice and Luck.' *Hypatia* 24/4: 68–90.
Gheaus, A. (2016). 'The Right to Parent and Duties Concerning Future Generations.' *Journal of Political Philosophy* 24/4: 487–508.
Gilabert, P. (2012). *From Global Poverty to Global Equality*. Oxford: Oxford University Press.
Gillies, A. (2010). 'Reputational Concerns and the Emergence of Oil Sector Transparency as an International Norm.' *International Studies Quarterly* 54/1: 103–26.
Gleick, P. (1998a). 'The Human Right to Water.' *Water Policy* 1/4: 487–503.
Gleick, P. (1998b). 'Water in Crisis: Paths to Sustainable Water Use.' *Ecological Applications* 8/3: 571–9.

Global Ocean Commission (2014). *From Decline to Recovery: A Rescue Package for the Global Oceans*. Oxford: Global Ocean Commission.

Goodin, R. (1992). *Environmental Political Theory*. Cambridge: Polity Press.

Goodin, R. (2010). 'Selling Environmental Indulgences.' In S. Gardiner et al. (eds) *Climate Ethics: Essential Readings*. Oxford: Oxford University Press, 231–46.

Gosseries, A. (2014). 'Nations, Generations and Climate Justice.' *Global Policy* 5/1: 96–102.

Gowa, J. and S. Y. Kim (2005). 'An Exclusive Country Club: The Effects of GATT on Trade, 1950–94.' *World Politics* 57: 453–78.

Green, S. (1989). 'Competitive Equality of Opportunity: A Defense.' *Ethics* 100/1: 5–32.

Haber, S. and V. Menaldo (2011). 'Do Natural Resources Fuel Authoritarianism? A Reappraisal of the Resource Curse.' *American Political Science Review* 105/1: 1–26.

Halperin, D. (1967–8). 'Human Rights and Natural Resources.' *William and Mary Law Review* 9: 770–87.

Halperin, M., J. Siegle, and M. Weinstein (2010). *The Democracy Advantage: How Democracies Promote Prosperity and Peace*, revised edition. London: Routledge.

Hanlon, J., A. Barrientos, and D. Hulme (2010). *Just Give Money to the Poor: The Development Revolution from the Global South*. Boulder: Kumarian Press.

Hansen, S. (1989). 'Debt For Nature Swaps: Overview and Discussion of Key Issues.' *Ecological Economics* 1/1: 77–93.

Harris, J. W. (1996). *Property and Justice*. Oxford: Oxford University Press.

Hassoun, N. (2012). 'The Problem of Debt-for-Nature Swaps from a Human Rights Perspective.' *Journal of Applied Philosophy* 29/4: 359–77.

Haubrich, D. (2004). 'Global Distributive Justice and the Taxation of Natural Resources: Who Should Pick up the Tab?' *Contemporary Political Theory* 3/1: 48–69.

Hayward, T. (2005). 'Thomas Pogge's Global Resources Dividend: A Critique and an Alternative.' *Journal of Moral Philosophy* 2/3: 317–32.

Hayward, T. (2006). 'Global Justice and the Distribution of Natural Resources.' *Political Studies* 54/2: 349–69.

Hayward, T. (2013). *Ecological Space: The Concept and Its Ethical Significance*. Just World Institute Working Paper 2013/02, University of Edinburgh.

Heath, J. (2005). 'Rawls on Global Distributive Justice: A Defence.' *Canadian Journal of Philosophy* Supplementary Volume 31: 193–226.

Held, D. (1995). *Democracy and the Global Order: From the Modern State to Cosmopolitan Governance*. Cambridge: Polity.

Herman, B. (2007). 'The Players and the Game of Sovereign Debt.' In C. Barry, B. Herman, and L. Tomitova (eds) *Dealing Fairly with Developing Country Debt*. Oxford: Blackwell, 9–39.

Hoekstra, A. and A. Chapagain (2008). *The Globalization of Water: Sharing the Planet's Freshwater Resources*. Oxford: Blackwell.

Honoré, T. (1987). 'Ownership (1961).' In his *Making Law Bind*. Oxford: Clarendon Press, 161–92.

Hossain, K. (1980). 'Permanent Sovereignty over Natural Resources.' In Hossain (ed.) *Legal Aspects of a New International Economic Order*. London: Francis Pinter, 33–44.

Hubbard, B. and S. Reed (2015). 'Saudis Moving to Reduce Dependence on Oil Money.' *The New York Times*, 2 April, A5.

Huseby, R. (2015). 'Should the Beneficiaries Pay?' *Politics, Philosophy and Economics* 14/2: 209–25.

Independent World Commission on the Oceans (1998). *Our Oceans: Our Future*. Cambridge: Cambridge University Press.

Inter-Agency Task Force on Gender and Water (2006). *Gender, Water and Sanitation: A Policy Brief*. New York: United Nations.

Intergovernmental Panel on Climate Change (2007). *Climate Change 2007: Impacts, Adaptation and Vulnerability*. Cambridge: Cambridge University Press.

Intergovernmental Panel on Climate Change (2013). *Climate Change 2013: The Physical Science Basis, Summary for Policymakers*. Cambridge: Cambridge University Press.

International Energy Agency (2012). *World Energy Outlook 2012*. Paris: International Energy Agency.

International Monetary Fund (2006). *World Economic Outlook*. Washington, DC: International Monetary Fund, September.

James, A. and D. Adland (2011). 'The Curse of Natural Resources: An Empirical Investigation of US Counties.' *Resource and Energy Economics* 33/2: 440–53.

Jentoft, S., H. Minde, and R. Nilsen (eds) (2003). *Indigenous Peoples: Resource Management and Global Rights*. Delft: Eburon Academic.

Jones, C. (2001). *Global Justice: Defending Cosmopolitanism*. Oxford: Oxford University Press.

Karl, T. L. (2007). 'Ensuring Fairness: The Case for a Transparent Fiscal Contract.' In M. Humphreys, J. Sachs, and J. Stiglitz (eds) *Escaping the Resource Curse*. New York: Columbia University Press, 256–85.

Kendall, J. and R. Voorhies (2014). 'The Mobile-Finance Revolution.' *Foreign Affairs* 93/2: 9–13.

Kennedy, R. and L. Tiede (2013). 'Economic Assumptions and the Elusive Curse of Oil.' *International Studies Quarterly* 57/4: 760–71.

Kerr, W. and J. Gaigord (1994). 'A Note on Increasing the Effectiveness of Sanctions.' *Journal of World Trade* 28/6: 169–76.

Kiss, A. (1985). 'The Common Heritage of Mankind: Utopia or Reality?' *International Journal* 40/3: 423–41.

Klosko, G. (1992). *The Principle of Fairness and Political Obligation*. Lanham, Md.: Rowman & Littlefield.

Knight, S. (2011). 'Caught Out.' *Prospect* magazine, 20 July.

Kolers, A. (2009). *Land, Conflict and Justice*. Cambridge: Cambridge University Press.

Kolers, A. (2012). 'Justice, Territory and Natural Resources.' *Political Studies* 60/2: 269–86.

Kolers, A. (2014). 'Reply to Armstrong.' *Political Studies* 62/1: 223–8.

Korsmo, F. (1988). 'Nordic Security and the Saami Minority: Territorial Rights in Northern Fennoscandia.' *Human Rights Quarterly* 10: 509–24.

Krasner, S. and J. Weinstein (2014). 'Improving Governance from the Outside In.' *Annual Review of Political Science* 17: 123–45.

Kymlicka, W. (2001). 'Territorial Boundaries: A Liberal Egalitarian Perspective.' In D. Miller and S. Hashmi (eds) *Boundaries and Justice*. Princeton: Princeton University Press, 249–75.

Lee, C. K. (2014). 'The Spectre of Global China.' *New Left Review* 89: 29–65.
Lippert-Rasmussen, K. (2012). '"Equality of What?" and Intergenerational Justice.' *Ethical Perspectives* 19/3: 501–26.
Lippert-Rasmussen, K. (2013). 'Offensive Preferences, Snobbish Tastes, and Egalitarian Justice.' *Journal of Social Philosophy* 44/4: 439–58.
Locke, J. (1960). 'Second Treatise' [1690]. In P. Laslett (ed.) *Locke: Two Treatises on Government*. Cambridge: Cambridge University Press, 265–428.
Lodge, M. (2006). 'The International Seabed Authority and Article 82 of the UN Convention on the Law of the Sea.' *International Journal of Marine and Coastal Law* 21/3: 323–33.
Luper-Foy, S. (1992). 'Justice and Natural Resources.' *Environmental Values* 1: 47–64.
McCallion, K. and H. R. Sharma (2000). 'Environmental Justice without Borders: The Need for an International Court of the Environment to Protect Fundamental Human Rights.' *George Washington Journal of International Law and Economics* 32: 351–65.
McCormick, J. (2001). *Environmental Policy in the European Union*. Basingstoke: Palgrave.
McGlade, C. and P. Ekins (2015). 'The Geographical Distribution of Fossil Fuels Unused When Limiting Global Warming to 2°C.' *Nature* 517: 187–93.
McIntyre, O. (2007). *Environmental Protection of International Watercourses under International Law*. Aldershot: Ashgate.
Mancilla, A. (2015a). 'What the Old Right of Necessity Can Do for the Contemporary Global Poor.' *Journal of Applied Philosophy*. doi: 10.1111/japp.12170.
Mancilla, A. (2015b). 'The Volcanic Asymmetry or the Question of Permanent Sovereignty over Natural Disasters.' *Journal of Political Philosophy* 23/2: 192–212.
Mancilla, A. (2016). 'Shared Sovereignty over Migratory Natural Resources.' *Res Publica* 22/1: 21–35.
Marinov, N. and S. Nili (2015). 'Sanctions and Democracy.' *International Interactions* 41/4: 765–78.
Marx, K. (1993). *Grundrisse*. London: Penguin Classics.
Mazor, J. (2010). 'Liberal Justice, Future People and Natural Resource Conservation.' *Philosophy and Public Affairs* 38/4: 380–408.
Meisels, T. (2003). 'Liberal Nationalism and Territorial Rights.' *Journal of Applied Philosophy* 20/1: 31–43.
Meisels, T. (2009). *Territorial Rights*. Dordrecht: Springer.
Milanovic, B. (2007). 'Globalization and Inequality.' In D. Held and A. Kaya (eds) *Global Inequality*. Cambridge: Polity, 26–49.
Mill, J. S. (2000). 'On Property and Taxation' [1848]. In P. Vallentyne and H. Steiner (eds) *The Origins of Left-Libertarianism*. Basingstoke: Palgrave Macmillan, 159–70.
Miller, D. (1995). *On Nationality*. Oxford: Clarendon Press.
Miller, D. (1996). 'Two Cheers for Meritocracy.' *Journal of Political Philosophy* 4: 277–301.
Miller, D. (1999). *Citizenship and National Identity*. Cambridge: Polity.
Miller, D. (2007). *National Responsibility and Global Justice*. Oxford: Oxford University Press.
Miller, D. (2009). 'Global Justice and Climate Change: How Should Responsibilities be Allocated?' *Tanner Lectures on Human Values* 28: 117–56.

Miller, D. (2012). 'Territorial Rights: Concept and Justification.' *Political Studies* 60/2: 252–68.

Moellendorf, D. (2009). *Global Inequality Matters*. Basingstoke: Palgrave.

Moellendorf, D. (2014). *The Moral Challenge of Dangerous Climate Change*. Cambridge: Cambridge University Press.

Moore, A. and R. Crisp (1996). 'Welfarism in Moral Theory.' *Australasian Journal of Philosophy* 74/4: 598–613.

Moore, M. (2012). 'Natural Resources, Territorial Right and Global Distributive Justice.' *Political Theory* 40/1: 84–107.

Moore, M. (2015). *A Political Theory of Territory*. Oxford: Oxford University Press.

Morrisette, P. (1989). 'The Evolution of Policy Responses to Stratospheric Ozone Depletion.' *Natural Resources Journal* 29/3: 793–821.

Moss, T. (2011). *Oil to Cash: Fighting the Resource Curse through Cash Transfers*. Center for Global Development Working Paper 237.

Mouawad, J. and A. C. Revkin (2009). 'Saudis Seek Payments for Any Drop in Oil Revenues.' *New York Times*, 13 October.

Nagel, T. (2005). 'The Problem of Global Justice.' *Philosophy and Public Affairs* 33/2: 113–47.

Narveson, J. (1999). 'Original Acquisition and Lockean Provisos.' *Public Affairs Quarterly* 13: 205–27.

Nili, S. (2011a). 'Conceptualizing the Curse: Two Views on our Responsibility for the "Resource Curse".' *Ethics and Global Politics* 4/2: 103–24.

Nili, S. (2011b). 'Democratic Disengagement: Toward Rousseauian Global Reform.' *International Theory* 3/3: 355–89.

Nili, S. (2016a). 'Liberal Global Justice and Social Science.' *Review of International Studies* 42/1: 136–55.

Nili, S. (2016b). 'Global Justice and Global Realities.' *Journal of International Political Theory* 12/2: 200–16.

Nine, C. (2008). 'The Moral Arbitrariness of State Borders: Against Beitz.' *Contemporary Political Theory* 7/3: 259–79.

Nine, C. (2012). *Global Justice and Territory*. Oxford: Oxford University Press.

Nine, C. (2013). 'Territory in a World of Limits.' In L. Leonard (ed.) *Environmental Philosophy*. Bingley: Emerald Group Publishing, 137–55.

Nine, C. (2014). 'When Affected Interests Demand Joint Self-Determination: Learning from Rivers.' *International Theory* 6/1: 157–74.

Nine, C. (2015). 'Compromise and Original Acquisition: Explaining Rights to the Arctic.' *Social Philosophy and Policy* 32/1: 149–70.

Nozick, R. (1974). *Anarchy, State and Utopia*. Oxford: Blackwell.

Oberman, K. (2015). 'Poverty and Immigration Policy.' *American Political Science Review* 109/2: 239–51.

Office of the High Commissioner for Human Rights. (2013). *Realizing Women's Rights to Land and Other Productive Resources*. New York: United Nations.

Orrego Vicuna, F. (1989). *The Exclusive Economic Zone: Regime and Legal Nature under International Law*. Cambridge: Cambridge University Press.

Ostrom, E. (1990). *Governing the Commons*. Cambridge: Cambridge University Press.

Ostrom, E. (2000). 'Private and Common Property Rights.' In B. Bouckaert and G. De Geest (eds) *Encyclopedia of Law and Economics. Vol. II: Civil Law and Economics*. Cheltenham: Edward Elgar. 332–79.

Ostrom, E. (2003). 'How Types of Goods and Property Rights Jointly Affect Collective Action.' *Journal of Theoretical Politics* 15/3: 239–70.

Ostrom, E. (2010). 'Polycentric Systems for Coping with Collective Action and Global Environmental Change.' *Global Environmental Change* 20/4: 550–7.

Otsuka, M. (2003). *Libertarianism Without Inequality*. Oxford: Oxford University Press.

Page, E. (2012). 'Give It Up for Climate Change: A Defence of the Beneficiary Pays Principle.' *International Theory* 4/2: 300–30.

Page, E. (2016). 'Qui Bono? Justice in the Benefits and Burdens of Avoided Deforestation.' *Res Publica* 22/1: 83–97.

Paine, T. (1835). *The Political Writings of Thomas Paine*. New York: George Evans.

Palley, T. (2003). *Combating the Resource Curse with Citizen Revenue Distribution Funds: Oil and the Case of Iraq*. Foreign Policy in Focus Special Report, December.

Parfit, D. (1984). *Reasons and Persons*. Oxford: Oxford University Press.

Parfit, D. (1997). 'Equality and Priority.' *Ratio* 10/3: 202–21.

Petterson, P. (2006). *Out Stealing Horses* (translated by Anne Born). London: Vintage.

Pevnick, R. (2008). 'An Exchange: The Morality of Immigration.' *Ethics and International Affairs* 22/3: 241–59.

Piketty, T. (2014). *Capital in the Twenty-First Century*. Cambridge, Mass.: Harvard University Press.

Pogge, T. (2001). 'Eradicating Systemic Poverty: Brief for a Global Resources Dividend.' *Journal of Human Development* 2/1: 59–77.

Pogge, T. (2002). *World Poverty and Human Rights*. Cambridge: Polity.

Pogge, T. (2008). *World Poverty and Human Rights*, second edition. Cambridge: Polity.

Pogge, T. (2011). 'Allowing the Poor to Share the Earth.' *Journal of Moral Philosophy* 8/3: 335–52.

Provost, C. and M. Kennard (2015). 'The Obscure Legal System that Lets Corporations Sue Countries.' *The Guardian*, 10 June.

Radon, J. (2007). 'How to Negotiate an Oil Agreement.' In M. Humphreys, J. Sachs, and J. Stiglitz (eds) *Escaping the Resource Curse*. New York: Columbia University Press, 89–113.

Rawls, J. (1971). *A Theory of Justice*. Cambridge, Mass.: Harvard University Press.

Rawls, J. (1999). *The Law of Peoples*. Cambridge, Mass.: Harvard University Press.

Rawls, J. (2001). *Justice as Fairness: A Restatement*. Cambridge, Mass.: Belknap.

Reglitz, M. (2015). 'Fairness to Non-Participants: A Case for a Practice-Independent Egalitarian Baseline.' *Critical Review of International Social and Political Philosophy*. doi: 10-1080/13698230.2015.1037574.

Risse, M. (2005). 'How Does the Global Order Harm the Poor?' *Philosophy and Public Affairs* 33/4: 349–76.

Risse, M. (2008). 'An Exchange: The Morality of Immigration.' *Ethics and International Affairs* 22/3: 241–59.

Risse, M. (2012). *On Global Justice*. Princeton: Princeton University Press.

Risse, M. (2014). 'The Human Right to Water and Common Ownership of the Earth.' *Journal of Political Philosophy* 22/2: 178–203.

Roark, E. (2013). *Removing the Commons.* Lanham: Lexington.
Robinson, J., R. Torvik, and T. Verdier (2006). 'Political Foundations of the Resource Curse.' *Journal of Development Economics* 79/2: 447–68.
Ross, M. (2001). 'Does Oil Hinder Democracy?' *World Politics* 53/3: 325–61.
Ross, M. (2006). 'Is Democracy Good for the Poor?' *American Journal of Political Science* 50/4: 860–74.
Ross, M. (2012). *The Oil Curse: How Petroleum Wealth Shapes the Development of Nations.* Princeton: Princeton University Press.
Sachs, J. and A. Warner (1995). *Natural Resource Abundance and Economic Growth.* NBER Working Paper series 5398.
Sala-i-Martin, X. and A. Subramanian (2003). *Addressing the Natural Resource Curse: An Illustration from Nigeria.* IMF Working Paper WP/03/139.
Sandbu, M. (2006). 'Natural Wealth Accounts: A Proposal for Alleviating the Natural Resource Curse.' *World Development* 34/7: 1153–70.
Sangiovanni, A. (2007). 'Global Justice, Reciprocity and the State.' *Philosophy and Public Affairs* 35/1: 3–39.
Schrijver, N. (1997). *Sovereignty over Natural Resources.* Cambridge: Cambridge University Press.
Schrijver, N. (2008). 'Unravelling State Sovereignty? The Controversy on the Right of Indigenous Peoples to Permanent Sovereignty over their Natural Wealth and Resources.' In I. Boerefijn and J. Goldschmidt (eds) *Changing Perceptions of Sovereignty and Human Rights: Essay in Honour of Cees Flinterman.* Antwerp: Intersentia, 85–98.
Schuppert, F. (2014). 'Beyond the National Resource Privilege: Towards an International Court of the Environment.' *International Theory* 6/1: 68–87.
Schwebel, S. (1963). 'The Story of the U.N.'s Declaration on Permanent Sovereignty over Natural Resources.' *American Bar Association Journal* 49/5: 463–9.
Segal, P. (2011). 'Resource Rents, Redistribution, and Halving Global Poverty: The Resource Dividend.' *World Development* 39/4: 475–89.
Sen, A. (1980). 'Equality of What?' *The Tanner Lecture on Human Values* 1: 197–220.
Sen, A. (1999). *Development as Freedom.* Oxford: Oxford University Press.
Shue, H. (1980). *Basic Rights.* Princeton: Princeton University Press.
Shue, H. (2014). *Climate Justice: Vulnerability and Protection.* Oxford: Oxford University Press.
Simmons, A. J. (1994). *The Lockean Theory of Rights.* Princeton: Princeton University Press.
Simmons, A. J. (2000). *Justification and Legitimacy.* Cambridge: Cambridge University Press.
Simmons, A. J. (2012). 'States' Resource Rights: Locating the Limits', online symposium on resource rights: http://territorynetwork.wordpress.com/
Singer, P. (2002). *One World.* New Haven: Yale University Press.
Slack, K. (2004). 'Sharing the Riches of the Earth: Democratizing Natural Resource-Led Development.' *Ethics and International Affairs* 18/1: 47–62.
Slaughter, A.-M. (2004). *A New World Order.* Princeton: Princeton University Press.
Smith, A. (1999). *The Wealth of Nations* [1776]. London: Penguin Classics.
Smith, A. et al. (2000). 'Contamination of Drinking-Water by Arsenic in Bangladesh: A Public Health Emergency.' *Bulletin of the World Health Organization* 78/9: 1093–103.

Smith, R. J. (1981). 'Resolving the Tragedy of the Commons by Creating Private Property Rights in Wildlife.' *CATO Journal* 1: 439–68.
Snyder, J. (2000). *From Voting to Violence: Democratization and Nationalist Conflict*. New York: Norton.
Sovacool, B. and M. Brown (2009). 'Scaling the Policy Response to Climate Change.' *Policy and Society* 27: 317–28.
Spencer, H. (1851). *Social Statics*. London: John Chapman.
Sreenivasan, G. (2012). 'What is Non-Ideal Theory?' In M. Williams, R. Nagy, and J. Elster (eds) *Transitional Justice—NOMOS LI*. New York: New York University Press, 233–56.
Steiner, H. (1994). *An Essay on Rights*. Oxford: Blackwell.
Steiner, H. (2005). 'Territorial Justice and Global Redistribution.' In G. Brock and H. Brighouse (eds) *The Political Philosophy of Cosmopolitanism*. Cambridge: Cambridge University Press, 28–38.
Steiner, H. (2009). 'Left Libertarianism and the Ownership of Natural Resources.' *Public Reason* 1/1: 1–8.
Steiner, H. (2011a). 'Sharing Mother Nature's Gifts: A Reply to Quong and Miller.' *Journal of Political Philosophy* 19/1: 110–23.
Steiner, H. (2011b). The Global Fund: A Reply to Casal.' *Journal of Moral Philosophy* 8/3: 328–34.
Sterner, T. (2007). 'Fuel Taxes: An Important Instrument for Climate Policy.' *Energy Policy* 35: 3194–202.
Stevens, P., G. Lahn, and J. Kooroshy (2015). *The Resource Curse Revisited*. Chatham House Research Paper on Energy, Environment and Resources, August.
Stiglitz, J. (2006). *Making Globalization Work*. London: Penguin.
Stijns, J.-P. (2006). 'Natural Resource Abundance and Human Capital Accumulation.' *World Development* 34/6: 1060–83.
Stilz, A. (2009). 'Nations, States and Territory.' *Ethics* 121/3: 572–601.
Stilz, A. (2013). 'Occupancy Rights and the Wrong of Removal.' *Philosophy and Public Affairs* 41/4: 324–56.
Stokke, O. and D. Vidas (eds) (1996). *Governing the Antarctic: The Legitimacy and Effectiveness of the Antarctic Treaty Regime*. Cambridge: Cambridge University Press.
Stone, C. (1997). 'The Crisis in Global Fisheries: Can Trade Laws Provide a Cure?' *Environmental Conservation* 24/2: 97–8.
Sutcliffe, B. (2007). 'The Unequalled and Unequal Twentieth Century.' In D. Held and A. Kaya (eds) *Global Inequality*. Cambridge: Polity, 50–72.
Swing, J. T. (1976). 'Who Will Own the Oceans?' *Foreign Affairs* 54/3: 527–46.
Tan, K.-C. (2004). *Justice without Borders*. Cambridge: Cambridge University Press.
Tan, K.-C. (2012). *Justice, Institutions, and Luck*. Oxford: Oxford University Press.
Temkin, L. (2015). 'Equality as Comparative Fairness.' *Journal of Applied Philosophy*. doi: 10.1111/japp.12140.
Tideman, N. (2000). 'Global Economic Justice.' *Geophilos* 00: 134–46.
Tideman, N. and P. Vallentyne (2001). 'Left-Libertarianism and Global Justice.' In B. Leiser and T. Campbell (eds) *Human Rights in Philosophy and Practice*. Aldershot: Ashgate, 443–57.
Tobin, J. (1996). 'A Currency Transactions Tax: Why and How?' *Open Economies Review* 7/1: 493–9.

Tomlin, P. (2013). 'Choices, Chances and Change: Luck Egalitarianism over Time.' *Ethical Theory and Moral Practice* 16/2: 393–407.
Tully, J. (1993). *An Approach to Political Philosophy: Locke in Contexts*. Cambridge: Cambridge University Press.
United Nations (2002). *Oceans: The Source of Life: United Nations Convention of the Law of the Sea 20th Anniversary*. New York: United Nations.
Vallentyne, P. (2012). 'Left-Libertarianism.' In D. Estlund (ed.) *Oxford Handbook of Political Philosophy*. Oxford: Oxford University Press, 152–68.
van Duffel, S. and D. Yap (2011). 'Distributive Justice before the Eighteenth Century: The Right of Necessity.' *History of Political Thought* 32/3: 449–64.
Van Parijs, P. (1995). *Real Freedom for All: What (If Anything) Can Justify Capitalism?* Oxford: Oxford University Press.
Van Parijs, P. (2009). 'Egalitarian Justice, Left-Libertarianism and the Market.' In I. Carter, S. de Wijze, and M. Kramer (eds) *The Anatomy of Justice*. London: Routledge, 145–62.
Vanderheiden, S. (2009). *Atmospheric Justice*. Oxford: Oxford University Press.
Vig, N. and M. Faure (eds) (2004). *Green Giants? Environmental Policies of the United States and the European Union*. Cambridge, Mass.: MIT Press.
Vogler, J. (2012). 'Global Commons Revisited.' *Global Policy* 3/1: 61–71.
Wade, R. (2003). 'What Strategies are Viable for Developing Countries Today? The World Trade Organization and the Shrinking of "Development Space".' *Review of International Political Economy* 10/4: 621–44.
Waldron, J. (1979). 'Enough and as Good Left for Others.' *Philosophical Quarterly* 29: 319–28.
Waldron, J. (1988). *The Right to Private Property*. Oxford: Clarendon Press.
Waldron, J. (1989). 'Rights in Conflict.' *Ethics* 99/3: 503–19.
Waldron, J. (1992). 'Superseding Historic Injustice.' *Ethics* 103/1: 4–18.
Waldron, J. (1993). 'Property, Justification and Need.' *Canadian Journal of Law and Jurisprudence* 6/2: 185–215.
Wenar, L. (1998). 'Original Appropriation of Private Property.' *Mind* 107/428: 799–820.
Wenar, L. (2006). 'Why Rawls is Not a Cosmopolitan Egalitarian.' In R. Martin and D. Reidy (eds) *Rawls's Law of Peoples: A Realistic Utopia?* Oxford: Blackwell, 95–113.
Wenar, L. (2008). 'Property Rights and the Resource Curse.' *Philosophy and Public Affairs* 36/1: 2–32.
Wenar, L. (2010). 'Realistic Reform of International Trade in Resources.' In Alison Jaggar (ed.) *Thomas Pogge and His Critics*. Cambridge: Polity, 123–50.
Wenar, L. (2016a). *Blood Oil*. Oxford: Oxford University Press.
Wenar, L. (2016b). 'Natural Resources.' In D. Held and P. Maffetone (eds) *Global Political Theory*. Cambridge: Polity, 198–212.
White, C. and C. Costello (2014). 'Close the High Seas to Fishing?' *PLOS Biology* 12/3: 1–5.
Widerquist, K. and M. Howard (eds) (2012). *Alaska's Permanent Fund Dividend: Examining Its Suitability as a Model*. Basingstoke: Palgrave Macmillan.
Wiens, D. (2014). 'Natural Resources and Institutional Development.' *Journal of Theoretical Politics* 26/2: 197–221.

Wiens, D. (2015). 'Natural Resources and Government Responsiveness.' *Politics, Philosophy and Economics* 14/1: 84–105.
Wiens, D., P. Poast, and W. R. Clark (2014). 'The Political Resource Curse: An Empirical Re-Evaluation.' *Political Research Quarterly* 67/4: 783–94.
Wisor, S. (2012). 'Property Rights and the Resource Curse: A Reply to Wenar.' *Journal of Philosophical Research* 37: 185–204.
Wisor, S. (2016). 'Conditional Coercion Versus Rights Diagnostics: Two Approaches to Human Rights Protection.' *Politics, Philosophy and Economics* 15/4: 405–23.
Wolf, A. T. (1998). 'Conflict and Cooperation along International Waterways.' *Water Policy* 1: 251–65.
Woo, E. (1999). Obituary of Arvid Pardo. *Los Angeles Times*, 18 July.
World Bank (2006). *Where is the Wealth of Nations?* Washington, DC: World Bank.
World Bank (2014). *State and Trends of Carbon Pricing*. Washington, DC: World Bank.
Worm, B. et al. (2006). 'Impacts of Biodiversity Loss on Ocean Ecosystem Services.' *Science* 314/3: 787–90.
Young, O. (2002). *The Institutional Dimensions of Climate Change: Fit, Interplay and Scale*. London: MIT Press.
Ypi, L. (2012). *Global Justice and Avant-Garde Political Agency*. Oxford: Oxford University Press.
Ypi, L. (2014). 'A Permissive Theory of Territorial Rights.' *European Journal of Philosophy* 22/2: 288–312.

Index

ability to pay principle 38, 77–8, 223, 225–6, 233
Abu Dhabi 195–7
accountability 52, 151–65, 178
Africa 1, 13, 48, 50, 52, 158, 160, 168, 235, 237, 240
agriculture 88, 158, 188–9, 238, 240
air 15, 80
animals 20, 130n15, 240
Antarctica 205–6
appropriation 29–39, 41, 75–8, 82, 181, 205, 210–12
Arctic 1, 203
attachment 17–18, 55–6, 93–4, 98, 113–29, 136–8, 204

Bangladesh 220
Barry, Brian 27n7, 190, 199n37
bees 222–3
Beitz, Charles 8n4, 27n7, 29, 35, 62, 69, 89n3, 105, 119–22, 177, 220
beneficiary pays principle 232
biodiversity 21, 80–1, 206, 214–16, 225, 230, 240
Brazil 96, 176n84
Britain 166, 192, 203–4

Caney, Simon 8n4, 90n25, 91n27, 149n27, 197–8n4, 225, 244–5n9, 245n11, 245n19, 246n25
capital 62, 90n17, 169–70, 176n76, 183–5, 189, 196–7, 237
carbon dioxide 13, 14, 95, 230–1
  carbon emissions 34, 37–9, 57n16, 77, 86, 90n23, 192, 194–5, 230–2, 235, 241, 245n19
  carbon sinks 76–7, 215, 225, 230, 233
  carbon taxes 192–5, 235, 240
Carens, Joseph 112n37, 172n1, 197n2
Casal, Paula 58n20, 90n22, 197n1, 199n30, 199n36
China 104, 112n26, 135, 169, 203
climate change 57n5, 185, 187, 192, 230–1, 234–6
  mitigation 38–9, 77, 194, 236
coal 14, 22, 114, 192–3, 235
Cohen, G. A. 57n15, 92n43, 92n44, 92n52, 111n15, 112n36, 112n37
Collier, Paul 50, 61n78, 91n38, 218n23

colonialism 55–6, 152, 161–3; *see also* decolonization
common heritage principle 205–7, 212–14
conservation 139–42, 147, 186, 220–44
  non-exploitation 221, 233–8
  protection 221–33, 235
  restoration 221–4, 226, 230, 235
contribution to the problem principle 226–8, 232–3

debt 48, 168, 177, 240
decolonization 132, 150–2, 165–7
democracy 47, 49, 155–6
disability 64–5, 68, 85, 90n16
duties 2, 9, 24
Dworkin, Ronald 27n10

economic growth 47–8, 50, 52, 80, 176n83, 185, 203
ecosystem services 15, 141, 222, 224, 229–30
education 46–8, 72, 169, 188, 220
egalitarianism 3, 31–2, 39–43, 46, 55–6, 62–88, 73–7, 93–4, 106–8, 116–17, 125–7, 145, 152, 165, 171
  equal access to wellbeing 3, 65, 71, 73–7, 79–88
  equality of resources 64–7, 85–6
  equality of status 39, 72–3, 84–5
  luck egalitarianism 64–7, 82–5
  scope of egalitarian concern 2, 41–5
energy 11, 81, 95, 228
environmental degradation 2, 21, 241, 243
equality *see* egalitarianism
European Union 25–6, 142, 170
Exclusive Economic Zones 202–9, 212, 216–17
extraction of natural resources 13, 52, 54–5, 102, 110, 135, 138, 154–5, 169, 189, 212, 220, 240

fish 121–2, 127, 156–7, 191, 202, 204–9, 225–8
forests 14, 17, 123, 230–2, 238, 240–1
fossil fuels 81, 95, 110, 187–8, 192–7, 205, 228, 234–7, 239–41
  fossil fuel industry 81, 246–7n36
  see also coal, oil, subsidies
free-riding 194, 229–33
Fried, Barbara 57n11, 112n31

Ganges, River 114–15, 138
gender inequality 73–4, 187, 220
general claims 53, 98
genes 66–7, 206, 215–16, 218n12
George, Henry 62, 65, 183
Gheaus, Anca 78–9, 91n28
Global Environment Facility 195, 241–2
Global Resources Dividend 90n24, 144, 155, 159, 177, 189
Goodin, Robert 27n8, 91n40, 199n42
Green Climate Fund 195, 241–2
greenhouse gases 15, 77, 180, 192, 227; *see also* carbon dioxide

Hayward, Tim 90n18, 189
Heath, Joseph 183, 185
High Seas 76, 188, 206–10, 212, 216, 219n43, 223, 241
Honoré, Tony 24, 28n17
human rights 15, 43, 74, 125, 234

Iceland 156–7, 203–4, 244n3
improvement 11, 18–19, 53–5, 94–110, 134–6, 204
India 116
indigenous peoples 1, 113–14, 125–7, 138, 143
inheritance 30, 66, 69, 105, 227–8
institutions 45–6, 48–9, 64, 242
intergenerational justice 20, 78–81, 83–4, 87, 105, 221, 227–8
international law 12, 76, 122, 132–3, 141–2, 152, 160–5, 167–8, 202–6, 213
International Monetary Fund 168
International Seabed Authority 212–16
international trade 52, 64, 152–60, 168, 177–8, 239–40

jurisdiction 22, 24, 111n22, 118, 135–6, 139–46, 167, 191, 205, 218n7
justice 2, 17–19, 127–9

Kant, Immanuel 114–15, 117, 136
Kolers, Avery 18–19, 128–9
Kuwait 30

land 1, 2, 11, 26, 27n4, 73, 75–6, 91n29, 96, 99, 111n15, 113, 117, 134–5, 138–9, 238, 240
Latin America 47, 168, 176n84, 235
left-libertarianism 41, 63–8, 183, 189
Lippert-Rasmussen, Kasper 91n33 92n49, 92n54
Locke, John 29–30, 32–3, 57n9, 57n10, 57n11, 65, 76, 96–8, 109, 111n15, 117, 206
luck egalitarianism *see* egalitarianism

Mancilla, Alejandra 148n16, 198n4, 244n3
Marine Protected Areas 188, 208, 216, 225–7, 241
Marx, Karl 94, 96
Middle East 1, 193, 196, 237
migration 150, 158, 178–9, 197n4
Mill, John Stuart 96–7
Miller, David 36, 38–9, 42, 44, 61n82, 104, 111n18, 111n24, 136, 246n25, 247n40
minerals 52, 76, 157, 170, 202, 204
seabed minerals 191, 209–13
minimalism about global justice 35–9, 42–3, 54–5, 214
mitigation *see* climate change
Moellendorf, Darrel 8n4, 245n12, 246n29
Moore, Margaret 58n24, 129n4, 131n29, 145, 148n12, 214, 218n7

nations 99–100, 134–8
national responsibility 38, 53–5, 83–5, 99–105, 134–6
national self-determination 142–6, 162–3, 204–5, 214
Native Americans 56
natural resources
defined 11–13
fugacious and non-fugacious resources 119, 223
renewable and non-renewable resources 15–16, 79
stock and flow resources 93
see also resource rents, resource taxes
nature 13, 19–20, 94
New International Economic Order 166–7, 177–9, 214, 219n40
Nili, Shmuel 45–6, 59n59, 172n10, 173n17, 183–4
Nine, Cara 58n24, 111n22, 149n24, 149n29, 211, 213n7
non-relationism 41–5, 106–7
non-renewable resources *see* natural resources
Norway 47–8, 132, 170, 195–6, 202, 237
Nozick, Robert 33–4, 37, 57n7, 57n14, 58n19, 245n15

oceans 9, 191, 201–17, 227, 230
oil 1, 47–9, 52, 86, 101–2, 127, 150, 170, 193, 195–6, 201–4, 235–7
Ostrom, Elinor 28n18, 28n24, 139–41, 148–9n20
Otsuka, Michael 57n7, 57n15, 90n16

Page, Edward 245n17, 246n23
Paine, Thomas 62, 65, 96, 98
Pardo, Arvid 206, 211, 217

Parfit, Derek 40, 58n34, 91n34
Permanent Sovereignty 24, 132–47, 150–2, 161–5, 243
Piketty, Thomas 176n76, 196–7, 198n11
Pogge, Thomas 8n7, 27n7, 90n24, 144, 149n34, 151, 153–6, 159, 172–3n11, 177, 187, 189, 197, 200n59
pollution 180, 182–3, 192–4, 227, 230
popular sovereignty 151–3, 160–5
poverty 38, 51, 77, 112n39, 157, 159, 184, 188, 234
private property 22, 25, 30, 75, 97–8, 140, 148n15
proximity principle 222–4
public goods 14–15, 47, 180, 224, 229–32, 234
  collective goods 14, 191–2, 207, 229–31
  pure public goods 14, 207, 229
  public goods argument 228–33

rainforests *see* forests
Rawls, John 36, 38, 42, 45, 102, 108, 112n38, 116, 139–42, 183
REDD 241
Reglitz, Merten 45
reindeer 20, 121–4, 137–8
relationism 41–5, 106–7
renewable resources *see* natural resources
resource curse 2, 45–53, 174n39, 184, 198n21
resource rents 47, 51–2, 68, 101–2, 107–8, 151–4, 178, 183, 195–7
resource taxes 155, 158–60, 183–97, 209, 240–1
responsibility 63, 81–8, 94–5, 98–9, 101–5, 226–8
right-libertarianism 32–4, 37–8, 64–5, 211
rights 22–7, 123; *see also* human rights
Risse, Mathias 27n7, 35–8, 42, 44–6, 55, 57n7, 59n51, 61n82, 70, 183, 197n4
rivers 22, 114, 132, 141–2
Ross, Michael 48, 59n54, 172n5, 173n30
Russia 203, 215, 217n2, 219n43

Saami 121–2, 124, 131n22, 137–8
Saudi Arabia 52, 203, 236–7, 239, 247n37, 247n41
Schrijver, Nico 27n5, 149n23, 162, 174n50, 175n52

self-determination *see* national self-determination
Sen, Amartya 89n5, 156
Shue, Henry 27n11, 57n16, 91n42, 92n55, 199n44, 244n7, 246n26
Simmons, A. John 57n9, 130n6, 130n10, 130n20
Sovereign Wealth Funds 195–7, 203, 247n41
sovereignty 141–2, 165–71, 202, 204; *see also* Permanent Sovereignty, popular sovereignty
special claims 53–6, 93–4, 134–42, 201; *see also* improvement, attachment
states 99–100, 139–44, 162–3, 202, 244
Steiner, Hillel 27n4, 57n6, 61n83, 65–8, 89n4, 89n10, 177, 189
Stilz, Anna 117–18, 149n29, 149n30
subsidies 81, 177, 193, 207–8, 240

taxation 17, 47, 67, 70–1, 75, 82, 177–197, 240–1; *see also* resource taxes
technology 12, 81, 87–8, 103, 188, 192–3, 203, 210–13, 216, 240–1
tragedy of the commons 139–41, 148n15, 208
trees 11, 13, 15, 119, 230; *see also* forests

United Nations 91n29, 149n24, 195, 202, 204, 207, 213, 216, 217n2, 241
United States 35, 37, 44, 49, 55, 104, 157, 167, 202, 207, 212–13, 215–16, 231

Vallentyne, Peter 57n7

Waldron, Jeremy 58n17, 110n11, 111n13, 111n15, 131n23
water 2, 9, 13, 30, 80, 88, 92n56, 132, 181–2, 186, 191–2, 220
wellbeing 3, 33–4, 41, 48, 51, 62, 64, 68, 82–3, 85–8, 124, 184, 187, 220, 225–6, 236–7
Wenar, Leif 8n2, 8n7, 27n7, 151–65, 218n6
Wiens, David 158, 174n39
Wisor, Scott 154–5, 173n16
World Bank 168, 241
World Trade Organization 170, 195, 208, 235

Ypi, Lea 59n47, 114, 130n8

Zambia 169–70

What do we owe to environmental refugees?

- Taxes CH8 → Discourage activities (PAN!)
  - Reduce inequality
  - raise revenues
  - user charges (181)

- Fines and Penalties when harm is severe p. 181

- P. 86 → deliberately cultivated tastes v not.
- P. 88 expensive tastes

the example of the Parade of cat may be treated/viewed like an expensive taste: — fulfill it or
  - Change it (by persuading or promoting change in conversion factor).

They deserve resources of help in changing (other kind of resources)

Food security (FAO) and attachment

Why is attachment supporting food security? What kind of control does attachment generate?